EL CHAPO

EL CHAPO

THE UNTOLD STORY OF THE WORLD'S MOST INFAMOUS DRUG LORD

NOAH HUROWITZ

ATRIA BOOKS

NEW YORK • LONDON • TORONTO • SYDNEY • NEW DELHI

ATRIA
BOOKS

An Imprint of Simon & Schuster, Inc.
1230 Avenue of the Americas
New York, NY 10020

First Atria Books hardcover edition July 2021

ATRIA BOOKS and colophon are trademarks
of Simon & Schuster, Inc.

For information about special discounts for bulk purchases,
please contact Simon & Schuster Special Sales at
1-866-506-1949 or business@simonandschuster.com.

The Simon & Schuster Speakers Bureau can bring authors
to your live event. For more information, or to book an
event, contact the Simon & Schuster Speakers Bureau at
1-866-248-3049 or visit our website at www.simonspeakers.com.

Interior design by Dana Sloan

Map design by Stella Ioannidou

Manufactured in the United States of America

1 3 5 7 9 10 8 6 4 2

Library of Congress Cataloging-in-Publication Data

ISBN 978-1-9821-3375-7
ISBN 978-1-9821-3377-1 (ebook)

This book is dedicated to all victims and survivors of the war on drugs, in the hope that they may find peace and justice.

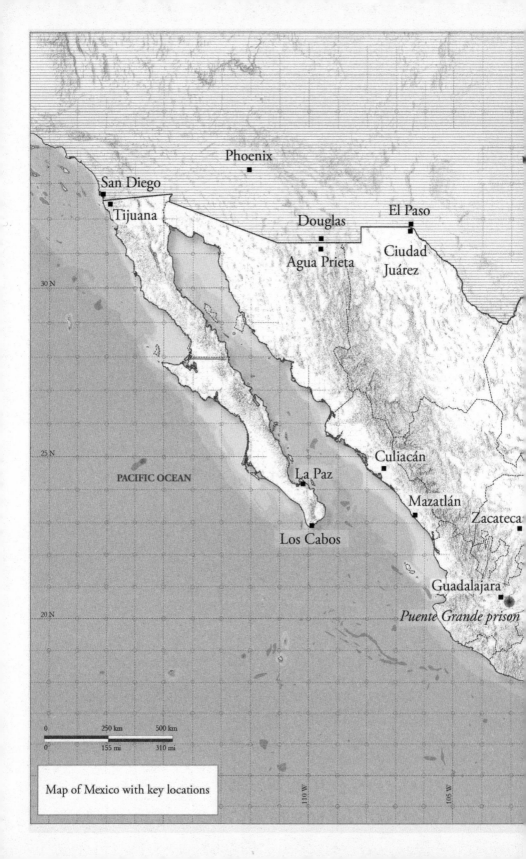

Map of Mexico with key locations

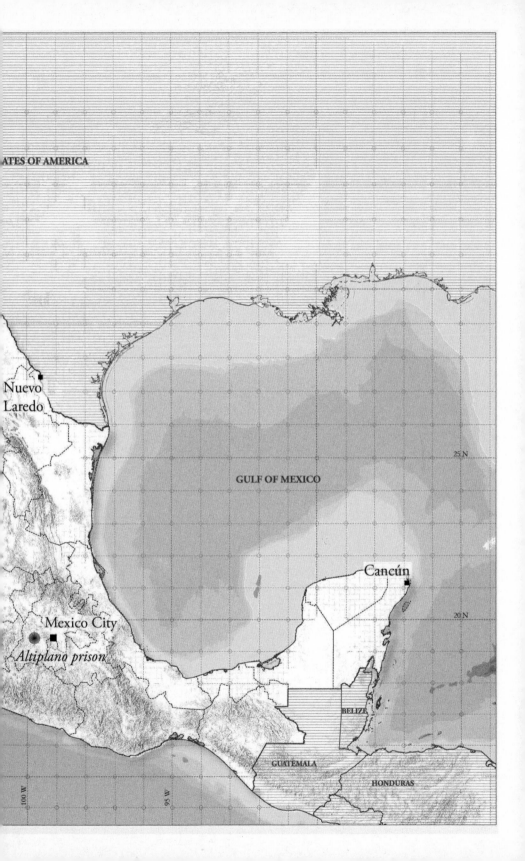

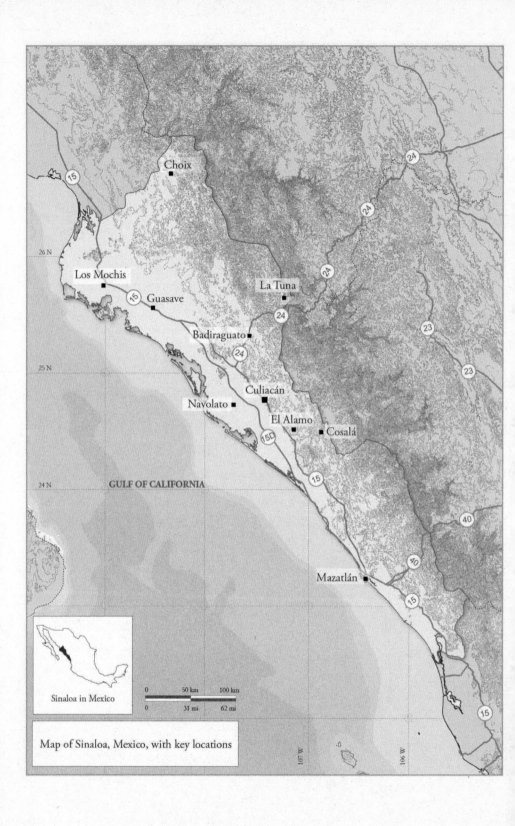

Choix

La Tuna

Los Mochis

Guasave

Badiraguato

26 N

25 N

24 N

Culiacán

Navolato

El Alamo

Cosalá

GULF OF CALIFORNIA

Mazatlán

Sinaloa in Mexico

0	50 km	100 km
0	31 mi	62 mi

Map of Sinaloa, Mexico, with key locations

CONTENTS

EL CHAPO

INTRODUCTION

THE SIERRA MADRE Occidental range sweeps down from the Rocky Mountains, across the Arizona border, and south through the states of Sonora, Chihuahua, Sinaloa, and Durango, forming the spine of northwestern Mexico. Little is known of the first inhabitants of the mountains, but thanks to archeological clues left behind in the form of pottery and subterranean pit houses, we can pick up the trail around 300 CE of scattered communities that grew into a society calling itself the Rarámuri, "those with light feet," or "foot runners." The Rarámuri, now known as Tarahumara, the Spanish corruption of their name, originally settled the plains to the east of the Sierra Madre, where they developed a culture of ritual endurance races, twenty-four-hour ultra-marathons run barefoot or in *huarache* sandals, a tradition that persists to this day. As Spanish missionaries first began arriving in the mountains in the 1500s, bringing with them misery and death in the form of smallpox and imperial cruelty, the Tarahumara rose up in successive revolts, moving deeper and deeper into the Sierra and bestowing upon the area a reputation as an untamable wilderness. But it wasn't enough to keep outsiders from coming in. Home to rich veins of silver, gold, copper, and other precious minerals, the mountains drew prospectors and mining companies for centuries, and many of the current inhabitants of the Sierra Madre can trace their presence in Sinaloa to ancestors who arrived as miners and never left. Now many of them make a living from the figurative gold mines of marijuana and opium. It is this, not mining, that has earned this region spanning portions of the states of Sinaloa, Chihuahua, and Durango a new name: the Golden Triangle.

The steep peaks and deep valleys were carved over millennia by rivers, which flow west to the ocean, tumbling down in torrents during the rainy season and in trickles—if at all—during the dry season. These waters irrigate the fertile lowland plains of Sinaloa, a long and narrow state against whose northern shores lap the waves of the Gulf of California, and whose southern beaches look out on the vast expanse of the Pacific. About an hour inland, the state capital of Culiacán sits nestled at the foot of the Sierra Madre mountains, which form a striking backdrop on the horizon.

Long a provincial backwater, Culiacán began to see a steady influx of people and money beginning in the 1940s, first as newly built dams made large-scale agriculture possible, and later as a few native Sinaloans began to take their talent for illegal import and export to a global scale. Culiacán now boasts a population of nearly a million people. The city is a magnet for people fleeing the countryside, and at its margins many of these newcomers live in ramshackle huts and often make a living picking through trash heaps. As you get closer to the center, dirt side streets and overgrown vegetation give way to a modern sprawl of glittering shopping malls, luxury sports cars, and late-model pickup trucks racing down broad thoroughfares, before turning into prim middle- and upper-class neighborhoods of two- and three-story homes, all signs of a place where people know how to spend money.

Culiacán is home to a professional baseball team, the Tomateros (named for one of Sinaloa's most important *legal* cash crops), and a sprawling botanical garden, nearly twenty-five acres of architecturally designed walkways and palm groves resplendent with thousands of plant species; at the heart of the gardens sits one of artist James Turrell's gorgeous "skyspace" sculptures, with an interior that changes color as the angle of the sun changes. At sunset, it glows an incandescent pink.

The city is vivisected by three rivers, the Humaya, the Tamazula, and the Culiacán, which meet just west of the downtown, allowing for a verdant *malecón*, or waterfront boardwalk, where families stroll in the shade and street musicians set up shop. At the center of it all stands a blindingly white, neoclassical cathedral overlooking the main plaza, a shady green oasis named for the revolutionary hero Álvaro Obregón that serves as a focal point for the town's street life. On the weekends, it is common to find live bands playing in the plaza's gazebo, while elderly couples dance in pairs.

About a kilometer away from downtown, perched on a wall of green glass tiles atop a long, low-slung shack with a corrugated metal roof, and wedged between a rail yard and a busy thruway, the mustachioed face of the bandit-saint Jesús Malverde scowls down on the traffic funneling in and out of the city. Devotees come here to pay their respects and leave a small offering at the shrine in the hopes that the spirit of Malverde will bring them good fortune in business, rain in a drought, the safe return of lost or stolen property, or safe passage to the United States. Merchants peddle trinkets, votive candles, and rosaries with Malverde's image, a sign of the fusion of Catholic faith and reverence for the legendary thief who has gained a semi-sacred status as a protector of the poor and, most infamously, as the patron saint of drug traffickers.

The story goes that Jesús Malverde entered the world as Jesús Juárez Mazo around 1870, when Sinaloa and the rest of Mexico were under the thumb of the dictator José de la Cruz Porfirio Díaz Mori. Born to a peasant family, Mazo grew up in poverty so severe that his parents starved to death. He swore revenge on the elite and took to the hills for a life dedicated to robbing rich landowners and passing out the loot to poor highlanders throughout the Sierra Madre. Among his wealthy victims, the acts of banditry earned him the nickname Malverde, meaning evil-green, supposedly due to an association between misfortune and the color green. But among the impoverished residents of the Sinaloa highlands, he gained a reputation as a Robin Hood figure at a time in which local and foreign investors were gobbling up low-lying, communal agricultural land to meet U.S. demand for sugarcane and other cash crops, while subsistence farmers in the mountains were losing land to wealthy ranchers.

Malverde is said to have met his end in 1909, at the hands of a gang of enforcers in the employ of the local strongman, after a traitorous friend tipped them off to his hideout. The killers promptly executed Malverde and hung his body from a tree as a warning to any other would-be rebellious peasants, but by extinguishing the threat, Malverde's killers created a martyr. His sympathizers are said to have given him a proper burial, and covered the grave with stones. Over time, the grave marker grew into a cairn that grew taller and taller as more and more peasants—or *campesinos*, as they're known in Spanish—arrived to drop a token of thanks, a blessing on his name that they hoped would give Malverde a reason to look kindly on them and bring them good fortune. There's scant documentation of Malverde's life, and historians believe his myth grew out of the combined exploits of two real-life bandits, but the legend of a single saintly highwayman persists. His alleged powers have kept pace with technology, too: on one of my visits to the shrine, a local man helpfully informed a visiting TV crew that their footage would come out black-and-white unless they made a donation to the saint.

Believers hold an annual feast at the shrine on May 3, the supposed date of Malverde's execution, and a cult of devotion has sprung up around it. The walls of the little chapel are bedecked with placards paid for by families and individuals from Culiacán, other towns in Sinaloa and nearby states, and those from afar, including placards from North Hollywood, California, Las Vegas, Nevada, and beyond. Many of them are emblazoned with favors and thanks—blessings for an easy road ahead, gratitude for a son's release from prison. Dollars from the United States and Canada, peso notes, even a few bills from China and Japan paper the walls, with messages scrawled on them in Spanish, English, and at least one in Arabic.

At the shrine, which was erected in the 1970s, another visage has begun to appear in recent years: the defiant, mustachioed face of Sinaloa's most famous native son, Joaquín Archivaldo Guzmán Loera, better known as El Chapo. To the extent that people outside Mexico are familiar with Malverde, it's often because of El Chapo and other drug traffickers like him.

Outside, mixed among the Malverde merch, are items that nod to this connecton. On one visit, I found a small statue of El Chapo—holding an assault rifle, his chin jutting up defiantly beneath his trademark baseball cap—standing on a table out front. Hanging from a rack and available for sale were several hats emblazoned with "CDS" (Cártel de Sinaloa), or "Private Pilot," or "701"—the rank given to El Chapo by *Forbes* magazine in 2009 when the magazine included him on its list of billionaires.

The number has become a shorthand for El Chapo, and can be seen on T-shirts, hats, and in graffiti scrawled on walls all around Culiacán.

The proliferation of merch bearing El Chapo's name and image—and its place of honor at the shrine of the bandit-saint—illustrates this particular drug lord's status in the popular imagination. El Chapo Guzmán is a flesh-and-blood human, unlike the semi-mythical Jesús Malverde, but the legend of El Chapo can appear just as fantastical. With his image as a local boy who hit it big while thumbing his nose at the gringos—an image bolstered by a media eager to simplify the sprawling, unruly, and complex tale of drug trafficking, corruption, violence, and misery into a one-man show—El Chapo has reached mythic proportions not unlike the fabled underdog Malverde. As the placards and foreign currency make clear, both the legend of Malverde and his devotees have spread far and wide. Jesús Malverde candles and statues have made their way north, appearing at alternative-medicine *boticas* in Latino neighborhoods in the United States, and retailing on Amazon for $27.96. He even showed up at El Chapo's trial in Brooklyn federal court, where reporters spotted a six-inch statue of Malverde on the defense team's table.

"It miraculously appeared," one of El Chapo's lawyers quipped to a tabloid reporter.

On my first visit to the shrine in April 2019, a young boy noticed my interest in the El Chapo merch on sale, and walked over to strike up a conversation.

"That's *El Señor*," he explained helpfully, as if I or anyone else could somehow be here and not know. "Chapo Guzmán."

When I told the kid that I had recently spent three months sitting in a courtroom just a few feet away from this fabled native of Sinaloa, his eyes went wide.

"How is he?" he asked, with a genuine concern that I heard frequently from residents of Culiacán and Sinaloa when discussing the trial of *El Señor*. I told the boy that El Chapo appeared alert and had followed the proceedings closely; I feigned a note of regret when I reported that El Chapo would likely spend the rest of his life in prison.

On another visit to the Malverde shrine, I found a two-man band playing for a small audience. A family sat watching on a bench several feet away, a little girl fanning her baby brother in the sweltering humidity that cloaked the city like a blanket. After pausing to wipe their sweaty faces, the two men, armed with an accordion, a guitar, and a small portable amp, struck up a tune, the rhythmic wheezing of the accordion keeping time as the guitarist banged out the melody.

> *Joaquín lo era lo es y será*
> *prófugo de la justicia*
> *el señor de la montaña*
> *también jefe en la ciudad*
> "Joaquín was what he is and will be
> A fugitive from justice
> The lord of the mountain
> And a boss in the city"

They were singing *narcocorridos*, songs recounting the exploits of notable figures in the drug trade. *Narcocorridos* often get a bad rap. Like the culture warriors in the United States who blame poverty and marginalization on hip-hop lyrics rather than addressing the structural issues that are the root of the problem, some commentators in Mexico have lambasted *narcocorridos* for glamorizing so-called narco culture. At first glance, it's easy to find it distasteful how the songs turn the abject violence of the drug war into the stuff of legend and the actions of blood-stained criminals into tales of heroism. But they're also a vital form of storytelling, and in a country where members of the press—those who haven't been killed or intimidated and forced out of business—are viewed with suspicion, *narcocorridos* are often seen as more honest chroniclers of the drug trade.

Baldomar Cáceres, a Culiacán-based singer born in Badiraguato, the rural municipality from which El Chapo hails, can belt out an a cappella ballad about nearly any narco you name, telling stories of their lives, notorious moments in their careers, and sometimes of their deaths. On my first day in Culiacán, Baldomar accompanied me on a drive around town, including a walk along an industrial canal to check out a drainage tunnel that El Chapo once used to escape a raid by Mexican Marines and the Drug Enforcement Administration (DEA). Standing at the mouth of the tunnel, Baldomar spontaneously burst into song.

Un túnel de alto criterio
Como kilómetro y medio
Por bajo de la tierra
Construcción sofisticada
Gracias ingenieros
"A tunnel of highest quality
About a kilometer and a half
Underneath the earth
Sophisticated construction
Thanks to the engineers"

The image of drug trafficking as a form of social banditry in the tradition of Jesús Malverde fits nicely with the rugged self-sufficiency of the inhabitants of the Sinaloa highlands, who eke out a hardscrabble life with little help from the state. Many local boys, El Chapo among them, have certainly distributed portions of their illegal largesse after hitting it big, helping to fund roads, electricity, and water pipes in their hometowns and earning a reputation as swaggering Robin Hoods—or Malverdes. Countless people I spoke with in Culiacán had stories, all virtually impossible to verify, of being at this wedding or that *quinceañera* at which El Chapo showed up to buy a round of drinks or hand out cash. El Chapo may have done that, but it's not hard to guess the real reasons a guy like El Chapo, with product to move, might want to buy local support, or build roads through remote mountains. And this narrative—the hard men taking on the government and giving back to their communities—obscures the real networks of power here.

Origin stories of the drug trade in Sinaloa often highlight the region's legacy of upheaval, banditry, and rebellion. But unlike the doomed bandit Malverde, early drug-trafficking clans of Sinaloa were hardly treated as outlaws. The Mexican sociologist Luís Astorga writes that early Mexican drug traffickers emerged *from within* the state power structure, rather than as actors outside of it. They came along at a time when that power structure itself was just taking shape, and managed to negotiate for themselves a cozy little cubby within it, one that worked for the state, for the wealthy elite, *and* for the drug traffickers and cultivators. To a more limited extent, it also worked well for the poor peasants living in areas like Sinaloa. There is a proud tradition of independence and autonomy in the Sierra, and the cultivation and trafficking of drugs allowed the people of the Golden Triangle to continue to fend mostly for themselves without posing a true threat to the core legitimacy of the government. The drug traffickers who came before El Chapo acted as local power brokers, playing a key role as unofficial intermediaries between the government and the people of the Sierra. The government allowed them to get rich trafficking drugs as long as the traffickers kept a relative peace in rural areas and made sure the local peasants showed up to vote for the ruling Institutional Revolutionary Party, or PRI.

These traffickers and the men like El Chapo who followed in their footsteps served for decades as pillars of support in the complex patronage system that kept Mexico a de facto one-party state for most of the twentieth century. When violence did arise, it typically came down not on the major traffickers who held power in drug-producing regions but rather on the heads of peasants. Sometimes that was because local authorities or their backers in Mexico City had decided that this town or that communal land project, or *ejido*, had become too troublesome. Later it came in the form of anti-drug raids pursued in an effort to appease the United States as Washington put the screws to the PRI to attack marijuana and opium production at the source. The system they maintained was orderly, if not entirely peaceful.

Things have changed in the past two decades. The violence of the contemporary drug trade in Mexico is bloodier, more indiscriminate, and more depraved than anything the early drug smugglers of Sinaloa could have imagined. The breakdown began in the 1990s, as the PRI lost its grip on power, and conflict among traffickers increased as the lines of communication with the state grew blurrier. But most scholars of this period date the true starting point to 2006, when then-president Felipe Calderón declared war on the so-called cartels, and sent the military into supposed "cartel strongholds" across the country. To write that this effort has failed is so obvious as to insult the intelligence of the reader, and does not do justice to the scale of the brutality, or to the depth to which it has traumatized Mexican society. In the decade and a half since the current drug war began in Mexico, hundreds of thousands of people have been murdered; tens of thousands more have been forcibly disappeared. Many areas of the country have become unrecognizable as people flee their homes and violence becomes commonplace.

At the heart of the violence and instability is a perpetual crisis of impunity and a core failure of the nation's criminal investigations and judicial system: nationwide, in 2018, 90 percent of homicides went unsolved; in the state of Guerrero, that figure stood at 98 percent. In the same year, an arrest was made in just 11.5 percent of criminal cases—and this typically when a suspect was caught in flagrante at the scene of the crime. Less than 4 percent of crimes resulted in some kind of judicial resolution, and less than 1 percent of those were from an actual trial.

In a system where killers, extortionists, and kidnappers are overwhelmingly able to commit crimes with little fear, in which the vanishingly small number of resolutions take place without any kind of transparency, civilians have a fundamental distrust of the authorities. As a result, the overwhelming majority of crimes are never reported.

The United States is inextricably involved in this violence in nearly every way: As the world's largest consumer of illicit drugs, it is North Americans' demand that drives the market and pours billions of dollars each year into the pockets of traffickers; for virtually the entire history of the prohibition of illicit drugs, Washington has directly pressured Mexican governments to comply with its anti-drug policies, violating Mexican sovereignty and denying its people the right to form their own policies; and the United States has provided direct operational support to the war on drugs in Mexico. By selling arms through official channels to security forces and allowing the traffic of illegal weapons to armed groups, the United States has effectively been providing cash and guns to all sides of the conflict, ensuring that confrontations grow ever more violent and deadly. This economy of death ramped up with particular ferocity in the first two decades of the twenty-first century: between 2008 and 2019, under an accord known as the Mérida Initiative, the United States provided more than $3 billion in anti-drug aid; during the same period, direct commercial arms sales to Mexico stood at $1.5 billion; sales of military hardware to Mexico for those years totaled more than half a billion dollars; ongoing human rights abuses committed by Mexican security forces, which began to accelerate dramatically in 2006, never proved an impediment to direct U.S. assistance.

Scary words have been thrown around like "insurgency," or "failed state." But drug traffickers like El Chapo have never sought the power of government, aside from making sure they have contacts in the government who can protect their business interests. Unlike the legendary Jesús Malverde, or left-wing guerrillas in the latter half of the twentieth century, drug traffickers in Mexico have never truly challenged the legitimacy of the state; on the contrary, they have often worked *with* security forces to suppress such uprisings, and there has long been a revolving door between trafficking networks and police agencies, particularly those agencies tasked with crushing political dissent—and those tasked with fighting the drug trade itself, which naturally brings them into contact with drug traffickers.

El Chapo may enjoy widespread support back home in Sinaloa, but he bears little resemblance to Jesús Malverde.

. . .

I first began writing about El Chapo in the fall of 2018, when I was assigned to cover his trial for *Rolling Stone*. When I think back now to my life before El Chapo, it gets a bit fuzzy trying to separate the bits and pieces I knew back then from what I have learned since. I likely knew more than the average American, having spent some time living in Latin America and picking up enough Spanish from a few stints living in Peru to read Spanish-language newspapers and take deep, autodidactic dives researching niche subjects like organized crime, drug lore, and fringe revolutionary movements. I knew who he was when he escaped for the second time from a Mexican prison in 2015, and I had some ambient sense of the terrifying violence that had consumed Mexico over the past two decades, and thanks to an interest in Mexican social movements, I had a baseline understanding of the political system in Mexico. But I was no expert. When I got the gig with *Rolling Stone* after applying for a different job there—they weren't hiring just yet, they said, but I spoke Spanish, and I had experience covering courts, they said; did I want to cover the El Chapo trial?—I embarked on a frantic mission to learn everything I could about the guy who, as it turns out, I didn't know a whole lot about. I say that to say this: in my initial breakneck catch-up sessions, and in the deeper research I've done since, I am entirely indebted to the work of Mexican journalists who have risked everything to write about drug traffickers and the state forces who enable them.

The trial began in early November 2018, and after a day or so I realized it was going to be a day-in, day-out affair. For three months, I sat in court each day, as El Chapo's former friends, associates, employees, and one tearful ex-lover recounted in painstaking detail his thirty-year career in drug smuggling.

We heard from Miguel Ángel Martínez Martínez, a former pilot and longtime partner of El Chapo who had survived repeated attempts on his life while in prison—assassination attempts he blamed on El Chapo— and then done his time in the United States, cooperated extensively, and been rewarded with an early release date. He was in witness protection by the time he testified in Brooklyn, and in order to protect him from retaliation the judge barred courtroom sketch artists from depicting his likeness. Martínez was a former cocaine addict who at the height of his game had been hoovering up as much as four grams of uncut coke a day, a fact that the defense tried to use to discredit his testimony. In a memorable moment, one of El Chapo's lawyers held up sugar packet to give jurors an idea of exactly how much cocaine that is. It's a lot.

One of the most revealing moments of the trial occurred during the testimony of Martínez, although it received little notice at the time. The topic of discussion was El Chapo's famous tunnel, the one he dug under the border between Agua Prieta, Sonora, and Douglas, Arizona, in 1990. Why, the prosecutor asked, had El Chapo chosen Agua Prieta?

It was simple, really:

"It was the city that the police had assigned to Mr. Guzmán in exchange for money so that he could work there with the drugs," Martínez replied, casually corroborating the long-held assertion that it was the state that controlled the drug trade in those days, rather than the traffickers themselves.

We heard from Jesús Reynaldo Zambada García, the brother of El Chapo's closest partner, Ismael Zambada García, aka El Mayo. Zambada walked jurors through notable events in his former associate's life, including his 2001 escape from prison. We also heard from Dámaso López, the former prison administrator who'd made El Chapo's life behind bars as comfortable as possible, and later went to work for El Chapo after his escape.

The assortment of former business associates included Jorge and Alex Cifuentes Villa, a pair of Colombian brothers who'd shipped cocaine to El Chapo and worked closely with him in Mexico. The two Cifuentes brothers made particularly fascinating witnesses, in part because of the apparent glee they took in sparring with El Chapo's attorneys, who did their best to draw the jury's attention to the brothers' villainous backstories.

In one memorable exchange, defense attorney John Lichtman highlighted countless examples in which Alex Cifuentes had admitted to lying to friends, family, colleagues, police, and prosecutors, pretty much everyone he had ever come into contact with.

LICHTMAN: And part of being a drug dealer, as we've seen today, is being a good liar, correct?

CIFUENTES: Yes, sir.

LICHTMAN: You lied all the time, didn't you?

CIFUENTES: Yes, sir.

LICHTMAN: You lied to other drug dealers?

CIFUENTES: Yes, sir.

LICHTMAN: You lied to your co-conspirators, correct?

CIFUENTES: Yes, sir.

LICHTMAN: You lied to your friends?

CIFUENTES: Yes, sir.

LICHTMAN: You lied to law enforcement.

CIFUENTES: Yes, sir.

LICHTMAN: You lied to immigration officials.

CIFUENTES: Yes, sir.

LICHTMAN: You lied to prosecutors.

CIFUENTES: Yes, sir.

LICHTMAN: You lied to lawyers.

CIFUENTES: Yes, sir.

LICHTMAN: You lied to your family.

CIFUENTES: Yes, sir.

LICHTMAN: You lied to your siblings.

CIFUENTES: Yes, sir.

LICHTMAN: You lied to your wife.

CIFUENTES: Yes, sir.

LICHTMAN: Your girlfriends.

CIFUENTES: Yes, sir.

LICHTMAN: And you didn't just lie about your drug dealing business, you lied about personal affairs as well; isn't that true?

CIFUENTES: Yes, sir.

Why, then, Lichtman was implying, should jurors believe him now? At times, the repetition became almost hypnotic, ping-ponging back and forth until finally Lichtman drove home his point and the jurors and members of the public snapped out of it to see where he had been aiming for all along.

LICHTMAN: You lied about Mr. Guzmán, didn't you?

CIFUENTES: No, sir.

LICHTMAN: He's the only person you didn't lie about?

CIFUENTES: That's right, sir.

In the first days of 2019, another Zambada arrived in court: Vicente "Vicentillo" Zambada Niebla, the eldest son and onetime heir apparent of El Mayo. Vicentillo is a handsome man with arrogant eyes and a majestic chin, and he held a commanding presence as he stared out at the courtroom. In calm detail he spoke of his life growing up at the center of his father's organized-crime empire, teenage jaunts to sit-downs with some of Mexico's most fearsome criminals, and contacts with some of its most powerful security officials. What he didn't talk about—or rather was not allowed to talk about—was the fact that he himself, as well as El Chapo, had met with DEA officials in order to drop the dime on rivals.

All electronic devices were barred in the courtroom, so reporters had to write notes by hand, something, which I admit is a tough job for my millennial fingers, accustomed as they are to tapping out notes on my phone. The task of scribbling as much you could, as verbatim as possible, for nearly eight hours every day, was exhausting. At times we would take turns going to the media room and swapping notes later, but it was a risky gambit to miss even a minute of the testimony. On some days, a witness would drone on for hours about boring minutiae, only for the prosecution or the defense team to pivot to an earth-shatteringly newsworthy subject with no notice whatsoever.

On the afternoon of January 15, I had ducked out of the overflow room and headed downstairs to the media room to call a source. As I was chatting with the guy, a retired DEA agent, I heard in the hall-way a sudden staccato pitter-patter, and then a stampede as reporters—particularly the Mexican reporters—charged into the room and began frantically calling their editors. Upstairs, under questioning from Licht-man, Alex Cifuentes had moments ago accused former President Enrique Peña Nieto of soliciting a bribe of more than $100 million dollars from El Chapo. Now, at the midafternoon break, my colleagues and I had less than twenty minutes to phone in the basic details to their editors and dash off a couple tweets before heading back to the courtroom.

"I'm gonna have to call you back," I told the retired DEA agent, hang-ing up and tossing my phone aside as I swung around wildly to try to figure out what might have just emerged.

By the time we headed upstairs to hear more, "El Chapo" and "En-rique Peña Nieto" were trending on Twitter as the bombshell allegation ricocheted around the web. Upstairs, Lichtman dove back into questions about the alleged bribe, while a supremely uncooperative Alex did his best to stonewall and deflect. The dynamic between the two was a result of the curious dance between witness and prosecutor, and witness and defense attorney: while Alex and other witnesses had freely admitted to every misdeed under the sun when asked by the prosecutors who had called them to the stand, they were less forthcoming when the questions came from the defense team, particularly when it was an issue that prosecutors had not brought up at all. Alex had originally made the Peña Nieto bribery allegation during proffer sessions, marathon sittings at which he agreed to tell U.S. investigators everything he knew, absolutely everything, as a condition of his guilty plea.

Slowly, haltingly, Lichtman pried the information out of Alex, who in a 2016 proffer session had told investigators that Peña Nieto had reached out to Chapo in 2012 during his presidential bid, pledging that if he were elected he would call off the manhunt and allow Chapo to live and work in peace; all Chapo had to do was "donate" $250 million to Peña Nieto's campaign coffers. Chapo, never one to say yes without some negotiating, responded with a counteroffer: $100 million in cash. According to Alex, Chapo sent the money through an intermediary nicknamed Comadre (Godmother) Maria, who delivered the cash-stuffed suitcases on the private jet of a prominent political consultant working for Peña Nieto's campaign. (Peña Nieto has forcefully and repeatedly denied the accusations, and no corroborating evidence has been found to support Alex's explosive claim.)

At the center of everything, always, was El Chapo. At the beginning of the trial he seemed almost bored at times, but as it wore on he began to engage more: sitting there at the defense table, leaning over to listen to his translator, or discussing something with his lawyers, or staring intently at a witness, or scanning the faces of the reporters and tourists and lawyers sitting in the gallery. His beady little eyes seemed to take in everything.

Many of the cooperating witnesses were well-known former drug traffickers, arrested years ago and extradited to the United States. But some were a surprise, like Christian Rodriguez, a young Colombian man who, it turned out, had played perhaps the most crucial role among all the informants at trial in building the case against El Chapo. A pudgy, soft-spoken young man, Christian was still in his twenties when he testified, years after he'd worked for El Chapo as something of a chief technology officer, with all the day-to-day headaches of an IT guy building communications systems for a particularly demanding boss, and then some. His testimony, and the evidence he'd gathered, revealed the most solid proof anyone had ever seen against El Chapo, and we hung on his every word.

Along with the two dozen or so reporters who formed the daily press corps, I watched intently to see how El Chapo would react to each co-operating witness, many of whom he had worked with closely for years, but might not have seen in decades. When El Rey Zambada entered, El Chapo appeared to greet him by raising his arms and crossing them as the two men locked eyes; as Dámaso López took the stand, he nodded at El Chapo, and held his hand to his heart; Vicentillo Zambada gave his compadre a smug little smile as he entered. Others seemed frightened, such as Christian Rodriguez, who tried to avoid looking in the direction of his former boss at all costs.

The most outrageous—and tabloid-worthy—reaction came on January 22, the second day of testimony by Lucero Sánchez López, a onetime state legislator in Sinaloa and, before that, El Chapo's lover. On her first day of testimony, she had presented a pitiful sight, speaking in a meek, low voice, appearing afraid even to be in the same room as El Chapo. Then, the following Monday, El Chapo appeared resplendent in a red velvet smoking jacket, seemingly matching his outfit to his glamorous young wife, Emma Coronel Aispuro, who strolled into the courtroom in a similar, if considerably more formfitting jacket. They appeared to be sending a message: in the face of testimony from his former lover, El Chapo's wife remained on his side.

On the day that the jury began deliberations, reporters threw out predictions for how long it would take them to reach a verdict; some guessed a few hours, arguing that the avalanche of evidence would convince even the most thorough juror of El Chapo's guilt; others guessed that for that very reason it could take days, if jurors were going to make an honest go of assessing the evidence.

Finally, at around 2 p.m. on February 12, the sixth day of deliberations, the press officer for the Department of Justice sent out an urgent email: the jury had sent a note; they'd reached a verdict.

After more than two long months, this was it. But no one was surprised with the result: Joaquín Archivaldo Guzmán Loera was found guilty on all counts. El Chapo took it in stride, and if he had a reaction, I couldn't see it on his face.

The jurors filed out, and after a few closing remarks, Judge Brian M. Cogan adjourned the court. Rising to his feet, El Chapo shook the hands of his lawyers, and turned to face his wife. Nodding at her a few times, he smiled, gave her a thumbs-up, and then turned around as the marshals led him out a side door.

A reporter approached Emma and asked her in Spanish how she felt. She was dry-eyed.

"Nobody's dead," she said, as she bustled past us and out the door.

. . .

A few months later, during my second trip to Sinaloa, I found myself in a half-empty coffee shop in Culiacán, stammering out questions to a guy named Beto. It was late, nearly 10 p.m., and the staff were eyeing us in hopes that we'd clear out so they could close up shop for the night. I was exhausted as well. Working with my fixer, a local reporter named Miguel Ángel Vega, I'd already done three or four hours of interviews that day, all in Spanish. My Spanish is okay, but it takes all the concentration I can muster to follow along and ask follow-up questions, and by the end of a day like that one, I was half-delirious, ready to drop. So when Beto and his two bodyguards strolled into the cafe, all tight jeans, polo shirts, flat-brim caps, and a lazy air of coiled menace around them, I was not only dead tired but also a little intimidated. They sat down and muttered darkly that they'd seen some men in the parking lot outside, didn't like the looks of them, and had waited until they left. That's why they were late.

At Beto's request, we moved from the table by the window where Miguel Ángel and I had been sitting to another one farther inside, so Beto could have his back to the wall. A few minutes later it became clear that the interview wasn't going well; it was my fault, and Beto seemed mildly annoyed. Shifting occasionally around in his seat, he looked uncomfortable, and during one of these fidgets I saw why, as he tugged the hem of his black polo shirt down to cover the handle of the semiautomatic pistol sticking out of his waistband.

He said he was a nephew of El Chapo, but that's a vague term, and

I figured he was probably more like a distant cousin. Still, he knew El Chapo better than almost anyone else I'd spoken with, and was particularly familiar with El Chapo's later years. Raised in the tiny village of Nogalito, a few miles from El Chapo's hometown of La Tuna, he worked closely with El Chapo, first as part of his security entourage and later as a pilot. I asked him something stupid: "Did you know your uncle well?" and he responded with a hint of mockery in his voice.

"I should," he said with a smirk. "I practically slept in the same bed as him every night."

I laughed nervously and tried to come up with a response, or at least my next question, but before I could do so, Beto looked up from his phone and locked eyes with me.

"I have a question for *you*," he said. "Why do gringo journalists always want to come here to Sinaloa to ask about drugs?"

You'd think I would have had a ready answer for this. It was my second trip to Culiacán, and I'd been working on the same story now for more than six months. But what he said gave me pause. Why did U.S. journalists come here? Why was *I* here?

Good question.

The only other gringos I ran into in Culiacán during all of my trips there was a film crew working on a documentary, and it was no coincidence that I ran into them at the Jesús Malverde shrine, a seemingly required stop on the "narco tours" of Sinaloa that reliably shows up in nearly every book or documentary on the region. You know the ones: a tough host whispering to the camera about the danger he's in, wondering if this pedestrian or that street juggler is a *halcón*, or falcon, the term for a cartel lookout; the masked dealers speaking in digitally altered tones near piles of drugs and weapons. I've watched them all, and I rarely come away from them feeling more knowledgeable about the situation in Sinaloa. There's little hard information, little context, hardly any discussion of the role of the police and military outside of a cops-and-robbers dynamic. (Over time, as Miguel Ángel and I got to know one another better, we made a game of mocking this self-serious genre, pointing to sillier and sillier candidates to identify as potential *halcónes.* My favorite was the inflatable dancing tube figure outside a car dealership.)

I came to Culiacán to do something different. When I first set out to write this book, I was asked the same question again and again: How are you going to find new information? Well-meaning friends, know-it-alls on Twitter, even a Customs and Border Protection agent at JFK Airport asked me this, pointing out as he stamped my passport that he'd already seen *Narcos*. What more was there to find out? For one thing, I knew that El Chapo's story needed to be cast in a more nuanced light, offering a better understanding not just of his exploits but of the place he came from, the time in history he inhabited, the forces of prohibition and foreign policy that shaped the drug trade and helped make him wealthy and left tens of thousands of Mexicans dead and tens of thousands more disappeared.

But sitting there next to Beto, I didn't know how to articulate that. I know better now, and I wish I could have explained myself to Beto. Here was a rough man, almost certainly with blood on his hands, asking me a simple question without malice or mockery. Why was I here in Culiacán, asking him questions about his uncle?

In response, I stammered something corny about finding the truth, telling the story of El Chapo, explaining how the opioid crisis was ravaging communities in the United States and it was important to understand where the drugs came from and what motivates the people here to send the drugs north. But I could tell Beto wasn't satisfied with my answer. *I* wasn't satisfied with my answer.

In the end, I never got the second interview with him; I never got to answer his question. A month or so after we first met, I was standing in the kitchen of my apartment in Mexico City, about to go for a walk with a friend, when my cell phone rang: it was Miguel Ángel. We'd been discussing plans for an upcoming trip to Sinaloa, which was to be my third. Among other meetings, I'd been pestering him to get me in touch with Beto again, to give me a chance to do a more thorough interview after blowing it the first time. But when I picked up, Miguel Ángel's voice sounded different, strained, stressed out.

"Dude, they fucking killed Beto," Miguel Ángel said in Spanish. "Beto's dead."

"What the fuck," I said, walking into another room. I asked Miguel to slow down, and then asked him to speak in English, as I was having trouble understanding his rapid-fire report filtered through a shitty phone connection.

Miguel Ángel didn't know much at that point, but over the next few days, word trickled out. One Sunday, July 21, Beto had received a call from someone claiming to be a cop, who told Beto that he'd arrested one of Beto's guys, that Beto would need to show up at a meeting place with ten thousand dollars if he wanted his man to come home alive. Beto had gotten the cash, and with two other men had gone to meet the cops. None of them were ever seen alive again. Two days later, Beto and his aide, the first guy to be "arrested," were found in a construction site on the outskirts of town, their bodies disfigured with signs of torture, bullet holes in their heads. Like so many other young men in Sinaloa, Beto was now a victim, a statistic, one of dozens of people murdered in the city that month.

Miguel Ángel and I never figured out why someone decided to kill Beto. Maybe it was a routine shakedown operation by crooked cops; maybe he pissed someone off; maybe someone owed him money and they didn't want to pay up. People like Beto have enemies, they live danger-ously, and they die for a lot of different reasons. At thirty-four, Beto was an elder statesman in narco years. Shortly before he died, Beto gave an interview to a British journalist with little experience working in Mexico, and in a parking lot in broad daylight Beto had shown the reporter the weapons he had stashed in the back of his truck. Maybe someone had seen this exchange and found it concerning. The British journalist wrote up the interview in breathless terms, laughably referring to Beto as a "drug baron." When word of Beto's death reached him, the reporter all but bragged about having spoken to Beto just days before he disappeared, recalling Beto's "last supper with me." (Miguel Ángel was not involved in setting up that interview.) Later, I would head up to the mountains to visit the little cemetery where Beto was buried, perched on a peak high above the village where he was born. I sat with his family as they spoke of the young man they had loved, the one who used to buzz his Cessna over their house whenever he flew back home for work or for a visit. They spoke with bitter anger at the way he had been killed, disappeared and dumped in a parking lot, rather than shot down like a man.

When I learned of Beto's death, I was upset that he had died violently; I was upset that his family was left grieving; I was upset that for a kid born in a tiny village deep in the mountains of Sinaloa, the life that Beto chose was virtually the only way for him to find respect and material comfort, and that this same life condemned him to an early death. And I felt regret that I never got to fully answer his question, to explain to him why I was reporting this book, why people so far away in the States would care about what's happening in his hometown.

From the outset, I intended to use the myth of El Chapo to tell a larger story: that of the drug trade in Mexico, how its interactions and entanglements with the state went far beyond the common assumptions of the cops-and-robbers dynamic, the brave cops and heroic soldiers and federal agents pursuing the dastardly, death-loving drug traffickers.

I hope this book serves as some sort of answer to Beto's question. But it's not just Beto who deserves an answer. My greatest hope is that I may add a bit of clarity to a complex story. Not just the story of El Chapo, but of Sinaloa, Ciudad Juárez, and of Mexico: the story of the chaotic, futile, and bloody mess of the so-called war on drugs.

This is a story I am able to tell only because of the unfathomably brave work of a small army of honest journalists in Mexico, many of whom faced grave danger and vile threats—and too many of whom paid with their lives—simply for committing the crime of telling the truth. I will be grateful to them as long as I live.

This book deals with a narrow slice of life in Mexico. The goal of it is to illustrate the mechanisms of power, corruption, and violence that influence and perpetuate the drug trade, and the society in which it exists. But this narrow view is a violent one, a dark one, and it cannot encompass the joyous, brilliant, vibrant and exhilarating aspects of life in Mexico. It is my greatest hope that readers of this book will seek out Mexico for themselves, and that they love what they find.

1

THE BOY FROM LA TUNA

I**T'S A HOT** and sunny day in mid-April 2019, and I'm sitting in the passenger seat of a borrowed Honda Pilot SUV driven by Miguel Ángel Vega, a jovial reporter born and raised in Culiacán. We're on our way to La Tuna, the birthplace of El Chapo, and like many of the towns and villages in these parts, it is not an easy place to get to. For people who don't want to be found, that's what makes it such a good place to hide. Driving along the twists and turns of Highway 24 as it hugs the curves of the hillsides, I can see why Sinaloans pride themselves on autonomy: in a place this remote, you can't look to the outside world for help. As I was about to find out, they take matters of security into their own hands out here.

It's an hour just to get from Culiacán to the municipal capital of Badiraguato, a town of about 3,700 people that spreads out on either side of the highway, which forms a main drag through town. Crossing the last bridge on the way out of Badiraguato, our cell phones lose service, and we drive for another hour up the highway before our next turn. Miguel Ángel and I pass the time chatting about the job, him quizzing me on my experience reporting on El Chapo's trial and me asking him questions about the area, obscure figures in the drug trade, his life reporting on the violence in his hometown. It's early afternoon now, and I'm forced to reapply sunscreen to my skin, still pale from winter in New York, and eventually I drape a spare shirt over my right arm to keep it from burning in the sun. Finally we come to the turnoff that will lead to La Tuna. This is where we hit the first checkpoint.

Miguel Ángel eases his foot off the gas and cuts the wheel left to turn onto a narrow dirt track headed off the highway and deeper into the mountains. By the side of the road, lounging in the shade of a tree, three men sit cradling AK-47-style rifles. As we pull up, they go bolt upright and eye us with sudden attention. A few feet away up a slight hill, a fourth man hops out of the cab of a bulldozer, an AK in one hand and a walkie-talkie in the other. With the walkie-talkie hand, he waves at us to stop, as his pals get to their feet. Apart from the tactical vests that hold extra magazines of ammo, all four men are dressed in street clothes. These men are not soldiers, and they're not cops, although they might be the closest thing to cops or soldiers around here.

Years after a team of Mexican Marines and a couple of DEA agents captured El Chapo in the coastal Sinaloan city of Mazatlán, and years after he made his second escape from a maximum-security prison, and years after another team of Mexican Marines captured him in the Sinaloan city of Los Mochis, and years after Mexican authorities washed their hands of him and handed him over to U.S. agents and he was loaded onto a plane and flown to New York, where he was convicted on all counts to face life in prison, the valley where El Chapo spent his youth remains solidly under the control of his brother Aureliano Guzmán Loera, a rotund and fearsome man known by his nickname, "El Guano."

El Guano was never much of a kingpin, nor even a second-in-command to El Chapo, who had always favored another brother, Arturo. El Guano's not much of a kingpin now, either; his domain extends about as far as the highway, and he's mostly in control of the drug cultivation in the area, while others make the real money smuggling drugs north and wield the real power, paying off entire police departments and city governments. But on this road, in this valley, El Guano is the man, and it's with his permission, granted on a semipermanent basis through a contact of Miguel Ángel, that we're allowed to enter the area.

The lead gunman appears to be in his late twenties, his arms covered in tattoos. Gripping the AK by its distinctive curved magazine—referred to in Mexico as a *cuerno de chivo*, or goat's horn—he keeps the muzzle pointed at the ground as he strolls up to the passenger-side window and motions for me to roll it down.

He wants to know who we are, what we're doing there. Do we have permission to be there?

I'm not sure how to respond.

When Miguel Ángel picked me up at the airport twenty-four hours earlier, the first thing he told me was the importance of being honest with these guys: as long as you're straight with them, they'll be straight with you. If you tell the truth, you don't have to worry. Miguel Ángel should know. After working for years as a journalist in Culiacán for the local weekly paper *Riodoce* (and a stint directing movies), he now makes his living as a "fixer," driving international reporters around the state setting up interviews with all manner of shady characters. Around here, he's the best in the business, and does a brisk trade as one of the only reporters with the contacts necessary to gain access to La Tuna.

When the gunman asks me if I speak Spanish, the first thing that comes out of my mouth is a lie.

"No," I say, feigning a look of regret.

My heart is pounding. Although I had known we might come across checkpoints like this, and I had heard stories of other reporters being turned away, Miguel Ángel and I have not discussed what I should say in such a situation. It seems wise to let him do the talking.

After giving me a hard stare for a moment, the gunman turns to Miguel Ángel and asks him who we are, if we're journalists. In a cheerfully deferential tone, Miguel says that yes, we're reporters, but explains that we're just here to see a friend.

Not a lie! Over the years, Miguel Ángel has cultivated a relationship with our host, an evangelical Christian who lives and raises cattle in La Tuna, just a short walk from the home of El Chapo's mother, and who graciously hosts Miguel Ángel and his rotating cast of guests.

"He's expecting us, ask them on the radio," Miguel Ángel tells the gunman with the tattoos and the hard stare.

Without taking his eyes off us, the young gunman takes a step back and mutters something into the radio. After a moment, he receives an answer that seems to satisfy him. He turns to me again, nearly blinding me with his gaze.

"¿Cómo te llamas?" he asks. "What's your name?"

Although I've been following the conversation fine, I perk up at this, as if the question is the first thing I understand, a relic of some Spanish 101 class in high school, and answer like I'm proud to pass a test.

"Noah, me llamo Noah," I chirp with only partially feigned relief, heart still racing.

The gunman gives me a close look, as if trying to determine if I'm lying.

"Okay," he says finally, with a raise of his eyebrows. After one more squint for good measure, he waves us along.

Miguel Ángel waves at the men as we pass. I dig into my backpack, pull out a pack of cigarettes, and light one, taking a long drag in relief.

"Dude," Miguel Ángel says happily, "were you so fucking scared?"

• • •

From the highway, we follow a dirt track as it curves and plunges and climbs its way deeper into the hills. The drive is punctuated now and again by small ranches and villages, some with names that would be familiar to a knowledgeable scholar of Mexico's drug lore, in which Sinaloa plays a central role. This area spawned enough big-name narcos to field the starting lineup of a baseball team (along with a healthy portion of the bullpen), and we pass through a series of villages that were once home to many of the men whose names have dominated most-wanted posters and newspaper headlines at one time or another for decades: Huixiopa, the birthplace of Juan José Esparragoza Moreno, alias El Azul; La Palma, hometown of the brothers Beltrán Leyva; and finally, La Tuna, home of El Chapo.

As we enter the village, it's immediately apparent that, among the impoverished villages of the region, this little community has received special attention. Dirt roads give way to paving stones, and most of the houses are in better shape than those in the villages we've passed. A group of young men in skinny jeans and polo shirts sit on all-terrain vehicles clustered around one of the stores. Most have walkie-talkies clipped to the belts of their jeans, and some of them have pistols sticking out of their waistbands, and they turn to give us a hard stare from under their flat-brim baseball caps as we roll past.

La Tuna is laid out in something of a horseshoe shape, and at the end of the valley, the road bends sharply and heads up the hill before curving back around. Above the midpoint of the bend in the road there sits a walled compound, the roof of a red-tiled pagoda poking above it, overlooking the valley: the home El Chapo built for his mother, now in her nineties. At the top of the ridge, about fifty yards from the compound, sits a beautiful blue and white church, which El Chapo financed in the late 1980s as a gift to his mother. Like many in La Tuna, she has been a devout born-again Christian since missionaries began spreading the good word here in the eighties, prompting a wave of conversions to the Apostolic Church, a breakaway Pentecostal movement. Just below the church sits the home of our host, and we climb out of the SUV and stand on the patio stretching, taking in the view.

· · ·

Joaquín Archivaldo Guzmán Loera was born on April 4, 1957, in La Tuna to Emilio Guzmán Bustillo and María Consuelo Loera Pérez, and he grew up there with his brothers Miguel Ángel, Aureliano, Emilio, and Arturo, and sisters Armida and Bernarda. Like most of their neighbors in La Tuna, the Guzmán family didn't have much, but with a few head of cattle inherited from El Chapo's grandparents, they were still better off than some of their neighbors. Little Joaquín was a short kid, squat, earning himself the nickname El Chapo—meaning "Shorty"—that would stick with him for life. During my visit to La Tuna, I find a first cousin of El Chapo wrangling cows into a wire cattle pen, and when he takes a break, I ask him to describe young El Chapo to me.

"Ever since he was a child, he was a talented and bright kid, he wanted to get ahead," he told me. "I'm telling you, this guy was a real fighter, a good worker and everything."

When it comes to El Chapo's early home life, it's hard to separate mythology and fact. Some versions paint El Chapo's father as a vicious and brutal man, a mean drunk who beat the young future kingpin at every opportunity and spent the little he earned on booze and prostitutes. Most of the relatives I speak with deny any abuse by Emilio's hand, although some do acknowledge that El Chapo's father was never one for hard work.

"Just like in any big family, there's one lazy one, one dumb one, one wild one, and so on," the cousin says. "Emilio just didn't like to work very much, but he was a good person."

María Consuelo, El Chapo's mother, on the other hand worked herself to the bone, tending to the family's small herd of cattle and raising young Joaquín and his siblings. El Chapo took after his mother's work ethic.

"Even as a little child he had ambitions," María Consuelo recalled in an interview published in 2014.

"I remember he had a lot of paper money—little notes of fifties and fives," his mother told the reporter. "He'd count and recount them, then tie them up in little piles. He'd say, 'Mama, save them for me.' It was just colored paper, but they looked real. He piled them up carefully. . . . Ever since he was little, he always had hopes."

With an eye toward business at an early age, legend has it that he would sell oranges to people along the winding, hilly walk between La Tuna and Huixiopa. On Sundays, his sister has said, he would get dolled up in cheap, fake gold chains and go out visiting family members and chatting up his neighbors. No matter that the fake gold would often give his skin a greenish hue.

El Chapo would continue to be a bit of a mama's boy even as he rose to prominence as one of Mexico's most notorious drug traffickers. In his only known interview, he described the relationship with María Consuelo as "perfect . . . lots of respect, affection, and love." For years, even when he was the most wanted man in Mexico, El Chapo would make regular visits back to La Tuna to see his mother. And as his wealth and status increased, he saw to it that she lived in comfort; he built the spacious compound in the center of La Tuna that she occupies to this day and installed on a hill above town a massive tank that continues to deliver running water to his mom's house, along with the rest of the village.

El Chapo never grew taller than five feet six inches tall, but he was a lively kid who loved to play volleyball, as long as he wasn't busy helping with the cattle or heading out on his sales rounds. It was that inner drive, that motivation and entrepreneurial spirit, that pushed him to look for opportunities beyond selling bread and oranges. As with so many other young men in the Golden Triangle, opportunity came in the form of opium and weed.

· · ·

The hemp plant arrived in Mexico in the sixteenth century, introduced by an emissary of the Spanish Empire who realized the crop would grow well in the colony, straddling the Tropic of Cancer, where temperate and tropical climates meet. The marijuana plant was in great demand at the time for the fabrication of the hemp ropes and sails necessary to maintain the Spanish crown's world-conquering navy, but over time the plant's flowers and the THC they contained began to be used for their psychoactive properties.

The red and pink flowers of opium poppies were also imported, from the Far East; government officials first made note of the presence of the plant growing in Sinaloa in 1889. In the mountains of the so-called Golden Triangle, where persistent droughts, thin topsoil, and steep slopes limit agricultural yield, poppies presented an attractive option to poor subsistence farmers. They could be harvested as many as three times per year and brought a significantly higher price at market than corn or beans. Many local farmers started to augment their subsistence crops with small plots of poppies and marijuana, while landowners and ranchers began to see large-scale promise in them as cash crops. A terminology sprang up around the trade: in these mountains, the opium poppy is known as *amapola*; the sap that is harvested for opium is called *goma*, or gum; and the growers and harvesters are known as *gomeros*, or gummers.

Before long, opium dens could be found in cities across northern Mexico, and opium and its derivative morphine began appearing in tinctures and patent medicines, as a brisk trade grew between the Sinaloan port city of Mazatlán and merchants in San Francisco. With the prohibition of opium in the United States in 1914, and in Mexico in 1920, the early drug runners of Sinaloa saw their profits soar when selling the stuff on the black market. Throughout the nineteenth and early twentieth centuries, opium (along with cocaine) had been legally available to consumers in a wide array of medicinal forms. In a pattern that would grimly repeat itself nearly a century later in the OxyContin-to-heroin pipeline, many consumers who had gotten hooked on formerly legal opium tinctures soon began turning to heroin. Thus demand increased, which in turn increased cultivation of opium in the Golden Triangle and other opium-producing regions across the globe.

The early drug trade in Sinaloa and the smuggling routes to the United States were initially dominated in part by pharmacists, but also by Chinese-Mexican syndicates who by at least 1916 were ferrying tins of raw opium north to Mexicali and across the border into Southern California, where they sold it to a Los Angeles–based Chinese man with connections up the West Coast. Even in these nascent, mom-and-pop days, there was a tremendous amount of money to be made in the illegal drug trade, and members of the Chinese syndicates could be seen rolling around Tijuana and Culiacán in the most expensive late-model cars Detroit had to offer. It wasn't long before Mexican gangsters began looking for a way to wrest the business from their Chinese counterparts.

Mexico during this time was in the midst of an identity crisis. After years of turmoil, the federal government was faced with the challenge of uniting a racially diverse nation divided into thirty-one states, many that were essentially ruled by the landowners who had survived the revolution or revolutionary generals who had used it to seize power. The early state builders and founding intellectuals of post-revolution Mexico set out to craft a unified national identity, celebrating the mix of indigenous and Spanish heritage that had no room for minorities like the Chinese or culturally distinct indigenous communities. Throughout the 1920s, anti-Chinese propagandists churned out newspapers such as *El Nacionalista* (The Nationalist) and *Pro-Patria* (Pro-Fatherland), blaming any social ill imaginable on the Chinese, whom they depicted as spreaders of disease and peddlers of vice, contaminating the purity of Mexico's youth with illegal gambling parlors, brothels, and opium dens. The campaign, directly inspired by similar ethnic violence against Chinese communities in the United States, reached its brutal apex in Sonora and Sinaloa, where anti-Chinese committees and nationalist gangs looted Chinese homes and expropriated businesses, forcibly deporting hundreds of residents and making life so unpleasant for others that they packed up and left. Between 1926 and 1940, more than three quarters of the Chinese population of Mexico either fled or were driven out by nationalist mobs and local police. Of the nearly 25,000 Chinese or Mexicans of Chinese descent living in the country in 1930, fewer than 5,000 remained a decade later. In Sonora, just 92 people remained from a community that once numbered 3,571 inhabitants. In Sinaloa, the Chinese population plunged from 2,123 to 165. Despite feeble attempts to repatriate some victims of the ethnic cleansing, the Chinese community of Mexico never recovered.

Sensing an opportunity, Mexican smugglers leapt into the fray. Taking advantage of—or actively fomenting—the chaos and racial tension of the moment, they swiftly and forcibly expropriated the businesses of the Chinese drug traffickers who until then had controlled the opium trade in northern Mexico. Working with their patrons in local government and forging ties with North American mafiosi, these Mexican gangsters set about building the modern drug trade.

• • •

The people of the Golden Triangle have long had a complicated relationship with the Mexican state. Many of its sons fought in the Mexican Revolution, that series of rebellions, military coups, peasant land grabs, and betrayals that began in 1910 and by the 1920s gave birth to the modern Mexican state. And in the decades afterward, Sinaloa was a rough place, rife with conflicts between peasants, landowners, and ranchers, as peasants agitated for land reform and local elites responded with waves of savage terror. It was not until the 1940s that the region began to stabilize, and the sticky paste of the poppy plant functioned as the glue that held together the fragile peace between peasants, village elites, political officials, and law enforcement.

By the time El Chapo was born in 1957, drug trafficking was essentially a state-controlled industry, and there existed a social order rooted in the drug trade: at the bottom, as always, were the peasants who grew drugs on small plots of land or did seasonal labor picking weed or scraping poppies. But rather than scratching a meager living from the thin mountain topsoil, peasants harvesting two opium crops per year from just one hectare of land saw enough cash to put them in the top 17 percent of wage earners in the state. Seasonal workers earned the state's average annual wage in just four weeks of work. These earnings, inflated by the black market, helped to keep local peasants pacified.

Above the peasants were the very same men who just years earlier had been hell-bent on stopping land reform through terror and violence. And at the top, local and state elites profited from the money kicked up by traffickers, which pumped cash into the state economy and filled the campaign war chests of local and national political leaders in Mexico City alike.

The very existence of anti-drug laws made control over rural areas a more manageable task, allowing government forces to collect profits from and maintain control over the production of opium and marijuana while keeping the peace, however violently. Whenever soldiers or local cops needed to meet an eradication quota, nip a peasant rebellion in the bud, or take out an overly violent or ostentatious trafficker, they could simply remember to enforce the law against their target while instilling in the surviving growers and traffickers fear, discipline, and a willingness to pay the "tax," according to historian Nathaniel Morris.

"If the soldiers know they're only ever going to be able to destroy 20 percent of the [opium] plantations, and the peasants know that too, it's very easy for them to just make a deal," Morris said. "The only people who could have any complaints about this are the people who are having their opium destroyed, and because they're opium growers, they don't really have any recourse."

The unspoken approval of these tactics by Mexico City did not necessarily mean that the president of the republic was directly running a drug cartel, but the structure of the state relied on the stability this relationship ensured. The Institutional Revolutionary Party, which ran Mexico as a de facto one-party state from 1929 until 2000, perpetuated its power by showering rewards and patronage on the wealthy who supported it and co-opting unions to capture and kill any potential radical labor agitation. This was as true of poppies as it was of petroleum.

Wary of drawing undue attention to any one dictator or president for life, the PRI maintained a veneer of democracy while holding a vise grip on power in virtually all sectors of government, an autocratic project once labeled the "perfect dictatorship." Each president served a six-year term, known as a *sexenio*, and chose his anointed successor in a process known as the *dedazo*, or tap of the finger; for seventy years, the PRI successor always won. But in many areas of the country, such as in the highlands of Sinaloa, the state had little presence and allowed communities to run themselves in a semiautonomous fashion as long as they did not challenge the legitimacy of the government. And when the state reasserted itself, it often did so with brute force.

When El Chapo was in his teens, his hometown got a firsthand taste of the violence the government could inflict in poor areas where illicit crops were grown, as documented by the historian Froylán Enciso. On February 8, 1975, Enciso writes, three army helicopters descended from the sky and alighted outside the hamlet of San José del Barranco, just a short walk down the road from La Tuna. Piling out of the choppers, soldiers and police agents rampaged through the village and, apparently finding no men to arrest, contented themselves with beating and tearing the clothing off the women they encountered, and opened fire at a pair of preteen boys, injuring one of them. When a group of women gathered up the courage to head to Culiacán and protest this outrage, officials released a different version of the story, claiming that soldiers had come under fire from the villagers and recovered two pistols when sweeping the hamlet.

In a 2018 interview, El Chapo's sister Bernarda, three years his junior, described these years as deeply frightening, and recalled sitting in the dark while soldiers stomped outside, as dogs barked in the night. According to Bernarda, El Chapo had run-ins with soldiers during this time.

"They hit him," she told reporters from Vice News, adding that the beating took place in front of their mother. "And they didn't allow us to say anything."

During my first trip to La Tuna, I heard a similar story: that any hope El Chapo may have had for pouring his ambitions into a legitimate business was beaten out of him by soldiers. The abuses showed him and countless others that they were on their own, and would have to make their own way in the world, by whatever means available to them.

In Sinaloa, the cultivation and trafficking of opium and marijuana emerged as a key pillar of stability for the burgeoning patronage system, allowing for the peace and quiet that Mexico City demanded and the limited self-rule that the proudly independent *serranos*, or highlanders, saw as a way of life. This was the world into which El Chapo was born, but by the time he began working in the drug trade, the old order was already starting to break down as federal authorities began to rethink the amount of autonomy its *serrano* subjects enjoyed, and began to contemplate how they could wrest control of the lucrative drug trade from state officials. The raids on La Tuna and countless other Sierra villages in the mid-1970s were a warning shot of what was to come.

. . .

By the time of El Chapo's birth the cultivation of these illicit crops had become entrenched in the region, and *gomeros* passed the tradition from father to son. At every rung of the ladder, from growers to buyers to smugglers, the business functioned along clan lines, and names like Carrillo, Quintero, Payán, Fernández—and later, Guzmán—popped up again and again throughout the decades as one generation took over from the last. For El Chapo, it was no different. He first entered the drug trade with his father, working as a hired hand on poppy and marijuana plots in the mountains around La Tuna, and sometimes traveled farther afield to sell the product in other areas of the state.

El Chapo left formal education for good after elementary school. For years, rumors have abounded that he remains nearly illiterate, although this is an exaggeration. Still, letters penned by El Chapo in later years show a spidery, uneven handwriting full of spelling mistakes. This shortcoming, however, did little to hinder his ability to advance in the drug trade, which requires a different kind of cunning than the traditional schooling he left behind. Many people who knew him over the years described a striving ambition and a calculating mind, and it was likely these attributes that helped ensure that young El Chapo was not destined to remain a poor rancher in La Tuna, nor anyone's hired hand.

At some point in his youth, El Chapo relocated from the deep rural outpost of La Tuna to the somewhat more happening town of Badiraguato, where he became close with the brothers Beltrán Leyva—Arturo, Héctor, Alfredo, Carlos, and Mario—who had grown up not far from La Tuna and would for decades be among his closest collaborators. According to a former lover, his decision to move out of his hometown in the mountains was motivated in part by a desire to escape his home life, and in part by a visceral terror of remaining in poverty, a motivation that would propel him for the rest of his life. In time, El Chapo would outgrow Badiraguato as well, and in his early twenties he relocated to Culiacán, where he threw himself into his work.

Myths and legends abound regarding these early years of El Chapo's drug career: according to some sources, El Chapo was related to or at least in the employ of the veteran drug lord Pedro Áviles Pérez, aka "The Lion of the Sierra," who in the 1970s was deeply embedded with the Sinaloan political elite and was busily rising a head above the rest as a pioneer in the use of airplanes to smuggle drugs; other versions have El Chapo working as a driver for a visionary ex-cop named Miguel Ángel Félix Gallardo, who would dominate the scene in the 1980s. I distrust these stories, in part because they very conveniently put El Chapo in the employ of two of the best-known traffickers of the time, and because they assume that a job in the drug trade functions along the organizational principles of a normal company: get a job, rise through the ranks. In truth, even as traffickers like Áviles and later Félix Gallardo grew more powerful than others and oversaw vast operations, the drug trade—at least on ground level—was fairly decentralized, countless crews working together sometimes and in opposition other times. All that mattered, really, was paying off the right cops, the right politicians, and you could probably make some good money trafficking drugs.

When El Chapo married his first wife, Alejandrina María Salazar Hernández, in 1977, at the age of nineteen or twenty, there was little fanfare in the Sinaloa tabloids—which covered some local narcos like high society—indicating that El Chapo was still a small fish at the time. El

Chapo and Salazar had three children together: César, Iván Archivaldo, and Jesús Alfredo. But like many drug traffickers before and since, his eye soon wandered: a few years after his marriage to Salazar, he is said to have been so taken by a beautiful young bank teller that he kidnapped her in order to "marry her." This was soon followed by a third marriage, to Griselda López Perez, with whom he had four children: Édgar, Joaquín, Ovidio, and Griselda Guadalupe. It's unclear if he ever divorced any of his wives, but this never stopped him from marrying again and again.

According to a psychological profile sketched out by a psychiatrist for the attorney general's office in the 1990s, the young trafficker from La Tuna was narcissistic, but feared "being the center of attention," likely because he had seen firsthand that being at the center of attention often didn't work well for long in his line of business. He was a quick thinker, swift to "analyze and synthesize . . . capable of relating facts and ideas and drawing logical conclusions from them," and knew how to keep composed, even when things didn't go his way. He was not quick to fly off the handle like some violent and powerful men, but that didn't mean he was someone you wanted to piss off.

"[Revenge] is not something that he exacts with the immediacy of an impulsive person," the PGR report found. "His response is calculated, intentional, his vision is to hurt his adversary using his weaknesses to produce the most harm possible."

El Chapo knew the importance of family, and preferred to work with people who shared his roots in Badiraguato, even better if they were related by blood, or by marriage. As much as he could, he partnered with people he had known for years, people with whom he had shared baptisms and weddings; he often delegated his most sensitive tasks to his brother Arturo, or to one of his brothers-in-law.

As his family expanded, so too did El Chapo's responsibilities as a drug trafficker, and his mind was never far from his work.

"Chapo always talks about drug business wherever he is," one former lieutenant later recalled. "With whatever people he's with, he's talking about drugs."

El Chapo was rising fast, part of a new cohort of Sinaloan traffickers in the Guadalajara Cartel who were headed for positions of power. His closest partners were the brothers Beltrán Leyva, Héctor, Arturo, and Alfredo, with whom he had grown up in Badiraguato; Ismael "El Mayo" Zambada, a collected and coolheaded man about a decade older than El Chapo who was born south of Culiacán; and Héctor Luís Palma Salazar, known as "El Güero" for his light complexion, an ex–car thief and steely-eyed murderer from Mocorito, Sinaloa.

These men would continue working with one another for decades, and later formed the leadership of what is now commonly known as the Sinaloa Cartel.

2

EXODUS

IT MAY HAVE been ambition and brains and a spasm of violence that helped propel El Chapo out of the mountains at a young age in search of a better life, but his trajectory in life had as much or more to do with the time period he was born into as with his raw talent. The old way was dying, new kings were being made, and young guns like El Chapo had an opportunity to rise fast.

In the years that El Chapo was entering the drug trade, Mexico was coming under increasing pressure from the United States to combat the production and trafficking of opium and marijuana. In 1969, less than a year into his term, President Richard Nixon ordered a dramatic show of force along the entire length of the U.S.-Mexico border, in which Customs agents searched every single car driving into the United States. Dubbed Operation Intercept, the move came with little warning, and caused massive traffic jams at virtually every port of entry from Tijuana to Brownsville. The message was clear: the United States could cause Mexico a great deal of pain if it wanted to, so Mexico City had better play along. The PRI had long resisted overt anti-drug mandates from Washington, but now its leaders saw that they would have to play along.

In 1973, President Nixon declared a "war on drugs" and combined a number of federal police agencies under one roof to create a new agency whose singular purpose was to fight the scourge of drugs: the DEA. As

Washington made it increasingly clear that Mexico would need to clamp down on traffickers, Mexico City likely saw a way to placate their neighbor and seize control of local protection rackets all at once: Operation Condor.

. . .

Since its inception, drug trafficking in Mexico had functioned as a sort of loosely connected network of fiefdoms, each overseen by a feudal baron, or *cacique*, who ruled his roost through a combination of patronage (earning loyalty by injecting money into the local economy and sponsoring public works); corruption (kicking in drug money to fund PRI campaign coffers in Mexico City); and violence (killing or arresting rogue traffickers unlucky or stupid enough to not receive protection). This was known as the "plaza system."

Perhaps the best anatomy of the so-called plaza system comes in *Drug Lord*, by Terrence Poppa. This masterful chronicle of the rise and fall of the Chihuahuan trafficker Pablo Acosta describes the "plaza" as a sort of jurisdiction overseen by a "plaza boss" who in turn acts as the point of contact for whichever police commander was tasked with taking bribes and instructing his underlings not to touch the traffickers.

"To stay in the good graces of his patrons in power, the plaza holder had a dual obligation: to generate money for his protectors and to lend his intelligence gathering abilities by fingering the independent operators, those narcotics traffickers and drug growers who tried to avoid paying the necessary tribute," Poppa writes. "It was a system that enabled the Mexican political and police structures to keep a lid on drugs and profit handsomely from it at the same time."

This or that trafficker may have been the boss of a given plaza, but it was clear they were just renting. The real owners were the local authorities to whom they paid bribes. These local authorities tolerated, protected, and even participated in the drug trade because it kept peasants from pushing for serious land reform, put money into their own pockets, and injected a huge amount of capital into the state economy. In Sinaloa, the business community was well aware of the potential riches to be found in opium, and for a time some local notables agitated for the legalization of opium crops for the production of morphine and other pharmaceutical drugs. United Nations treaties on drug trafficking allowed for legal opium crops in countries like Turkey, Iran, and Yugoslavia, they reasoned; why not in Sinaloa? In one editorial, a pro-legalization author even offered a fig leaf to anti-drug crusaders with the suggestion that some of the tax revenue from legal opium could be used to fight the true scourge of marijuana, a drug of degeneracy, madness, and crime. Thanks in part to the drug trade, Sinaloa had enjoyed a major economic boom in the decades following World War II: between 1950 and 1960, heads of cattle increased from about 590,000 to more than a million, while the number of cars and trucks zooming along the roads of Sinaloa more than doubled, from just 16,743 in 1960 to 35,539 in 1970. All the while, levels of violence remained low.

This system functioned on a local basis for decades, with little centralized coordination, and drug lords like Eduardo "Lalo" Fernández, Pedro Áviles, and other top traffickers of his generation were deeply embedded with local elites and enjoyed near total impunity. But by the mid-1970s, this "Pax Sinaloa" had already begun to break down. Demand for marijuana was at an all-time high thanks to the hippie boom in the United States, and heroin dealers there were clamoring for a new source of product after the United States and its allies dismantled the so-called French Connection heroin pipeline from Europe to the United States in 1972. Both factors caused production of marijuana and opium to surge in Sinaloa, and the drug trade expanded rapidly. And because it was an illegal industry, disputes between traffickers jockeying for a slice of the action could only be mediated through violence. The Culiacán to which El Chapo moved in the mid-1970s was overflowing with newcomers from the Sierra, and it was overrun with new money, drugs, and violence. Murders soared, and the state saw a resurgence in left-wing agitation from students and radical peasant groups—a development perhaps more disturbing to Mexico City than the rise in drug production.

As the federal government sought to rein in local autonomy in all its forms and extend its centralized power to every corner of Mexico, there began a concerted campaign by federal law enforcement agencies like the Federal Judicial Police (PJF) to seize control of the state-run protection rackets. In those days, Sinaloa was known as a plum posting for federal police, most of whom were paid wretchedly, saw little hope of retirement, and could not trust their bosses or their government to have their back. Working with drug traffickers was as close to a retirement plan as they were going to get, and Sinaloa offered the most enticing benefits package around, leading some cops to fight for the opportunity to do a tour of duty in the state. It could mean the difference between scraping by on a lowly civil servant's salary and the high stakes and fast life of a cop on the take. PJF agents earned such a reputation for avarice, corruption, and brutality that local outlets took to referring to them as "Attila's Hordes."

The name Operation Condor referred to a series of campaigns by federal police under the umbrella of the PGR (Spanish initials for the attorney general's office) and soldiers under the defense ministry. Billed as a broad and sustained campaign against the drug trade, it was equal parts counterinsurgency campaign, hostile takeover, and a nasty episode of corporate raiding on the part of federal police against the local and state authorities who had previously run the show.

The first phases of Operation Condor, consisting of aerial defoliation spraying and an increased military presence, began in 1975 under President Luís Escheverría, who was already mounting an eventually unsuccessful scheme to be named Secretary-General of the United Nations when his term ended. His successor, President José López Portillo, went a step further in maintaining a facade of coordination with U.S. anti-drug policy, and allowed on-the-ground support from advisors with the fledgling DEA. This concession by López Portillo came as a huge victory to U.S. officials, who felt like they were finally getting the cooperation they had long sought from Mexico City.

"This is my third year here but never have we had the working relationship with Mexican officials that we've had since launching this year's campaign," said one DEA agent in January 1976. "In this respect it's a new and much better ball game."

But for residents of Sinaloa, it was a different story. People who lived through those years recall the arrival of Operation Condor as a time of siege, with military vehicles choking the streets of Culiacán as soldiers headed to and from the highlands, or rushed to bust clandestine heroin labs in the city. Human rights abuses, including illegal detentions, disappearances, and torture, were commonplace.

In the mountains, it was even worse.

Several top military commanders overseeing Condor had cut their teeth in repressive campaigns against the PRI's political opponents, including the 1968 Tlatelolco massacre of student protesters in Mexico City and the dirty wars against left-wing guerrillas in the state of Guerrero (sometimes in collaboration with local drug traffickers). In these campaigns, the military disappeared hundreds of civilians. The army's tactics took on a similarly brutal form during Operation Condor.

With crop dusters spewing poison from on high, legal crops were destroyed along with drug plots, and troops swept through the area spreading terror to nearly everyone in their path. These scorched-earth tactics mostly fell on the heads of poor farmers, while the leading traffickers often managed to avoid losses by paying bribes and marking their fields with colored flags so corrupt pilots knew to avoid them on defoliation missions. And in the face of indiscriminate violence, peasants fled the mountains in droves, leaving two thousand hamlets in highland areas of the Golden Triangle as ghost towns. Despite a pronounced population growth in other areas of Mexico between 1970 and 1980, municipalities such as Badiraguato saw an overall loss of residents that decade. El Chapo was one of countless *serranos* who fled the crackdown in the mountains and began living and working in the city, where there was more opportunity and less indiscriminate violence from the authorities.

Mass killings occurred with little investigation from higher authorities, including the deaths of thirteen alleged drug traffickers in a village near the coastal resort city of Mazatlán. Near Badiraguato, in the village of Santiago de los Caballeros, soldiers mowed down ten alleged smugglers and wounded a handful of civilians. In the first year of Operation Condor, civilians filed more than four hundred complaints against anti-drug troops, but like the angry protest by women from La Tuna who complained of the violent raid in 1975, the complaints were mostly ignored or dismissed.

One of the metrics by which Mexico City (and its backers in Washington) measured the success of Condor was the number of individuals locked up on drug charges in the Golden Triangle region, but this too fell hardest on the poor, rather than established drug smugglers. Of the 1,300 prisoners being held at the main jail in Culiacán, 85 percent were poor *campesinos* or laborers, and the remainder were overwhelmingly urban youngsters, according to a report by the state bar association. Few prisoners, if any, received due process: according to the same report, 90 percent of detentions were carried out illegally, with no warrant or probable cause. But this posed little problem for investigators, who were happy to torture prisoners into confessing to whatever misdeed of which they found themselves accused. Adding insult to insult, and injury to injury, the arresting agents helped themselves to the looted belongings of many arrestees. A few weeks before the report came out, federal police detained the organization's vice president and tortured him as well.

Operation Condor involved a veritable alphabet soup of law enforcement agencies active in Sinaloa—both military and civilian—all jockeying for supremacy, and who sometimes came into violent conflict with one another. At the beginning of Condor, federal officials with the military, the PJF, and the Federal Security Directorate (a secret police agency that protected the interests of the regime) set out to uproot the power of the Judicial Police of Sinaloa, or PJS. Over the course of the operation, the military tortured and disappeared at least seven PJS officers, and at one particularly tense moment, federal troops were prepared to launch a full-frontal assault on PJS headquarters in Culiacán.

By the end of Condor, everything had changed. While the local cops still took bribes and worked on behalf of drug traffickers, they no longer ran the show. The operation wiped many of the old generation of drug traffickers off the map, particularly those who had begun attracting attention from the United States, including Pedro Áviles, whose name came up in scores of DEA investigations and was becoming a potential embarrassment to the politicos in Mexico City. Áviles and seven of his henchmen died in a hail of gunfire in a northern area of Culiacán, an ambush that looked a lot like a massacre. His death left room for the likes of Miguel Ángel Félix Gallardo—and eventually El Chapo—to rise up in their place. But Culiacán was too hot; they would have to relocate.

So Félix Gallardo and other young guns pulled up stakes and headed for Guadalajara.

. . .

Chronicles of the late 1970s and early 1980s drug trade in Mexico typically fixate on the singular genius of Félix Gallardo, known in later years by his nickname of "El Padrino," or the Godfather. Born in 1946 on a ranch outside Culiacán, Félix Gallardo got his start in the drug business as a cop with the state Judicial Police. He had the good luck or political favor to end up on the security detail of Leopoldo Sánchez Celis, who served as governor of Sinaloa from 1963 to 1968. Sánchez Celis was widely believed to have close connections with the drug trade in the state, working as an intermediary between his PRI bosses in Mexico and the chosen traffickers he allowed to work in Sinaloa. Félix Gallardo formed such a close bond with his boss that the governor later stood as best man at Félix Gallardo's wedding, and Félix Gallardo was godfather to the governor's son. Félix Gallardo undoubtedly learned much during his time protecting Sánchez Celis, and likely made the most of the connections his friendship with the former governor offered.

Félix Gallardo left the PJS sometime in the early 1970s to be a full-time drug trafficker, and worked with Pedro Áviles, which put him in a good position when Áviles outlived his usefulness in 1978. With the federal police now calling the shots, Félix Gallardo was up for a promotion and became one of the go-to intermediaries between traffickers and the government. Everyone kicked up to him, and he made sure they were protected.

The third relationship that helped catapult Félix Gallardo above the shoulders of lesser narcos was an introduction to Juan Ramón Matta Ballesteros, a Honduran businessman and airline owner with close links to both drug traffickers and anti-communist forces in Central America.

It was through Matta that Félix Gallardo first made contact with the leaders of the burgeoning cocaine "cartels" in Colombia, and it was on the Honduran tycoon's airplanes that he first began to fly cocaine into Mexico before sending it along long-established smuggling routes to the

United States on which he had primarily been moving marijuana and heroin.

Above all else, Félix Gallardo recognized the wisdom in keeping his head down while cultivating relationships with the political elite who made his success possible. Obsessed with gadgets, he dropped tens of thousands of dollars at a time on the latest radio equipment, and snapped up properties around Culiacán and Guadalajara, posing as a hotel mogul. He was making astronomical amounts of money and acquiring ranches and homes across Mexico, but he had a stingy side, too, and he jealously guarded his immense personal fortune. Always willing to exploit an opportunity, he once agreed to buy an older cousin's plot of land outside Culiacán, but spent years stringing her along with promises to pay up.

Along with Félix Gallardo, a clique of up-and-coming Sinaloans set up shop in Guadalajara, the capital of the central state of Jalisco and Mexico's main financial and banking center outside of Mexico City. His two main collaborators were the thuggish and cunning Ernesto "Don Neto" Fonseca Carrillo, a native of the Badiraguato village of Santiago de los Caballeros who had clawed his way to lead the group's heroin operations, and Rafael "Rafa" Caro Quintero, of La Noria, Sinaloa, a hotheaded young marijuana grower and scion of a long line of drug traffickers whose flashy lifestyle made up for Félix Gallardo's modesty. Félix Gallardo, Neto Fonseca, and Caro Quintero have since achieved such fame that they are often considered the undisputed leaders of the Guadalajara network, but countless other traffickers were in the mix as well, allowed to operate as long as they made sure to pay up to Félix Gallardo's friends in the PJF and the DFS. And among that influx of Sinaloans into Guadalajara and other areas outside of the Golden Triangle was a young El Chapo.

• • •

While Félix Gallardo was building an empire on cocaine and making connections with the political and social elite of Guadalajara, El Chapo, then aged about twenty-seven or twenty-eight, headed to Zacatecas, a state located smack-dab in the middle of the country.

In the center of Zacatecas, just north of the state capital, lies Fresnillo, an agricultural town that sits more than a mile above sea level on the *altiplano*, the high plain that runs down the spine of central Mexico. The area emerged in Spanish colonial times as a center of Mexico's mining industry, and for centuries workers have dug deep to tap into rich veins of silver and gold, along with other valuable (if a bit less shiny) minerals like lead, zinc, and phosphorite. Mining is still an important industry in the region, but Zacatecas also began to distinguish itself in agriculture, thanks to the lush summers it enjoys, and Fresnillo is surrounded by miles of productive fields, where farmers grow corn, peppers, tomatoes, and other food crops. In the early 1980s, it also became a center of the marijuana trade as traffickers and drug producers streamed out of Sinaloa in the exodus spurred by Operation Condor.

El Chapo arrived in Zacatecas in 1984, accompanied by his longtime friend and collaborator Arturo Beltrán Leyva, as well as a cousin from La Tuna. By this time, a seemingly endless number of loosely connected crews were developing a sprawling network of large-scale marijuana plantations northeast of Fresnillo. There was occasional infighting among the crews—in one instance, the theft of a water pump resulted in bloodshed—but for the most part the growers worked together, developing their farms near one another in difficult-to-reach areas scattered across the plains and paying off the same corrupt cops for the protection they needed to work so brazenly in the open. While some of the farms were owned by local Zacatecan traffickers, the largest operations were directly financed by members of the Sinaloan diaspora, such as Rafa Caro Quintero and Neto Fonseca, and operated by middle managers working on their behalf.

Among the midlevel operators in Zacatecas at this time was a Sinaloan native by the name of Juan José Esparragoza Moreno, whom everyone called "El Azul," or the Blue One. He hailed from the village of Huixiopa, which lies in the valley leading to El Chapo's hometown, but El Azul was nearly a decade older than El Chapo and considerably more established by this point, having worked closely with the core leaders of the Guadalajara syndicate since at least the early 1970s.

A few miles north of Fresnillo, El Azul and his crew were developing a 2,000-hectare marijuana farm (about 500 acres), and he was also involved in the heroin trade. It was under his wing that El Chapo and Arturo Beltrán Leyva worked sowing poppies and harvesting opium, the start of a long and fruitful relationship. Over the ensuing decades, both men would continue to work closely with El Azul and other members of the crew.

. . .

Marijuana and opium have always been labor-intensive affairs; weed needs room to grow, and poppies must be painstakingly cut open and the sap scraped off. In Zacatecas, this required armies of laborers—often bussed in from Culiacán, two states away—who would remain on-site for the duration of the job. For their work, they earned about 2,000 pesos per day, or about $11.57 in dollars; that might sound like a pittance, but comparable legal work planting and harvesting sugarcane in the area brought in about $3 per day, without food or lodging. For a poor peasant, it was likely an easy choice between sugarcane and marijuana. For producers like El Azul and his bosses, however, it was a huge operating expense.

Cocaine, on the other hand, made for a more streamlined operation. It required fewer workers to manage loads, but not just any hotheaded young *serrano* could get in the game. It required international contacts, like those that Félix Gallardo maintained through his Honduran pal Matta Ballesteros.

Before cocaine roared back in popularity in the 1970s as a glamorous disco drug, it had remained much of a niche market, particularly in Mexico, where consumption was low and few traffickers moved the stuff in any serious way. From 1960 to 1970, officials in Mexico seized less than 30 kilograms of coke during the entire decade; beginning in 1971, Mexican cops were confiscating more than 100 kilos of coke each year. In 1985, authorities seized more than five tons of coke in Mexico, and by 1989 that amount had tripled. Drug seizures are an imperfect measurement of the scale of the drug trade, but they do tell part of a story; and in Mexico, it was clear: cocaine was here to stay.

Back then, smugglers employed human mules to carry the coke into the United States on commercial airlines. But the market for cocaine soon grew far too large for this relatively rinky-dink method, and traffickers like Carlos Lehder and the Boston-born hippie dope dealer George

Jung began shipping it in ever-larger quantities by private plane and boats through the Caribbean, buying up islands like Norman's Cay in the Bahamas as latter-day pirate bays to store the drugs before the final leg of the journey. As the DEA cracked down on the route through the Caribbean, the Colombians looked to Mexico as an alternative.

The smugglers in Colombia needed to move coke, and in Mexican traffickers, they found willing partners with well-established smuggling routes. This pattern became known as the Mexican "trampoline," as bricks of coke flew in from Colombia, landed in Mexico, and, with a great and satisfying *boing*, continued on to the United States. For producers, traffickers, and street dealers, coke just made sense. Without the headache of growing seasons, irrigation, and land that went along with weed and opium, trafficking cocaine was a simple matter of shipping. As a bonus, traffickers and dealers could cut it as much as they wanted with laxatives, lactose powder, or whatever else stretched one brick of coke into two or three. By the time it reached the streets of Chicago or New York, a kilo that fetched $3,000 in Colombia, sold for $10,000 in Mexico, and went wholesale in the states for $30,000 could easily earn retail sellers as much as $100,000, justifying the risk they took by selling on the street at high volume in small quantities. At first, the Mexicans were glorified—and very well paid—couriers for the Colombians. The margins for coke were astonishing: without even having to lift a finger cultivating a field on a hilltop miles from any paved road, Mexican traffickers could make exponentially more money than they had in the past simply by moving it from one destination to the other.

• • •

DEA agents based in local branches in Guadalajara and elsewhere were sounding the alarm about the growing power of drug traffickers, but for years, Washington didn't want to hear about it. As far as they were concerned, Operation Condor had been a success; it had indeed led to a drop in drug production in Sinaloa, and a corresponding plunge in the purity of Mexican heroin in the United States, despite growing evidence that production zones had simply moved outside the Golden Triangle. To have said otherwise would have been to contradict Mexican officials at a time that diplomatic tranquility and the ongoing fight against left-wing agitation was a higher priority to Washington than the warnings of a few DEA cowboys in a provincial office in Mexico. Much of this realpolitik was based on whom Félix Gallardo had chosen as his benefactors.

The main source of political protection for the traffickers in Guadalajara came from the Federal Security Directorate, or DFS, a shadowy secret police force that acted as the enforcement arm of the regime, murdering left-wing students and disappearing agitators. Unlike the PJF, which despite its corruption was still a bona fide police force, the DFS existed to ensure the political stability of the PRI government. Its criminal activities were an open secret, according to a former DEA agent who worked in Mexico at that time.

"[The DFS] became involved in drug trafficking, murder, stealing properties where they would go onto a ranch and just kick people out," the former agent said, speaking on condition of anonymity. "It became nothing more than a criminal organization, without question."

As the DFS became more involved in the drug trade, its ranks swelled with thuggish crooks looking to get rich. Beginning in 1977, the agency expanded exponentially, from just under 500 agents in 1977 to more than 3,000 agents in 1984. Droves of those new recruits came from the PJF, perhaps seeing in the DFS an opportunity to commit more fully to lucrative criminal pursuits without the pesky police duties required by their previous jobs. While corrupt PJF agents continued to provide cover for drug trafficking, it was the DFS that took the lead in offering political protection.

Just as Félix Gallardo and pals benefited from their ties to the DFS, the DFS also had its own friends in high places, including the Central Intelligence Agency. Despite its clear involvement in criminal pursuits, the DFS and its drug-trafficking assets were useful to American interests in the region, keeping tabs on leftists and perceived Soviet interests in Mexico, and helping to funnel arms to right-wing forces in Central America. It was just a few years since left-wing rebels had toppled the U.S.-backed regime in Nicaragua, and many of the people who ran Guadalajara seemed to be involved in the U.S. effort to fund and arm the right-wing Contra rebels trying to overthrow the Sandinistas there. Matta Ballesteros's SETCO airline was a veritable Contra Airways, ferrying arms and other supplies from airstrips in Honduras to encampments on the border with Nicaragua; Félix Gallardo was described as a "big supporter" of the Contras and made hefty monetary donations to the cause; Neto Fonseca was seen in the company of CIA pilots active in shady pro-Contra flights of arms and cocaine; and the CIA saw the DFS as so essential to its interests in Central America that it actively protected DFS leaders from scrutiny, even when they popped up on the radar of U.S. law enforcement agencies.

It might seem a paradox for one arm of U.S. foreign policy, like the CIA or the State Department, to engage in activities in direct opposition to the activities of another, like the DEA. But from its origins in the wake of World War II, the CIA and its backers in Washington have repeatedly turned a blind eye to the drug-smuggling activities of local players in geopolitical hot spots who, at one time or another, served as a bulwark against the spread of communism. Sometimes, the CIA even played a direct role in drug trafficking, most notably during the events that became known as the Iran-Contra scandal. As far as I (and many others) can tell, there is no evidence to suggest that the CIA was actively trafficking drugs with Félix Gallardo and his allies during this era, but they undoubtedly were working with people who protected the traffickers, and this undoubtedly made it next to impossible for the DEA and honest Mexican cops to muster the political will required to arrest them. To the delight of the drug traffickers in Guadalajara, and to the frustration of the DEA agents pursuing them, it was clear that Washington's priorities lay in the Cold War, not the drug war.

• • •

Guadalajara, meanwhile, was becoming transformed by its status as the headquarters of one of the most lucrative financial engines in the country. Cocaine money served as a foundation for construction projects, restaurants, and other businesses that began to restore some of the glamour Guadalajara had lost in the decades after the revolution. Félix Gallardo was a shareholder of the state-owned investment bank SOMEX, and despite his desire to keep a low profile, he had begun appearing in the society pages, hobnobbing with the wealthy elite of Guadalajara at weddings and baptisms. As he rose in stature, an audience with him became highly sought after. At a rotating series of headquarters, located around Guadalajara, he would receive a steady stream of visitors and petitioners, who sometimes crammed into waiting rooms and sat about for hours until it was their turn to speak with the boss.

The traffickers had the run of the city, sometimes carrying military-grade weapons in public despite Mexico's strict gun laws. They had the complete backing of the DFS, whose agents would escort them while transporting drugs, and they were paying regular bribes to the local branch of the PJF, including an agent who kept a lion cub in a motel bathroom and on occasion could be seen conversing with Félix Gallardo in the open.

Even the few cops foolish enough, brave enough, or honest enough to stand up to an AK-toting thug in this town would be sure to slink away in the face of a DFS badge, which gave its bearer the de jure ability to carry automatic weapons and the de facto ability to do whatever the fuck he wanted with them. It was a license to traffic drugs, as sure a sign as any that the guy holding the tin plate had the backing of big money, the backing of big men, and the backing of the state.

Félix Gallardo and his partners were linked so closely with state and federal cops in Guadalajara that it was sometimes difficult to tell where the line between traffickers and cops was, or if there was a line at all, according to Lawrence Victor Harrison, a gringo living in Guadalajara at the time. Harrison had drifted down to Mexico after auditing a few university classes at the University of California, Berkeley, in the late sixties, and early seventies and eventually settled in Guadalajara. Standing over six feet tall, he stuck out there, earning himself the nickname "Torre Blanco," or White Tower, but he liked Mexico, and never really left. A keen hobbyist (and alleged CIA agent), Harrison loved tinkering with radio equipment and electronics, and by 1981 he'd found work setting up communications equipment for state cops and a local DFS commander. It was through his DFS contacts that he met Neto Fonseca, who hired him to set up a security system and a high-frequency radio network. For about four months in late 1983 and early 1984, Harrison lived at one of Neto Fonseca's homes in Guadalajara, where he observed the large entourage of local cops and federal agents on his payroll who hung about, and saw Don Neto's relationship with all sorts of unsavory characters, including American pilots who claimed to be trafficking weapons and cocaine on behalf of the right-wing Contra rebels in Nicaragua.

Like Neto Fonseca, Félix Gallardo, and countless other traffickers, Harrison was able to travel freely with DFS credentials, and later told DEA agents that he and Neto Fonseca's DFS pals helped escort shipments of drugs, blowing through police roadblocks on the highway with the flash of a badge. Sometimes, he said, Neto and his associates would snort lines of cocaine off the badges, in lieu of a mirror.

They were all doing a lot of cocaine.

While Félix Gallardo was projecting the image of a successful young CEO, his partners were having a bit more fun. Rafa Caro Quintero spent much of his time in Chihuahua and Sonora, where he had teams of engineers and agronomists designing sophisticated irrigation systems that allowed multi-acre marijuana plantations to sprout up from the desert, capable of churning out untold tons of marijuana per year. On visits to Guadalajara, where he purchased a twenty-five-acre estate on the outskirts with $4 million in cash, Caro Quintero lived the wild life of an untouchable young prince. Neto Fonseca, meanwhile, was running his operation out of a villa in Guadalajara that on most days was teeming with a large retinue of bodyguards and various hangers-on, a group that typically included a handful of DFS agents; some men from another arm of PRI's secret police known as the Department of Political and Social Investigations, or IPS; and a rotating cast of PJF agents, state judicial cops, and soldiers.

In his time working for Neto Fonseca, Harrison got a firsthand glimpse of the gang's inner workings, occasionally accompanying Neto's gunmen on missions to escort convoys of trucks. He also began to see some internal divisions, resulting from the differences in style between the buttoned-up Félix Gallardo and his more rough-and-tumble partners.

"Mr. Félix Gallardo told me that both Mr. Fonseca and Mr. Caro were too wild, that they were attracting too much attention," Harrison said later. "Though he had to continue business with them, that he didn't want to be around them any longer because they were too rowdy."

Félix Gallardo had a vision, and the cowboy antics of his pals were quickly becoming a liability, risking attention from the United States and upsetting the careful balance required to maintain a relationship with corrupt soldiers and agents of the PJF and DFS. In one instance, an informant told the DEA that a brother-in-law of Caro Quintero had pistol-whipped an army captain in charge of protecting a smuggling route in Sonora; the captain retaliated by setting up roadblocks in the area and seizing thirty tons of marijuana belonging to Caro Quintero. Despite the deference that their DFS badges earned them, and despite all the money they were pouring into the pockets of cops, military officers, and politicians, Félix Gallardo and the others were about to learn that their protection had its limits.

. . .

On the afternoon of February 7, 1985, a group of *pistoleros* unwittingly set in motion a series of events that would result in the downfall of Don Neto, Caro Quintero, and Félix Gallardo, reshape the drug trade, and eventually make room for El Chapo and others of his generation to take charge. Just as Félix Gallardo had feared, the out-of-control violence of his partners was about to ruin everything they had worked for when they came for DEA Special Agent Enrique "Kiki" Camarena.

Kiki Camarena, a Mexican-born American citizen and former marine, had arrived in Guadalajara in 1980, volunteering for a foreign posting after three years on the border in Calexico and another four making bust after bust in the dusty barrios and farm towns of California's Central Valley. Camarena had a charming smile that belied the crusader's zeal with which he waged his drug war, a mission informed by seeing friends succumb to heroin overdoses in his youth in California. Mike Vigil, a DEA agent stationed in Hermosillo in the early 1980s, had met Camarena when both were stationed on the border, and later worked some investigations with him when both were working in Mexico.

"He had a great sense of humor, he was very athletically built, and he got along with everybody," Vigil recalled. "I don't think anybody had a bad thing to say about him."

Camarena had put in for a transfer because he was sick of petty busts, sick of putting one guy in jail and seeing him replaced the next day, of seizing a few pounds of weed and never putting a dent in the supply. Many DEA agents working abroad had a similar scorn for drug interdiction on U.S. soil, and like them, Camarena wanted to attack drugs at the source. Since his arrival in Guadalajara, Camarena and his fellow agents began trying to piece together an idea of what Félix Gallardo and his cronies were up to, according to journalist Elaine Shannon, whose book on Camarena remains the definitive account of his time in Mexico. Camarena was a regular visitor to the local office of the Federal Judicial Police, or PJF, where he'd consult with the agents, track down leads, and try to cultivate sources.

He and the other DEA agents in Guadalajara had followed the money, tracing checks from the United States to Peru, trying to get a picture of how much cash might be flowing through Félix Gallardo's coffers; they harangued Mexican officials to hand over account numbers, and tracked a paper trail stretching from San Diego to Guadalajara to Lima, eventually forming a portrait of a vast money-laundering scheme. According to the picture they had put together, money mules on the West Coast were packing cash into trucks in California and driving it to Guadalajara, where Félix Gallardo's pencil pushers would deposit the money before wiring it *back* to a Bank of America branch located in San Diego. Then, the kingpin's money guy in California would withdraw the drug proceeds as cashier checks that he'd send to coke producers in South America as payment. In one month, the investigation showed, as much as $20 million had moved through Félix Gallardo's bank accounts.

And that was just the money that DEA agents had managed to track; the real figure was likely far higher. A cousin of Félix Gallardo who in the early 1980s helped his relative manage stash houses in California and who later ferried drug proceeds from Los Ángeles to Guadalajara in a motor home stuffed to the gills with cash estimated that he personally delivered $150 million in cash over an eight-month period from July 1984 to February 1985.

. . .

Camarena and the other agents had begun to believe that the official story from Mexican officials of continued drug-eradication flights was a smoke screen. DEA agents had briefly been allowed to monitor these efforts at the beginning of Operation Condor, but in 1978 the Mexican government revoked access, and the DEA now had to rely on the good word of Mexican antinarcotics agents to confirm that planes were still crop-dusting the marijuana and poppy fields of the Golden Triangle. As Camarena and the other agents in Guadalajara gathered more and more evidence of large-scale cultivation of marijuana—and saw with their own eyes DFS men escorting suspected drug shipments—they were less and less inclined to trust that good word. So Camarena had struck out on his own, conducting undercover investigations and posing as a drug trafficker to try to lure Mexico-based smugglers into selling heroin to agents in Texas. And working with a Mexican pilot named Alfredo Zavala, he had managed to locate massive marijuana plantations growing in the desert. One such plantation that Camarena is often —but perhaps erroneously— credited with discovering was an operation in Chihuahua known as Rancho Búfalo. The field belonged to Caro Quintero, and it was a sprawling operation, covering nearly 2,500 acres, employing hundreds of workers, and capable of producing astronomical amounts of weed. When Mexican troops raided it and a handful of other ranches in November 1984, they captured and destroyed more than 10,000 tons of marijuana in the process. Government agencies in the United States had previously estimated that about 14,000 tons of marijuana were consumed nationwide each year, and the seizure in Chihuahua was so immense that it "throws all those numbers askew," and prompted stunned officials to wonder out loud if they had been seriously underestimating all along the amount of weed being smoked. The destruction of Rancho Búfalo—which was later estimated to be worth as much as $8 billion—was a serious blow, but Camarena and his DEA colleagues weren't done causing problems for Félix Gallardo and his powerful cronies. Camarena wanted to follow the money further.

But on February 7, 1985, he vanished.

• • •

Once Camarena's fellow DEA agents realized he'd been taken, they leapt into action, desperately scouring Jalisco for the missing agent as DEA men poured into the city from near and far to help with the search. While his comrades were buzzing about the city in search of him, Camarena was being held at a home in the Jardines del Bosque section of Guadalajara, alongside his pilot Alfredo Zavala, whom the hit men had also abducted. With both men in their custody, the captors began to torture them in an attempt to get whatever information they could out of them. The interrogator, later identified as an agent of the IPS, a sister agency to the DFS, took a particular interest in Camarena's investigations into Félix Gallardo and the corrupt cops on his payroll. Camarena told them what he knew. Begging for mercy, he remained respectful. He called his tormentor "*comandante*." At times, the interrogators paused to beat Camarena, ignoring his cries. The torture lasted for three days before someone finally caved his skull in with a pipe or tire iron.

• • •

Weeks after the kidnapping, officials announced they had issued warrants for the arrest of "six or seven" people suspected of having a role in Camarena's disappearance, including two state cops who helped hustle him into the car that day. But there was still no trace of Camarena or Zavala.

Finally, on March 7, one month after Camarena and his pilot disappeared, investigators found two badly decomposing bodies wrapped in plastic, lying in a ditch on a ranch southeast of Guadalajara. The bodies, which appeared to have been left in that spot recently, were "truly unrecognizable," according to one Mexican official, but their identities were confirmed when one of the bodies matched Camarena's fingerprints on file. It took an autopsy and Camarena's fingerprints to confirm that the bodies were those of Camarena and Zavala.

• • •

The murder of Camarena turned him into a martyr for the DEA, part of the agency's foundational mythology, and helped legitimize the DEA as a serious agency deserving of the respect given to other federal law enforcement branches. Over the years, the story took on a life of its own; it holds center stage in the fictionalized Netflix series *Narcos: Mexico*, and has been the subject of several books. But for decades, controversy has lingered over the motive behind the plot. According to the official narrative, Caro Quintero ordered Camarena's abduction as revenge for the agent's supposed role in the destruction of Rancho Búfalo; but for years, dark rumors have swirled around the case, accusations that CIA agents had some role in the murder of the hardheaded young DEA agent when he got too close to the links between Mexican drug traffickers and the CIA's efforts to fund the Contras in Nicaragua. This theory, based in part on accusations by former DEA agents, was whispered widely enough to be turned into a *narcocorrido*, and has remained an open question. In 2019, it emerged that the Justice Department had opened a new investigation into the allegations, but as of this writing, it remains unclear what role, if any, the traffickers' connections to the CIA had in the murder of Camarena.

• • •

Whatever spurred the murder of Camarena, the fallout was immediate and furious, an unmitigated disaster for the vision that Félix Gallardo and his pals in Mexico City had envisioned for a centrally controlled monopoly of the drug trade. By early April 1985, both Caro Quintero and Neto Fonseca were in handcuffs. When police in the Pacific Coast resort town of Puerto Vallarta swept onto the property of a nearby town's security chief, they found Neto Fonseca hunkered down with a small army of henchmen, including current and former agents of the PJF and DFS, further underscoring the agency's ties to the cartel. As for Caro Quintero, he was arrested in a luxurious mansion in Costa Rica, where he'd shacked up with the daughter of a *PRIista* power broker. Over the next seven years, U.S. prosecutors would charge numerous suspects with taking part in the conspiracy to kidnap and murder Camarena, including multiple PJF agents, the brother-in-law of a former Mexican president, and the doctor who kept Camarena conscious during the interrogation. Witnesses at the trials testified that they had seen high-ranking Mexican politicians and military officials in a room with Félix Gallardo, Neto Fonseca, and Caro Quintero to plan the murder, although some critics have questioned the validity of the testimony, and convictions against two of the plotters (including Matta Ballesteros) were later tossed out.

After just a few years of being Mexico City's chosen traffickers, the Guadalajara network as it had existed was finished. Under pressure from the United States, President Miguel de la Madrid initiated a purge of the DFS before shuttering the agency and rebranding it as the Center for Investigation and National Security, or CISEN. The days of open involvement in drug trafficking by PRI spooks appeared to be over, but on the ground there wasn't much difference. Perhaps some drug traffickers would be forced to turn in their DFS badges for CISEN badges, or exchange them for PJF shields.

Miguel Ángel Félix Gallardo did not go to jail just yet. Of the three leaders of Guadalajara, he had always been the one with the political connections, with the backing of the PRI elite, the connections with Colombia, and it appeared he was still useful to somebody. Neto Fonseca with his heroin, Rafa Caro Quintero with his weed: they were disposable, they represented the old days. Cocaine was the future.

•   •   •

After the arrest of his two partners, Félix Gallardo went underground, fleeing his stronghold of Guadalajara for some seaside solitude in the Sinaloa resort town of Mazatlán. He found a refuge there, amid the beaches, *cevicherías*, and *banda* music, protected by local police in exchange for using his status and muscle to control local criminals and "discourage" them from committing robberies, car thefts, and other crimes that might scare off tourists or draw federal attention.

But eventually, even Félix Gallardo outlived his usefulness to his protectors. In the United States, where the Reagan administration's so-called war on drugs was already a front-page story thanks to the rising tide of crack cocaine flooding the streets and the ensuing hysteria over crime supposedly driven by crack users, the furor of the death of a federal agent helped push that effort to a fever pitch. In 1986, the U.S. Congress passed legislation that would add a new weapon to Washington's arsenal in its drive to force countries like Mexico to align with U.S. anti-drug policy. Under the new law, any country that failed to be "certified" as taking an active role in combating the production and transport of drugs in or through its territory would be cut off from any foreign aid. If Mexico wanted to continue receiving help from the United States in the form of military equipment and economic aid packages, it would have to prove it was dealing with drug traffickers. Despite being in power during the years in which the DFS and PFJ were rising to new heights of power and corruption, President de la Madrid was learning how to speak Washington's language: in 1987, he was the first Mexican president to label organized crime a national security threat, a Very Serious Term that indefinitely justifies heightened security measures, and allows for little dissent.

In 1988, in an election widely viewed as fraudulent, the chosen *PRIista* successor Carlos Salinas de Gortari squeaked to victory, barely beating out a left-wing challenger. Among Salinas's chief concerns was ensuring that Mexico anti-drug efforts be "certified" by the United States. In one of the first initiatives of his *sexenio*, Salinas pushed through judicial reforms that mandated a fifteen-year minimum sentence for drug trafficking. He also gave word to top PJF agents that the capture of Félix Gallardo was now a priority. Who better to serve up on a platter than Félix Gallardo, the highest-ranking narco connected to the Camarena killing still on the loose?

On April 8, 1989, federal cops strolled into the mansion in Guadalajara where Félix Gallardo was lying low. Without firing a shot, they forced him to the ground at gunpoint and took him into custody, ignoring his bribes and threats.

That evening, in a coordinated sweep, the military arrested more than six hundred members of the Sinaloa State Judicial Police and the Culiacán municipal police force for allegedly colluding with drug traffickers. Among those arrested were nine high-ranking law enforcement officials in Sinaloa and several other areas across Mexico accused of accepting thousands of dollars a month in protection money from Félix Gallardo.

At a preliminary hearing a few days later in Mexico City, Félix Gallardo denied any ties to the drug trade, insisting that he was nothing but the owner of a couple of hotels in Guadalajara. An initial tally of the humble hotelier's assets seized by the government included three jets, a Thoroughbred horse stable, a handful of condo buildings, ranches, hotels, and stores in Culiacán and Guadalajara, a discotheque, and a collection of more than fifty luxury cars.

Félix Gallardo, like his partners arrested four years prior, was now sitting in prison, charged with bribery and drug trafficking and soon to be charged with the murder of Camarena, for which he would ultimately be convicted and sentenced to decades in prison. He's still in prison. But the drug trade kept chugging on.

The emerging leaders of the new order divvied up their responsibilities over new territory. Anyone trafficking drugs through those areas would have to pay the plaza bosses in order to benefit from their protection agreements with local, state, and federal cops. In Tijuana, the brood of brothers named Arellano-Félix assumed command; and in Ciudad Juárez, Amado Carrillo Fuentes—the nephew of Neto Fonseca nicknamed "the Lord of the Skies"—consolidated control.

And in Sinaloa and along a swath of the border with Arizona, El Chapo, Ismael "El Mayo" Zambada, the brothers Beltrán Leyva, and other allies held sway. This corridor was considerably less lucrative than the huge border crossings in Juárez and Tijuana. But El Chapo always had a way of making do with what he had.

3

SINALOA COWBOYS

AGUA PRIETA DOESN'T look like much, not at first. Tucked on the northern edge of the Mexican state of Sonora, this border town has few buildings that reach more than two stories, and some of the streets near the center of town are barely paved. But as Keoki Skinner drives me through town, he tells me to peer a bit closer. Certain things start to stand out: sprawling houses left and right, manicured cactus gardens out front, brand-new trucks on the curb.

Keoki and I chat about this and that as we cruise along, him pausing to point out landmarks. With his shock of white hair, a slight stoop, and hard-to-place American accent, he could be any other Arizona-dwelling retiree; but his knowledge of the town gives him away as a local. Putt-putting through Agua Prieta in his rickety green VW Beetle emblazoned with a bumper sticker that reads "Make America Mexico Again"—"that's for the ICE guys at the border, drives them crazy," he says—we roll by mansion after mansion, as Keoki offers commentary on their owners' aesthetic choices and backstories. One is decked out with Grecian columns, another studded with domes straight out of a cocaine-fueled *1001 Arabian Nights*, and many feature walled-in swimming pools and huge solar panels, to offset the tremendous power suck of running air-conditioning 24/7 in this hot, desert town. A born entrepreneur, Keoki mourns the fact that he didn't get into the solar panel business a few years back, before they started popping up on roofs all over town.

One of Keoki's side hustles is running tours to show off the local cuisine and lore to visitors, many of them "snowbirds," retirees who spend their winters in Arizona. He has made this little desert town his home for longer than I've been alive, and he can recite its recent history with the attention to detail of a local reporter and the pride of a tour guide sharing his love of his adopted home. Cruising by a particularly ostentatious mansion near the center of town, he pauses his running commentary to note that the owner of this house is "clean," having made his fortune as a dentist. Keoki loves Agua Prieta, and it shows: people know him here, and in the time I'm with him numerous people stop him in the street to chat. His positive feelings do not extend across the border to Douglas, Arizona, about which he has little good to say. The two towns sit side by side, straddling the border, but their fortunes have diverged over the years. Douglas has never been the same since the closure in the 1980s of a pollution-spewing copper smelter, which wiped out many jobs in the area.

Agua Prieta, on the other hand, is home to several factories, known as *maquiladoras*, which churn out the kinds of odds and ends whose creation consumers rarely consider. One *maquiladora* is exclusively dedicated to the fabrication of Velcro strips and employs about twelve hundred people here. In another, workers toil over auto parts for the Japanese company Takata. The workers make lower wages than factory workers in the States, of course, but the factories still attract job seekers from all over Mexico. But that's not where the money for mansions comes from.

"This doesn't exactly look like a town built by *maquilas*," Keoki says, driving past a store whose main products appear to be stone columns and other gaudy home decor.

For decades now, Agua Prieta has been a key node along one of the most important smuggling routes in northern Mexico. It's also home to an indelible piece of the legend of El Chapo, whose people have long controlled the town and kept it calm, even as other areas along the border have changed hands between rival smugglers and fallen prey to catastrophic violence.

The Agua Prieta that Keoki found when he first arrived in the mid-1980s was not studded with the mansions that line its streets today, and there were few if any of the late-model cars and souped-up pickups that now rev their engines down the city's main drag. After a few years of youthful wandering in Mexico (and a bit of gray-market smuggling of dental equipment), he'd begun working as a fixer and later as a freelance reporter for the *Arizona Republic*. In the mid-1980s, the paper sent him to Agua Prieta to report on a period of political upheaval that was unfolding in the mid-1980s between militants with the ruling PRI and the then-up-and-coming National Action Party (known by its Spanish acronym the PAN, a clever acronym that's also the Spanish word for bread). At the time, the two parties were at one another's throats, duking it out over a contested mayoral election; the PRI claimed victory, the PAN wouldn't let the mayor take office, someone set city hall on fire, and a young cameraman from a Phoenix TV station got snatched off the streets by Mexican security forces. It was a mess, and Keoki couldn't get enough of it.

"There was just all this stuff going on," Keoki tells me over a dinner of enchiladas at a little restaurant where he addresses the waitstaff by name. "So once that happened, I said, 'I want to stay here. This place has got a lot of action. I'll have plenty of stories here.'"

Plenty of stories, perhaps, but a sore lack of *licuados*, a smoothie popular in southern Mexico, for which Keoki had developed a taste in his travels. During a break in the action one day, Keoki found himself eating at the bar of a restaurant in town and struck up a conversation with a *PANista* who had taken a liking to him, and would sometimes give Keoki a tip-off about actions the party's activists were planning. Turning to his *PANista* pal, he asked where a guy could get a *licuado* around here. Nowhere, the man told him; Agua Prieta didn't have a smoothie shop. But his friend, whose father was a wealthy businessman and owned all the liquor stores in town, had a solution: Maybe Keoki wanted to open one up?

Sweetening the pot, the *PANista* said he just happened to have a perfect building downtown with some retail space available. With his characteristically entrepreneurial spirit, Keoki took a look around, spied the ample foot traffic going past the vacant storefront, and considered the possibilities it would present to a newsman like himself to operate a place where people could gather and swap gossip. Before he knew it, he was in the *licuado* business.

"I'd love to become part of the community," Keoki remembers thinking. "People could come to me with tips and I'm not being parachuted into places and digging up stories."

He named the shop "El Mitote." The name came to him on a trip he took with one of his new employees to buy supplies in Nogales, another border town about two hours west of Agua Prieta. They were chatting, and she noted his penchant for gossip, exclaiming, "*¡Eres un mitotero!* You're a gossiper!" In Mexican slang, *mitote*—an indigenous loanword—means something like "hubbub," as in, you hear a shouting match down the block and quiz your friend: "What's the *mitote?*" In the context of a location—a juice bar, say—it's a "gossip spot," and a *mitotero*, a label Keoki wears with pride, is a collector and dispenser of gossip. And so El Mitote was born.

At first, the people of Agua Prieta didn't know what to think of Keoki. Unlike Mexico's resort towns on the Gulf Coast or the beaches of the Pacific, Agua Prieta has never been a hot spot for vacationers from the north, and so he stuck out as one of the only gringos in town. But as his business got off the ground and he began raising a family, it became clear he was there to stay. Folks started opening up.

"My worry always was they'd think I was a DEA agent or something, you know, 'What's this fucking gringo doing in our town?'" Keoki says. "But once I got settled in my business, and I met my future wife, and then we bought a vacant lot, I built a house here. So that kind of dispelled any suspicion I think."

As he was running El Mitote, people got to know him well. Even today, he says, years after he sold the business, he'll still occasionally get stopped at a gas station or in a convenience store by someone who remembers him from back then.

"The name really stuck," he says. "People here always had trouble with my name, Keoki, but they always knew me as *el Güero Mitotero*, the blond gossiper. I'll see someone up in Tucson and they'll say 'Hey, *Güero del Mitote!*'"

. . .

Not long after Keoki opened up shop, another crop of newcomers began to arrive in Agua Prieta. They wore fancy boots and spoke quickly, with the heavy, nasal twang of the Mexican northwest. Their cars often had Sinaloa license plates—when they had license plates at all. Keoki called them "Sinaloa Cowboys," for the way they carried themselves, brash and confident, flashing a lot of cash. But it was clear they weren't making their money riding horses.

Keoki wasn't particularly fond of the new influx of drug traffickers in town. They liked to double-park outside his shop, they were loud and demanding, and they wouldn't stop harassing the young women who worked behind the counter. But, ever the hustler, he saw a chance to make some money off them, and he started marketing certain drinks to them, like an alfalfa smoothie, or another concoction he labeled the "AR-15." He told the loud young men that they were the perfect cure for a hangover, or *just* the trick to rejuvenate oneself after a sleepless night. The Sinaloa Cowboys had plenty of hangovers to cure and late nights to recover from, and they began to come to El Mitote more often, buying drinks with crisp hundred-dollar bills. It was a revealing lesson in the ways in which drug money makes its way into every corner of a border town like Agua Prieta, and adds up over the years.

"I always talk about Reaganomics, you know, 'trickle-down,' " he says. "Well, in drug towns like this, that money trickles down. You know, nice restaurants, you saw the gym, I mean we have a really nice theater here outside of town where I saw *Roma* on the big screen before it was even in Arizona."

Among the newcomers, not everyone stuck out like the brash, alfalfa-guzzling Sinaloans, or like Keoki, *El Güero del Mitote*. When Francisco Rafael Camarena Mácias showed up in town around 1988 or 1989, he defied easy categorization. He told folks he was a lawyer, up from Guadalajara, and talked about a plan to build low-income housing in Agua Prieta. In no time, he started to throw money around, getting in good with the local bigwigs on both sides of the border. He snapped up a vacant lot for $90,000 in cash and built a house into which he moved his family; across the way in Douglas, he set about ingratiating himself with local judges, businessmen, and politicos who played golf and conspired with one another at the country club. He also bought a local construction company, Douglas Redi-Mix, which just happened to operate a warehouse a couple hundred feet north of his new home, on the Douglas side of the border.

The first thing that got the local *mitoteros mitote*-ing about Camarena Mácias was the price he paid for the lot in Agua Prieta, located on Calle Internacional, the straightaway street that runs along the border fence, Keoki recalls.

"When somebody pays ninety thousand dollars cash for a vacant lot, that word gets around pretty quick," he says. "I mean, I bought a vacant lot, and it was right on the fence as well, and I paid six thousand dollars for mine."

Then there was the hole Camarena Mácias dug in the backyard. Initially, when neighbors asked why he was digging behind his new home, Camarena Mácias told them it was for a swimming pool. Fair enough: Agua Prieta is a hot and dry place. And what well-to-do businessman wouldn't want a place to cool off, a place for his kids to splash around? But then his workers filled the hole right back up. Hmm.

The neighbors were right to be suspicious. Camarena Mácias was in fact a lawyer, and he was even telling the truth about being from Guadalajara. But what he didn't mention was that his last job in Guadalajara was running an office in the city for a young drug trafficker named Joaquín Guzmán Loera, better known as El Chapo.

Before he decamped for the border, Camarena Mácias, known by his narco buddies as "El Caballo," or the Horse, worked out of an office secretly tucked in the second story of a supermarket, where El Chapo's men operated a warehouse to store drugs and money.

Alongside the Beltrán Leyvas and El Mayo, El Chapo had graduated from lackey to boss, and he was quickly growing wealthy. But the revenue coming in from the territory he controlled, stretching up from Sinaloa to a swath of the border between the state of Sonora and Arizona, paled in comparison to the money being made by other factions in Tijuana and Juárez who controlled lucrative border crossing routes. Unlike the massive border crossings in those cities, the ports of entry at Agua Prieta and

Nogales to this day consist of just a few lanes of traffic, and could never handle the volume of vehicles and goods that cross from Mexico into San Diego and El Paso. So El Chapo would have to get creative if he hoped to build his organization beyond the twenty-five or so employees and the two offices he controlled at the time, in Guadalajara and Agua Prieta.

In the Guadalajara office, Camarena Mácias's job consisted of taking and sending messages for El Chapo. When he got to Agua Prieta in the late 1980s, he had a new task. Arriving with his family in tow, money to burn, and local backs to scratch, he snapped up the properties on either side of the Douglas–Agua Prieta border and set about digging a tunnel connecting his newly built ranch house to the warehouse on the Arizona side belonging to the construction company he'd bought, Douglas Redi-Mix. Hence the disappearing pool hole in the backyard.

The tunnel was a feat of engineering, designed by an architect whose handiwork El Chapo so admired that El Chapo allowed him to use the informal pronoun *tu* in Spanish when they spoke. (He was the only one, according to an underling of El Chapo who always used the formal *usted*.) The entrance on the Mexican side was located in the recreation room of the new house, concealed by a pool table that sat on a hydraulic platform sealing the tunnel up. With the flip of a switch, a dummy hose spigot hidden in plain sight, the platform wheezed up to reveal a hole that dropped down to the tunnel floor. Below sat a wheeled cart hitched to a rope on which workers could roll the drugs about two hundred feet north to the other end of the tunnel, which opened up into the Douglas Redi-Mix warehouse, where another hydraulic platform disguised as a drainage grate hid the exit. The roof of the tunnel was about five feet four inches high, so most adults had to stoop while guiding the contraband through, but it did the trick. El Chapo now had a literal pipeline spewing cocaine into the United States. Before long, the tunnel became the primary route through which El Chapo sent cocaine into the United States, more than three tons passing through it each month.

When the tunnel was up and running, El Chapo was elated, crowing to a lieutenant about the "fucking cool tunnel" his team had built.

Camarena Mácias wasn't the only guy El Chapo sent to Agua Prieta, and he wasn't even the first. Starting around 1987, El Chapo's men, the guys whom Keoki had noticed, had begun settling down in Agua Prieta and the surrounding area, turning it into one of their main bases along the United States border. Well within their area of control, it was far from the border crossings held by other factions, but still offered a straight supply line into the United States, just a few hours away by car from Phoenix and Tucson. The team running the Agua Prieta operation included El Chapo's brother Arturo Guzmán—nicknamed *El Pollito*, or little chicken—and Héctor and Arturo Beltrán Leyva, brothers who had worked closely with El Chapo since their days growing up together in the mountains of Sinaloa. Between 1988 and 1991, El Chapo and his crew smuggled thirty-five tons of cocaine over the border into Arizona, according to one estimate.

In order to get drugs to the border, the gang opened an airstrip in Cumpas, Sonora, about one hundred miles south of the border, where Arturo Guzmán and the Beltrán Leyva brothers were in charge of receiving drug shipments by plane, unloading the goods, and ferrying them north to the crossing point in Agua Prieta. After selling the loads in Arizona, they would smuggle cash back into Mexico. To meet the sudden demand for clean cash, a swarm of currency exchange shops popped up in town.

The man in charge of this bustling operation was a pilot named Miguel Ángel Martínez Martínez, a former contraband smuggler who had begun working for El Chapo in 1986. His first job, an attempt to buy weed in Colombia, had ended in failure. Martínez had been forced to fly home to Mexico on a commercial flight after whiling away several fruitless months awaiting a connection who never showed. But he had behaved himself, and his composure impressed El Chapo, who offered him another shot. Martínez flew some loads of cocaine from Colombia to Mexico for El Chapo, but after just a few short months his career as a pilot-trafficker sputtered to a stop on a short gravel landing strip in the state of Durango, where Martínez landed hard on the nose of the plane. El Chapo took the accident in stride, but he no longer wished to entrust his life or his precious cargo to Martínez's flying skills.

"Mr. Guzman told me that I was a really bad pilot and that he didn't want me to continue working for him as a pilot," Martínez recalled later.

Assuming he was fired, Martínez thanked his boss for the opportunity, but El Chapo told him there was a misunderstanding: he wasn't firing Martínez, but rather giving him a promotion. So Martínez failed upward, and soon found himself working as a coked-up air-traffic controller, snorting endless white lines as he coordinated an endless line of planes arriving from Colombia loaded down with bricks of cocaine.

They spoke in code over high-frequency radio: "wine" meant jet fuel, "girls" referred to the planes, "documents" meant money, and the precious cargo, the cocaine, they called "shirts." Between 1987 and 1991, shipments would arrive on a small fleet of airplanes, each carrying hundreds of kilos of cocaine. They were moving as much as the Colombians could send them. Martínez, who had standing orders from El Chapo to receive as many planes as possible per shipment, recalled how pleased El Chapo was in one instance when the Colombians flew in more than ten planes in one night.

"*Compadre*," El Chapo said to Martínez. "Now it's a great party."

El Chapo bestowed on Martínez tremendous responsibility, sometimes tasking him with holding as much as $30 million in cash at a time. But his trust was not absolute, and occasionally he would test his lieutenant's integrity.

"He would send me suitcases with $1,200,000 inside them and then just tell me there was a million inside," Martínez said. "He would say, 'Well, how much arrived? There is eight suitcases, *compadre*, so that is eight million.'"

But Martínez counted every time. And when he found $80,000 extra, $100,000 extra, $200,000 extra, he would tell his boss. Every time. El Chapo never acknowledged the fact that he was testing Martínez, but Martínez knew.

Still, Martínez had become an indispensable part of El Chapo's operation, one of a handful of aides who answered directly to the boss and worked day and night to ensure El Chapo's orders were carried out. Even then it was clear El Chapo had big plans.

"I wasn't the right hand of Chapo Guzmán," Martínez recalled. "He's an octopus, Chapo Guzmán. He must have about five right arms and five left arms."

. . .

As El Chapo and his allies were emerging as an independent organization in the late 1980s, their main connections in Colombia were members of Pablo Escobar's Medellín Cartel: the Ochoa family and Gonzalo Rodriguez Gacha. Miguel Ángel Martínez made frequent trips to Colombia to meet with Rodriguez Gacha and the other suppliers, and on occasion El Chapo would join him, to put a personal face on the business. But El Chapo and his allies were also looking to branch out, especially as some of their former Colombian contacts began to be arrested or killed, including Rodriguez Gacha, who was gunned down alongside his son and a handful of devoted bodyguards on December 15, 1989, in a shoot-out outside the Colombian town of Tolú.

In early 1990, El Chapo forged a new relationship that would make him rich beyond his wildest dreams. His new contact was a young Colombian trafficker named Juan Carlos Ramírez Abadía. Ramírez, who went by the nickname "Chupeta," or Lollipop, was just twenty-seven years old at the time, but was already a rising leader of the faction of the Cali Cartel that would soon become known as the Norte del Valle Cartel. The two men met for the first time at a hotel in Mexico City, and nearly thirty years after his first meeting, Chupeta could still remember the bravado with which El Chapo presented himself. In 1990, the prevailing rate most Mexican smugglers charged to move Colombian coke was 37 percent of each load, but El Chapo came in driving a hard bargain: he wouldn't do it for any less than 40 percent. In exchange for the extra 3 percent, El Chapo promised that not only could he move the coke faster than other smugglers, but he would also guarantee its safety while it was under his control, and pay Chupeta back for anything that was lost in Mexico.

"I'm a lot faster," El Chapo told Chupeta during that first meeting. "Try me, and you'll see."

Chupeta saw. In under a week, El Chapo's men moved the first load of 4,000 kilos from its landing spot in Mexico to its destination in Los Ángeles, while other traffickers typically took a month, or more. From then on, the Colombians had a new name for the young capo from Sinaloa: "*El Rapido.*"

The key to El Chapo's speed, to his reputation as "El Rapido," was the tunnel. It allowed El Chapo's men to move huge loads of merchandise under the border in one go, rather than breaking it down into smaller shipments that could cross the border hidden in vehicles. Once the cocaine was brought under the border, workers at the warehouse on the U.S. side stuffed it into hidden compartments in cars and trucks, and ferried it north to Phoenix, Arizona, the hub from which it was shipped to distribution points throughout the country.

And thanks to El Chapo's connections with corrupt Mexican security forces, he proved himself to be more reliable than his competitors.

"With him, in Mexico, you seldom lost, because of their corruption agreement," Chupeta recalled.

The absurd profits from cocaine had sent the amount of bribe money paid by Mexican traffickers skyrocketing, from as much as $3.2 million a year in 1983 to an estimated $460 million a decade later. That was more than the annual budget of the Mexican attorney general's office, and more than half the annual budget allocation of the entire U.S. Drug Enforcement Administration. They would hand over the bribe money to the officials overseeing a given area, who would pocket some and distribute the rest to the rank and file, ensuring a systemic protection for the area they covered. This money bought off street cops, who either knew to look the other way or were sometimes recruited to actively aid in drug trafficking by working as muscle and escorting drug convoys along the highway. They bought off judges, prosecutors, mayors, anyone who might stand in the way of their operation. Not every cop or public servant was directly paid off, but enough key players took kickbacks to make honest cops unable to do their jobs. Many took bribes just to stay alive— refusing that monthly envelope of extra pay put a target on your back.

In exchange for all that money, traffickers like El Chapo and his pals enjoyed the steadfast protection of officials in virtually every law enforcement agency in the country. Once, Martínez said, when he and another trafficker were flying back from Thailand after a meeting to connect with heroin traffickers there, they spent the whole flight home chatting to a couple of fellow passengers. Unbeknownst to them, they were talking to DEA agents. When Martínez and his pal arrived in Mexico City, they were promptly arrested, but the representative of the PGR detaining them quickly changed his tune when they mentioned El Chapo's name.

"You work for Joaquín?" an agent said, before letting them go with a warning that the men they'd been chatting with on the plane were U.S. federal agents.

· · ·

In the decades since El Chapo's men were pushing coke through the Agua Prieta tunnel, the domestic market for drugs in Mexico has dramatically expanded. But at the time, virtually every gram the cartel ferried north was destined for the United States. It's not hard to see why: a kilo of cocaine in those years cost between $2,000 and $3,000 at its origin point in Colombia, and with every step along the smuggling chain, the price of that kilo rose dramatically, as traffickers factored in the cost of fuel, manpower, protection bribes, and risk of seizure. At its next stop, unloaded off a boat or plane in Mexico, the kilo born in the high Andean jungle of Colombia now cost about $6,000 at its landing spot in Cancún, or at an airstrip in Sinaloa or Sonora. If it made the trip to a warehouse in Mexico City, that kilo was now worth about $10,000. Across the border is where the traffickers started to make real money: if the kilo ended up in Los Ángeles, it was now worth a cool $20,000; in Chicago, it sold for $25,000; if it was destined for the dance floors of Manhattan, traffickers would flip it in New York for a staggering $35,000, netting themselves about $26,000 in profit, nearly double what they earned after costs for a kilo sold in Los Ángeles.

Once a month, Learjets loaded with as much as $10 million in drug money from the United States would take off from the border and head to Mexico City, where workers would offload the cash and stash it in homes and apartments, before stuffing it into Samsonite briefcases and taking it to the bank. On the rare occasion anyone dared ask Martínez where the money came from, he said he imported tomatoes. (Coincidentally, or perhaps not, tomatoes are one of the major legal exports of Sinaloa, and the hometown baseball team in Culiacán is named *Los Tomateros*, or the Tomato Growers.)

But getting the money back across the border to Mexico was as risky as it was cumbersome.

On November 10, 1989, a United States Customs agent named Michael Humphries spotted a young man driving north into Douglas from Agua Prieta. Less than an hour later, Humphries spied the same young man, looking jittery and this time piloting a black Ford Bronco with California plates, inching forward in one of the southbound lanes at the port of entry, headed back into Mexico. Humphries decided to take a closer look. As he tossed the vehicle, Humphries made an astonishing discovery: peeling back a panel on the driver-side door, he came upon a staggering amount of cash, all neatly stacked as if it were in a bank vault. He found more behind the panel of the passenger-side door, and still more cash stashed in a secret compartment at the tailgate.

In a photo taken that day, Humphries can be seen grinning as he holds aloft black trash bags sagging with the weight of $1.2 million in drug money.

The nervous young man whose careless, speedy return across the border had tipped Humphries off was Arturo "El Pollo" Guzmán, El Chapo's younger brother.

The seizure smashed the record at the time for the largest cash haul reported at any port of entry in Arizona. It was bound to attract attention. But El Chapo was more concerned for his brother than for the money, and was delighted when El Pollo posted bail a few days later and vanished back into Mexico.

Martínez was with El Chapo in La Tuna the day Arturo left jail. They were there to consecrate the new church that El Chapo had built for his mom, that gorgeous little building on a hilltop just fifty yards from Doña Consuelo's house, and everyone was in good spirits. When El Chapo got the news about his brother, he approached Martínez, bubbling with excitement.

"*Compadre*, they already set Arturo free," El Chapo crowed.

El Chapo, as yet unencumbered by infamy, started to enjoy the fruits of his labor. El Chapo had grown up with nothing, and in later years he would return to a simple lifestyle, but in the early days, his relative anonymity allowed the poor boy from La Tuna to see the world: in just a few years of working with El Chapo, Martínez had seen him go from being a workaday trafficker with a few dozen men to a rising kingpin overseeing a sprawling network of international suppliers and distributors.

"When I met Mr. Guzmán, he didn't have a jet," Martínez said. "In the nineties, Mr. Guzmán already had four jets, he had houses at every single beach, he had a ranch in every single state."

They looked abroad for new business opportunities. In Thailand, a kilo of ultra-pure "China White" heroin cost just $10,000 and retailed in New York for $130,000. If El Chapo could set up a pipeline from Southeast Asia to the States, he could make a fortune without having to mess around with production in the Sierra, just the way he moved coke for the Colombians. Using an array of fake passports, Martínez traveled with El Chapo throughout Latin America and took trips to Southeast Asia for both business and pleasure. They gambled in Macau and Las Vegas, bought jets in Los Angeles, visited Hong Kong, Japan, and Europe. According to Martínez, El Chapo took trips to Switzerland to undergo a clinical procedure in which "they put some cells in you so that you keep young." El Chapo even got himself a California driver's license under the name Max Aragon, a frequently used pseudonym. Like the kingpins of Guadalajara a few years prior, they were all doing a lot of cocaine. Martínez recalls snorting up to four grams a day in those years, a habit that he could afford given his access to the stuff, but which permanently destroyed the mucous membranes in his nose, for which he later required plastic surgery. El Chapo indulged, too, Martínez recalled, although with far more moderation, and he later gave it up.

Life was good for them back then, and the money started to add up.

El Chapo had a $10 million house in Acapulco. On a ranch in Guadalajara he built a zoo and stocked it with lions, tigers, panthers, and deer. He even outfitted his narco zoo with a little train, so visitors could ride around the property and admire the animals in comfort.

El Chapo took to showering his most loyal henchmen with gifts, presenting Martínez with a diamond-studded Rolex and rewarding employees with luxury cars as Christmas bonuses. One December, Martínez said, he bought more than fifty cars, and allowed the men to choose between a Thunderbird, a Buick, and a Cougar, each costing more than $30,000. He paid Martínez $1 million a year in cash each December.

El Chapo's crew was pushing tens of thousands of kilos of cocaine a year, with a street value of hundreds of millions of dollars, pocketing the profits on four out of every ten kilos, and Martínez estimated that 95 percent of that was going through the tunnel. But Agua Prieta was a small town, and people talked, and soon Customs officials in Douglas were hearing whispers about suspicious activity around Camarena Macias's warehouse. On May 9, 1990, federal agents in a suburb of Phoenix, Arizona, busted a truck loaded with cocaine, and managed to connect it back to the warehouse in Douglas. On May 17, Customs agents raided the place and discovered the tunnel.

Martínez remembered getting a phone call from the boss in the wake of the raid. El Chapo was irate that his main smuggling route had been busted—along with millions of dollars' worth of coke—and he had an idea of who might be to blame, unaware of the stakeout by Customs.

"This is fucking over. They found the tunnel," El Chapo raged to Martínez on the phone.

Fables abound of El Chapo murdering employees and meting out savage punishments for small infractions, but many of these are hard to verify. He certainly grew quicker to enforce discipline with violence in later years, but at the time, he could be a surprisingly forgiving boss. As angry as El Chapo was with Camarena Macias, he allowed the lawyer from Guadalajara to escape with his life. Thanks to corrupt cops on Guzmán's payroll, they knew that the American authorities were looking for Macias in connection with the coke bust, and he sent the lawyer packing, first to Mexico City, and then to the Sinaloan resort town of Mazatlán.

In Agua Prieta, not all was lost: there were still about 900 kilos of cocaine sitting in a warehouse in town, waiting to be moved. No longer feeling very trusting of his lieutenants on the border, El Chapo immediately headed to Agua Prieta to take charge of the situation, and upon landing came up with a plan to load the cocaine onto trucks and drive it nearly three hours west to cross the border in Nogales.

The federal agents who discovered the tunnel were shocked by its sophistication. And despite its short lifespan, the tunnel proved to be a valuable experiment for El Chapo. It would not be his last tunnel. But there is no resting on one's laurels in the drug trade, and for now, El Chapo had a problem: he had too much cocaine on his hands to reliably move on trucks going through legal ports of entry. The delay threatened to tarnish El Chapo's reputation with the Colombians, who began to wonder if "El Rápido" was a one-trick pony, if maybe they'd have to start calling him *"El Lento,"* the Slow One.

4

THINGS FALL APART

On APRIL 21, 1993, a team of Mexican Federal Judicial Police stopped a tractor trailer in Tecate, a border town in the state of Baja California about half an hour west of the outskirts of Tijuana. At first, the vehicle appeared to be a run-of-the-mill commercial truck transporting foodstuffs for wholesale in the United States. In the trailer sat pallet after pallet loaded with orange and yellow cans of pickled jalapeño chile peppers bearing the name La Comadre, with the logo of a whimsical-looking Mexican girl sporting twin braids tied with red bows. Nonetheless, the PJF agents began to inspect the chile cans, and after some time they hit pay dirt. Opening one of the cans, an officer discovered not the soupy mix of oil, brine, and jalapeños packed into a normal can, but rather in its place a kilo of cocaine stuffed into the can with some sand to weigh it down. As officers ransacked the rest of the pallets of chile cans, they found one can after another stuffed with coke and sand. By the end of the day, they stood gazing at a mountain of cocaine weighing in at more than seven tons. At the time, it was one of the largest-ever seizures of cocaine on the record.

While the cops had been ransacking the truck, Miguel Ángel Martínez Martínez—El Chapo's logistics whiz—was fielding increasingly panicked calls from his contact in Los Angeles. The man had been waiting for the tractor trailer to arrive at their warehouse that day, and had become alarmed when it failed to show up. It was not until the following day that Martínez learned of the seizure, and called his boss.

"Fuck it, compadre," El Chapo said when he heard the news. "That [route] is now finished."

All in all, the scheme to smuggle coke in chile cans had had a good run. It had begun in early 1990, in the wake of the discovery of El Chapo's tunnel in Agua Prieta. At the time of the raid, they had been sitting on more than seven tons of cocaine at a warehouse, but thanks to a tip-off from a police contact, they'd moved it before swarms of DEA, Customs, and Mexican police arrived in town and shut down the tunnel. They were left, however, with a whole lot of coke on their hands and no way to get it north.

A new tunnel would have been ideal, but it would have taken time to scout locations, buy property, design the thing, and get it operational. After some brainstorming, one of El Chapo's lieutenants had an idea: What if they hid cocaine in chile cans? The smell of the real chiles could help throw drug-sniffing dogs off the scent, and the shipments would easily blend in with the millions of dollars in goods crossing the border every day. And it had been done before. While this method is often held up as proof of El Chapo's singular genius, newly rediscovered evidence suggests he was not the first to try this method. As early as 1984, the owners of a pair of chile canneries in the state of Zacatecas were said to be using their facilities to smuggle marijuana in chile cans, around the same time that a young El Chapo was working on a grow operation in the area.

At first El Chapo considered just buying a pepper factory and converting it into a coke-processing plant, as the guys in Zacatecas had done with weed; but to do that they would have to go to the trouble of actually getting approval from the Food and Drug Administration to import their "peppers," and that seemed like a pain in the ass. Instead, they began to clone the packaging of an existing company, La Comadre, which already had FDA approval. So, using the existing brand, they rigged up a packaging machine bought in the United States, and set about canning the drugs in workshops in Guadalajara and Mexico City.

To simulate the weight and feel of a real pepper can, they would stuff a kilo into each can and fill it up with a particular type of sandy gravel that did a good job of mimicking the sound and feel of chile oil sloshing about in the cans. Soon the packagers were able to churn out hundreds of cans a day, which would be loaded onto pallets with real chile cans and placed on eighteen-wheelers headed for the border. Any Customs agent inspecting the load would have to get through a few layers of real chile cans to get to the drugs.

"If you picked up a can from the top part of it, it was chile peppers," Martínez said later. "If you picked one up from the side, they were chile peppers. The ones in the middle had cocaine."

And for a while, it worked fantastically. The chile idea was such a smash hit that others seem to have copied it. According to El Chapo's contact in Los Angeles, a friend of his had gone to the store to buy pickled jalapeños but instead found sixteen kilos of cocaine in the cans he had purchased, albeit of a different brand than La Comadre. According to the contact, who laughingly retold the story to Martínez, the friend had returned to the store and bought their entire supply of the chiles in question. Over the next few years, El Chapo and his people pulled in nearly a quarter of a million dollars by sending tractor trailers through Baja California, packed to the brim with dummy chile cans, Martínez estimated.

But he did so without paying the taxes that were typically demanded by the people who controlled Tijuana. And the people who controlled Tijuana were not happy about it.

• • •

Before 1994, when the North American Free Trade Agreement threw open the gates of commerce between Mexico and the United States, tariffs on consumer goods crossing the border prevented a wide range of items from appearing on shelves, from Levi's jeans to Sony television sets. As a result, there existed a vast constellation of smuggling outfits all along the border from Brownsville, in southern Texas, to Tijuana, on the Pacific Coast, who snuck goods across the border for sale on the black market.

One such family of smugglers was the Arellano-Félix clan. A brood of seven sons and four daughters born to a mechanic, they had begun their career smuggling clothing and electronics before graduating to trafficking drugs. Like nearly all the other high-level traffickers of their era, the

Arellano-Félix siblings hailed from Sinaloa, but soon went forth into the wider world to seek their fortune. They landed first in Guadalajara, and later, in the early 1980s, they set up in the city of Tijuana, a city whose reputation as a den of hedonism dates back to Prohibition, when a cottage industry of bars serving legal booze to American customers popped up and stuck around even after that ill-fated experiment ended in the United States. In the 1980s, it made a good base for traffickers like the Arellano-Félixes, located just across the border from the immense drug market of Southern California and the freeway network to parts north and east in the United States.

Of the eleven children in the family, six would work in the drug trade; but only three were worth mentioning in those early days in Tijuana: Francisco Rafael, Benjamín, and Ramón. The eldest brother, Francisco Rafael, was in the family business, but was never at the center of the action. His main thing was Frankie Oh's, a palatial nightclub in Mazatlán that held a crowd of 2,500, was outfitted with indoor waterfalls and exotic fish and animals, and would become the cornerstone of the family's money-laundering operation. Francisco rode a Harley, palled around with champion boxers, and was said to wear a large scorpion medallion in a nod to his astrological sign.

The youngest of the three, Ramón, was the muscle. In addition to his slaughtering any snitches, rogue smugglers, honest cops, and nosy journalists who got in the way of the family's business, stories abound of Ramón attacking strangers at the slightest provocation—a bouncer who told him to pour a beer from a bottle into a cup, say, or some poor sap who just looked at him wrong. Some traffickers, like El Chapo, were known for their innovation in smuggling methods. Ramón, on the other hand, made a name for himself in the creative application of violence, torture, and dismemberment.

The brains of the operation was baby-faced Benjamín, frequently pictured with his prominent chin jutting out and his bangs swept forward. Benjamín had an unnerving habit of staring right at people when he spoke, barely blinking. He may not have been the eldest, but from early on it was his strategic thinking that propelled the brothers forward.

The Arellano-Félixes were deeply embedded in Tijuana, and the political protection they acquired through rubbing elbows with powerful people and doling out bribes to cops, politicians, and military officers formed the first firewall against any serious investigation into their operation. One DEA informant reported to his handlers that he had been aggressively questioned by police during an attempt to follow buses that were suspected of transporting drugs across the border. His body was later found on a hill overlooking town. Kidnapping victims lucky or crafty enough to escape one of Ramón's torture chambers were reportedly delivered back to their captor posthaste by the very cops they thought would be their saviors.

When they began working in Tijuana, the brothers—like El Chapo in Sinaloa and Sonora, and like Amado Carrillo Fuentes in Ciudad Juárez—did so under the umbrella of Miguel Ángel Félix Gallardo. Even after the events surrounding the murder of Kiki Camarena, when the connections between the various factions under Félix Gallardo began to fray, there was room enough in Tijuana for other factions in town. The local representative for El Chapo and his allies was Jesús Reynaldo "El Rey" Zambada, the younger brother of El Mayo Zambada.

According to Luis Astorga, the reigning dean of Mexican drug-war letters, the lines began to be drawn between "*los urbanos*," suave city kids like the Arellano-Félix clan, and "*los serranos*," rough-and-tumble guys like El Chapo, El Mayo, Héctor "El Güero" Palma, and their allies, who carried themselves with a cowboy swagger that belied their rural upbringing. By the late 1980s, El Chapo and his crew were on a collision course with the brothers Arellano-Félix.

According to some tellings, the trouble began with an unforgivable violation of El Güero's family. El Güero—whose nickname, meaning "Blondie," came from his fair skin and light brown hair—was of the old guard; he was an early collaborator with Félix Gallardo, and also a mentor to El Chapo. A Venezuelan trafficker connected with the Arellano-Félixes had seduced his wife and eventually forced her to withdraw $7 million from her bank account before he decapitated her. For good measure, he threw the couple's two children off a high bridge in Venezuela. The Arellano-Félix brothers protected the Venezuelan, and Félix Gallardo was widely believed to have approved the atrocity.

Other stories trace the feud back to a birthday party held in Tijuana for El Mayo in 1988, at which Ramón Arellano Félix murdered a friend of El Chapo named Armando "El Rayo" Lopez. The murder caused an uproar. But everyone had money to make, so, not long after, El Chapo and the brothers came together for a sit-down on relatively neutral ground in Mexico City, where they managed to shake hands and make up. For a time, everything was all right.

• • •

Personal feuds have often played a role in gangland conflict, and it's possible that the humiliation of El Güero and the slaughter of his family, or the murder of Rayo Lopez, were enough to set El Chapo and the Arellano-Félix brothers on a path toward war. But the cause of violence is rarely so simple or cinematic as one powerful psychopath sending his gunmen to kill the gunmen of another powerful psychopath. The bloody beef between El Chapo and the Arellano-Félix family came at a time of upheaval in Mexico. It was the beginning of the end of the days in which the lines of communication between traffickers and their government accomplices were clear, the beginning of the end of the time in which there was no question about who answered to whom. With the dismantling of the DFS in 1985, and the capture of Félix Gallardo in 1989, the remaining factions began to grow more territorial. And to hold territory, you need an army.

Of all the factions that rose with the fall of Félix Gallardo, it was the Arellano-Félixes who took the idea of territory most seriously. While El Chapo and El Mayo continued to work closely with Amado's crew in Juárez, investing in drug loads together, shipping through one another's territory, and essentially functioning as one organization, the Arellano-Félixes began to charge exorbitant fees on anyone moving drugs through Tijuana. For many traffickers, the tax was a worthy price to pay to be able to ship drugs through the mammoth border crossing there, directly to customers in Southern California. But for those who didn't pay, the family needed to make an example.

To control the plaza, Ramón began recruiting foot soldiers from among the bored children of Tijuana's wealthiest families. Many of them had U.S. passports, making it easy to cross between Tijuana and San Diego. On the U.S. side, the brothers forged ties with street gangs in San Diego, particularly a crew of hoods known as the Logan Heights Gang, whose leaders were close with the powerful Mexican Mafia prison gang. With these two disparate groups of recruits—rich kids from Tijuana, poor kids from San Diego—the Arellano-Félixes had enough muscle to force independent traffickers into paying the necessary taxes, and to pose a lethal threat to any outside smugglers looking to use Tijuana as a no-toll throughway for drug shipments.

To get the men in fighting shape, Ramón organized training camps in the mountains outside the city, and brought in ex-soldiers, corrupt cops, and even a Syrian mercenary to drill the motley assortment of San Diego gangsters and Tijuana playboys on the finer points of interrogation and murder.

Despite the bad blood between El Chapo and the Arellano-Félix family, El Mayo and his brother El Rey managed for several years to maintain cordial relations with the brothers. El Mayo knew violence was bad for business, and hoped the situation would work itself out. But the tenuous peace between El Chapo and the brothers in Tijuana was pushed to the brink once more in the wake of the discovery of the tunnel in Agua Prieta in the spring of 1990, as El Chapo felt the need to move product through the brothers' territory in Tijuana. Trouble was inevitable, El Rey recalled.

"The Arellano-Félixes thought they were the kings, the owners of Tijuana, and they didn't want anyone to cross drugs on their border without their authorization," said El Rey, who at the time was living and working in Tijuana.

El Chapo, however, was less convinced of the Arellano-Félixes' royal status. And he had coke to move. As he continued pushing the dummy peppers cans north, he soon set his sights on Tijuana as the location for his next big project: a tunnel far bigger and more sophisticated than the one in Agua Prieta. Buried sixty-five feet belowground, the tunnel stretched more than a quarter of a mile, from a hidden entrance in the floor of a warehouse on the Mexican side to another in a warehouse just north of the border. One Customs official later quipped to a reporter that it was the "Taj Mahal" of tunnels.

· · ·

In an effort to starve the Arellano-Félix brothers out of business, El Chapo and his allies made it clear to their suppliers that no one was to do business with Tijuana. In one meeting with the Colombian drug lord Chupeta, El Chapo explained the beef with the Arellano-Félixes, and Chupeta did not have to be told: it would be wise, he surmised, to cease dealings with the brothers.

"I saw that the Sinaloa Cartel people were stronger," Chupeta later said. "There were more people in it, and they were all united in that problem against the Arellano-Félixes."

This was bound to end in bloodshed. The Arellano-Félix brothers were not ones to go hungry without putting up a fight.

Scattered violence warned of what was to come. In September 1992, in Iguala, Guerrero, gunmen working for El Güero murdered a lawyer who had worked for Félix Gallardo, who was seen as backing the Arellano-Félix brothers from prison, and gunned down eight of the lawyer's family members; months later, a group of Ramón's shooters abducted six of El Chapo's men in Tijuana, shot them in the head, and dumped their bodies by a highway outside the city; in Culiacán, a car bomb blew up on a property belonging to El Chapo. The final straw came in 1992 as El Chapo was driving through Guadalajara, and by chance ran into Ramón Arellano-Félix in traffic. To Ramón, the encounter was an opportunity to end the pesky feud once and for all. El Chapo was less wary, and as he pulled over the car to greet his former ally, Ramón and his men opened fire. El Chapo barely escaped with his life and swore revenge. When his loyal lieutenant Miguel Ángel Martínez tried to offer words of caution, El Chapo responded with a grim declaration.

"Either your mom is going to cry, or their mom is going to cry," he told Martínez.

El Chapo didn't want his mother to cry, so it would have to be Benjamín and Ramón's mother.

Not long after the violent encounter in Guadalajara, El Chapo got his shot at revenge. In November 1992, the son of a longtime associate of El Chapo, who happened to go to university with Francisco Javier Arellano-

Félix, learned that Benjamín, Ramón, and young Francisco Javier, along with a handful of their most trusted hit men, were going to be in Puerto Vallarta, a popular resort town on the Pacific coast of Jalisco, on the night of November 7, 1992.

Ramón and his brother Francisco Javier were inside the club, blowing off steam with their men. It was a Saturday night and the place was packed when, sometime after midnight, El Chapo and his men arrived. Piling out of the truck, El Chapo's men made a frontal assault on the club, storming inside and opening fire on their rivals, along with hundreds of innocent club-goers.

Unfortunately for El Chapo, someone had also tipped off Ramón, and his gunmen were ready, returning fire as Ramón, Francisco Javier, and their top lieutenants fled through an air duct in one of the bathrooms. When the smoke cleared, six people were dead, including several of Ramón's hit men and a handful of innocent revelers.

. . .

Two months after the debacle in Puerto Vallarta, Amado Carrillo Fuentes once again tried to act as a peacemaker in a last-ditch effort to prevent war. A few years older than El Chapo, he was widely respected by nearly everyone involved in the drug trade in Mexico, and in a few years would be by far the most powerful trafficker in the country. But this time, Amado may have underestimated the level of tension between El Chapo and the Arellano-Félix family, and he made the mistake of inviting the son of El Mayo to come along. It soon became clear that this was a dangerous miscalculation.

It was early 1993, and Vicente "Vicentillo" Zambada Niebla, age sixteen, was living with his uncle El Rey and attending high school in Tijuana, where he regularly socialized with the Arellano-Félix family. So when Amado headed to Tijuana, he decided to bring Vicentillo with him to the meeting, which was being held at a mansion that the Arellano-Félixes used as a safe house.

The atmosphere was tense as the pair rolled up to the house, where Benjamín Arellano-Félix was waiting for them surrounded by armed guards. He was surprised to see Vicentillo Zambada by Amado's side.

"What are you doing here?" he snarled at Vicentillo.

"He's with me," Amado replied. "He doesn't have anything to do with this, he's just with me."

Vicentillo followed the men into the house, and headed to the kitchen to wait while the adults talked. Finally, he was called into the living room, where the atmosphere had only gotten more tense. As Vicentillo entered the room, Benjamín Arellano-Félix was in the middle of demanding that Amado ally himself with Tijuana against El Chapo, before turning his wrath on the teenage son of El Mayo.

By now, Benjamín had completely lost his cool, spitting profanities and death threats inches from Vicente's face.

"El Chapo and your father are going to regret not having killed us at the discotheque," he shouted.

Finally, around 1 a.m., Amado and Vicentillo managed to extricate themselves from the house, and without swinging by the hotel to pick up their things, they headed straight for the airport, where Amado had a Learjet waiting on the tarmac. The streets of Tijuana where Vicentillo had strolled after class were now enemy territory, and it was time to beat a hasty retreat. Even Amado was shaken; he knew what the Arellano-Félix brothers were capable of, the manpower they had at their disposal, and the casual sadism with which the brothers meted out punishment. Amado did not trust the Arellano-Félixes, particularly Ramón. Even though Ramón had not been present at the meeting, Amado suspected he was waiting in the wings for a possible signal to attack. After failing in his peacekeeping mission, the Lord of the Skies only felt safe again once he and his young friend were in the air, the lights of Tijuana receding into the distance behind them.

Amado and Vicentillo flew southeast, crossing the Gulf of California to Hermosillo, the state capital of Sonora, where Amado had a home. After a few hours' rest, he put Vicentillo on a plane to Culiacán, where one of El Mayo's lackeys picked up the boss's son and took him to Mayo's house. Vicentillo may have just hours before witnessed the final rupture between Mexico's most important drug-trafficking families, but he was still a teenager and El Mayo was still his father. When the younger

Zambada arrived at his father's house and debriefed him on the disastrous meeting, Mayo assured his son that he was not in danger. Then he scolded Vicentillo for not being in class.

With Amado and Vicentillo safely out of Culiacán, the battle lines were drawn. On one side of the conflict were El Chapo, El Mayo, and other Sinaloan allies; on the other were the Arellano-Félix brothers and their army of well-to-do cutthroats and American-born gangsters. In Sinaloa, the war made itself known as the number of murders skyrocketed and kidnappings became commonplace.

The rift was complete, and no amount of diplomacy could heal the enmity between El Chapo and the Arellano-Félix family.

• • •

On May 24, 1993, a month and two days after the seizure of the cocaine chile cans in Tecate, the brothers made their move, and the war came to a head in the parking lot of the Guadalajara airport.

Despite the danger of the gunmen whom Ramón had looking for him, El Chapo was traveling light that day, with only a few bodyguards, one of whom he had sent ahead to drop off his luggage. As El Chapo's car pulled up to the departures terminal, Ramón and a team of gunmen from San Diego sprinted forward, guns raised.

"They're coming, they're coming!" El Chapo's bodyguard cried, just before the hit men opened fire, raking El Chapo's car with automatic gunfire.

His driver sprang from the car to return fire, and as he planted one shoe on the ground, a bullet slammed into his foot. In the backseat, El Chapo grabbed a suitcase full of cash and leapt from the car, running hunched over as he desperately sought cover inside the terminal. As he and the bodyguard burst through the door, El Chapo slipped and fell hard. The suitcase in his hand clattered to the ground and burst open, spewing cash across the ground.

Frantically stuffing cash back into the suitcase as outside gunshots continued to ring out in staccato bursts, El Chapo and his henchman ran toward the baggage carousel, scrambled through its mouth, and dashed out onto the tarmac. Leaving the chaos and bloodshed behind them, they ran across the runways to the far end of the airport. From there, they hiked along a local access road until they came to a highway, where they commandeered a taxi and were driven to safety.

As El Chapo was making his escape, the gunmen who had ambushed him simply dropped their weapons on the pavement and calmly but quickly walked toward the departures terminal. They breezed through security and walked right onto an Aeromexico flight bound for Tijuana. Conveniently, the flight was running late. For some reason, it had waited at the gate twenty minutes past its departure time, just long enough for the assassins to board.

Back in the parking lot, a white Mercury Grand Marquis sat riddled with bullets. Slumped in the front seat was Archbishop Juan Jesús Posadas Ocampo, a popular official in the Catholic Church in Mexico who had championed the rights of the poor and spoken out against corruption. He had made the mistake of arriving at the airport at the wrong time, in a car identical to one that El Chapo sometimes traveled in, and now he was already dead, his blood beginning to slow its rapid flow out of the fourteen bullet holes in his plump body.

The death of the archbishop drew more attention than even the massacre at the discotheque in Puerto Vallarta, more than all the back-and-forth shootings across Sinaloa and Baja California over the last few years. They had crossed a line. In the blink of an eye, El Chapo and the Arellano-Félixes were the most wanted men in Mexico and were running for their lives. The Mexican government announced a $5 million bounty for anyone who could offer up information leading to the capture of the major capos, including El Chapo and El Güero of the Sinaloa faction and several Arellano-Félix brothers of Tijuana.

Miguel Ángel Martínez had warned El Chapo of the danger of going to war. Now, to his horror, he watched as his warning came to pass.

"It was too much pressure," Martínez recalled. "They were putting their photographs on the national TV every five or ten minutes."

The murder of a high-ranking official in the Catholic Church could not be ignored. It brought into devastating focus the violence of the drug trade, and spelled disaster for the men whose reckless disregard for the law, for civilians, and for the norms of civil society led to such a brazen gun battle in broad daylight. But it also raised suspicion in Mexico, and accusations immediately began to swirl that the archbishop had been the real target of the attack, the victim of powerful forces who disliked his public statements critical of Mexico's corrupt elite and who used drug-smuggling gunmen to do their dirty work. Nothing has ever been proven, and for their parts, both sides denied culpability. In one of the strangest episodes of the affair, Benjamín and Ramón, two of the recognizable fugitives in Mexico, actually met in person with the Vatican's representative in Mexico. Despite the $5 million bounty on the heads of the visitors, Benjamín and Ramón made it out of the meeting without trouble, and disappeared once more.

El Chapo did his best to disappear as well. After his madcap dash through the Guadalajara airport terminal and across the tarmac, El Chapo headed to Mexico City. It might seem counterintuitive for a Sinaloan fugitive with his face plastered on every newspaper and television screen in the country to head for the capital, but *El Distrito Federal*, DF for short, had long functioned as something of a neutral ground for drug traffickers, a metropolis of such overwhelming size and density that it offered a place to lie low, to conduct business away from prying eyes. They called it *El Humo*, or the Smoke, both for the smothering haze of air pollution and for the cover it provided to traffickers looking to do their business in anonymity.

El Chapo lay low for two days there, gathering a few men—and one woman—and some cash. Then he, one of his wives, a bodyguard known as "*El Tigre*," and two other henchmen headed south, toward Guatemala and, eventually, El Salvador. They had business in El Salvador, where a five-ton load of cocaine was just sitting there, waiting for pickup.

Perhaps if El Chapo had headed back to Sinaloa and hidden out in the mountains, he might have been okay. But Guatemala was not Sinaloa, and he was arrested shortly after his arrival. A few days later, a team of Guatemalan soldiers arrested the Mexican fugitive and his entourage and handed them over to Mexican troops just across the border.

. . .

Flanked by a pair of prison guards in black uniforms, El Chapo stood in a courtyard of Federal Readaptation Center #1, in Almoloya de Juárez, about fifty-five miles from downtown Mexico City. In later years, these guards would have been wearing face masks to protect themselves and their families against retaliation; but back then, traffickers still followed something of a code. Families were still off-limits, and the guards showed their faces alongside that of their prisoner.

El Chapo appeared dazed at first, his downcast, thousand-yard stare betraying a man lost in thought, but he soon seemed to take in his surroundings, his alert, beady eyes sweeping from right to left and back again. Dressed in a puffy beige jacket and prison-issue beige slacks, he was clean shaven, and his hair fell limply across his forehead. Apart from his somewhat bulbous nose, diminutive stature, and unflattering prison clothes, he struck a handsome figure, thinner at age thirty-eight than he would appear in later years, a well-defined jawline leading to a defiant chin. In his hands, cuffed in front of him, he held a stiff, Elmer Fudd–like baseball cap as reporters shouted questions at him.

"Are you engaged in drugs?" one reporter asked.

"No, señor," El Chapo replied softly.

"What do you do?"

"I'm a farmer," El Chapo said, with a straight face.

"What do you grow?"

"Corn and beans," El Chapo said.

"And what are the guns for?" another reporter jabbed.

"I've never used weapons," El Chapo replied, his laserlike gaze shifting from one reporter to the next.

"Listen, you obviously have a lot of money," a reporter shouted. "Why?"

"No, señor," the drug lord insisted. "I don't have money."

According to El Chapo, the whole thing was a misunderstanding. Yeah, he knew the Arellano-Félix family, but not through drug trafficking. They were all from Sinaloa, he said; he knew them socially. This was all a stark departure from the conversation he'd had with interrogators on the flight to Mexico City, during which he had spoken freely, and given in great detail information on his competitors and named the corrupt officials on his own payroll. But he seemed to have had a change of heart, or someone had convinced him to shut up, and now he proclaimed his innocence.

A judge did not agree, finding Joaquín Guzmán Loera guilty of drug trafficking and bribery, sentencing the boy from La Tuna to twenty years in prison. A year later, he was also convicted for the murder of the archbishop, although another judge later threw that ruling out.

With the exception of Francisco Rafael, who was arrested in December 1993 in Tijuana, the Arellano-Félix brothers had better luck, and most of them managed to evade the bounty on their heads—although escaping capture in Mexico rarely comes down to luck. Still, they had to go underground for years following the shoot-out in Guadalajara. Never again would they be able to live as publicly, flaunt their wealth so openly. (Curiously enough, the next time Ramón was seen in public, he appeared unwittingly in a man-on-the-street segment on a 1995 episode of *The David Letterman Show*. On the lam in LA, pale and pudgy in a Chicago Bulls shirt and sporting sunglasses and a blond wig, he looked annoyed as the camera zoomed in on him and pranky correspondent Rupert Jee mockingly asked Ramón if he was Michael Jordan. "I don't understand," Ramón muttered in Spanish.)

El Chapo's imprisonment seemed to have little effect on the war, which continued with deadly consequences for both sides. People associated with the Arellano-Félixes had a habit of getting shot, gunmen and lawyers alike. El Chapo's side took hits, too: El Rey, the younger brother of El Mayo, narrowly escaped an assassination attempt in Mexico City, and another Zambada brother was murdered in Cancún.

What had once been a business defined by relatively hegemonic control was now suffering from violent competition between rivals in an open market. And the violence was hurtling beyond the control of the cops and politicians who had long sought to keep a lid on such bloody mayhem while lining their own pockets.

While the outside world began to disintegrate, El Chapo began to get settled in prison.

5

I AM TITO

PRISON WASN'T SO bad for El Chapo, all things considered. As soon as he arrived at Puente Grande, a maximum-security prison on the outskirts of Guadalajara, he began spreading money around left and right, bribing everyone he could to make sure he was comfortable. For the guards and administrators of Puente Grande, it paid to do El Chapo's bidding: the prison cook pulled in a cool 15,000 pesos (about $1,518 at the time) a month to prepare special meals for the special inmate; custodial supervisors could earn as much as 40,000 pesos a month (about $4,210), while the warden allegedly earned more than 50,000 pesos a month (about $5,260) for tending to the needs of his powerful guest. When El Chapo wanted lobster, he ate lobster. When he wanted new shoes, a change of clothes, a cell phone, he got them. El Chapo had always had a voracious sexual appetite, and this did not change during his time locked up at Puente Grande, where he arranged for conjugal visits with his wives, and passed his days pursuing several of the women who made up the tiny group of female inmates serving time there.

But El Chapo was not content to sit in prison and rot, however much lobster he could eat, however many women he could sleep with. El Chapo needed to see to it that his affairs outside the prison walls continued smoothly. So he turned to his trusty lieutenant, Miguel Ángel Martínez Martínez.

In the immediate aftermath of the shoot-out at the Guadalajara airport and El Chapo's subsequent arrest, Martínez had fled to Europe,
where he stayed for about six weeks until things had cooled down a bit in
Mexico. El Chapo trusted Martínez immensely, and had given his lieutenant instructions on how to support El Chapo's family if he were taken
out of commission. He had given Martínez control of a wide range of
his properties and possessions, including warehouses, ranches, trucks,
planes, and stockpiles of drugs. In the event that the government got its
hands on him, El Chapo had instructed Martínez to transfer the drugs to
Juan José Esparragoza Moreno, aka El Azul, the old trafficker and fellow
Badiraguato native who had been a longtime mentor and partner to El
Chapo. When Martínez returned to Mexico in the summer of 1993, he
met with El Azul in Cuernavaca, the picturesque state capital of Morelos,
southwest of Mexico City. Arriving at the meeting, he found Amado Carrillo Fuentes had joined El Azul there, too. Martínez was holding on to
3,500 kilos of cocaine, left over from a shipment that he and El Chapo
been planning to get across the border in chile cans prior to the April 22
bust in Tecate, Baja California, when PJF agents finally uncovered the
scheme, and were hoping to sell it to El Azul.

The meeting did not go as planned.

El Azul was taken aback by the huge quantity of drugs El Chapo was
trying to unload, Martínez recalled. "He just opened his eyes and he said,
'You're scaring me with all those amounts,'" Martínez recalled. "He told
me, 'I cannot accept anything from you. I will call you later on and I'll
tell you what we're going to do.'"

Martínez was learning about the limits of mutual aid in the drug
trade. El Azul and El Chapo had been close, sure, they had worked together frequently since the days growing weed and opium in Zacatecas,
but such partnerships were only as good as the money it made them. And
El Azul was wary of sticking his neck out for El Chapo when it appeared
his old friend was down for the count. But he hadn't written El Chapo off
for good; he just needed some time.

Soon after the meeting in Cuernavaca, Martínez reunited with
El Azul again, this time alongside Arturo Guzmán, El Chapo's younger
brother whom everyone called El Pollo. El Pollo instructed Martínez to

hand everything over to him, and the former pilot was glad to oblige. But when they sent the load north, hidden in a train car full of molasses, the DEA seized it at the border crossing in Mexicali.

Down in Colombia, El Chapo's suppliers were getting angry and impatient. Chupeta, the North Valley Cartel kingpin, was furious. In the span of a few months, his main customer in Mexico—the one with whom he'd gone all in when he agreed to cut out the Arellano-Félix brothers—had been arrested over a stupid turf battle; the authorities in Mexico and the United States had seized more than ten tons of their cocaine; his deal with "El Rápido" was beginning to look like a colossal clusterfuck.

Finally, after speaking on the phone with El Pollo, Chupeta agreed to continue sending coke to El Pollo on the condition that the Mexicans would pay for the merchandise that had already been lost.

Aside from El Pollo and Martínez, El Chapo's biggest allies outside of prison were the Beltrán Leyva brothers, the trafficking clan originally from La Palma, a tiny hamlet nestled along the dirt road that leads to La Tuna. Arturo Beltrán Leyva, known as *"El Barbas,"* or the Bearded One, was the oldest of the three brothers. He was a killer, a heavyset man with a mean scowl who oversaw the family's security operation with a ruthless determination. Héctor Beltrán Leyva was a smoother customer than Arturo, and was known as *"El H"* or *"El Elegante."* He largely handled the money-laundering side of things, pumping the family's cash into front businesses and buying expensive art, a scheme that allowed him and his wife to hobnob with Mexico's elite. Alfredo was the youngest, born in 1971. With a squat build and a dark beard and a mop of black hair, he liked to party, a habit that would later earn him undue attention from the law.

The brothers became some of El Chapo's staunchest allies as the new generation of traffickers began to rise in stature in the chaos of the late 1980s and the fallout of the kidnapping and murder of Kiki Camarena. They had sided with him against the Arellano-Félix family as war broke out, and were now helping to run coke on his behalf while El Chapo was behind bars. El Chapo had seen some capos slide into irrelevance after their arrest. And El Chapo had no intention of being irrelevant.

Héctor "El Güero" Palma remained an important ally as well, and he continued to move drugs with the help of Miguel Ángel Martínez, allowing El Chapo to invest in his loads. But El Güero wasn't free for long, either: on June 23, 1995, he was on his way to a wedding party when the Learjet he had been flying in crashed near Zapopán, Jalisco. It was a miracle anyone survived, according to a DEA agent posted to Mexico City at the time who saw photos of the crash.

"It looked like a beer can that had been run over by a semi," the agent recalled.

But El Güero was a survivor, and he did walk away from the crash, albeit badly banged up. When a convoy of soldiers fanned out to search the surrounding area, they came across the injured El Güero and uniformed *federales* acting as his bodyguards and hiding out at the home of a PJF supervisor. El Güero, who was carrying federal police credentials, was identified in part by a pistol he was carrying, a .38 super with a palm tree on the handle made of precious gems. El Güero, too, was soon living it up at Puente Grande, enjoying many of the same perks as El Chapo.

• • •

With El Chapo and El Güero in prison and the Arellano-Félix boys on the run, the center of gravity shifted to Juárez, which was under the control of Amado Carrillo Fuentes, the Lord of the Skies. Amado had originally arrived in the state of Chihuahua in the late 1980s to coordinate with the boss of Ojinaga, Pablo Acosta Villareal, and taken over when Acosta had gained a bit too much notoriety for anyone's liking and been gunned down in an ambush by PJF agents in 1987. The main beneficiary of Acosta's death was Amado, along with everyone who profited from a more discreet plaza boss. By the mid-1990s he was one of the most powerful drug traffickers in Mexico, with mansions and ranches scattered throughout the country. He was moving untold tons of cocaine across the border each year, and held such power that many journalists in Mexico did not even dare print his name. Working with Amado were allies of El Chapo such as El Mayo and El Azul.

The only major faction that didn't originate in Sinaloa was the Gulf Cartel, one of Mexico's oldest trafficking networks and the one that likely had the closest ties to the administration of President Carlos Salinas de

Gortari. The boss of the Gulf Cartel, Juan García Ábrego, had close ties to the family of the president, and controlled the Gulf Coast and ports of entry along the southern Texas border in an uneasy alliance with Amado and other Sinaloans.

The violence between the Arellano-Félix clan and Amado's crew (including the remnants of El Chapo's group) made it somewhat difficult for El Chapo to maintain contact with his people on the outside. Martínez, who had visited him some six months after the 1993 arrest, could no longer come in person thanks to the Arellano-Félix gunmen lurking around Guadalajara, nor could El Chapo's brother El Pollo. El Chapo had a cell phone, but when he needed to get important messages out with no fear of surveillance, he was reduced to relying on a brother-in-law to visit him and pass messages along. He needed a way to deal with the Arellano-Félix brothers once and for all. He decided he would talk to the DEA.

•   •   •

While El Chapo sat in Puente Grande, big changes were taking place outside the prison walls, and not only in the drug game. The Mexican economy had long been undergoing a steady trend of liberalization, but under President Salinas de Gortari, this had leapt into overdrive as the administration privatized hundreds of state-run companies, bringing billions of dollars in foreign investment capital flowing into the country. In the process, Salinas helped create a new class of hyperwealthy Mexicans in just a few short years: in 1991, three years into Salinas's term, Mexico had just two billionaires; by the time he left office in 1994, the country had twenty-four individuals or families worth a billion dollars or more. The newly minted billionaires knew whom to thank for their wealth, and in case they didn't, Salinas was sure to remind them, especially as the PRI made a bid to stop relying on government funding and self-fund its own campaigns, part of an effort to appear more democratic. This marriage of big business and the PRI, however, was anything but democratic, and took place behind literal closed doors.

Salinas had helped make these men rich. Now it was time to shake the tree. At one supposedly confidential gathering held in 1993 at the home of the former finance minister—and memorably described in a book by the *Miami Herald* columnist Andrés Oppenheimer—the guest list included such luminaries as the telecommunications baron Carlos Slim and Carlos Hank Rhon, an old PRI kingmaker. At that banquet, Mexico's thirty richest people—all men—gathered at a U-shaped table in a cavernous room decked out with multimillion-dollar paintings by Diego Rivera and other luminaries of the Mexican art world, and here they pledged their ongoing support to the regime. When someone suggested that each of the men should bundle no less than $25 million for the party, one attendee stood up and swore to double that sum.

"I, and all of you, have earned so much money over the past six years that I think we have a big debt of gratitude to this government," the guest said. "We owe it to the president, and to the country."

· · ·

Despite the fact that his term was nearly over, Salinas and his backers in Washington were not yet done enriching their friends in the plutocratic stratosphere of the Mexican elite. On January 1, 1994, the North American Free Trade Agreement went into effect, freeing up the exchange of goods and capital between the United States and Mexico. For wealthy industrialists, this new order was like having access to a money printer. For Salinas, it cemented his legacy as the great liberalizer of Mexico's economy. For the poor in both countries, it was a nightmare: cheap, subsidized U.S. agricultural products flooded the market in Mexico, wiping out countless small farmers whose incomes had long been protected by tariffs. In the United States, good union jobs evaporated and reappeared in Mexico, paying far lower wages.

Like any outgoing *PRIista* president, Salinas had plans for the future of the country and the party. But not all plans go off without a hitch, even those of the PRI. In early 1994, Luís Donaldo Colosio, the man whom Salinas had tapped to succeed him, started getting out of line. He gave speeches about the rights of the indigenous communities of Mexico while an indigenous peasant group, the Zapatista Army of National Liberation, was staging a rebellion in the southern state of Chiapas; he talked about the rights of the poor. Then, on March 23, 1994, a gunman with ties to the local branch of the PRI gunned him down in at a rally in Tijuana.

The assassination opened up the race to a new successor named Ernesto Zedillo, and opened the floodgates for a wave of conspiracy theories, never proven, that the PRI had murdered Colosio after he spooked the party with his left-wing speeches. Zedillo, a relatively low-ranking party member who had resigned from his post as education minister in order to work on Colosio's campaign, was no Colosio, but he was also far enough from the core Salinas faction that he never would have otherwise received the *dedazo* if not for the shooting. As a parting gift to the man he was reluctantly handing power, Salinas did little to mitigate a growing economic dip that was devastating the middle and working classes of Mexico.

Zedillo started his term amid a severe economic crisis and a steep devaluation of the peso, but he quickly showed that such tribulations wouldn't prevent him from being a different—slightly different—kind of *PRIista* than previous presidents. This began in February 1995 with a bang, when prosecutors ordered the arrest of Raúl Salinas de Gortari, the previously untouchable brother of the former president. A civil engineer by training who later worked closely with his brother in politics, Raúl has sometimes been referred to in the press as *"el hermano incómodo,"* or the awkward brother, named so for the embarrassment he drew his family with his corruption. Think Billy Carter—if Billy Carter had amassed a fortune of more than $120 million in Swiss bank accounts, allegedly used his proximity to the presidency to help a drug trafficker's failed bid to buy a pair of seaports, and maybe ordered the murder of his own brother-in-law. (Raúl was convicted of that, along with "illegal enrichment," but both judgments were later tossed out.)

In the run-up to NAFTA, the United States had bigger priorities in Mexico than taking their government pals to task for alleged collusion with drug traffickers. Especially when one of the chief suspects of official corruption was Raúl Salinas, the brother of the president.

"Back in 1993, it was very unpopular to say anything against Mexico, basically because of NAFTA," one U.S. official said later. "Who was going to go and do a direct investigation against the President's brother? You just put it away, and it goes into the batter."

But now Raúl was in trouble.

Another high-profile target of the new administration was the outgoing deputy attorney general, Mario Ruíz Massieu. As the top lawman tasked with fighting drug traffickers, he had accepted millions of dollars in bribes in exchange for providing the Gulf Cartel with political protection, and stuffed the ill-gotten cash into a closet in his home in Mexico City, prosecutors alleged. As the Salinas *sexenio* drew to a close, Ruíz Massieu seemed to see the writing on the wall, and in the final months of 1994 he dispatched a bag man to make repeated trips to the States, hauling cardboard boxes stuffed with twenty- and one-hundred-dollar bills to be deposited in a bank in Houston, federal prosecutors said. When he learned that prosecutors in Mexico were about to indict him for taking bribes, Ruíz Massieu fled to the States, but no sooner had he scurried off the plane at Newark International Airport than he walked straight into the cold embrace of handcuffs, placed under arrest by federal agents operating on an indictment in Texas. In a statement following his arrest, Ruíz Massieu claimed that the money consisted of a $500,000 "bonus" awarded by Salinas, along with cash entrusted to him by relatives. He denied that there was anything at all strange about keeping $9 million in a closet. Really, those were his exact words: "It's not at all strange to keep it in the closet." (Ruíz Massieu died by suicide in 1999, before he could fully defend his good name in court. In a suicide note, he blamed Zedillo for his ruined reputation and untimely death.)

• • •

Political changes were under way in the United States as well. In 1992, Bill Clinton took the White House, the first Democrat to hold the presidency since Jimmy Carter lost to Reagan twelve years earlier. Intent on shedding Carter's bleeding-heart image, Clinton tacked to the right on domestic issues like welfare, as well as tried-and-true "law-and-order" initiatives. With the sensational headlines of the crack epidemic still on the minds of many Americans, the Clinton administration largely hewed to the status quo on drugs and crime, pushing through legislation that would lead to the imprisonment of untold young black and brown men, and maintaining the Reagan and Bush administrations' posture of all-out "war" on drugs. In the run-up to NAFTA, Mexico largely got a pass, but the larger drug-war machine rumbled on at ever-greater speed.

The DEA and the U.S. war on drugs had changed in the years since undercover agents like Kiki Camarena were running around Mexico with little in the way of backup. The agency had grown more muscular, better funded. Unlike in the 1970s and 1980s, when it played second fiddle to the Cold War foreign policy priorities dictated by the State Department and the CIA, the antinarcotic effort was now central to U.S. policy in the region, a cudgel with which to get Latin American governments in line.

Throughout the Cold War, and particularly under President Reagan, and then George H. W. Bush, the budget for defense and national security had barreled along like a runaway train. The budget for the DEA had been creeping up steadily as well, but as the agents in Guadalajara found out the hard way, the priorities of the DEA frequently came a distant second to the priorities of the CIA, the State Department, and anticommunist hawks perched in various positions throughout the superstructure of the U.S. government and diplomatic corps. When the "need" to fight communism trumped the "need" to combat drug trafficking, it was rarely an even contest. Even in the twilight years of the Cold War, the United States always seemed to prioritize its preoccupation with halting the spread of communism over its stated mission of fighting the drug trade, to the delight of drug traffickers and the deep frustration of DEA agents in Mexico.

"They don't give a damn," the former DEA agent in charge of the Guadalajara in the early 1980s said later. "They turn their heads the other way. They see their task as much more important than ours."

Now, however, with the Soviet Union in full-on retreat, all that defense spending had to go somewhere. As a rule, bigwigs at the Pentagon and law enforcement honchos—from chiefs of police on up to administrators at the DEA or Department of Defense—do not like to see their budgets decreased, and they rarely have to. In 1988, as glasnost was taking hold in Moscow and the threat of global war receding, the Pentagon announced its expansion of counternarcotics missions, and Congress happily chipped in a $300 million appropriation to help out. In 1989, Congress bumped the appropriation up to $450 million. That's peanuts compared with modern DEA budgets—the agency requested nearly $3 billion for the 2020 fiscal year—but at the time, it represented a considerable increase in both funding and mandate as the perceived threat of the Soviet Union faded into history.

"With peace breaking out all over the place, it gives us something to do," one two-star general quipped at the time.

And here's what they did: the new budget assigned the Pentagon to take the lead on all aerial and maritime monitoring of suspected drug routes. Analysts with the Air Force began looking into the use of spy satellites to keep track of suspected drug labs in Latin American jungles. Navy budget planners recommended shifting some training operations from the Atlantic to the Caribbean to monitor drug shipments sailing north from Colombia. Then–defense secretary Dick Cheney assigned a new group called Task Force 6 to monitor trafficking activity along the border with Mexico. The Pentagon authorized Delta Force hostage-rescue teams to capture drug traffickers abroad. A team of troops with helicopter support scrambled in Puerto Rico when a tip came in that Pablo Escobar was lying low at a beach villa in Panama, but aborted the mission when the informant's story fell apart.

In anti-drug warfare, the bloated military had found not only a new way to use the toys and manpower it already had, but also an excuse to rattle their alms cup at Congress year after year. And they weren't shy about it either. Just ask Lawrence Korb, who served as assistant defense secretary during Reagan's first term.

"Getting help from the military on drugs used to be like pulling teeth," Korb said at the time. "Now everybody's looking around to say 'Hey, how can we justify these forces?' And the answer they're coming up with is drugs."

As Washington began to take a national security approach to the fight against the drug trade, and as the military stepped up its support of anti-drug efforts, the DEA was able to develop an increasingly militarized strategy, including a program called Operation Snowcap, in which teams of agents underwent special-forces training and deployed to foreign countries like Colombia, Bolivia, and Guatemala, to conduct recon and search-and-destroy missions against coca fields and cocaine laboratories.

One of the DEA agents taking part in these special-ops missions was a young Mexican American agent named Joe Bond.

Now, with his graying hair and kind, deep-set eyes, Bond casts an unassuming figure. He could be anyone's father or a spry grandfather. He's also one of few U.S. law enforcement agents to have met with El Chapo in person before his extradition to the United States. Unlike some ex-DEA agents who have a connection to El Chapo, Bond has done little to capitalize on this—no ghostwritten memoir, few media appearances beyond the occasional Spanish-language interview on Telemundo. He's happy to tell his story, however, including portions of it that he had previously needed to keep under wraps. With the trial of El Chapo behind us, he's now freer to speak.

Joe Bond was born in Mexico City to a North American father and a Mexican mother, part of a sprawling family whose patriarch, Bond's grandfather, was a well-connected member of the PRI. He recalls fondly how his grandfather would spoil him, allowing Bond as a young teen to drive his car. Bond went to high school in Mexico City, but headed to the States for college. When he graduated from college with a degree in finance and marketing, he initially began working in the shipping business, but changed course when he met a commander of the Mississippi Highway Patrol, who told Bond they needed troopers who spoke Spanish. On a whim, he applied to the academy, and found law enforcement to be his calling. Working as a state trooper in Mississippi, he began regularly teaming up with the DEA, whose agents, like the Highway Patrol, found his knowledge of Spanish useful. After four years of interagency work, he joined the DEA, and after a year or so working out of an office in Jackson, Mississippi, Bond volunteered for Operation Snowcap. He underwent training with Army Rangers and Navy SEALs, and went on to do a handful of ninety-day tours as part of that operation, trekking through the jungle to locate and destroy drug labs and clandestine airstrips, spending months at a time essentially serving as a special-ops soldier abroad. Eventually, he rotated back stateside and returned to the resident office in Jackson, Mississippi, but when a posting in Mexico City opened up, he jumped at the chance to head back to his hometown and work out of the embassy there.

Within two weeks of his arrival in Mexico City, the country's most powerful drug lord, Amado Carrillo Fuentes, died on the operating table while undergoing plastic surgery. Unlike some narcos who go under the knife to change their appearance and avoid capture, it appeared Amado was seeing the doctor for a tummy tuck. And thanks to an anesthesiologist, he succumbed to an acute overdose of an anesthesia cocktail and a sedative drug. This cost the anesthesiologist his life—he and his assistant were found on the side of a highway on the outskirts of the capital, encased in cement.

Unlike many in Mexico who suspect that Amado never died but rather fled to Cuba to shack up with a mistress, Joe Bond is sure of the fate that befell the boss of Juárez. He saw the body. He even has a photo of the dead drug baron, his face bloated but still recognizable.

· · ·

On November 7, 1997, Joe Bond was in his office at the U.S. embassy in Mexico City when he received a call from one of the U.S. Marines standing guard outside. There was a guy, the Marine told him, who had a message for the DEA. Bond threw on a jacket and went downstairs to see what was up.

The visitor, whom Bond referred to by the code name "Electra," was the brother-in-law through whom El Chapo sent important messages. And he had a message for Bond, he said.

"Really," Bond replied, at once interested and suspicious.

Yep, Electra said. El Chapo wanted to talk to the DEA.

That was going to be a challenge. DEA agents could not easily waltz into Puente Grande the way they might enter a prison in the United States.

Through Electra, El Chapo told them to use a code name: "Tito."

Bond's bosses back in Washington needed some convincing; they were fearful of "another Kiki Camarena incident," Bond recalled. Over the next several months, he worked on developing a plan that would allow them to access the prison as safely as possible. But in order to do that, he would need permission from the Mexican government.

The only person Bond trusted enough to speak to, and powerful enough to give permission, was José Luís Santiago Vasconcelos, the PGR official tasked with tackling drug trafficking. Of all the Mexican officials Bond dealt with, he had found Vasconcelos to be the most honest, the most willing to share intelligence, even allowing Bond to sometimes sit in on his briefings. With the utmost secrecy, Bond and another DEA agent, an intelligence officer named Larry Villalobos, began discussions with Vasconcelos and his boss.

They would have to go to Puente Grande undercover. El Chapo had stipulated that no one—not the prison warden, not the guards—could know that he was reaching out to the DEA. If word got back to other traffickers that he was talking to the gringos, he worried that his life, and the lives of his family members, would be in grave danger. He may have had much of the prison staff on his payroll, but he was not the only one. As for the agents, they knew that their safety inside the prison depended on keeping their true identities as tightly guarded as possible to prevent the possibility of being kidnapped or assaulted inside Puente Grande.

Finally, on March 2, 1998, Vasconcelos told Bond that the plan could move forward, as long as they agreed to bring along a representative of the PGR named José "Pepe" Patiño Moreno, for whom Vasconcelos vouched personally. Like Vasconcelos, Patiño had a reputation as being a rare honest prosecutor and had been involved in the investigation into the murder of Cardinal Posadas Ocampo, along with other high-profile crimes linked to the Arellano-Félix organization.

Vasconcelos had arranged for agents Bond and Villalobos to pose as sociologists, telling the prison warden that Pepe Patiño was accompanying them while the "sociologists" conducted psychological profiles of prominent Mexican criminals. He did not say ahead of time who they wished to meet, and El Chapo would not have advance notice of the specific date on which they were to arrive. They didn't want anyone to be able to plan any hijinks ahead of time.

On March 4, Bond reached out to Electra and told him to get word to El Chapo that they would be coming at some point in the future. The next day, the little delegation flew to Guadalajara and drove to Puente Grande.

· · ·

As Joe Bond, Larry Villalobos, and Pepe Patiño pulled up to the outer perimeter of Puente Grande, they found they had a welcoming party, a group of heavily armed guards awaiting their arrival.

The two DEA agents and the Mexican prosecutor spilled out of their car and presented themselves to the officer in charge, who solemnly checked each man's credentials.

Bond handed over a fake driver's license that he carried with him for undercover assignments, identifying him as "José Bonillas," a pseudonym he had been using since his first days as a cop back in Mississippi. It was just similar enough to his real name that if some unsuspecting pal or acquaintance greeted him with a hearty "Hey, Joe!" while he was on assignment, he could shrug it off; some people called him Joe, José Bonillas would explain.

Both DEA men had credentials identifying them as sociologists, and as both were native Spanish speakers, both of Mexican descent, so they didn't seem too out of place posing as Mexican sociologists. The officer in charge of the security detail nodded for them to follow him to the entrance of the prison.

Puente Grande cuts a foreboding silhouette, a sea of gray concrete walls, razor-sharp concertina wire, and grim watchtowers nestled in the verdant Jalisco countryside, like some kind of menacing, reverse oasis. At the time, it was home to some of the most dangerous men in Mexico (or at least, the most dangerous men who had fallen afoul of the police), and was notorious for corruption and for being run by wealthy inmates. Definitely a no-go zone for men like Joe Bond and Larry Villalobos.

Arriving at the entrance of the prison's administrative area, a guard ushered them into the office of the warden, who waved them in with a chilly welcome. Once again they presented their passes and their credentials, and gave him the spiel, claiming that they were there to conduct psychological profiles of prominent Mexican criminals. The man on their agenda that day was El Chapo.

Bond could tell immediately that the warden did not believe them. The official gave them a knowing grin, looked them up and down, but said nothing.

"You could tell, like, 'These guys are bullshitting me, but I have no choice,'" Bond recalled.

The warden may have been in charge of Puente Grande, but when the attorney general's office in Mexico City told him a couple of sociologists needed access to the prison, he had no choice but to comply. So he welcomed them, however icily, and escorted the group to a private room in the medical wing of the prison that he had set aside for their visit, before excusing himself to go fetch the inmate.

While they waited, the DEA agents and the Mexican prosecutor took in their surroundings. The room really was set up for psych evaluations, complete with a sofa, a table and chairs, and two windows with metal bars on them overlooking the prison yard. After about fifteen minutes, maybe half an hour, a guard opened the door and in walked the man they had come to see.

As the door closed behind him, El Chapo shook his visitors' hands one by one. He was dressed in government-issue prison khakis, like those he had worn in front of the press scrum back in 1993 when officials had first paraded him before the nation following his arrest in Guatemala. He looked better than he had then, like he had lost weight, was eating all right, had been getting exercise.

Once Bond was sure the guard had left, he introduced himself.

"Good afternoon," Bond greeted the prisoner. "I am Tito."

As soon as the code name left Bond's mouth, the imprisoned drug lord went pale, his beady eyes narrowing. He'd known the agents would come at some point, but not when; he was unprepared, caught unawares.

Without saying a word, El Chapo dropped to the floor in a push-up position, and lowered himself down to peer under the door, checking to see if anyone was standing close and listening in, while Bond, Villalobos, and Patiño looked on.

Once El Chapo seemed certain no guards were snooping, he rose to his feet once more and gave the group another once-over. He began to mumble something, almost in a whisper, clearly thrown off.

Bond hastened to assure El Chapo once again that he was safe, and introduced himself, Villareal, and Patiño, stressing that although Patiño was with the PGR, they had complete faith in him.

El Chapo shot Patiño a glare, but nodded in acceptance.

He began to speak in a nervous torrent, ranting about his enemies, of the threats against him.

"They're everywhere," El Chapo said. "They," people belonging to the

Arellano-Félix network, were in Mexico City, Guadalajara, and Aguascalientes, and he worried they were going to try to kill him, kill his family members, anyone they could get their hands on associated with him.

"He was ranting," Bond recalled. "I was like, 'Just slow down, man.'"

Bond could see that El Chapo was used to being in control, and he knew he needed to assert himself, show El Chapo that they were calling the shots here.

"He had great charisma, I'm not kidding you," Bond told me later. "He obviously had the temperament to take control of things. He thought that, because we knew who he was, that he was gonna intimidate us. But he wasn't going to intimidate us."

After he finally calmed down, El Chapo began to bring the agents up to speed, and spoke bitterly of his distrust of Mexican officials. When El Chapo was first arrested, he said, he had offered the PGR information on the Arellano-Félix brothers, but had waited with growing dismay while the agency took more than a week to act on his tip. When they finally raided the house where he said the brothers would be, his enemies had had time to flee, and the PGR agents found nothing besides some cash. After that, he said, he had resolved to never again provide information to Mexican law enforcement. He simply couldn't trust them.

Before he could say more, El Chapo made clear what he wanted: to be placed in a prison where he could speak face-to-face with an associate he trusted to gather up-to-date information on his enemies that El Chapo could feed to the DEA; he asked for a guarantee of safety for his family; and he asked that his outstanding charges in the United States be "resolved," in order to fend off the possibility of extradition.

At this, Patiño got tough. El Chapo was in prison, he reminded the inmate, serving a twenty-year term. The group was there in good faith to hear information that might help the Mexican government and the United States fight drug trafficking, but had no interest in banter, and had nothing to lose by walking back out the door and leaving El Chapo to sit out the rest of his sentence.

Bond cut in, telling El Chapo that he would have to provide information that proved his willingness to cooperate before the U.S. government even began to consider his requests.

El Chapo nodded solemnly.

"I will speak honestly to you, and I will give you my word on everything I am about to say," he pledged.

He spoke of the Arellano-Félix brothers, of the events that had led to the war between his faction and theirs. The brothers, he said, were "intelligent, wealthy, and extremely dangerous," according to a classified DEA report written later directly based on the notes Bond and Villalobos took at the meeting. The brothers, El Chapo warned, were in the practice of sending double agents to work as informants for the DEA and collect intel through their interactions with the gringos. Within the last six months, El Chapo said, he had learned that the group was smuggling drugs and cash under the border of Baja California and California. He named the men he said were responsible for dealing with the group's Colombian contacts.

When the agents asked him about political protection of the Arellano-Félix clan, however, El Chapo clammed up. He refused to talk about politicians. "They're too dangerous," he said.

At this point, El Chapo changed the subject. He wanted to discuss El Güero Palma.

This came as a surprise, Bond recalled. As far as they knew at the time, El Güero and El Chapo were still friends and partners here in Puente Grande, as they had been on the outside for years.

According to El Chapo, however, they had not spoken in nearly four years. They had broken ties back in 1994, after El Güero had ordered the killing of El Chapo's brother-in-law Sal López, the brother of El Chapo's second wife, Griselda López, he said. El Güero had ordered the murder without sanction, without El Chapo's blessing, and for this El Chapo said he was forced to break ties with his longtime friend and partner, despite their years of working with one another and their shared hatred of the Arellano-Félix brothers. They had not spoken since then, although outside of prison, El Chapo's brother El Pollo and his former pilot Miguel Ángel Martínez Martínez had both worked with El Güero in some capacity. And they were not speaking now, despite being incarcerated together at Puente Grande.

El Chapo told the agents that because of this rupture in his alliance with his former friend, he was willing to provide information on El Güero if that would help his case. In twenty-four hours, he said, he could give the DEA and the PGR information on the whereabouts of drug storages and weapons caches; with a week's notice, he could provide information on the group's entire infrastructure, including the corrupt officials protecting them in their home base of Tepic, in the state of Nayarit, as well as along the border, in the city of San Luis Río Colorado, where El Güero's people often crossed drugs.

In order to do this, however, El Chapo would need to be moved. He refused to summon any of his former associates to visit him at Puente Grande, for fear that Arellano-Félix killers would identify them and murder them. He suggested a move to a prison in Mexico City, pointing out that the open court case he faced in the capital would provide a handy cover for the transfer.

The meeting lasted around two hours. As it was winding down, El Chapo gave the agents and Patiño a warning. The Arellano-Félix brothers, he claimed, were planning to assassinate the former attorney general and current ambassador to France, and planning to frame him for the killing. He wanted to go on record that he was not involved in any threat against the former prosecutors.

• • •

They never did meet again. Shortly after the visit to Puente Grande, Bond got word from prosecutors in the United States that any further meetings could harm future court cases against El Chapo, and ordered him to cease contact. Bond was livid.

"They're territorial, these fucking U.S. attorneys. I hate them all," Bond told me, the order still clearly stinging more than twenty years later. "I said, 'Man, what do you want? A feather in your hat? We're the ones making the case, not you! You're just writing it up!'"

Of the men whom Bond trusted to collaborate on the mission, most are now dead. Jose Luís Vasconcelos survived multiple assassination attempts before his death in a suspicious plane crash in 2008; Mariano Herrán Salvatti, Vasconcelos's boss at the time, died in 2009, after his conviction—and subsequent exoneration—on corruption charges; but the worst fate among them was the grisly death of Bond's friend Pepe Patiño, the man Bond had trusted enough to go inside Puente Grande with him to see El Chapo.

Patiño had been leading the PGR's charge against the Arellano-Félix organization, a case that he had worked on and off since 1993, in the wake of the killing of Cardinal Posadas Ocampo. Joe Bond and other law enforcement officials described Patiño as one of the few officials in Mexico they could fully trust.

"If you needed any kind of help, he was there," one U.S. prosecutor who worked with Patiño said later. "He was absolutely courageous. He was extremely bright. He did everything that was promised and more."

On April 10, 2000, about two years after his trip to Puente Grande with Bond and Villalobos, Patiño and two colleagues, a federal prosecutor named Oscar Pompa Plaza and a Mexican Army captain named Rafael Torres Bernal, were crossing the border into Mexico after attending a meeting with the FBI and the DEA in San Diego. For some time now, the team had been working largely out of San Diego, rather than at their office in Tijuana, preferring the United States because they had more freedom to operate away from any prying eyes. The downside of this arrangement is that they were unarmed when they crossed the border. Their weapons were stashed just a short distance into Mexico, at a border guard outpost, but that short distance was all it took. Video cameras at the border crossing in Otay Mesa, California, showed the trio driving into Mexico, but then they vanished.

Two days later, the three men were found in their car, which appeared to have swerved—or been steered—into a ditch. But one look at the group showed they had not died in a car crash. An autopsy report later showed that they had suffered massive damage to their internal organs; two of them had had their heads crushed by a pneumatic press; someone had slashed them with knives; then, for good measure, the killers had run over them with a heavy truck.

Bond still wonders if his friend's gruesome death came as a result of the meeting at Puente Grande.

"They found out through the warden that Pepe Patiño was there with the DEA," he said. "They wanted to know what El Chapo Guzmán said about the [Arellano-Félix organization]. So, they tortured him, and then they killed him."

That was the price so many honest cops paid in Mexico, before and since.

• • •

While El Chapo was in prison, the world outside continued to change drastically.

On July 2, 2000, the people of Mexico made history when they voted to elect Vicente Fox Quesada as their next president, the first time a party other than the PRI or its forebears controlled the presidency since 1929. A member of the center-right National Action Party, or PAN, Fox won the election with just 43 percent of the vote; the runner-up PRI candidate received 36 percent, while the candidate for the center-left Democratic Revolution Party, or PRD, got 17 percent.

A businessman who had worked his way up the corporate ladder, Fox got his start at Coca-Cola as a route supervisor and eventually was in charge of the company's operations across Latin America, before serving as the governor of the central state of Guanajuato. With this common-man image—he once sparked controversy among Mexico's hyperliterate elite by mixing up the name of the Argentine author Jorge Luís Borges—he ran as a plainspoken populist, albeit a probusiness one. Pushing hard against the tarnished image of the ruling party, Fox cast himself as an anticorruption reformer and pledged to power-wash seventy years of *PRIista* rot from the halls of the federal government. It helped that his opponent was Francisco Labastida Ochoa, a former governor of Sinaloa and interior minister under Zedillo who had for years been dogged by whispers of corruption. The allegations against Labastida included accusations that he had used the state police to do the dirty work of Miguel Ángel Félix Gallardo during his 1986–92 *sexenio*, and a secret CIA report leaked in 1998 that accused Labastida of taking bribes from traffickers. But more than anything, it was the legacy of the PRI's entanglement with drug traffickers that Labastida could not shake, rather than whiffs of personal scandal. Fox knew this, and drilled into the point again and again during his campaign, telling reporters at one press conference that "drug lords took over the PRI years ago."

In addition to the liberalization of the economy by latter-day *PRIistas* in the late 1980s and 1990s, which helped shake the party's control of big business (while also putting state assets in the hands of a few politically connected families), a series of political reforms under Zedillo had made it possible for a more genuine election to take place, largely free of the usual outright fraud employed by the regime. And the PAN had been carefully laying the groundwork for a national victory, capturing offices in state and local elections across the country over the previous twenty years. The PAN began as a reaction to the anticlerical policies of the Mexican Revolution and postrevolutionary governments, and is to this day often cast as right-wing or "center-right." But such political labels meant little in a country where the ruling party was marked more by a big-tent commitment to its own power than to any of the guiding left-wing principles of the revolution whose legacy it claimed. In Latin America, the term "right wing" summons images of death squads of Augusto Pinochet's Chilé, or the depraved purges of anticommunist dictators in Argentina, Nicaragua, or El Salvador; but in Mexico, the work of containing communists fell to the PRI, a member of the Socialist International. And while the PAN was right-wing in the sense of being "business friendly" and supporting neoliberal trade policies like NAFTA, by 2000 it had styled itself as a party of liberal-democratic rule of law, human rights, and the free market, an alternative to the venal, self-dealing authoritarianism of the PRI. At long last, the "perfect dictatorship" had fallen, and for many Mexicans, Fox's victory seemed to promise a new era of economic growth and political openness.

At the same time, however, the drug trade was entering a new phase, one marked by a sudden uncertainty and a breakdown in the lines of communication between smugglers and security forces. This began in northern states like Chihuahua and Baja California, as well in Jalisco, the former home of the Guadalajara network, where opposition candidates began in the 1990s to wrest away control from the PRI in state and municipal elections and, upon taking office, replace midlevel and senior officials in state prosecutor offices and police agencies. With this breakdown of the traditional state-sponsored protection rackets, drug traffickers in areas where the PRI lost power were forced at once to re-negotiate the terms of their operations with officials and, increasingly, rely on their own muscle to settle disputes and deal with competitors. Just as the Arellano-Félix brothers had done in Tijuana, more and more traffickers began to develop private militias and fight more openly with their rivals rather than relying on crooked cops and soldiers to arrest the competition. The rise of democratic elections and successful opposition parties in Mexico was indisputably a net positive. But in the underworld of organized crime, it shook the old "plaza system" to its core, a deadly side effect. The nation stood on the eve of one of the darkest periods in its history, an era of widespread violence and mayhem from which it has yet to extricate itself. But when Fox took power on December 1, 2000, none of this was known. Hope abounded for a new day in Mexico.

Less than two months later, El Chapo would make a mockery of those dreams.

6

AN EXCELLENT SURPRISE

After eight years of incarceration, El Chapo Guzmán decided he didn't want to be in prison any longer. So on January 19, 2001, he left, and nobody saw fit to stop him.

El Chapo had been doing all right in prison. He had enjoyed many of the same creature comforts during his years in Puente Grande as he had on the outside—good food, women, volleyball—and unlike his life on the outside, he even got to sleep in the same place every night. Toward the end of El Chapo's incarceration, he took a particular liking to twenty-three-year-old Zulema Yulia Hernandez, who was serving time for her part in the armed robbery of a security van. Photos of Zulema show a pretty young woman with almond eyes and hair swept back in a high ponytail, a cocky smile on her face, but she had lived a tragic life, abandoned by her mother at an early age and growing up destitute. Things only got worse when she crossed paths with El Chapo. Zulema first caught the kingpin's eye during family visitations, and he soon began to woo her with the help of guards, to whom he dictated love letters and arranged for flowers and a bottle of whiskey to be sent to her cell.

Through long, intimate conversations about El Chapo's hardscrabble upbringing in La Tuna, his resolve to never return to such a life, and their shared experience behind bars, the relationship blossomed,

Zulema said years later. Anabel Hernandez, an investigative journalist who has written extensively on the drug war, tells a darker story. In her book *Narcoland*, Hernandez describes a brief period of infatuation on El Chapo's part, followed by an unending series of degradations. According to Hernandez, Zulema was forced to have an abortion during her relationship with El Chapo, and later was repeatedly raped by prison staff and inmates alike.

In April 1999, a new crew of guards and administrators arrived at Puente Grande, led by Dámaso López Nuñez, who took over as deputy director of security and immediately proved even more pliant than his predecessor in seeing to it that all of El Chapo's needs were met. When Dámaso López arrived, El Chapo immediately began to shower money and gifts on the new deputy director of security: ten thousand dollars in cash here, a house there. When one of Dámaso's children was injured in an accident, it was El Chapo who paid the child's medical bills.

"When I needed anything, I would ask and he would give it to me," Dámaso said years later.

With Dámaso and his men on the payroll, El Chapo was able to communicate more freely than ever with his brother, the Beltrán Leyvas, and other allies as they worked to keep him in the game, and he had access to nearly every luxury imaginable.

His legal situation seemed to be improving as well. When a judge threw out El Chapo's conviction for the murder of Archbishop Juan Jesús Posadas Ocampo, speculation swirled in the press that he might not be imprisoned for much longer, speculation the government tried to tamp down.

"[Rumors that] Mr. Guzmán Loera could soon gain his freedom are absolutely false and inaccurate," a representative of the attorney general's office said in a press statement dated October 12, 2000.

In fact, El Chapo didn't need any help from the legal system, as he had been laying the groundwork for his own release for some time. He planned his escape with a tight circle of co-conspirators that included his lawyer, his brother Arturo "El Pollo" Guzmán, and his longtime partner "El Mayo" Zambada García. It also included at least one prison guard, a man nicknamed El Chito who oversaw the prison laundry, and likely required the acquiescence of any number of prison officials above El Chito's pay grade. In a letter to Zulema Hernandez dated November 28, 2000, and published later in the weekly magazine *Proceso*, El Chapo bid a sentimental farewell to his lover.

"I say goodbye sending all my greatest sentiment that a man can feel for a woman he loves," he gushed. "Soon there may be an excellent surprise. I love you. JGL."

Several events seem to have prompted El Chapo to move forward with the escape when he did.

In September 2000, Dámaso López had resigned from his post amid mounting rumblings of an investigation into corruption at the prison. The corruption hadn't begun with him, but he was unlucky enough to be in charge when investigators finally got to poking around, and his departure threatened to leave El Chapo without access to the perks that made his life worth living and allowed him to stay in contact with his cronies on the outside.

Then, in early January, newly sworn-in president Vicente Fox ordered an investigation of the rampant corruption at Puente Grande. It was an absurdly belated response to years of complaints from honest guards about the power that El Chapo and other wealthy inmates wielded in the prison, and compounded El Chapo's fears of losing his privileged status. In response to Fox's directive, officials ordered that El Chapo and two other high-profile drug traffickers be moved to a different wing of the prison.

Finally, one day before El Chapo's escape, there came the most pressing development yet.

For most of his time in prison, El Chapo's worst fear, facing trial in the United States, had been kept at bay. Despite the two countries sharing an extradition treaty that dates back to the Civil War, there were significant legal hurdles against extradition, namely the possibility of a defendant like El Chapo facing the death penalty in the United States. But on January 18, 2001, the Supreme Court of Mexico ruled that extradition of inmates such as El Chapo could proceed as long as the United States pledged that they would not face execution.

With extradition suddenly a real possibility, and the likelihood of prison officials finally cracking down on El Chapo's luxurious suite of perks and privileges, the time had come for him to leave.

On January 19, around 8 p.m., the guard nicknamed El Chito rolled a laundry cart up to El Chapo's cell. El Chapo climbed in, nestling himself below layers of sheets and blankets. Once his stowaway was concealed, El Chito began the nerve-racking trip from the cell to the prison gates, while El Chapo held his breath beneath the sheets.

Puente Grande is divided into eight different security units, each separated from the other by checkpoints that the guards and inmates called "diamonds," four-sided glass enclosures manned by a guard who could open the locked doors on each side of the diamond with the push of a button.

To get to the prison gates, El Chito would have to roll the laundry cart through several of these checkpoints. For Chito, who could see where they were going, it must have been a heart-pounding trip for fear that his secret passenger would be discovered; for El Chapo, who could only guess as to their progress as he scrunched himself lower beneath the blankets, it must have felt like an eternity. At each diamond, El Chapo heard the muffled click of the door opening, knowing he was one step closer to freedom. At one diamond, his heart nearly froze when El Chito stopped to chat with the checkpoint guard, briefly letting go of the cart. Free of Chito's guiding hand, the unusually heavy cart slowly began to roll away. For a moment, El Chapo wondered if his escape would end then and there, before he could even make it past the prison walls.

Chito managed to grab the cart and he continued the trip to freedom. After a few more diamonds and no further snags, El Chito rolled the cart into the night air and made a beeline for his car. El Chapo pushed himself free of the dirty laundry, scrambled out of the cart, and dove into the trunk. After shutting the trunk door over the escaped kingpin, Chito climbed into the driver's seat and steered as calmly as he could toward the final checkpoint, where a guard stood manning a metal lift gate known as a *pluma*, the last barrier between El Chapo and freedom. The guard did a cursory search of the interior of the vehicle and waved his colleague along without checking the trunk. Soon Chito was watching the prison recede in his rearview mirror.

In *Narcoland*, Anabel Hernandez argues that the laundry cart story was a tall tale cooked up in the wake of the escape to hide the real story: that El Chapo had simply walked out the door. Others have joined Hernandez in speculating that the laundry cart story was a fanciful tale ginned up to cover up a more mundane escape made possible by systemic corruption. As far as excuses go, however, the laundry cart theory—which was retold repeatedly in trial testimony by multiple former accomplices of El Chapo—never did much to obscure the simple fact that El Chapo managed to escape Puente Grande due to rampant corruption. Regardless of whether El Chapo was rolled out by El Chito or El Chapo walked out on his own two feet in a stolen guard uniform, it was his ability to buy the right people that allowed him to escape.

El Chapo was back.

• • •

More than five hundred cops fanned out across the state of Jalisco in search of El Chapo, but he seemed to have vanished into thin air.

For President Fox, the escape was more than just a black eye, it was a disaster. Here was proof that corruption continued to permeate nearly every level of his country's criminal justice system and political life. Six days after the escape, Fox flew to Sinaloa, where he promised to recapture El Chapo and confront the problem of corruption head-on.

"Today I reaffirm our war without mercy against the pernicious criminal mafias," he said, promising a "great reform to ensure that every family can sleep peacefully, so we all can live without fear of going out into the street, without assaults or humiliation, without the fear of losing everything at the hands of the criminals."

Mexican government officials pointed fingers angrily in all directions, but mainly at one another, as the political reverberations of El Chapo's escape spread throughout the country. Jorge Enrique Tello Peon, a former CISEN agent who for the past two years had been the second-in-command of the Public Security Secretariat, which oversaw Mexico's prison system, blamed pervasive corruption at Puente Grande. State human rights officials in Jalisco blamed the federal human rights commission for systematically ignoring whistle-blowers who tried to come forward about that corruption. Prosecutors and state police officials in Jalisco and Sinaloa complained that they were being sidelined by the feds. Opposition politicians blamed everyone currently in power.

Despite his post as head of the agency that was charged with keeping El Chapo in prison, Tello Peon—a holdover from the previous administration—came out swinging, laying the blame on lower-level prison officials, accusing them of complicity.

"What happened in Jalisco is evidence of the capacity of corruption, shall we say, the structural erosion of national institutions by organized crime, particularly drug trafficking," he thundered. "The prison bars and millions of pesos in security systems won't do anything if prisoners leave through the doors. They say that Mr. Guzmán didn't escape, that they let him out. They're right."

Tello Peon clearly did not count himself among the "theys" who aided and abetted El Chapo's roll to freedom, despite being in charge of the very prison from which El Chapo had escaped.

• • •

A few days after the escape, Jesús Reynaldo Zambada Garcia, aka El Rey, got a call from his big brother El Mayo. El Rey had been living in Mexico City for a few years now after fleeing the Arellano-Felix clan in Tijuana, and kept busy running warehouses, overseeing the smuggling of drug shipments through the airport, and bribing whoever needed bribing.

On that day in January, El Mayo summoned El Rey to his house in Mexico City to give him an urgent task. El Mayo had just learned from one of his military contacts that there was a special-forces operation in the works to recapture El Chapo at a temporary hideout in the state of Querétaro. El Mayo needed his little brother's help finding coordinates for a spot in which a helicopter could land outside Mexico City after a rescue mission scooped up their fugitive friend, El Chapo.

The next day, El Rey, his wife, El Mayo, and a few of his men drove out to a flat, deserted area that El Rey had chosen in the state of Querétaro, which neighbors Mexico State. They arrived at the landing area just before 7 a.m., and not long after, a helicopter appeared over the horizon, touching down near where they stood. El Chapo hopped out of the chopper and joyfully embraced El Mayo, before introducing himself to El Rey, whom he had never met in person.

The group bundled into a car, El Chapo in the backseat, El Rey driving, and chitchatted on the two-hour drive back to Mexico City. At El Rey's suggestion, El Chapo held a newspaper up to his face as they drove through a tollbooth, to keep his now-famous face away from the cameras at the toll plaza. The two-bit cloak-and-dagger ruse worked.

As they entered the outskirts of the capital, El Rey's prearranged escort of municipal police on motorcycles and PJF agents in a car pulled up on either end of the vehicle that El Rey was driving, to make sure they had no problems getting their guest into the capital. El Chapo was alarmed when he saw the police, but El Rey reassured him.

"Don't worry about it," El Rey recalled telling El Chapo. "These are our people. They are here to protect us. No one is going to touch us from here now."

When they arrived at El Mayo's house in the ritzy residential neighborhood of Lomas, El Mayo and El Chapo began plotting their future.

"Everyone was super happy," El Rey recalled.

•   •   •

When the news broke of El Chapo's escape, Special Agent Joe Bond was in his office at the American embassy in Mexico City. As chaos erupted around him, his phone began to ring off the hook.

"I got telephone calls from [the Federal Investigations Agency], I got calls from the prosecutor's office, 'What do you know? Who are you contacting? Do you know anything?'" he recalls. "They didn't believe me, but I didn't know shit."

DEA officials in Washington were asking him the same question as well.

"No, no, no, no, and no," he recalls telling his bosses. "I don't know how he escaped."

Months later, in early summer, a surprise visitor showed up at the

U.S. embassy: Griselda López Pérez, El Chapo's second wife, had come to get visas for herself and her children. Bond had put in place a "BOLO" alert—"be on the lookout"—in the event that any of El Chapo's family surfaced, so when Griselda gave her name to embassy staffers, they pinged him. Racing downstairs, Bond approached Griselda and introduced himself to her. It had been years since he had met her husband at Puente Grande, but it seemed there was no need for an introduction.

"I know who you are," Griselda told him.

In addition to getting the visas, she also had a message for Bond: El Chapo's brother El Pollo wanted to reach out on behalf of the fugitive drug lord. El Pollo would be in touch soon.

About two weeks after his encounter with Griselda, Bond's phone rang.

"It's El Pollo," a voice announced.

Startling to attention, Bond told El Pollo he would call him back. After the arrest of "Electra," the source who had connected him to El Chapo last time, he had to assume that his counterparts in Mexican law enforcement were listening. Using a burner phone, he called Arturo back a short while later.

Bond did not have to think that hard to guess what El Chapo had in mind. El Chapo's goal in having his brother reach out to the DEA once more was not a mystery to Bond. In a repeat of El Chapo's unsuccessful attempts to offer up information on the Arellano-Félix brothers and Güero Palma during his meeting with the agents at Puente Grande in 1998, Bond suspected that El Chapo was again looking to use the DEA to mop up anyone who might stand in his way.

"He wanted to get rid of the competition," Bond said. "And they can't blame it on him, because the DEA is the one who took care of it."

Bond was intrigued, but he knew he couldn't sit down with El Chapo's brother without letting his Mexican counterparts know about the rendezvous. While less well known than his brother, El Pollo was a fugitive with indictments in the United States and charges against him in Mexico, and Bond could meet him only if he got permission from the Mexican government. He was reticent, however, to involve his Mexican counterparts, for fear that they might undermine any guarantee of safety—however temporary—he gave to El Pollo. But the opportunity to meet with an envoy of El Chapo was too good to pass up, so he decided to call José Luís Santiago Vasconcelos, the by-the-book prosecutor who was Bond's most trusted contact in Mexican law enforcement.

Then there was Genaro García Luna, a man Bond had fewer reasons to trust, but whose permission Bond would need if he were to meet with El Pollo. Only thirty-three years old, Genaro García Luna was something of a rising star in Mexican law enforcement. He enjoyed a good relationship with much of the U.S. diplomatic community, who sang the praises of García Luna as a no-nonsense reformer, a "big picture guy" who tackled problems with an eye toward long-term strategy. Sporting a buzz cut, a square jaw, and the tough glare of a cop's cop, he spoke a staccato Spanish and impressed U.S. envoys with his "intense personality" and friendly attitude toward Washington.

Armed with degrees in mechanical engineering and business administration, García Luna had climbed swiftly through the ranks of the intelligence agency CISEN, and by his early thirties he had commanded top posts in the Federal Preventive Police and the PJF. In 2000, incoming president Vicente Fox tapped García Luna as director of strategic planning for the PJF. At the time of El Pollo's call, he was tasked with reorganizing the PJF into a new, consolidated police bureau that was to be called the Federal Investigations Agency (of which he would be named founding director). Like his predecessors in the PRI, Fox was seeking to remove the stain of corruption from his top law enforcement agencies and was pursuing a cosmetic rebranding under the guidance of this American-backed wunderkind.

But García Luna also had a reputation for being territorial with investigations, and everyone knew that many of his underlings were corrupt to the bone. Later, much more serious allegations would surface against García Luna, including that he was actively siding with El Chapo's Sinaloan faction while targeting its enemies. But speaking with me in early October 2019, Bond told me that he had never seen proof. The two had a decent relationship, despite the fact that Bond's counterpart was in the habit of tapping his phone. Bond knew to be tight-lipped around the guy (or while talking on the phone), but that didn't stop them from working together.

Still, Bond was wary of informing García Luna about his meeting with El Chapo's brother, for fear that the hard-charging top cop would use the meeting as a way to arrest Arturo. Bond had no problem with seeing El Pollo in handcuffs—it would be a win for Mexican law enforcement and the DEA alike—but at this moment, his priority was the potential intelligence he could gather from speaking with El Chapo's brother. And if a meeting with El Pollo ended in his arrest, he'd be hard-pressed to get any future informants to trust him.

Given the rumors that many of García Luna's men were on the take, Bond was equally worried that word of the meeting would filter from García Luna's subordinates to any one of the rival traffickers said to be paying protection money to top PJF officials. But without García Luna's say-so, the meeting was not going to happen.

"I had to dance with the devil," Bond told me with a shrug. "What am I going to do?"

In a huddle with Bond and Vasconcelos, García Luna agreed to the DEA meeting with Arturo, under one condition: that Garcia Luna accompany Bond to the meet.

Bond told them that he thought this was absurd. García Luna was one of the most prominent cops in Mexico, and Arturo or one of his goons was sure to recognize him on the spot, Bond said.

"Everybody fucking knows you, are you kidding me?" an incredulous Bond recalled telling García Luna.

"I'll do something," García Luna assured him. "Just tell them I'm your bodyguard."

With permission from his Mexican counterparts, Bond called El Pollo back and let him know the meeting was on. For a location, they settled on an upscale hotel fifteen minutes on foot from the U.S. embassy. Bond told El Pollo to pick the room and to text him the number five minutes in advance of their meeting. The meeting was on.

On an evening in early September Bond and his "bodyguard" strolled into the lobby of the hotel. He immediately saw Mexican federal agents milling about in the lobby, trying to blend in with the tourists and other patrons of the hotel. El Pollo also appeared to have placed men in the lobby, guys who on another day Bond would have loved to nab. But not tonight.

With García Luna trailing him slightly, Bond headed up to the suite and knocked on the door. One of El Pollo's men greeted Bond with one word.

"Tito?" the henchman asked.

Bond nodded.

"Come on in," the henchman said.

García Luna, playing the part, followed Bond deferentially, losing for a moment his usual air of imperious police commander.

"Genaro was good, because he just looked at me like, 'You're the boss,'" Bond recalled

García Luna stayed back, and Bond entered the living room of the suite to find El Pollo sitting at a table. He was even smaller than his brother, standing about five feet five inches tall, skinny, with deep-set eyes, a boyish mop of black hair, and a thin mustache, and little to none of his older brother's charisma. But what El Pollo lacked in leadership qualities he made up for in brute-force loyalty. He had remained a trusted servant to his brother during El Chapo's incarceration, once commenting to a friend that freeing his brother was his "first purpose in life." Now he was putting himself at immense risk in order to act as his fugitive brother's envoy.

Greeting the agents, El Pollo explained the purpose of the meeting: El Chapo wanted to sit down with the DEA and talk about having his charges reduced, or at least the possibility of taking extradition off the table. In exchange, he could provide information on his rivals, particularly the Arellano-Felix family.

As Bond expected, El Pollo's overture was similar to the proposal El Chapo had made during his sit-down with Bond and Larry Villalobos back in 1998 at Puente Grande, although now that he was a free man, El Chapo had considerably more leverage with which to bargain. El Pollo insisted that he had no idea of El Chapo's exact location, that he had intentionally been kept in the dark to avoid the possibility of giving up his brother under torture, but that El Chapo wanted to talk.

The meeting lasted about half an hour, and ended somewhat inconclusively, with Bond telling El Pollo that it was unlikely that his own supervisors and his Mexican counterparts would approve a meeting with El Chapo. Still, he wanted to keep communication lines open, and exchanged new phone numbers with Arturo so they could speak again.

Bond headed back to the embassy and began to write up his report on the encounter. Less than two hours later, his phone rang. It was García Luna.

"Joe, we had to pick him up," García Luna said.

"What the fuck?" Bond asked angrily.

"Yeah," García Luna said. "We had to pick him up. The pressure is too intense."

Bond was furious. He had no problem with a career drug trafficker like El Pollo being in handcuffs, but by arresting Arturo so soon after he had met with Bond, García Luna was all but ensuring that no one else would trust Bond enough to come forward as El Pollo had. The Mexican lawman tried to reassure Bond that the arrest would not be traced back to him, but Bond felt as if he had betrayed El Pollo after giving him word that the meeting would be secure.

"It felt really bad," Bond said, still seeming to feel the sting of García Luna's betrayal more than fifteen years later. "I gave my word, you know? That's the one thing, my integrity. I didn't want to be doubted, and [El Pollo's arrest] obviously brought doubt."

In El Chapo Land, the natural response to the arrest of El Pollo was to try to break him out. El Pollo had been El Chapo's lifeline throughout his time in Puente Grande, and El Chapo did not want to let his little brother rot. In a series of meetings in the weeks following the arrest, his partners had begun hatching a wild escape plan that involved flying a helicopter over the prison yard, dropping a rope down to El Pollo, and hoisting him to freedom. When someone pointed out that El Pollo was liable to be shot to death if he was just dangling in the air from a rope, someone suggested attaching to the rope a steel bubble in which El Pollo could take cover. Somehow, this brilliant plan never came to fruition. Three years later, on December 31, 2004, El Pollo was murdered in prison, an act of revenge against El Chapo that would serve as a catalyst for the final schism with some of his oldest allies.

. . .

In the weeks and months after his escape, El Chapo held a series of meetings with his allies at the ranch of Francisco Aceves Uriah, better known as Barbarino, a veteran hit man known for his loyalty to El Chapo and infamously accused—mostly in *narcocorridos*—of numerous high-profile slayings.

Present at the meetings were some of El Chapo's oldest friends and partners, including Mayo Zambada and his brother El Rey, the Beltrán Leyva brothers, and Juan José Esparragoza, the elder-statesman drug trafficker known as El Azul. El Chapo's position was far from secure: the Arellano-Félix brothers were still in charge of Tijuana, and a low-intensity war had been bubbling up now and again over the past eight years that he had been in prison; Amado Carrillo Fuentes was dead, and although his brother Vicente Carrillo Fuentes, aka El Viceroy, was still in charge of Juárez, the Sinaloa federation's relationship with El Viceroy was far chillier than it had been with the Lord of the Skies; to make things worse, El Chapo was running out of money.

For all his loyalty, El Pollo had not been the most skillful manager during El Chapo's stay in prison, and the empire he had ruled at the time of his arrest in 1993 was significantly reduced. The Beltrán Leyvas had been of enormous help to him during his incarceration, but he didn't want to work for the Beltrán Leyvas; he wanted to run the show.

At one of the first meetings at Barbarino's ranch, El Mayo made it clear that he was backing El Chapo to the hilt.

"I'm with you one hundred percent," El Mayo said. "I'm going to help you with anything you need. And any kilo of coke that I receive from Colombia, I'm going to give you half. So for now, just take care of yourself, stay in hiding."

In conversations with El Rey, El Chapo said he was looking for a nice quiet ranch where he could lie low for a while.

"El Chapo was concerned about where he should settle down,"

El Rey recalled. "He was thinking about a ranch in the area of, say, Tejupilco."*

El Rey, however, didn't think that was such a good idea. He told El Chapo that he was happy to take him in for a while at one of his ranches, but that El Chapo's large security entourage might cause a problem if they were trying to stay under the radar.

El Mayo had a better idea.

"Let's go to Sinaloa," El Mayo told El Chapo. "Let's go back to your native lands."

---

*Tejupilco de Hidalgo is a municipality in western Mexico State, near the borders of Michoacán and Guerrero.

7

LET'S GO TO SINALOA

PERCHED ATOP A peak that looms over La Tuna, a ring of cypress trees sits like a crown, blowing faintly in the breeze. From below, across the valley, the trees are all you can see of "El Cielo," or the Heavens, the home El Chapo built for himself. It's a sanctuary he never got to truly enjoy, but which he visited from time to time, sneaking back into his hometown to throw a party or visit his mother.

It sits unoccupied now, like it has before, and El Chapo will likely never set foot here again. (But don't tell his mother that—the family once threw out a television reporter who had the temerity to ask Doña Consuelo directly how she felt about her son spending the rest of his life in prison.) If he were to get out of prison, however, a visit to this little village and the mountaintop retreat above it might be one of the first items on his itinerary. Indeed when he escaped from Puente Grande prison in January 2001, it was to El Cielo that El Chapo returned, to plot his new empire—and to see his mom.

When El Chapo arrived in La Tuna sometime after his escape, things were looking good for him. He was free, back in the mountains in which he had grown up, where he had gotten his start, where much of the population loved and supported him, and where the remoteness and the rugged terrain provided a natural defense that shielded him and allowed him to move about with relative ease. He was moving coke again, thanks to the start-up help of Mayo Zambada and the Beltrán Leyvas. And he began to reinvest in the trafficking of marijuana and heroin as well—there was always more money to be made in cocaine, but the local economy of his sanctuary still relied heavily on the production of those two trusty cash crops, the hills dotted with red poppy flowers and redolent stalks of cannabis. By purchasing these drugs from local farmers, he could make a handsome profit, prop up local business, and buy an enduring base of support. Who's going to give up the guy who pays wholesale for their crops?

Among the farmers El Chapo bought from in those days was a man named José,* an affable father of three born, raised, and still living in a small town just off the highway that leads from the municipal seat of Badiraguato toward La Tuna. Like El Chapo, José learned how to grow weed and opium from his father, while his friends learned from their fathers, each growing up in a family tradition, using their family's own tried-and-true methods to grow the crops on little plots of land in the hills above their village. In the early 2000s, he was working an area of land totaling about two hectares, roughly equal to the size of about five football fields. The area was under the protection—or the control—of El Chapo, to whom José and other growers paid a tax of about 30 percent of their income in exchange for protection from the soldiers who might otherwise raid the area, burning crops and sending months of work up in smoke.

For several years after the escape from Puente Grande, José did not meet the man to whom he paid taxes. But that finally changed in 2005, when, short on funds, he decided he wanted to make a proposition to El Chapo. A friend agreed to make the introduction, and they drove together up the highway, onto the dirt road, and on to La Tuna. When El Chapo received them, José made his proposal: Rather than pay the 30 percent tax, what if El Chapo covered the expense of planting, and then they split the eventual profit fifty-fifty?

El Chapo readily agreed; that's just the kind of guy he was, José recalled.

---

* Names marked with an asterisk are pseudonyms.

"He was a very simple man, and very natural," José said. "You just felt like talking to him, never found him to be aggressive."

The relationship between local trafficker-strongmen and the people who grow opium and weed is more complex than José's tale lets on. It's rarely an even one, and can sometimes be downright feudal: growers rarely have much choice in whom they sell to, so the people buying are able to set the asking price. The exchange is one of constant negotiation, and often features a certain degree of coercion—whether through the direct threat or deliverance of violence, or through the local boss withdrawing his protection and opening the farmer up to the full fury of a state that is, technically, dedicated to wiping out the farmer's livelihood.

When El Chapo was operating out of a series of hideouts in the mountains of the Golden Triangle, he saw to it whenever possible that the crops of farmers like José were spared, according to a former lieutenant of El Chapo.

"Well, if it was a small group of about twenty-five men, he would send an icebox with food and he would tell them that that's what there was in exchange for them not to cut the crops," the underling recalled. "Otherwise, they would have to face bullets."

Until very recently, small-time, self-employed farmers like José formed the backbone of the opium and marijuana industries. (This status quo has been upended in recent years as widespread legalization of marijuana in the United States and the introduction of synthetic opioids like fentanyl into the heroin supply have caused prices of both crops to plummet.) As in any good capitalist system, farmers did most of the work, and were exposed to the most risk at the hand of the state. It pays well, better than most legal work; but by the time a stamp of heroin or a dime bag of weed has been sold on the streets of New York or Philadelphia, only about 1 percent of the total profits find their way back to the farmer. The real profits, the billions of dollars that flow from the street sales to the money launderers to the front companies and bank accounts of traffickers, don't trickle all the way down to little villages nestled in the mountains of Sinaloa or Guerrerro, or to the streets of the border towns through which the drugs pass on their way north. But it's on the heads of these small-timers that most of the violence of the drug war falls.

Still, José and others in the highlands of Sinaloa talk of those years right after El Chapo's escape as something of a golden age, when you knew who ran things and you could look the boss in the eye, make a deal with him, and then have a pleasant chat all afternoon. In his spare time, José plays in a band, and El Chapo would often pay them to perform at parties up in La Tuna or as far afield as Durango. It felt good to hang out with a guy like El Chapo, José said, to be in the presence of someone regarded in these parts as a great man.

"He is a legend, truly, a legend," José said. "It was a privilege to speak with him, to have a friendship with him like I did."

If José's description of El Chapo appears at odds with the things El Chapo is known for, was known for even back in those days, it is probably in part because he was telling what he wanted a gringo reporter to hear, and in part because, whether or not he was giving the sanitized-for-gringo-reporters version, many people in the mountains of Badiraguato knew only this side of El Chapo, the magnanimous local chieftain. This area of Sinaloa was, for many years, spared the violence that the drug trade—and the war on drugs—wreaked on other areas of Mexico. And when violence did arrive, it usually came in the form of the heavy hand of the state, rather than the cruelty of narco hit men.

But even as El Chapo was spreading his goodwill around his hometown and surrounding villages, he and his allies were inflicting violence elsewhere. For when El Chapo arrived back in La Tuna in 2001 and began to rebuild his empire, he was a man hell-bent on revenge.

. . .

Ramón Arellano-Félix was first. Cops on the payroll of El Mayo cornered the notorious butcher in Mazatlán on February 10, 2002, when they tried to pull him over in a traffic stop. Ramón, true to his nature, opened fire on the cops and fled, then tried to hole up in a nearby hotel. The cops shot him down in the street. One of the most wanted men in Mexico after El Chapo, Ramón was carrying false documents, and the day after he was shot, someone showed up at the morgue and spirited away his body. Ramón's identity was confirmed only after investigators scraped a bit of his blood off the sidewalk and ran a DNA test.

El Chapo and El Mayo had gotten revenge the old-fashioned way, using dirty cops to do their dirty work. El Chapo was so elated that he wouldn't shut up about Ramón's death for some time after.

"On occasion, up in the mountains, we would talk about that," recalled El Mayo's brother, El Rey. "That if anything had really given him pleasure, it was to have killed Ramón Arellano."

Benjamín Arellano-Félix was next. Working with the DEA, Mexican police had tracked Benjamín down in part by keeping tabs on his daughter, who was in the United States being treated for a rare facial deformity, and located him by tracing phone calls that his wife made from the hospital. On March 9, 2002, police raided a home where Benjamín was staying in the state of Puebla, east of Mexico City, and took him into custody safely. Just like that, the leaders of the family, the bosses of Tijuana, were out of the game. The rest of the family remained a force in Tijuana for years, but never at the same level of power, and never posing the same threat to El Chapo and his allies.

Rumors and accusations have repeatedly surfaced that elements within Vicente Fox's administration helped orchestrate El Chapo's escape, part of a plan to return to the days of federal control over a more monopolistic drug trade. Some, like the investigative reporter Anabel Hernández, have accused Fox outright of supporting El Chapo's return to power, pointing in part to the quick demise of the leading Arellano-Félix brothers after he got out as supporting—if circumstantial—evidence.

While there's no hard evidence of the administration as a whole supporting El Chapo's return to power—informal pacts between state officials and drug traffickers are rarely put into writing—numerous members of Fox's government were implicated in or convicted of grievous acts of corruption throughout and after his *sexenio*. Among El Chapo's most important friends in Mexico City may have been none other than Genaro García Luna, the top federal cop who arrested Arturo back in 2001. García Luna's star had continued to rise, and throughout the first half of the decade he oversaw the newly created Federal Investigations Agency, or AFI, which he had been handpicked to launch and lead. It was the latest in a long string of rebrandings by Mexican law enforcement, an attempt to break with past scandals and outrages, or at least to break with the names and uniforms of the agencies that those scandals tarnished. But just as always, the AFI was rife with corruption, from the top down. And according to recent court documents, released in late 2019 and early 2020, the rot began at the very top, with Genaro García Luna himself. According to El Mayo's brother El Rey, García Luna personally accepted huge cash bribes in exchange for passing along information and allowing El Chapo and El Mayo and their allies to operate with impunity while he earned himself the image of a tough anti-crime crusader by pursuing their enemies. If he was indeed on their payroll, he was a very good friend to have. (García Luna has denied the accusations and pleaded not guilty in federal court. As of this writing, he continues to fight the case against him.)

. . .

From his base in Sinaloa, El Chapo oversaw the rebuilding and restructuring of his and El Mayo's empire, an alliance of various crews and factions that they referred to as "the Federation." Throughout the late 1990s and early 2000s, El Chapo's allies had coordinated closely with Amado Carrillo Fuentes's faction in Juárez, along with other, smaller networks throughout Mexico. This alliance had its roots in the late 1980s, when the various kingpins, nearly all of whom were born and raised in Sinaloa, gathered at a meeting in Mexico City to divvy up the territory that had once been controlled by the so-called Guadalajara Cartel under Miguel Ángel Félix Gallardo. And they grew closer still through a shared enmity with the Arellano-Félix organization in Tijuana.

In those years, the various crews collaborated so closely that many of the midlevel operatives working for one or the other leader considered it to be a single organization. When Amado died on the surgeon's table in 1997, his brother Vicente, known as "El Viceroy," took over. While he was not as close with Mayo and El Chapo as his brother had been, the federation continued.

At a meeting held in early 2002, El Chapo, El Mayo, and others had reunited with El Viceroy in Gómez Palacio, Durango, on the border of the state of Coahuila, where they had hashed out an agreement to continue working with one another. Of particular interest to El Chapo,

El Mayo, and the Carrillo-Fuentes family was the shared route the traffickers used to smuggle cocaine by train to Texas and then on to Chicago.

El Chapo and his allies had been moving cocaine into the United States by train since at least the late 1980s. One of the most important routes saw drugs moving up train tracks to the Texas border, before crossing into the United States for distribution. In about 1997, El Mayo and the Carrillo-Fuentes family gave control of the route to a trafficker by the name of Tirso Martínez Sánchez, an inveterate gambler whose love of soccer earned him the nickname "El Futbolista." Born in Guadalajara in 1967, Tirso had grown up destitute, selling candy on the streets to support himself before he got into the drug game and found himself possessing a knack for logistics that allowed him to move steadily more weight. By the turn of the millennium, he was earning so much money that he routinely threw away hundreds of thousands of dollars placing bets on cockfights, snorted prodigious amounts of cocaine on a daily basis, and was the proud owner of soccer teams in several states in Mexico. Standing five feet seven inches—about an inch taller than El Chapo—he had all the appearance of a businessman, complete with suit, tie, and gently receding hairline. This muted image belied his hard-partying, high-roller lifestyle.

Tirso began working the train route in 1997, and took it over in 2000 after an unfortunate incident in which his boss shot himself in a drug-fueled police chase. Soon Tirso was coordinating multiton loads belonging to the Carrillo-Fuentes family, El Mayo, the Beltrán Leyvas, and El Chapo, who had continued to buy a stake in the loads from prison.

A kilo of cocaine at that time sold wholesale in Chicago for about $20,000, netting the investors a total of about $30 million per trip, before expenses. Coordinators would be paid in cocaine, earning a couple hundred kilos off the top that they could flip to their customers when it arrived in Chicago. For these midlevel operatives like Tirso, each train shipment could mean a windfall of as much as $4 million before expenses. Cash from the wholesale customers was smuggled back into Mexico in cars and hidden in appliances carried by mules onto commercial airplanes, or used to buy diamonds and jewelry that would then be smuggled into Mexico and sold. Money launderers working with the traffickers would then move the cash laundered through currency exchanges known as *casas de cambio*, casinos, and other cash businesses.

The route provided a relatively secure method to get large amounts of drugs over the border; as innovative as El Chapo's tunnels were, moving product through them required workers to send shipments to the border, unload them, bring them through the tunnel, and load them back onto trucks before the drugs could move on to their destination. Trains, on the other hand, required less leapfrogging, and fewer workers. Working out of warehouses in Mexico City, laborers would weld sheets of metal onto a frame at either end of the tanker cars, load in the drugs, and spread a steel paste over the welding lines, before finally painting over the compartment to make it appear as if the compartment walls were actually the tanker wall. The workers would then pack the compartments with as much as 1,800 kilos, fill the tank with vegetable oil, and hook the car onto a freight train headed north.

With minimal inspection—thanks in part to reduced border inspection post-NAFTA—the train would cross the border from Nuevo Laredo, Tamaulipas, to Laredo, Texas. From Laredo, the trains headed north to Chicago, or to New York, where the tanker car would be offloaded into a warehouse leased in the name of a front company. There workers would break open the compartments with sledgehammers, remove the drugs, break up the load, and deliver portions in a fleet of cargo vans to wholesale customers.

In addition to being both stealthy and high-volume, pushing coke north in freight trains provided another bonus. Because the loads were welded into secret compartments in tanker cars, El Chapo's people had no need for much of a presence in the areas the drugs passed through, no warehouses in which to unload shipments, and therefore he saw no need to pay a tax to whoever controlled this or that border crossing.

Just as he had done in Tijuana in the early 1990s, El Chapo decided to begin sending cocaine shipments through the border crossings at Nuevo Laredo and Matamoros in the northeastern state of Tamaulipas. In doing so, he flouted the power of the so-called Gulf Cartel, which controlled the plaza in Tamaulipas, including the ports of entry between Nuevo Laredo and Laredo, Texas; Reynosa and McAllen, Texas; and Matamoros and Brownsville, Texas. But again, he picked a fight with a group of killers far better organized and willing to spill blood than he.

The group commonly known as the Gulf Cartel began in the 1930s as a smuggling outfit run by Juan Nepomuceno Guerra, a bootlegger and businessman who dressed like a well-to-do cowboy and cultivated deep ties to the *PRIista* elite in both the border region and in Mexico City. It was thanks to these connections that Guerra managed to stay out of jail for nearly his entire life—apart from "a few hours" one time—and embed his relatives and friends in top posts in local law enforcement, along with the judiciary and the political machine. Guerra's nephew, Juan García Ábrego, took the reins in the 1970s, capitalizing on the marijuana boom and the long-established smuggling routes of his uncle to turn a rag-tag border-town posse into one of the strongest organized-crime outfits in Mexico. García Ábrego's influence over much of the Gulf Coast, as well as his high-placed friends and the millions of dollars in bribes he spread around, made the Gulf Cartel such a force to be reckoned with that successive generations of Sinaloan traffickers, from Miguel Ángel Felix Gallardo to El Mayo to Amado Carrillo Fuentes, found it better to maintain an uneasy truce than to try to take control over the plaza. Ábrego was known to allow other traffickers to move drugs through his plaza if they paid a tax, but he responded with ferocious violence against those traffickers foolish enough to refuse to pay the tax. To maintain his smuggling routes and keep himself and his people out of prison, be bribed officials on both sides of the border, including Texas National Guard members, agents in the Immigration and Naturalization Service, and at least one FBI agent, along with the usual suspects in top jobs at the Federal Judicial Police and the state and federal attorneys general's offices. In 1994, the DEA estimated that García Ábrego's network was pulling in as much as $10 billion a year in profits.

García Ábrego's principal lieutenant was a man named Osiel Cárdenas Guillen, whose nickname "Mata Amigos," or "Friend Killer," gives a hint at how he got and maintained power. By the time he had muscled and backstabbed his way to a position of power under Ábrego, all he needed was for García Ábrego to go down to take the reins of the Gulf Cartel.

He didn't have to wait long. García Ábrego had maintained close ties with President Carlos Salinas and his brother Raúl when they were in power from 1988 to 1994, but the next administration had less patience for him, and found the political will and police muscle necessary to arrest him. The *federales* arrested García Ábrego in 1996 at a ranch outside the city of Monterrey, in the northeastern state of Nuevo León, and he was swiftly extradited to the United States, where he is currently serving eleven consecutive life sentences.

After a brief power struggle, control of the Gulf network passed to the Friend Killer. While García Ábrego and his uncle were part of a prominent family based in Matamoros that had extensive ties to the ruling elite at the state and federal level, Cárdenas Guillen was of more humble origin, and could not rely on family connections to enforce his will and maintain order as his predecessor had. To control the plaza, he needed an army.

The Friend Killer's first big hire was Arturo Guzmán Decena (no relation), a corrupt paratrooper born in the state of Puebla who made his name committing war crimes against indigenous Zapatista rebels in the southern state of Chiapas in 1994. He arrived in Tamaulipas in 1997, part of a deployment of soldiers sent under the authority of the PGR to reinforce (and bring to order) the Judicial Federal Police. Soon thereafter, he crossed over completely, and went from taking bribes to working directly for the Gulf Cartel. He took the code name Z-1, after a radio frequency used by his special-forces unit, and he named his new crew of enforcers Los Zetas.

With his prominent chin, muscular frame, straight-backed military posture, and commando training, Z-1 cut a figure not unlike a Mexican GI Joe, and brought to the Zetas a level of training, discipline, and brutality rarely seen before in Mexico—except by security forces. His initial recruits were fellow soldiers, wooed by the promise of earning more in a year as cartel hit men than they could dream of in a lifetime of military service, bribes notwithstanding. Later the group began to recruit more widely, first importing battle-hardened special-forces veterans from Guatemala known as *Kaibiles*, and later hiring among poor young men in the cities and countryside of northwestern Mexico who were willing to do bad things for money. Through strict training and shocking brutality, the reputation of the Zetas as a commando-like force would endure and helped spread the Zetas brand to semiautonomous criminal cells operating in states across Mexico.

In time, the Zetas would eventually split off from the Gulf Cartel and become one of the most widespread and brutally violent organized crime groups Mexico has ever seen, but back in the early 2000s, when El Chapo decided to start sending coke through Nuevo Laredo, the Zetas contented themselves with carrying out staggering public displays of violence on behalf of their boss, the Friend Killer. Midday shoot-outs, wholesale massacres, and bodies dumped in town squares became a facet of everyday life in areas in which the Zetas operated, even as other areas of Mexico grew markedly safer.

The old order of the drug trade in Mexico—corrupt but untouchable *PRIista* power brokers protecting select traffickers and arresting or killing their enemies—was coming to an end. The demise of this status quo correlated directly with the rise of paramilitary groups like the Zetas, who were unafraid of controlling the plaza through brute force, and foreshadowed the blood-chilling increase in violence that would sweep across Mexico a decade later. Under the PRI, traffickers had been incentivized to keep violence to a minimum, and keeping it out of sight when it was unavoidable. But as the PRI began to lose its grip on power in the later 1990s, criminal groups had to rely on their own fearsome might to maintain control of the criminal rackets. Rather than burying bodies out in the desert or dissolving them in acid, they began to leave headless torsos in town squares, often affixed with *narcomantas*, banners proclaiming the reason for the victim's mutilation. They also began to flex their muscle in public more and more.

One near tragedy made clear that a new type of narco had arrived.

On November 9, 1999, a pair of U.S. agents, one DEA, the other FBI, were taking a tour of Matamoros with an informant, who from the backseat pointed out homes linked to top Gulf Cartel narcos. As they cruised through a residential neighborhood, the agents realized they were being followed; first one car, then a second, then a third was tailing them. As the driver tried to speed up, the other agent pulled out his cell phone and dialed a state police commander in a panic. Before they could escape, however, a convoy of eight trucks and SUVs blocked the road, and more than a dozen AK-toting gunmen piled out, including several openly wearing insignia of the state police, undeterred by the consular plates on the agents' car.

Flanked by his bodyguards, Osiel Cárdenas Guillen, the Friend Killer himself, materialized from the group of killers and demanded that the agents turn over the informant. When they refused, the capo's men raised their weapons and prepared to fire. In a last-ditch attempt to save their skin, the agents again identified themselves, and shouted that to kill them would be a serious mistake.

Finally, Cárdenas Guillen relented, but sent them off with an angry warning.

"You gringos. This is my territory!" Cárdenas Guillen shouted. "You can't control it. So get the hell out of here!"

Deeply shaken, the agents and the informant sped immediately to the border crossing and took refuge in Brownsville. The incident set off alarm bells in Washington, and among many federal law enforcement officials raised the specter once more of the murder of Kiki Camarena.

"This was very, very close," one U.S. official said. "It was as close as you can get without a funeral."

The confrontation made clear that the drug game had changed. Unlike the old guard in Sinaloa, who for the most part understood the importance of keeping their heads down and avoiding direct confrontation with state security forces, the Zetas were as brazen as they were brutal, and they were unafraid to provoke the wrath of their neighbors to the north.

· · ·

As late as 2002, El Chapo, El Mayo, and the other Sinaloa capos maintained good relations with the Gulf Cartel and the Zetas. But El Chapo began eying the northeast for expansion, perhaps due to its key railroad and highway infrastructure. He dispatched Arturo Beltrán Leyva to Tamaulipas to begin recruiting people on the ground to coordinate smuggling and to prepare for war.

Arturo's best-known lieutenant in the area was an American named Edgar Valdez Villarreal, a former high school football star from across the border in Laredo who had been moving weed and coke into Texas since the late 1990s. Nicknamed "La Barbie" for his Ken doll–like blond hair and blue eyes, La Barbie set about creating a paramilitary force called Los Negros, which he and his patrons in Sinaloa hoped could stand up to the Zetas.

Tensions had already been running high in Nuevo Laredo, where La Barbie and other independent traffickers who paid taxes to the Gulf Cartel were beginning to buck the authority of the Friend Killer and the Zetas. As El Chapo and the Beltrán Leyvas began to muscle in, the lucrative plaza was primed to explode. As is often the case in murky conflicts between organized crime groups, the exact event that sparked the war for Nuevo Laredo is hard to pinpoint. Some, like El Rey Zambada, say the conflict began when La Barbie murdered the brother of a Zeta commando; others argue that it was the murder of an independent trafficker by the Zetas, which drove other independent traffickers like La Barbie to side with El Chapo and the Beltrán Leyvas. It probably didn't help the situation when, on March 14, 2003, Mexican soldiers in Matamoros arrested the Friend Killer after a lengthy shoot-out, creating an immediate power vacuum.

By August 2003, the place was racked by daily violence, with at least forty-five murders and at least forty kidnappings in a town that had once enjoyed relative stability. On August 1, a heavily armed convoy of La Barbie's men opened fire on agents of the Federal Investigations Agency with automatic weapons and rocket launchers, turning downtown Nuevo Laredo into a war zone for nearly an hour as terrified residents huddled indoors.

The brutality and public nature of violence that followed was unlike any that Mexico had seen before. Bodies left in the street with warnings to rivals; severed heads rolled into crowded public spaces; videos depicting torture and murder. As El Chapo and his lieutenants battled for control of Nuevo Laredo, violence was inflicted more broadly—and publicized more widely—than ever before. Even if the numbers didn't rise overall, the impact of these public displays was felt more broadly, more viscerally, and contributed to a feeling among many Mexicans that the situation was quickly spinning out of control.

. . .

As the Zetas made their presence known, expanding throughout Tamaulipas and beyond, it signaled a new phase of the drug trade, an arms race of sorts, as other trafficking networks began to form paramilitary-like security forces. El Chapo was no exception. Soon after his escape from Puente Grande he went on a hiring spree, looking specifically for ex-soldiers who knew their way around weapons and knew how to interrogate, torture, and kill.

One new hire who fit the bill was an unassuming young man named Isaias Valdez Ríos, who had spent years in the GAFE, a special-forces unit of the Mexican Army in which many of the original Zetas members had learned their brutal trade. Compared with the action-figure physique of Z-1, the founder of the Zetas, Valdez cut a relatively unassuming profile, with a slight build and wide-set eyes that gave him a perpetual look of melancholy. For some reason everyone called him Memín, the name of a comic-strip penguin drawn in racist caricature that was popular in the 1950s and '60s.

Memín enlisted with El Chapo in 2004, although he didn't know at first whom he was working for. It became evident on his first day on the job, when one of El Chapo's top enforcers, another ex-special-forces guy named Fantasma, picked him up and gave him a lift to an airfield on the outskirts of town, where a Cessna was waiting to fly him to La Tuna.

When Memín arrived at El Cielo, the mountain redoubt overlooking El Chapo's hometown, he was handed a tactical vest and an AK-47, and put to work on guard duty. For the first two weeks he kept his distance from the boss, just working his shift and sleeping on the ground, but eventually El Chapo summoned the new hire over so he could give him the once-over.

"*Chavalón*, dude, how are you doing? I heard you have been part of the special forces with the GAFE," El Chapo said, according to Memín.

"That's right," Memín replied.

"Well, you know, here you have to be on the lookout," El Chapo said, giving his version of an orientation speech.

All the while, El Chapo continued to rebuild. He liked to be involved and took an active role in planning drug shipments, new smuggling methods, and intrigues against rival traffickers. But he also had an innate understanding of how to work with local networks in far-flung places, creating a more horizontal structure than the hierarchical pyramid that many imagine when they hear the word "cartel."

While some of the smuggling outfits sometimes called cartels, like the Medellín and Cali cartels of Colombia, or the family-run Arellano-Félix organization were quite top-down, El Chapo's federation was more horizontally organized, with a great deal of decision-making latitude given to individual crews in their own locale.

The most succinct—and perhaps best—description of the so-called Sinaloa Cartel that I have ever heard came from a former attorney from Colombia who from 1998 to 2006 brokered hundreds of millions of dollars in business between his bosses in Colombia and El Chapo and his allies in Mexico: "The Sinaloa Cartel was a group of people who helped each other mutually in order to be able to get cocaine shipments into the United States successfully," the former trafficker said.

He was speaking of course of the big guys—not the small-time smugglers and crooks often referred to as "cartel members." This group, the kingpins who would later be referred to as the Sinaloa Cartel, mainly consisted of El Chapo, El Mayo, the Beltrán-Leyvas brothers, Juan José "El Azul" Esparragoza Moreno, and Ignacio "Nacho" Coronel—whom he referred to as the powerful traffickers, the ones with the capital to invest tens of millions of dollars at a time in loads of cocaine, the ones with the smuggling infrastructure to move that coke north to the United States, and the political connections to ensure that, for the most part, it got to its destination without interference from law enforcement. Each had his own crew of loyal gunmen, but they frequently shared logistics with semi-independent trafficking outfits located in key locations that would unload a boat in the southern state of Chiapas, say, or load it onto a train in Mexico City, or move it across the border in Juárez. Each had his own area of influence, his own plaza—Arturo Beltrán Leyva in Acapulco,

Nacho Coronel in Guadalajara—and in each plaza each had his own political and police contacts. Sometimes they worked together, sometimes they worked on their own; sometimes they pooled their money and invested in shared loads, sometimes they ponied up their own money and bought an entire shipment outright. But they never approached the level of corporate organization and hierarchy that is so often assumed when lazy or overly imaginative narrators set out to depict trafficking networks like El Chapo's.

In the old days, before his arrest, El Chapo and El Mayo had often dispatched trusted associates and family members to coastal regions in order to oversee maritime arrivals of cocaine loads. El Mayo had sent his brothers out, to Tijuana, to Mexico City, to Cancún, and El Chapo had done the same, installing his brother Arturo, El Pollo, in Agua Prieta back in the 1990s. But now they increasingly worked with local traffickers in coastal areas like Chiapas, or the Yucatán Peninsula in the state of Quintana Roo, or with smuggling families like the Salazar family in Sonora, who knew the lay of the land and had existing relationships with local law enforcement. They had a similar system abroad, linking up with local traffickers in Central American countries such as Panama, Honduras, and Guatemala, whose existing smuggling routes and knowledge of the local peculiarities were indispensable in hopscotching loads of cocaine from South America to Central America to Mexico.

They continued to work closely with cocaine producers in Colombia, including the organization of Juan Carlos Ramírez Abadía, alias Chupeta, the bloodthirsty young trafficker to whom El Chapo had boasted of "being a lot faster" during their first meeting back in 1990. Chupeta had continued working with El Chapo's friends and family throughout the 1990s, and after the escape, he reconnected with El Chapo. By the summer of 2002 Chupeta's men were sending multiple loads of cocaine, tons at a time, by speedboat from the Pacific coast of Colombia to the beaches of Chiapas in southern Mexico, where El Chapo would buy it outright for $6,000 per kilo. So strong was the relationship that on one occasion, when the coke that arrived was of poor quality, a lieutenant of Chupeta agreed to give El Chapo a discount, shaving $500 off the cost of each kilo. El Chapo always knew how to drive a bargain.

By partnering with local crews along the supply chain, El Chapo got access to local expertise, and the local traffickers got access to a staggering amount of investment capital, as well as the connections that El Chapo and his allies had forged with high-ranking cops, military officers, and politicians. By this time, in the early to mid-2000s, much of the cocaine coming to Mexico arrived by boat, as the increasingly sophisticated radar systems employed by Mexican authorities in southern Mexico made the old method of large-scale illicit flights from Central America or Colombia ever riskier. One exception, however, was the operation at Benito Juarez International Airport, in the heart of Mexico City, where El Mayo's little brother El Rey oversaw logistics and kept officials on their payroll. Using airline companies that appeared legitimate on paper, El Rey and his workers were able to fly massive shipments of cocaine into the airport, and unload it under the protection of the corrupt officials he was paying to look the other way. Several years after his escape, El Chapo began doing the same, using a company called Aero Postal (later renamed Aero Fox) to fly DC-8 cargo jets into Benito Juarez packed with as much as five tons of cocaine at a time.

At their most organized, they were a federation, a cooperative of individually powerful and wealthy men who, in the words of that Colombain envoy, helped each other mutually in order to be able to get cocaine shipments (and heroin and meth and weed) into the United States successfully. There it became the responsibility of distributors like Pedro and Margarito Flores, identical twin brothers based in Chicago who by the early 2000s were quietly building one of the largest drug distribution empires in the country.

8

THE FLORES TWINS

PEDRO AND MARGARITO "Junior" Flores got an early start in the drug game. Born to a midlevel pusher in a Mexican American neighborhood on the South Side of Chicago, the identical twin brothers were just seven or eight years old when they began helping their father by translating for him during drug deals, and helping him load and unload his product. Their father's reliance on a pair of prepubescent boys to help move Scarface quantities of blow was not without its farcical moments. Once, when their older brother Adrian ordered a young Junior—everyone called Margarito "Junior"—to get the keys from the car, Junior gave his big brother a brief moment of terror when he announced he couldn't find the keys. Racing out to the car, Adrian popped the trunk, and to his relief, the ten kilos of cocaine—keys, as they're often referred to in street slang—were still there.

By all accounts, the Flores brothers were quiet guys who avoided the excess of some drug dealers. An undated side-by-side mug shot of the twins shows two young men with a nearly identical appearance, both brothers sporting close-cropped buzz cuts, staring into the camera with a serious gaze under heavy eyebrows. In the side-by-side, Pedro is seen sporting a sparse mustache, stud earrings, and a chain, while Junior is slightly rounder, and clean-shaven.

The big break for the brothers Flores came in 1998, when their older brother was locked up on a drug-trafficking charge. His customers still had noses and arms to feed, so the young brothers, teenagers at the time, stepped up to keep the coke and heroin flowing while their older brother was away. They quickly showed a knack for the business that far surpassed the abilities of their father and brother.

The supplier who began working with them after the arrest of their father was a man they called "El Profe," or the Professor. El Profe, in turn, was coordinating with Tirso Martínez Sánchez, the guy down in Mexico who was known as El Futbolista. They were well connected, only a few steps removed from the big players down south; but back then, the Flores twins were still far enough down on the food chain that they had little knowledge of the larger logistics chain that delivered them their product. All they had to worry about was picking up their load from El Profe, whose men would drop it off for the twins in a beat-up old Ford Econoline cargo van in the parking lot of a Denny's off Interstate 55 in Bolingbrook, Illinois, a suburb of equal parts tree-lined streets and mall sprawl along Interstate 55, thirty miles west-southwest of downtown Chicago. The first time Pedro and one of his employees went to pick up the van, the worker was so unnerved by the sight of the old window-less beater—he called it a "kidnapper van"—that he refused to drive the thing, for fear local law enforcement would be on top of them just by eye-balling their ride. So Pedro hopped behind the wheel himself and, nerves on fire, began to drive it back to his warehouse, praying to God the whole time that the rickety old vehicle wouldn't die on him.

After driving the fifteen minutes back to the stash house, he ran into another problem: the van was too big to fit into the garage, and as he backed up, Pedro rammed the roof of the van into the garage ceiling. Jumping out of the driver's seat, Pedro ran around back, opened the doors, and began pulling plastic bags laden with cocaine bricks out of the back of the van, about 250 kilos in all. As Pedro hurriedly tried to unload the quarter ton of cocaine into the garage of the stash house, in full view of a handful of neighbors out for a morning stroll, one of the bags tore open, spilling kilos of coke across the driveway. It was, Pedro recalled ruefully, a "pretty hectic day."

Slapstick mishaps aside, that first pickup solidified the brothers' reputation and proved to El Profe that they were capable of handling significant shipments of drugs. Over the next several years, they returned repeatedly to that Denny's parking lot, where they'd hop into the grimy old kidnapper van, drive the quarter ton or so of cocaine to the stash house, and return the van brimming with cash. They soon caught the eye of a Mexican trafficker named Lupe Ledezma, an old-timer who knew their father, and he offered to cut the twins in a rung higher up the ladder, shipping directly to them and putting them in charge of distro. They went from being successful midlevel wholesale dealers to running one of the most prolific trafficking networks in the Midwest, shipping wholesale loads of coke and heroin up and down the interstate to dealers in Milwaukee, in Ohio, even New York City. They were making more money than they knew what to do with, but they were smart, kept a low profile—which is not to say they didn't enjoy the occasional trip to Vegas. And the coke and dope kept coming.

When it wasn't shipped by train, the drugs arrived in tractor trailers, tucked into loads of legal goods that disguised the real merchandise hidden away in secret compartments. The most common method the traffickers used to cover their tracks was to hide the merch in a load of fresh produce, fruits and vegetables and the like. Not ones to waste good products, the Flores twins even made an effort to unload the legal goods in local stores after unloading the cocaine, but by this time the brothers were moving such volume that they had to be careful not to call attention to themselves—with so much produce to sell on the cheap, they sometimes caused local prices to crash.

"At first we were trying to get rid of it at local markets, you know, but that started to become an issue, you know, we couldn't keep doing that," Pedro recalled. "We didn't want the people to get suspicious and the prices of produce would drop dramatically in certain areas. We were just kind of dumping out the produce for nothing, we were practically giving it away just to get rid of it. The prices would drop—it was practically free vegetables and produce."

If, to your delight, you came across an unbelievable deal on tomatoes or lettuce at a grocery store on the South Side of Chicago in the early 2000s, it is possible you have the Flores twins to thank.

It fell to the Flores twins and other distributors in local markets to cover their own tracks, making up for the remarkably cavalier actions of the traffickers who sent the cocaine. In 2003, one load in particular tested Pedro's patience: Lupe phoned to let Pedro know a load of cocaine had arrived on the outskirts of Chicago, but there was a "small issue" with the cover load. The problem became apparent when Pedro and his men showed up to unload the cocaine and were met by an entire herd of woolly, bleating sheep.

"There was about 150 heads of sheep, live sheep, and we were in a dilemma because the warehouse I had at the time was in the city," Pedro recalled. "So now I'm looking at a bunch of live sheep, like what are we going to do with them, because the driver explains he can't take the sheep back with him."

Pedro had to get the coke into the city for distribution, but the sheep posed an immediate problem. Chaos reigned as Pedro and his men, transformed for the moment into lowly shepherds, struggled to corral the animals back onto the truck on which they had arrived. Eventually, he called up a friend who owned a ranch outside the city. For ten thousand dollars the rancher agreed to take the sheep off Pedro's hands, but the episode left him concerned about the potential consequences of such sloppy cover-ups.

"These cover loads were kind of, you know, weak, man," he recalled. "They put no effort into really concealing the drugs, and the risk of that was that every time a load got dropped off in the city or got seized, I would lose people, you know?"

•   •   •

By the early 2000s, the twins were moving hundreds of kilos of cocaine at a time, selling wholesale to street-level dealers throughout Chicago and developing a customer base along the interstates that branch out from Chicago throughout the Midwest.

Chicago has long played an important role in American commerce, with nearly $1 trillion in freight passing through it each year by rail, by air, and by truck. Like the shrewd capitalists they were, the Flores twins seized on this advantage and ran with it.

"It's practically centered in the middle of our country, which makes it convenient, you know," Pedro Flores said. "You're halfway to everywhere and logistically the infrastructure of the railroad systems, highways, airports, waterways just makes it ideal, not just for drugs, probably for any type of goods."

Eventually, however, things got too hot for the brothers in Chicago. So after making sure that their operation could run smoothly in their absence, the twins pulled up stakes in the spring of 2005 and relocated to Guadalajara, the cradle of modern Mexican drug trafficking. Guadalajara was as attractive in 2005 to the twins as it had been to Miguel Ángel Félix Gallardo back in the late 1970s and early '80s: a world capital for banking (and money laundering), big enough to blend in, and an all-around nice place to live if you're a young drug trafficker with money to spend. But it wasn't long before trouble at home followed them to Mexico. Just a few months before the twins fled the country, a low-level dealer—who moonlighted as both a police informant and a stick-up artist—had raided several stash houses belonging to the Flores brothers, kidnapping a worker and making off with about 400 kilos of cocaine. Pedro reached out to Lupe Ledezma to let him know about the loss, and to tell him that he and Junior would need some time to set up new stash houses; but Lupe was unsympathetic. If the twins were not able to receive the next shipment, he told Pedro, there was going to be a "problem."

Pedro knew a threat when he heard one, and decided to comply with his longtime supplier despite their sudden loss of infrastructure in Chicago. When several hundred kilos of cocaine arrived soon after, they worked furiously to unload it onto customers, and resorted to stashing about 100 kilos at a friend's house. But their unlucky streak continued when the friend stole the 100 kilos, and they were now in debt even further. This time, Pedro put his foot down: no more shipments from Lupe until they were able to get new stash houses in Chicago.

Lupe was furious. Who was this little upstart, basically a gringo, in Lupe's eyes, who thought he could dictate the terms of their business? In response, Lupe demanded that the twins hand over their entire business—warehouses, workers, and all—in order to settle the debt. Pedro balked: to hand over his infrastructure in the States would be to hand over his entire business. Instead, he agreed to begin paying Lupe in installments to make good on the $12 million or so that he now owed his supplier.

A few months after the twins and their girlfriends arrived in Mexico, Lupe contacted Pedro to see about working together again, and invited him to a meeting in Zacatecas, about five hours north of Guadalajara by car. Pedro agreed to the meet and headed to Zacatecas with his girlfriend and one of their workers, but a bad feeling began to nag at him; he and Lupe had never really settled the bad blood between them, and the meeting was going to be in an area outside the city with poor cell service. Before heading to the meeting, Pedro called up Junior and arranged for him to pick up his girlfriend and take her home while he had the sit-down with their supplier.

Ten minutes into the meeting, the cops kicked down the door.

Two dozen heavily armed men burst into the room, headed straight for Pedro, and forced him to kneel on the floor, where he crouched helplessly as they rained down blows on him with the butts of their assault rifles. After stripping him to his underwear, the gunmen cinched his arms tightly behind his back with handcuffs and blindfolded him. They told him they were cops.

"You're going back to the U.S.," the gunmen said.

This was it, Pedro thought; his countrymen had finally tracked him down, and now he was headed back to the States to rot in an American prison, just like his older brother and his father had.

But these men, whether police or not, were not here to do the bidding of the North Americans. Instead, they tossed the blindfolded Pedro into the back of a truck and took off on a torturously bumpy ride careening along what felt like a dirt track into the mountains. After a while, they pushed Pedro out of the vehicle and barked at him to sit. So he sat. The hours dragged by, and he sat, until finally, around four in the morning, Pedro's captors bundled him into the truck once more and drove him to a shack the size of a jail cell. The men threw Pedro onto a cot, still handcuffed and blindfolded, and left him there.

For more than two weeks, Pedro's world was dark, as he lay wasting away in the locked room.

"I lost about thirty pounds," Pedro recalled. "I got sick. It was pretty traumatic."

After sixteen days of darkness, the men dragged their prisoner out of his cell, tossed him into the back of a truck, and drove for about half an hour, before stopping to switch vehicles. As they hauled Pedro into the next vehicle, Pedro managed to peek out from under his filthy blindfold to see the unmistakable black-and-white paint job of a Mexican federal police cruiser. Taking off once more, his captors continued on for another hour along a bumpy dirt road before finally stopping. One of the gunmen pulled Pedro, still trussed and blindfolded, from the car and marched him a few steps before he kicked Pedro in the knees, forcing him to the ground.

This was it, Pedro thought. If this was how he was going to die, he thought, he wasn't going to show any weakness. He would die like a man.

"At that point I felt like it wasn't even more worth [sic] for me to beg for my life," he said. "I just thought it was going to be over."

But instead of putting a bullet in Pedro's head, one of the men slipped something into the back pocket of his filthy jeans, and leaned down to whisper in his ear.

"You're lucky, your brother saved you," the guard spat. "I'm putting this handcuff key in your shoe. When I leave, I want you to count to one hundred, and don't get up, and don't turn around until I leave."

So Pedro counted, 1, 2, 3, 4, until he got to 100. Reaching into his sock, he pulled out the key, and twisted his hand until the key slid into the lock of the handcuffs, and freed himself. When he pulled the blindfold off, he saw it was night. In his back pocket, he found a cheap Nokia cell phone, and using the phone as a flashlight, began to make his way to an area where the phone would have service. After weeks of lying on a filthy cot in total darkness, he was so weak that he had to sit down to rest every few steps. In the pitch-black night around him, he heard what he thought was a wildcat prowling.

Finally, after stopping and starting for what felt like an eternity, he made his way to the highway, and managed to get a weak signal on the phone. He dialed his brother, keeping an eye out on the road and ducking for cover every time a car passed.

"I was pretty messed up," Pedro said. "I didn't want to bump into like, a cop or something like that and he sees me in that condition, you know?"

Pedro had no idea where he was, except that he could see across a wide-open valley, and across the valley there was a car with its lights flashing as it snaked back and forth along the switchbacks of the road going down the mountain. After a while watching the cars on the road, it dawned on Pedro that it was a road he had driven along many times, and he again called his brother Junior, who told Pedro to sit tight and wait. After another half hour of waiting, Junior finally arrived, and Pedro stood up to give his twin brother a joyous hug. Then he pulled back and gave his twin a once-over.

"You stink," Junior said.

Despite the sorry state in which Junior found his brother, emaciated, reeking of two weeks in the same filthy clothes, despite the fact that their longtime mentor had betrayed them, Junior greeted Pedro with good news. He had spoken with El Chapo, and the boss was on their side.

While his brother was languishing in a fetid shack in the mountains outside Zacatecas, Junior had been working frantically to locate him, an effort that had led him to Culiacán, where associates of El Chapo had agreed to connect him with the big man. When El Chapo received Junior at a mountain hideout in the Sierra Madre, and Junior had presented him with ledgers showing details of the brothers' regular payments to Lupe, El Chapo agreed to help get to the bottom of it.

Junior and one of El Chapo's men went to see Lupe, bringing along a voice recorder to get an unguarded Lupe on tape. At the meeting, Lupe proceeded to "slap the shit out of" Junior, pistol-whipping him and berating him until finally El Chapo's men intervened. When El Chapo heard the beating on tape, he ordered Lupe to release Pedro.

• • •

The first meeting the twins held together with the upper echelons of the Sinaloa federation was with El Mayo. By now, El Mayo was well aware of these twin brothers from Chicago, who without the usual hubbub of rich young traffickers drunk on money and power had managed to carve out a significant market share of U.S. drug distribution, and he was eager to meet them. El Mayo greeted the twins warmly, and congratulated them on their success. He had heard good things, that they had moved more than twenty tons of cocaine in the several years they had been active.

Not one to brag, Pedro corrected El Mayo. The real number, he pointed out, was probably somewhere between fifteen and twenty tons of cocaine, he said modestly.

Rising from his chair, the older man began to hold forth on his own early days slinging coke in the United States, even telling the brothers he was familiar with their neighborhood back home in Chicago. He had sold dope there, too, he said, back in the day.

"Any one of those idiots could sell drugs in Mexico, but very few could do it in the United States like that. You guys have my respect," El Mayo told Pedro and Junior, crossing the room to shake their hands.

"Imagine if you were triplets," he added with a laugh.

Sensing an opportunity, and eager to cut out unscrupulous middlemen such as Lupe, Pedro took a chance. How would you feel, he asked El Mayo, about working directly with us, no intermediaries?

"You know what, you guys have earned it," El Mayo said, according to Pedro. "From now on, I'm going to give the same prices as I give my top lieutenants. You guys are my people."

Before getting down to business, El Mayo had one request for the brothers.

"I want you to go meet my compadre tomorrow," he said. It was time for Pedro and Junior to meet El Chapo.

The next day, one of El Mayo's men drove Pedro and Junior out to a cornfield on the outskirts of Culiacán, where they boarded a small plane and flew about forty-five minutes up into the mountains to the west of the city; they landed on a rough airstrip cut at an incline into a mountain. A small greeting party was assembled there, and the men loaded Pedro and Junior into a pickup truck to head to the boss's house.

As they were driving up the mountain, Pedro glanced over his right shoulder and saw a sight that instantly told him everything he needed to know about the people he was now dealing with. By the side of the road was a man, stark naked, and chained to a tree. But the brothers didn't have time to dwell on this chilling sight: soon they arrived at a *palapa* near the crest of the mountain, and standing there, waiting for them, was El Chapo, dressed in jeans and a T-shirt, his trademark ball cap perched on his head, a pair of walkie-talkies in his hands, a jewel-encrusted .38-caliber pistol tucked into his waistband.

El Chapo said a friendly hello to the brothers, and with his observant little eyes, took in the two Americans, who were dressed in jean shorts and decked out with gold chains.

"With all that money, you can't afford the rest of the pants?" El Chapo quipped, according to Pedro. "The only thing you're missing is a dress!"

Pedro had brought as a gift a pair of gold-plated, .50-caliber Desert Eagles, the monstrous pistol often seen in the hand of John Rambo and countless other action heroes. They weren't the most practical weapons, however, weighing nearly five pounds apiece, and Pedro could tell immediately from El Chapo's reaction that he thought the guns to be silly.

"I guess I was watching too many movies, big, old, heavy handguns," Pedro said. "It was not, you know, something they would use."

After some other pleasantries, the three men took a seat under the palapa, while a small army of about forty armed guards prowled the perimeter. An AK-47 was propped up against the drug lord's chair. Despite his relaxed demeanor, he appeared ready for anything.

The conversation quickly turned to the problem of Lupe. After Pedro's kidnapping and hearing the secret recording of Lupe exploding at Junior, El Chapo had made up his mind that Lupe was untrustworthy, and now he offered the brothers his full support. He even had a plan for how to lure Lupe into coming to a sit-down with El Chapo and the Flores brothers.

"If I make him come, I'm going to give you a gun, and I want you two guys to shoot him once in each eye," he told the twins.

Until the kidnapping, the brothers had largely managed to keep themselves free of the violence inherent in drug trafficking. They didn't want to kill Lupe. They didn't want to kill anyone. But now they were dealing with a man who was used to killing people when he needed to. They politely declined El Chapo's offer of shooting Lupe in each eye, but settled the issue by agreeing to pay El Chapo the remaining $4.4 million that they owed. They'd let him handle Lupe. It wasn't exactly charity, but they were out of a bind.

Before the brothers left, El Chapo had another question for them: Could they read English? They could. Gesturing to one of his men to bring a sheet of paper, El Chapo asked them to take a look at a printed-out copy of a news article about a drug bust that had happened a few months earlier. He wanted to know if they thought it was real, or if the trafficker whose men had gotten caught had cooked up an excuse. Taking a glance at the article, Pedro thought it looked too simply written to be real.

"Man, it looks like anybody would type this up," Pedro told El Chapo.

The drug lord turned to one of his men.

"*Ejecútenlo*," he said. "Execute him."

Someone was going to die because of what Pedro had told the boss, and this didn't sit well with him. Later, when they were back in Culiacán, Pedro went down to the business center of their hotel and looked up the seizure on the internet; sure enough, there were accounts of the bust in several newspapers. Pedro was horrified: he didn't want anyone to die because of his snap judgment of the printout. He immediately got on the phone with his main contact for El Chapo, and explained to him that the story was in fact real.

"I was worried that someone might get hurt over a simple mistake," he recalled.

The twins never found out the fate of the man whom El Chapo had suspected of lying, but they did find out what happened to Lupe. When El Chapo learned of the way in which Lupe had double-crossed the twins, he ordered a hit man to kidnap Lupe and his sons, only releasing the sons when Lupe agreed under duress to sign over a number of properties to El Chapo in order to pay his ransom. When the sons reneged and went to the police, the hit man told Pedro he smothered Lupe to death with a plastic bag before tracking down and murdering the sons for going to the cops. Even after hearing this grim news, however, Pedro was feeling paranoid. Some months after his kidnapping, the twins' father—he'd joined them in Mexico—mentioned a rumor that Lupe had been seen. This worried Pedro, and he mentioned his concern to El Chapo, telling the boss that Lupe still posed a threat.

"You are seeing ghosts," El Chapo replied. "Worry about something else."

They were not so worried as to stop working. Despite their supposed aversion to violence, despite the rough start in Mexico, Pedro and Junior launched themselves into their work with their typical mix of discretion and logistical prowess, and it paid off. On the first shipment alone, a load of 500 kilos of coke delivered by El Chapo and El Mayo to Chicago and distributed by their workers from there, the twins made more than $1.5 million overseeing the operation from Mexico.

By the fourth time he met with El Chapo at the boss's mountain hideout, Pedro was getting used to the routine. As always, he came bearing gifts, which this visit included a pair of jean shorts, a jokey nod to El Chapo's comment about Pedro's fashion choices on the first visit. El Chapo received the shorts (delivered in a box with the Viagra logo) with a chuckle.

During a chat with the boss after arriving, Pedro told El Chapo about how nervous he had been on that first visit, how he hadn't known what to expect.

"I said I had this idea like the movies, that you had lines of people and guys would shoot them in the head and say 'Next!'" Pedro recalled.

Everybody laughed at that, including El Chapo, but then his demeanor changed.

"Only the ones we have to," El Chapo said.

.   .   .

While the Flores brothers were making themselves comfortable in Guadalajara, El Chapo's war for Nuevo Laredo and Reynosa had continued unabated. But in the end, El Chapo's push into Tamaulipas ended in failure. The Zetas, now working largely independently of the Gulf Cartel to charge taxes on drugs trafficked through the plaza, held total control of criminal activity in the area and enforced it with astonishing brutality. They also began to branch out, finding new streams of revenue by extorting legitimate businesses and trafficking migrants. And with their reputation as ruthless cutthroats with special-forces training, the Zetas brand spread quickly, as criminal cells took on their name—sometimes with permission, sometimes without—in states throughout Mexico.

The grinding war of attrition and eventual victory of the Zetas in Nuevo Laredo was the first major setback for El Chapo since his escape from prison. Until that point, most of the arrested and slain drug capos had belonged to rival groups like the Arellano-Félix organization, the Gulf Cartel, and the Zetas. But El Chapo did not lose sight of smuggling routes in the northeast, and soon set his sights on an even larger prize: Ciudad Juárez. This push, combined with a simultaneous surge of counternarcotics pressure from the federal government under newly elected president Felipe Calderón, was about to bathe Mexico in even more blood.

Within days of taking the oath of office, Calderón had sent more than 7,000 federal troops into his home state of Michoacán, which had seen more than 500 drug-related murders the year before. On January 7, 2007, President Calderón stepped up to a podium in Tijuana to address the nation. He praised the work of those soldiers already deployed, and announced a new deployment of 2,600 soldiers and 110 federal police to Tijuana. Soon he would do the same in Juárez.

"We will continue with the operations that let us reestablish the minimum conditions of security in some parts of the republic, so that little by little we can take back our streets, our parks, our schools," Calderón said.

The architect of Calderón's anti-drug strategy was none other than Genaro García Luna, the hard-charging founding director of the Federal Investigations Agency who accompanied Joe Bond when the DEA agent met with Arturo Guzmán Loera in 2001 (and arrested Arturo hours later). García Luna had continued his steady rise to power, and under Calderón took the lead in the new administration's pugilistic policy against drug traffickers, to the delight of his supporters in U.S. law enforcement. But according to federal prosecutors in Brooklyn, García Luna was already on El Chapo's payroll, and had been for years. In the ensuing years, Calderón's campaign would fall far heavier on El Chapo's rivals than it ever did on El Chapo.

In Tijuana, troops and *federales* would replace the city's 2,320 municipal cops, every one of whom the troops stripped of their weapons the evening of their arrival, ostensibly so the army could test their weapons to see if they had been used in drug-related gun crimes. To his supporters and to anti-drug hawks in Washington, this show of force was a godsend; finally, someone was taking seriously the threat posed by drug traffickers! Finally, a president whose policies lined up with the militarized anti-drug efforts of the United States.

But what was the problem at hand? And were the military and the federal police really able—or willing—to do the job?

Violence linked to organized crime had been rising during the 1990s and 2000s, particularly in areas along the border. But a singular focus on these conflicts obscures a larger truth: Mexico as a whole was actually getting less violent. When Calderón took office in 2006, Mexico was riding a historic downturn in homicides, beginning around 1993, when the country saw nineteen murders per 100,000 residents, and continuing until 2007, when the figure stood at just eight murders per 100,000 residents. That 2007 number is less than half the murder rate that Chicago was experiencing at the time, and no serious policy maker would have suggested sending troops to patrol the South Side.

Still, the discrepancy between that historic decline and Calderón's decision to send troops to cities like Ciudad Juárez—where the murder rate instantly skyrocketed—has led to accusations that he launched the war simply to prove his legitimacy in the wake of a bruisingly close presidential election. Calderón had defeated his opponent Andres Manuel López Obrador, the left-wing mayor of Mexico City often called by his initials AMLO, by less than a quarter of a million votes; AMLO had not gone down quietly, opting instead to contest the results based on believable but ultimately unproven allegations of fraud. AMLO, a born populist showman, had even thrown himself a mock inauguration. Calderón rode out the postelection challenges, but when he arrived in office he had little in the way of a mandate and a significant portion of the country believed he might have stolen the election. What better way to prove his power by declaring war on a problem that had for so long eaten away at Mexico and her institutions?

. . .

At the time of Calderón's inauguration, horrific acts of violence were grabbing national attention, and many Mexicans did live in fear of violence, regardless of the overall decline in homicides. The security crisis was very real for people living in areas plagued by drug violence, such as the disco in Michoacán where a group of killers dumped five severed heads on a dance floor in September 2006; or in Tamaulipas, where heavily armed convoys of Zetas drove down city streets in broad daylight and La Barbie was establishing himself as a pioneer of *narcovideos*, recording executions of his enemies that helped increase the ghoulish spectacle of the turf war there; or in Ciudad Juárez, where a mere mention by journalists of the name "La Linea"—the enforcement arm of the Carrillo-Fuentes crew— was enough to garner death threats or worse.

For all the talk of drug gangs as a kind of criminal insurgency, Mexican traffickers have never sought state power beyond the corruption required to operate. Unlike in Colombia, where traffickers like Pablo Escobar and Carlos Lehder actively involved themselves in politics and waged a war directly against the state, traffickers in Mexico have always been content to let the government handle governance, as long as that governance does not interfere with business. But it was that very coexistence, that blurring of the line between criminal groups and the state, that compounded the problem ever deeper. Impunity was rampant, and a vanishingly small number of crimes were ever solved. In many cases, the cops supposedly tasked with solving this kidnapping or that murder were the very ones committing them.

At the time Calderón took office, journalists in Mexico and U.S. diplomats in the State Department noted that he would need to act fast to confront organized crime, purge corrupt officers from the police, and reform the opaque, ineffective, and often compromised judiciary. He acted fast indeed, but only in terms of brute force—force that had full support of the United States. As for the rest of those necessary markers of progress? Not so much.

Calderón's answer of sending in the military and federal police against an asymmetric and deeply embedded "enemy" never had a chance of ending that impunity or defeating that corruption, and perhaps it wasn't meant to. Instead it brought unending misery to vast swaths of Mexico as increasingly fractured drug gangs simultaneously battled one another and fought security forces. Soldiers ill-equipped to handle law enforcement duties themselves became some of the greatest violators of human rights. Just as in Culiacán during Operation Condor, rates of nondrug crimes—the kind that target individuals and civilians far more than drug trafficking does—shot up, as atomized criminal networks spread like falling embers, starting fires wherever they landed.

The nightmare was just beginning.

9

JUÁREZ

WAR CAME TO Juárez on the backs of black military pickup trucks, black-clad soldiers, black masks hiding all but the slits of their eyes, riding in a convoy bristling with high-powered weapons. It was a show of strength welcomed by some residents, but it wouldn't be long until the soldiers began to look to many like occupiers, a new belligerent force in the hellish violence engulfing the city.

Juárez had seen a steady decline in violence in the 1990s and 2000s, with the murder rate wobbling up one year, down the next. The city had a startlingly high rate of murders of women, or *feminicidios* as it's known in Spanish. Women disappeared on the way to work; women disappeared on the way home from work; women went to the club and never came home; women got into taxis and never came home. This was not the work of some ultra-prolific serial killer; it was a symptom of wealthy, powerful, and untouchable men who used women for sport and killed because they could. It was not a problem that would be solved by a military invasion.

But Calderón had his plans. In March 2007, just as he had in Tijuana and Michoacán, President Calderón sent in the military, deploying thousands of troops to take over law enforcement duties in the city and, ostensibly, to root out drug gangs and restore order.

As if an earthquake had struck and cracked open the earth's mantle, all hell broke loose.

In 2007, there were 336 murders reported in Ciudad Juárez. By the end of 2008, the city had recorded at least 1,587 murders; in 2009, the number rose to 2,643, not counting disappearances. And in 2010, the bloodiest year yet, more than 3,000 people were murdered in Juárez, a tenfold increase from 2007. Other crimes skyrocketed as well, as civilians were targeted for kidnapping and business owners faced the choice of paying impossible extortion fees to local gangs and crooked cops or closing their shops altogether. Tens of thousands of residents in Juárez became refugees, fleeing across the border to El Paso or seeking safety in other areas of Mexico.

The cities of El Paso and Juárez straddle the Rio Grande river, nestled in a mountain pass some 3,700 feet above sea level. From El Paso, you can peer across the border and see the streets and low-slung buildings of Juárez fan out across the valley. From the Juárez side you can see the buildings of El Paso creeping up the slopes of the Franklin Mountains, a little range that sweeps down from New Mexico to their terminus at the river. The two cities are home to more than two million people, at once united and separated by fate, history, and a trickle of water. Several bridges span the Rio Grande within the city limits of El Paso and Juárez, where crowds bustle back and forth and cars line up at all hours to cross over. Like many border towns between the Pacific and Gulf coasts, Juárez and El Paso have a unique identity, a shared history, and the residents take pride in calling themselves *fronterizeros*, border folk.

I arrive in Juárez from El Paso on a Friday morning in June 2019, the air still slightly cool before the sun the chance to rise and bake everything in its sight. I had meant to cross by foot but get a lesson in the interconnectedness of the two cities when a friend giving me a lift accidentally drives straight over the border.

Driving through Ciudad Juárez, the wounds of the past thirteen years remain visible, even if much of the violence has retreated from the public eye once more. Buildings stand empty, abandoned years ago by their owners. The lucky ones were able to get out, to places where their names didn't appear on death lists, where their kids could go outside without seeing bodies hanging from bridges; the unlucky ones are dead, either buried in the city cemeteries or lost in one of the mass graves that dot the desert on the outskirts of town. Even in the short drive from the international bridge to my hotel, I see at least half a dozen clubs, bars, restaurants, and hotels with boarded-up windows, weeds growing tall through cracks in the parking lots. It's been a few years now since the worst of the violence, a time of unabating terror for residents of the city, many of whom lived for years under a self-imposed curfew, rarely venturing out after dark if they didn't have to. In 2018, there were 1,259 murders in the city, the first time the number jumped above 1,000 since 2011—including the massacre of eleven people found tortured and murdered inside a home. In the months prior to my visit in 2019, the murder rate has been creeping back up higher still; but it was nowhere near the level of mayhem that overwhelmed the city streets a decade ago, and not as public, not on main streets.

"Not everyone's talking about crime," one local reporter said. "There's more people out on the street."

The trauma of those earlier days remains. My guide is Miguel Perea, a local journalist who worked as a photographer during those awful years, and it's clear that driving from one crime scene to the next, day after day, he learned how to survive. The tricks he learned are hard to unlearn, and a decade later he still carries habits from that time. When a traffic light goes red, he leaves a car's length between his beat-up sedan and the vehicle in front; if shooting breaks out, or if someone comes for you, you're going to need that elbow room to peel away, bang a U-turn, swerve into the oncoming lane. When Perea parks, he backs into the space; if the appointment sours, if you've gotta leave in a hurry, if someone comes for you, you don't want to waste a few precious seconds peering over your shoulder as you back out. One young reporter to whom Perea introduces me, a photographer named Carlos Sánchez, almost died that way: his first month on the job, gunmen cornered him and a colleague in a parking lot and opened fire. The colleague died, and Carlos made it out by the grace of God, or by quick thinking, or by dumb luck; he's not sure. He still carries a bullet in his body, but he never even found out who the gunmen were, or why they attacked. The day after the shooting, the newspaper for which he and his fallen colleague worked printed a beseeching letter addressed to no one and to everyone asking a simple question: "What do you want from us?"

It wasn't always like this.

For decades, Juárez was a relatively sleepy town. Despite its position on an international border, it's actually located deep in the interior of the continent, an area that saw little large-scale development throughout much of its history. The economy largely revolved around minor trade— cattle, horses, and sundry goods—and the service industry, which expanded a great deal during the failed experiment of alcohol prohibition in the United States. A cottage industry bloomed here as El Pasans crossed over into Juárez in droves to drown their temperance in the bars and cantinas that line the main drag, a stone's throw from the U.S. border.

The city's expansion was tied to cyclical migrations: workers in the 1910s and 1920s headed to the United States, only to be expelled in the 1930s, many of them settling in border-region cities like Juárez. This expulsion, which took place during the lean years of the Great Depression, was one reason that politicians in southwestern states so avidly supported the anti-marijuana scaremongering of the drug warrior Harry Anslinger, and eagerly tied fact-free horror stories of marijuana use to racist stereotypes of the Mexican workers they sought to eject.

Facing a shortage of agricultural labor north of the border at the outset of World War II, the United States and Mexico launched the Bracero Program, which offered temporary work permits to Mexican laborers, drawing huge numbers of migrants north over the course of the program; between 1942 and 1964, more than three million Mexican workers received permits, and millions more crossed the border to work without documents. When the United States unilaterally ended the Bracero Program in 1964 and launched a mass expulsion of Mexican workers, many settled in Juárez, just as those expelled in the 1930s had. By 1960, these successive waves of migration had helped turn Juárez into Mexico's fourth-largest city.

In 1969, in an effort to force Mexico into compliance with his anti-drug policies, President Nixon brought the border to a standstill for weeks by ordering that every car driving north be searched. The stunt, code-named Operation Intercept, was a warning that the lax policies of yore were coming to an end, and had an indelible effect here in Juárez as the border policies of the United States became ever stricter and more punitive and a rising number of migrants unable to enter or remain in the United States began to settle in. Over the next several decades, the city continued to expand thanks in part to a concerted effort by Mexican and U.S. officials (egged on by a slick El Paso consulting firm) to develop the border's industrial sector, incentivizing the opening of factories with the establishment of a free-trade zone just south of the Rio Grande (or Río Bravo, as it's known in Mexico).

With the introduction of the North American Free Trade Agreement in 1994, dozens of new tariff-free factories, known as *maquiladoras*, sprouted in the city, drawing hundreds of thousands of new residents, who migrated from other areas of Mexico and Central America in search of work. Between 1990 and 2005, the city's population ballooned from 800,000 to 1.3 million. As migrants poured into the city seeking jobs at the multinational factories, new, poorly planned neighborhoods began to sprout up on the outskirts of the city. In just fifteen years, as the population swelled, the city's footprint expanded dramatically as these new neighborhoods, or *colonias*, began to stretch out into the desert. The new digs were spartan, with few of the amenities that make city life bearable, such as public gathering spaces or parks where children can play. In many cases, the streets of entire *colonias* went unpaved save for the road used to bus workers to and from the *maquiladoras*. With the majority of the factory jobs going to women, Juárez saw a huge growth in its population of unemployed young men, many of whom lived in the *colonias* on the edge of the city, with little social infrastructure. Making matters worse, a global economic downturn in the early 2000s hit the *maquiladora* sector hard. In Juárez, 65,000 jobs had vanished by 2002, and the companies that operated the plants began to slash the voluntary contributions they made to city coffers, further exacerbating the problem of crumbling infrastructure.

Another factor in the rise of violence was the increase in domestic drug use. For much of Mexico's history, the issue of drug trafficking and cultivation has largely concerned the smuggling of drugs to the United

States. But as successive waves of laborers found jobs in factories and began working inhumanly long shifts, methamphetamine use began to climb in cities like Juárez and Tijuana. By the early 2000s, border cities like Juárez and Tijuana were reporting a rate of methamphetamine consumption that was double the national average. Unlike trafficking, which relies on smuggling routes more than physical territory, the growth of *narcomenudeo*, or retail drug sales, in Juárez, led to local drug dealers jockeying for control of retail turf. And that led to bodies in the street. Ruthless economic expansion—and its eventual collapse—along with rising domestic drug use and local turf battles between gangs set the stage for the carnage to come.

"Workers in this model were not viewed as human beings with dreams and aspirations but rather as mere economic outputs," the scholar Tony Payan wrote in 2014. "Generations of these young people grew up in the streets, waiting for their parents to come back from the maquiladora. . . . The violence that plagued the city in the last decade has been committed by this generation of street kids, now aged in their 20s, 30s, and 40s."

If Juárez was a test of the viability of the neoliberal economics so in vogue in the 1990s, the violence that began to engulf the city in 2008 was proof of its failure.

• • •

Anyone with a passing knowledge of the war in Juárez has likely at one point or another heard the story cast as an epic struggle between two drug gangs, El Chapo Guzmán's Sinaloa Cartel on one side and the late Amado Carrillo Fuentes's Juárez Cartel on the other. That's not the whole story, but there's some truth to it: beginning in 2006, on the heels of their apparent defeat in Tamaulipas, El Chapo and his allies made a concerted push to seize the plaza in Ciudad Juárez, in hopes of gaining control over the city's ports of entry. If he could get his rivals out of the way, El Chapo could move untold quantities of cocaine, heroin, meth, and weed across the border there each year.

For most of El Chapo's career, his faction and the faction run by the Carrillo Fuentes family in Juárez were on such good terms that functionally they acted as one organization. In the old-school style of Sinaloa narco capos, the groups were bound by family ties and sacred baptismal rites. When Amado died on the surgeon's table in 1997, his younger brother Vicente, El Viceroy, took over, and for years the alliance persisted. But things started to go downhill after El Chapo's escape, as the fugitive kingpin moved aggressively to reestablish himself.

It's impossible to pinpoint the exact moment when things began to sour, but one factor was El Chapo's attempt in the early 2000s to cut Vicente out of major drug shipments on the shared train route the two organizations had been operating since the 1990s, according to Tirso Martínez Sánchez, alias El Futbolista.

For Tirso, working directly with El Chapo for the first time was a nerve-racking experience. His initial introduction to El Chapo took place sometime in mid-2001, months after El Chapo had escaped from Puente Grande. The trip was shrouded in secrecy: he was told only that he had to meet a "very important person." En route to the middle of nowhere west of Mexico City, Tirso was made to switch vehicles and wear a blindfold for the remainder of the trip. When they pulled to a stop, the driver ushered Tirso and a colleague named Alfredo Vasquez out of the van and removed their hoods. Tirso saw they were standing outside a cabin, nestled in a mountainous rural area. Armed guards patrolled the perimeter, and as they climbed the steps to enter the cabin, a woman was leaving—El Chapo always found time for women. Inside they found El Chapo. Tirso had never seen the boss in the flesh, but Vasquez, who had known El Chapo since the early 1990s, was greeted warmly, the old associates embracing in a hug. Then Vasquez gestured to Tirso.

"Compadre," he said to El Chapo. "Look, he's the one in charge of the train route."

Greeting Tirso, El Chapo began to ask him detailed questions about the route, showing evident pride in his own role in pioneering the method. El Chapo wanted to know how much they were capable of transporting, how many tanker cars they were operating at the time. He wanted to greatly increase the amount they were shipping, eager to regain his footing. After discussing the route for a bit, it was time to go, and Vasquez and Tirso left the way they came, blindfolded in a cargo van.

Soon after, Tirso realized that El Chapo's ambitions were going to cause trouble and put him, Tirso, in the middle of it. For years he had worked just as closely with El Viceroy as he had with El Chapo and El Mayo's people, and it had gone well for him. But at a second meeting with El Chapo, again in a remote area west of Mexico City, El Chapo laid down an ultimatum: from now on, Tirso would only coordinate loads through El Chapo's people.

When Tirso reported his meeting to El Viceroy, the boss of Juárez was furious that "that asshole" El Chapo was scheming to cut him out of major deals.

Tirso was terrified.

"I was in between a rock and a hard place," he said.

Throughout the early 2000s, the tensions would increase until they exploded in violence: El Chapo's people murdered El Viceroy's brother, Rodolfo Carrillo Fuentes, in Culiacán in September 2004; in retaliation, El Viceroy on New Year's Eve of that year arranged the murder of El Chapo's brother Arturo, El Pollo, in prison, where he'd been since being arrested in 2001.

El Chapo always knew how to make enemies.

• • •

If El Chapo had learned one lesson in his attempts to seize trafficking routes in the northeastern state of Tamaulipas from the Gulf Cartel, it was the importance of recruiting locally, part of his larger strategy of deputizing homegrown criminal networks to act in his interests. If the Sinaloa federation was going to make a move on Juárez, he would have to raise an army from inside the city to challenge the power of El Viceroy and his gunmen.

The Carrillo-Fuentes family had held control of Juárez since the early 1990s. They maintained their power with the help of an enforcement gang known as *La Linea*, or the Line, the core of which was made up of police, both former and active-duty. La Linea had built up a fearsome reputation, but existed as a whisper, a rumor you didn't want to be heard gossiping about; even mentioning it in the press could get you killed, just as Amado, in his day, had made sure his name rarely made it into print. Cops on the cartel payroll made sure that no rogue traffickers could work in Juárez without paying a tax to El Viceroy, arresting, killing, or disappearing anyone who violated the law of the plaza. They also ensured that shipments of drugs could pass through the city unmolested; one former government official recalled that he used to hear cops on the radio at night, telling one another to stay off a certain road, or to stay in the station house, in order to allow tractor trailers and their armed escorts to pass through town.

The Juárez Cartel also farmed out some of its dirty work to local street gangs, which had proliferated throughout the late 1990s and early 2000s as the population of poor, unemployed, and restless young men in the city ballooned. One such crew was Barrio Azteca, a collection of killers that initially took root in the Texas state prison system, and by the early 2000s had a strong presence on both sides of the border.

Despite their stranglehold on Ciudad Juárez, El Viceroy and his goons in La Linea and Barrio Azteca had plenty of enemies, and El Chapo eagerly began making overtures to them as he prepared for war. They didn't have to look for long before a potential partner, Mario Nuñez Meza, appeared of his own volition. Meza, who went by the alias M-10, was a former Juárez municipal policeman who had a falling-out with the Juárez Cartel. In late 2005 or early 2006, he traveled to the mountains of Sinaloa to seek support from El Chapo and his allies, and at a meeting there, M-10 laid out his plan for an alliance to take on their common enemy, El Viceroy. El Chapo liked what he heard, and so did El Mayo. Now that they had someone to work with in Juárez, they pledged to supply M-10 with weapons smuggled from the United States and to provide support through El Chapo's police and government contacts in the border region. With support from Sinaloa, M-10 began recruiting others like himself, people who knew Juárez, who wouldn't be seen as invaders, and who had a blood feud with El Viceroy and his men. They called themselves La Gente Nueva, or the New People. They also went by a more recognizable name: Los Chapos.

One such recruit working with El Chapo's people in Juárez was a trafficker and hit man named José Antonio Torres Marrufo, alias El Jaguar, a dead-eyed killer with massive biceps and a neck like a tree trunk. Jaguar had previously been closely allied with La Linea, but his relationship with them had understandably soured after some members of the crew, including El Viceroy's top lieutenant, had kidnapped him. When he made it out alive, he swore revenge.

As he began to set up smuggling infrastructure on either side of the border, Jaguar turned to an associate he had known for several years, an El Paso–based drug smuggler named Edgar Iván Galván. Galván was made of softer stuff than Jaguar and M-10. He had gotten involved in drug trafficking only in the last few years, after a divorce threw his life into disarray. The two men had gotten to know each other in Juárez, where Galván had a bachelor pad. In 2007, Jaguar hit up his old pal to help La Gente Nueva set up stash houses in El Paso to store drugs and weapons.

Galván told Jaguar he would think about the offer, and headed back to El Paso to mull it over. On the one hand, the gangster's obvious bloodlust was frightening to Galván, who despite his involvement in drug trafficking wasn't inclined toward violence. So the offer gave Galván pause. He knew Jaguar was a killer, and had gotten a firsthand look at just how vicious this guy was: once, when Galván had been driving around Juárez with Jaguar, the gangster decided to take a detour, and drove them to a nondescript house in town. It was a murder house, a black site to which Jaguar's henchmen would spirit away kidnapping victims to be tortured and dismembered. Inside, the white-tiled floor was built at a slight angle, sloping toward a drain.

"In that house, no noise came out if someone were to scream," Galván said.

The more he thought about Jaguar's "offer," the more he knew he had no choice.

"At first I didn't want to work with him, but a week later I told him yes," Galván said. "Jaguar is not the kind of person who asks questions. He orders you."

During one meeting in 2007 when they discussed Jaguar's work for El Chapo, the burly killer gave his friend a grim warning:

"He told me I shouldn't go to Juárez for a while," Galván recalled. "He said things were going to get really ugly."

. . .

Galván would play his own role in that ugliness. Over the next few years, Galván handled about four or five major shipments of weapons to Jaguar, pumping countless high-powered firearms into Juárez during the worst years of the fighting there. The shipments of weapons—which Jaguar referred to as *juguetitos*, little toys—included bulletproof vests and dozens of semiautomatic AR-15s and AK-style rifles, easily converted to full-auto capability with a few tweaks of the hardware.

But not all of Jaguar's "little toys" were so small. One haul included a monstrous .50-caliber sniper rifle, the kind that can hurl a slug through light armor and shatter concrete blocks.

When that batch was ready for pickup, Jaguar seemed especially interested in the sniper rifle, asking Galván if he liked the "special little toy."

"What a big animal," Galván recalled telling Jaguar on the phone.

"That's a .50-caliber," Jaguar replied. "Take care of it."

Galván was one link in a much larger ecosystem of weapons trafficking, one that directly supports the bottom line of U.S. gun dealers while fueling deadly conflict south of the border.

On paper, Mexico has quite restrictive gun laws, a policy that began in the 1960s as part of an effort to keep weapons out of the hands of dissidents and guerrilla fighters. Only the police and military are allowed to carry assault weapons, and the caliber of weapons that ordinary civilians may own is limited to .380 or less. But in practice, it's illegal to own anything more powerful than a .22. There's one legal gun store in the country, and it's located on a military base.

Despite all this, the country is flooded with illegal firearms, including an increasing number of high-powered guns, like 9mm handguns, AR-15 and AK-style assault rifles, and Jaguar's favorite special little toy, those .50-caliber sniper rifles capable of punching fist-sized holes in cars and causing unspeakable damage to human flesh. Of the estimated 15.5 million illegal guns in Mexico, one study found that 90 percent are used for criminal ends.

Proponents of gun rights in the United States might point to the well-worn adage that "when guns are outlawed, only outlaws will have guns," but in the case of Mexico this fails to take into account the extent to which lax gun laws in the United States directly undermine Mexican restrictions on firearms. Estimates vary, but anywhere from 80 percent to 90 percent of the 15.5 million illegal weapons in Mexico were bought in the United States and trafficked over the border in hidden compartments or tucked into commercial vehicles, often waved through by corrupt border guards.

For ten years following the 1994 passage of the Federal Assault Weapons Ban in the United States, firearms continued to drift across the border. But the illicit trade took off like a starting pistol in 2004 when the ban expired, and the guns being smuggled into Mexico were increasingly the kind of military-grade weapons that made possible the rise of disciplined paramilitary groups like the Zetas. The rate of violent deaths soon followed.

Despite his close relationship with Washington, President Calderón vented his frustration at the lax gun laws and uneven enforcement that allowed so many deadly weapons to float into the hands of hyperviolent criminal groups in Mexico.

"We seized more than 90,000 weapons. . . . I am talking like 50,000 assault weapons, AR-15 machine guns, more than 8,000 grenades and almost 10 million bullets," Calderón told a CBS reporter. "Amazing figures and according to all those cases, the ones we are able to track, most of these are American weapons."

As North American guns continued to flow across the border into the hands of criminal groups, the U.S. government committed hundreds of millions of dollars to the militarization of Mexico's fight against drug traffickers. In October 2007, President George W. Bush, Calderón, and the heads of state of several Central American nations announced the Mérida Initiative, a sprawling security pact aimed at tackling drug trafficking and named for the Yucatán Peninsula resort town in which the deal was hashed out. Under the terms of the agreement, the United States pledged to inject more than $1 billion into the anti-drug efforts of its southern neighbors in the form of military hardware, training, and cash. The lion's share of the money was destined for Mexico.

Conscious of the fact that the deal would result in vast sums of money pouring into institutions hardly known for their efficacy or respect for human rights, the architects of the deal mixed some sticks in with the carrots: the release of 15 percent of the funds would be contingent on Mexican security forces making sustained progress in curbing human rights abuses and increasing transparency. Despite all the evidence that Mexican security forces were as corrupt and brutal as ever, unleashing more indiscriminate violence than ever, the United States always found "progress" to highlight, and only once withheld that 15 percent—and even then only temporarily. This may have come as a surprise to people on the ground in Mexico during that time, who witnessed the behavior of the military and federal police firsthand. But then again, perhaps it was not such a surprise. Just days after both nations signed the historic accord, video emerged that appeared to show police practicing torture on one another, under the watchful tutelage of English-speaking trainers said to be private security contractors. A video of actual torture may be gruesome, but a video of torture training, of police "practicing" the art of squirting water up a mock detainee's nose and dunking another's head in raw sewage? This effectively proved a fact that to many in Mexico was common knowledge: torture was a routine and institutionalized tool of soldiers and police. The Mérida money arrived nevertheless, 15 percent and all: over the next decade, the United States would deliver $1.6 billion to Mexico's anti-drug fight, with a significant portion of it going to the military and police forces. It was a small portion of the money that Mexico was spending during that time, but a potent symbol that the United States supported and encouraged the aggressive strategy initiated under Calderón.

As the author Dawn Paley points out in her excellent 2014 book, *Drug War Capitalism*, the United States does not push for policies such as police training in Latin American countries out of a sincere desire for human rights, but rather as a means of pursuing its own foreign policy goals. And, as Paley and others have shown, that training has rarely, if ever, led to more security or democratic freedoms for the people living in recipient countries. In Mexico, police and military agencies with close ties to the United States have been some of the worst abusers of human rights; this was true of the CIA-backed DFS in the 1970s and 1980s as they went from kidnapping left-wing students to actively collaborating with drug traffickers; it was true of the GAFE special-forces units of the 1990s, many of whose members formed the core of criminal paramilitary squads like the Zetas; and it continued to play out in the twenty-first century, most notably with the Mexican Marines, whose operations became increasingly deadly as they grew into their role as the tip of the spear acting on U.S. intel in Mexico. From 2007 to 2011, the Marines engaged and wounded at least 200 civilians in armed skirmishes, with just one documented death occurring. Beginning in 2012, the picture underwent a ghastly reversal, with SEMAR units killing 445 civilians and injuring just 19 people between 2012 and 2018.

In Juárez, the aggressive strategy initiated under Calderón meant constant terror.

The killers seemed to be locked in a grim race with one another to top the brutality of their rivals' work, hanging bodies from bridges, leaving severed heads in public plazas, shooting wildly into the rare club or bar that could still draw a crowd after dark. One summer day in 2008, killers from one side or another hacked into an emergency radio frequency, spitting death threats at EMTs as they tried to treat a gunshot victim. The EMTs walked off the job in frustration, and henceforth refused to respond to scenes involving gunshot wounds unless accompanied by a troop escort. The Red Cross hospital in town suspended twenty-four-hour emergency services after a group of gunmen strolled in and killed four patients. If you caught a bullet after 10 p.m., or crashed your car? Tough luck, hope you make it to morning. Gunmen shot up the motorcade of the governor, killing a bodyguard. One group threatened to kill a cop every forty-eight hours until the police chief he resigned, and in Juárez, you can bet that the threat is real.

The mayor, meanwhile, tried to project strength.

"I'm not going to give in," he said defiantly. But he said it while sitting in a temporary office, across the river in El Paso.

10

THE YEAR OF SKINNY COWS

A S WAR BEGAN to rage to the north in Juárez, El Chapo remained ensconced in his stronghold in the mountains of Sinaloa. But El Chapo was stretched thin, and his control over his own home turf was beginning to crack. In early 2008, simmering tensions between his faction and those controlled by the brothers Beltrán Leyva—Arturo, Héctor, and Alfredro—boiled over into a bloody and protracted shooting war on the streets of Culiacán and in the surrounding cities and towns.

The Beltrán Leyva brothers' path to power was closely linked with El Chapo's and resembled his story closely. They grew up in La Palma, a tiny hamlet nestled along the dirt road that leads to La Tuna, and like El Chapo, they've left their mark on their hometown. From the road overlooking La Palma, it's impossible to miss the mansion they built there, a palatial villa that dwarfs the other buildings around it.

Along with El Mayo, they aided El Chapo following his escape from Puente Grande, their political connections proving crucial in helping him avoid being recaptured. And as the threat from the Zetas encroached, they had once again proven themselves to be among his most steadfast allies.

One of the most important contributions that Beltrán Leyvas brought to the table had always been their skill at bribery. Over the years they managed to get some of Mexico's top officials on their payroll, including a high-ranking federal police agent nicknamed "the Queen," a member of an elite, DEA-trained investigations squad who for years made himself useful to the Beltrán Leyvas by taking out rivals and using his close ties to U.S. law enforcement to help identify snitches; and officials even more senior than the Queen, who took millions of dollars in bribes, keeping some for themselves and spreading the rest among the men who followed their orders. One former federal cop who later became a high-ranking lieutenant of Arturo Beltrán Leyva estimated that hundreds of cops were on Arturo's payroll at any time. On occasion, the ex-cop said, he met in person with some of the highest-ranking police officials in the country on behalf of the Beltrán Leyvas to demand results.

• • •

The alliance between El Chapo and the Beltrán Leyvas began to unravel on January 21, 2008, when a team of Mexican soldiers arrested Alfredo— also known as *El Mochomo*, or the Desert Ant—in Culiacán. Mochomo had been raising a ruckus of late, causing trouble around town, and de-spite warnings from El Chapo to keep a lower profile, he'd stuck around, tempting fate. Now he was caught. When the cops cornered Mochomo, he was toting an AK-style assault rifle, eleven luxury watches, and two suitcases with nearly $1 million in cash. The next day, police in Mexico City raided a safe house reportedly belonging to Mochomo, where they arrested eleven alleged hit men and uncovered a terrifying arsenal of weapons, including twenty frag grenades, an array of assault weapons, and forty ballistic vests, eight of which bore the letters "FEDA," which officials said was likely an acronym for "Arturo's Special Forces."

Arturo, alias *El Barbas*, or "the Bearded One," could have an ex-plosive temper, and had been known to mete out violence against men, women, whoever, for the slightest insult. When his brother Mochomo went down, Arturo flew into a rage, and he focused his wrath on this old friend El Chapo, whom he accused of orchestrating the arrest. El Chapo swore then, and his closest aides have sworn ever since, that he had noth-ing to do with it this time.

"Arturo Beltrán was blaming my compadre," said Dámaso López Nuñez, the former prison official who'd become one of El Chapo's most trusted servants. "I told Beltrán—no one could make him come to reason about it. He held on to this, that my compadre was behind it, and he decided to fight against my compadre, to make war."

Whether or not El Chapo was actually behind Mochomo's arrest, Arturo wasn't coming out of nowhere with the accusation. Drug traffickers in Mexico have used cops and soldiers to do their wet work for decades, and vice versa. The line between them has often been fuzzy at best, and it was hardly seen as a breach of some omertà, some sacred oath of silence, to turn a rival over to the feds. El Chapo did it, the Beltrán Leyvas did it, and their contemporaries and their predecessors did it. For most of the history of the drug trade it was the traffickers' preferred method of enforcement, and it worked well for everyone (except the guy who got betrayed): the government got to parade narcos dead or alive in front of news cameras and pledge to continue the fight against drugs, and the traffickers who paid for the hit or arrest got to sleep a little easier that night. That had been El Chapo's goal in reaching out to the DEA from prison in 1998, and again in the wake of his 2001 escape, and ever since he had, through a lawyer, been in intermittent contact with the DEA and likely much more frequent contact with Mexican officials. Pretty much everyone assumed that El Chapo had been behind Mochomo's arrest: in a classified diplomatic cable sent a few months later, U.S. State Department staff cited "embassy sources" who also speculated that El Chapo had provided the military with the intel leading to the arrest of Alfredo.

In the wake of Alfredo's arrest, El Chapo hoped for a time that he could continue to keep his fingerprints off any violence that spilled over as a result. But as the situation got closer to all-out conflict, El Chapo did turn to friends in the police.

"My compadre was trying for there not to be any shoot-outs or confrontations between his gunmen and the Beltrán gunmen," Dámaso said. "He preferred for the government to be the one that did the work. So they would receive the locations where the gunmen for the Beltráns were located; this was given to the federal police with which there was a relationship already."

On April 30, three months after Mochomo's arrest, the simmering tension boiled over. A crew of federal police working for El Chapo rolled up to a home in Culiacán's Guadalupe neighborhood in an attempt to arrest or neutralize Beltrán Leyva men who were hiding out there. The gunmen opened fire on the cops, the cops returned fire, and suddenly Culiacán went up in flames as hostilities moved into the open.

In the first eleven days of May, the city saw fifty-two murders. The papers began running tallies of the dead reminiscent of casualty reports printed in the United States during the height of the war in Iraq:

May 5

1. Miguel Ángel Santa Cruz Armendaris, 45, commander of the State Ministerial Police
2. Candelario Baldenegro Leyva, 30

May 6

3. Alberto Javier Olivera López, 45, officer with the Directorate of Protective Services
4. Jaime Sarabia Zamora, 30
5. Guadalupe Inzunza Moreno, 35–45
6. José Manuel Peña López, 40, agent of the State Ministerial Police
7. Héctor Olguín Urías, 22

May 7

8. Unidentified, in Costa Rica [a neighborhood of Culiacán]
9. Unidentified, in Costa Rica
10. Efraín González López, 20

May 8

11. Patricia Córdoba
12. Modesto Beltrán Beltrán, 80
13. Lucrecio Almodóvar Elizalde, 40
14. Álvaro Lugo Cárdenas, 30
15. Arturo Meza Cázares
16. Édgar Guzmán López
17. César Ariel Loera Guzmán

Édgar Guzmán López. César Ariel Loera Guzmán. Those last deaths hit close to home for El Chapo. On May 8, just after 8:30 p.m., El Chapo's son Édgar—the second boy born to his second wife, Griselda López Pérez—pulled into the parking lot of the City Club supermarket in Tres Rios, a ritzy neighborhood of malls and mansions, accompanied by his cousin, César Ariel Loera Guzmán. Pulling their car up next to another car where two friends were standing—including Arturo Meza Cázares, son of the powerful money launderer Blanca Cázares—Édgar and César greeted their pals and stood there chatting in the warm night air.

They had only been there a few minutes before a convoy of five pickup trucks roared into the parking lot, the drivers screeching to a halt about thirty feet away from the young friends. At least twenty gunmen in tactical vests piled out of the trucks, leveled their AK-47s, and let loose with a hail of bullets. One of the attackers raised a rocket launcher to his shoulder and fired toward the victims, but the projectile veered off course and exploded against the wall of the supermarket across the parking lot.

The withering gunfire cut down the three young narco heirs instantly, while the fourth young man managed to dash across the parking lot and take cover in the shopping center, leaving a trail of blood behind him as the attackers raked his path with gunfire, damaging nearly two dozen vehicles in the process.

In a photo taken of the crime scene that night, Édgar can be seen facedown where he fell, blood pooling around his head, his car peppered with bullet holes. Investigators found at least one handgun on one of the victims, but it was unclear if they had managed to get off a shot at their attackers.

At the time, blame for the murder of Édgar Guzmán López and his friends fell squarely and quite reasonably at the feet of the Beltrán Leyva brothers. But according to local reporter and fixer Miguel Ángel Vega, the attack may have actually been a case of mistaken identity, carried out by gunmen loyal to El Chapo, who were so on edge that, upon seeing a couple of wealthy young men in late-model cars, they opened fire without a second thought. According to the lore that has sprung up in the years since Édgar's death, El Chapo was so devastated that he dispatched runners to buy up all the roses in Culiacán on the day of the funeral.

The killings continued.

May 9

18. Guadalupe Félix Munguía
19. Unidentified
20. Unidentified
21. Unidentified
22. Unidentified
23. Unidentified
24. Unidentified
25. Raymundo Velarde Urías, 35

May 10

26. César Manuel Armenta Franco, 25
27. Yani Gualberto Montoya Sánchez, 29
28. Paúl Román, 17
29. Jesús Sillas Zepeta, 35

May 11

30. Plácido Bruno Esteban, 60
31. Unidentified, decapitated
32. Alberto Taniyama Palazuelos, 38
33. Heracleo Sóto Félix, 30
34. Román Vidaca Robles, approximately 30

On May 11, a team of *federales* cornered a cousin of El Chapo, along with five gunmen, in a home in Culiacán. Following a shoot-out, the cops arrested the cousin and his men, and seized sixteen assault rifles, three grenades, more than one hundred magazines, and thousands of rounds of ammo.

Days later, on May 13, the federal police and the army launched a joint operation dubbed "Operation Culiacán-Navolato," mobilizing nearly three thousand soldiers, *federales*, and Marines in Sinaloa and mounting street patrols in Culiacán. The cops and soldiers began raiding businesses suspected of ties to drug trafficking, and hitting safe houses where they found arsenals of automatic weapons. In the city of Guamúchil, gunmen attacked the headquarters of the State Ministerial Police, spraying the building with gunfire from AK-47s and AR-15s, and tossing a couple of grenades. In an effort to disrupt illicit communications, soldiers dismantled twenty-three high-frequency radio antennas atop La Chiva, a mountain overlooking the city.

Splashed across the front page of one of the major daily newspapers in Culiacán that day was a grim declaration: ES LA GUERRA. It's war.

Just as in Juárez, the addition of a third belligerent force added fuel to the flames, and the bloodshed continued across the state.

May 13

   1. Celso García Morales, 30, shot in El Rosario

   2. Rodrigo León Sánchez, 19, stabbed in Mazatlán

   3. Gladis, 17, stabbed in Mazatlán

   4. Jimena Leticia, 2 months, stabbed in Mazatlán

   5. Rosendo Avilés Ramirez, 37, shot in Culiacán

May 14

   6. Julio César Saucedo Guzmán, 18, shot in Guamúchil

   7. Unidentified, shot in Elota

May 15

   8. Unidentified, shot in Elota

May 16

   9. Bonifacio Ruíz Gil, 24, shot in Choix

   10. Unidentified, approximately 30, in Mazatlán

   11. Juan Alonso Guerrero Fernández, 34, shot in Guasave

May 17

   12. Abel Castelo Baldenegro, 37, stabbed in Culiacán

   13. Unidentified, shot in Culiacán

   14. Unidentified, shot in Culiacán

   15. Jonathan Dahary Ibarra Parra, 19, beaten to death in Culiacán

   16. José Luís López Pérez, 57, shot in Culiacán

May 18

   17. César Omar Beltrán Flores, 29, shot in Culiacán

   18. Javier Alberto Chang Valle, shot in Guamúchil

May 19

   19. Eligio Duarte Araujo, 24, shot in Culiacán

   20. Unidentified, shot in Culiacán

   21. José Luis Beltrán Lafarga, shot in Guasave

22. Jesús Antonio López García, 39, shot in Guasave

23. Francisco Omar Olivarría Palma, 40, shot in El Fuerte

24. Armando Zavala Osuna, 47, shot in Mazatlán

May 20

25. Unidentified, *embolsado* [bagged], shot in Ahome

May 21

26. Luis Alberto Zamora, 27, shot in Culiacán

27. Urbano López López, 39, shot in Sinaloa de Leyva

May 22

28. Héctor Javier Doblantes Avendaño, 21, shot in Culiacán

29. Miguel Antonio Carrillo Gámez, 23 shot in Culiacán

30. Juan Fernando Zavala Peraza, 23, shot in Culiacán

31. Guillermo Cabada Zazueta, 32, shot in Culiacán

32. Amadeo Vega Vergara, 35, shot and decapitated in Culiacán

33. Hugo Abelardo Aispuro Aispuro, 27, shot in Culiacán

34. Unidentified

35. Unidentified, approximately 35, beaten to death in Mocorito

May 24

36. Miguel Ángel Sánchez Bobadilla, 46, shot in Culiacán

May 25

37. Ignacio Juárez Romero, dismembered in Culiacán

On the opinion page of *El Debate de Sinaloa*, the editors placed a photo of a window riddled with bullets. WELCOME TO CULIACÁN, the head-line read.

• • •

Many residents of Sinaloa will tell you that, in the old days, if you kept out of trouble you'd be all right. This has echoes of the government's sinister tendency to cast any victim of gun violence as a hood who had it coming; keep your head down and your nose clean and it'll be okay, and if you're not okay, you must not have kept your head down and your nose clean, right? But I've heard it from enough people that there has got to be some truth to it. In the spring of 2008, however, bullets were flying so thick that innocents started to get caught in the crossfire, or snatched off the street and dumped in some *pozole* barrel or mass grave outside the city.

Cops were a constant target. If they worked for El Chapo, the Beltrán Leyvas were gunning for them; if they worked for the Beltrán Leyvas, El Chapo's people were gunning for them; if they were honest cops, everyone was gunning for them. It got to the point where if you saw a police officer ordering lunch at your favorite taco stand, you'd go to the one down the block, recalls Fernando Brito, a photographer who was shooting for the newspaper *El Debate* when hostilities broke out between the two factions in 2008.

When he started as a photographer, Brito saw a side to his hometown that he had previously only known by rumor, or whispered innuendo. Born in Culiacán in 1975, and growing up here in the 1980s and 1990s, he came of age in something of a bubble; the narco stuff was always present, but for him it was a low buzz in the background, something he never paid much attention to. But now his job required him to see his city in a grim new light.

"I didn't realize what was happening in Culiacán," said Brito in a blend of Spanish and English, leaning forward in his chair and widening his eyes for emphasis now and again. "Since I entered to work on the newspaper, I realized that. And I knew about every part of Culiacán with that work. I went to every part of Culiacán because of murder."

Taking shelter in the air-conditioned lobby of my hotel on a blisteringly hot and humid mid-August day in downtown Culiacán, Brito runs his hands through his salt-and-pepper beard and adjusts his glasses as he describes the toll this work took on him.

"Every year was increasing the violence," he told me. "The first year I was working is like 470 [murders] just like that. The second year, it's like 500 [murders], just like that. In 2008, the violence was—it was a boom of the violence."

For news chasers like Brito, it was a busy time. And it left its mark.

"If they call me at three a.m., if they call me every hour, I go," he said. "It [made] me very sad, to see all those bodies. I never think [about] the body, I always think on their families."

The constant stress began to take its toll. He began to drink heavily, began to exhibit symptoms that he would, years later, recognize as telltale signs of post-traumatic stress disorder.

"You never are quiet, relaxed," he says. "Always tense, always thinking, looking. And that is not life."

To get a sense of the scale and timeline of the violence, I headed one day in August 2019 to the General Historical Archive in downtown Culiacán, a state-run organization whose preservation of local archives includes daily copies of Sinaloan newspapers bound up in great leather tomes. It's a sleepy place around a large stone courtyard, and the archivists were happy to help, fetching papers from this or that month, this or that year, and giving me tips about which paper I should trust most. Donning latex gloves and a face mask to protect the brittle pages from my breath and fingerprints, I dove in, starting with a volume containing the daily copies of *Noroeste* (less reliable than *Riodoce*, more reliable than *El Debate*, they tell me) from May 2008.

Pawing through the month's papers page by page, it is startling to pinpoint the explosion of violence. One day, crime coverage is limited to *La Nota Roja*, or the red news, the section of Mexican newspapers dedicated to splashy crime stories. The next, it's all over the front page, day in and day out. Shoot-outs, assassinations, bodies turning up left and right with skulls pierced by bullets, showing signs of torture. The well-worn truism "if it bleeds it leads" is particularly apt in Mexico, where gory pictures are splashed on front pages and strung up on newsstands, the headlines announced balefully by paper vendors hawking copies at traffic islands or on street corners.

This is life in a low-intensity war: you go about your life, obeying the local codes that keep you out of trouble, until the violence overwhelms everything. Eventually, hopefully, life returns to something like normal. But each time it reaches that boiling point, it chips away a little at the belief that there's really any way to stay safe.

• • •

It was a time of death and chaos for anyone involved in the drug trade in Culiacán, even those not actively fighting for one side or the other, according to one trafficker named Antonio.* Antonio grew up south of the city and started working in the drug trade in the early 2000s, moving mari-juana and heroin with a small crew that functioned semi-independently but maintained good relations with—and received protection from—the faction of El Mayo. Despite having no real dog in the fight, Antonio re-calls the constant fear that he would inadvertently find himself targeted by one side or the other, or get caught in an ambush alongside someone more involved than himself.

"You never knew which people to get close to because you never knew which people had stayed with Arturo Beltrán and you never knew which people had stayed with El Chapo's people," he said over a meal of french fries and cheeseburgers at a strip mall McDonald's on the outskirts of Cu-liacán. "There were many deaths. If you were in a place like we're in now, they'd arrive to kill someone and they'd kill innocent people eating."

To make matters worse—for people like Antonio, that is—the fight-ing was bad for business.

"For us it was a year of *vacas flacas* [skinny cows], as they say," he recalled. "You had to go around very carefully. There was a lot of loss of money, of product, of lives, and such."

Antonio managed to survive those years, and he continues to smug-gle marijuana and heroin. But for Pedro and Junior Flores, the identical twin brothers from Chicago, the war was the final straw. The brothers had been an integral part of El Chapo's stateside distribution network since the early 2000s and key associates of El Chapo in Mexico since their ar-rival in Guadalajara in 2005. They had been making tens of millions of dollars a year moving El Chapo's coke, heroin, and meth north and sell-ing it to wholesalers across the United States. But by 2008, the danger of narco life was beginning to wear thin.

With notable exceptions, most of the smugglers in El Chapo and El Mayo's orbit had always had a reputation for restraint that their ri-vals lacked, cognizant of the fact that dead bodies brought scrutiny, and scrutiny brought heat, and heat forced even the most compliant and cor-rupt authorities to take some kind of action against drug trafficking. But whereas El Chapo, El Mayo, and their allies had been willing to roll their sleeves up and dish out deadly violence when they needed or wanted to, Pedro and Junior had never shared that willingness to solve problems through bloodshed. In the years since they'd arrived—however violent their initial time in Mexico had been—they had continued to avoid the bloodier aspects of their profession, even as this typically deadly business made them rich men.

But now that El Chapo was at war with the Beltrán Leyvas, bodies were dropping in Culiacán, and traffickers who had once worked with both El Chapo and the Beltrán Leyvas as one were forced to make a choice. The leaders of both factions began calling to demand loyalty from their various distributors, smugglers, gunmen, and corrupt cops and soldiers. The warning to the Flores twins came directly from El Mayo, who told them during a business meeting that, if they wanted to continue working for him and El Chapo—and, it was implied to continue living—their relationship with the Beltrán Leyva brothers was finished as of that day. El Mayo made it clear; there would not be a second warning.

Pedro and Junior were in a bind. Until this point they had been allowed to operate in a "sweet spot," Pedro said, focusing only on money and ignoring the gunplay and political intrigue around them. Adding to their stress levels, Pedro was about to become a dad. The twins' father, Margarito Sr., had been in prison when the twins were born, and they knew the hardship of growing up without a dad around.

"My wife became pregnant in 2008, and I began to think about our future or the lack of a future and the life I was living," he said. "I couldn't promise my family tomorrow, you know. I couldn't see a future with them. I couldn't even imagine being a husband or a father to my children, to my unborn children."

It was time to look for a way out. They would be risking their lives if they continued working for one side or the other involved in the Sinaloa civil war. The only other option they saw was to become informants for the DEA; they'd be risking their lives doing this, perhaps even more so than by simply picking a side, but if they had to risk their lives, they figured they might as well choose an avenue that provided a means to escape the drug trade once and for all.

Over the decade in which the twins had run their business, they had imported a staggering sixty tons of cocaine into the United States and distributed it in more than a dozen cities, raking in countless millions of dollars and helping El Chapo and El Mayo maintain dominance in the U.S. drug market. They knew the feds would be interested due to the scale of their criminal misdeeds, which made them fantastic informants, but which also heightened the risk of spending more time than they would like to behind bars, should they make it out alive at all. To have any shot at getting out of prison in this lifetime, they were going to need to give the DEA their full cooperation. That would mean not just incriminating the bosses and their gunmen down in Mexico; they would also need to give up their own ill-gotten wealth, and they would have to hand over their friends, their workers, people who had served them loyally for years.

The brothers had been on the DEA's radar for several years now, largely due to a federal indictment in Wisconsin, the one that had originally prompted them to flee to Mexico in 2005. But for years, the DEA had been in the dark as to the full extent of the Flores network. That began to change in the summer of 2007, when a police informant made a controlled buy of fifty grams of heroin from a West Side Chicago dealer. As investigators worked that case, they moved higher up the food chain to another dealer pushing a bit more weight, and in early 2008, an informant recorded the second dealer on a phone call talking business with Pedro Flores.

Despite having a growing case against the Flores twins, the DEA had little way of reaching them in Mexico. Then, in the spring of 2008, a lawyer for the brothers based in Chicago knocked on the DEA's door and told the agency they wanted to cooperate.

• • •

It's not an easy decision to cooperate with the DEA. It's not so much that it goes against a criminal code of secrecy—snitching in Mexico is deadly for normal folks, but for the top traffickers it's just called doing business. But turning yourself in requires total surrender, with no guarantee that you will benefit personally. When an informant as high-ranking as Pedro or Junior turns himself in, he still has to face the music, typically by pleading guilty and hoping that their handlers will prevail upon the judge to grant a more lenient sentence in light of cooperation. Often-times sentencing is delayed for years as cooperators continue to provide useful intel, and only ends once investigators decide they've given enough to earn a shot at a second chance. But Pedro and Junior had been trafficking tons, literal tons, of coke and heroin for the better part of a decade; the DEA assured them that they would not walk away from this without serving significant time in prison, and that a judge could always ignore any recommendation for a lighter sentence. But the twins saw it as their only way out, and threw themselves at the mercy of the U.S. government.

From the time that they began cooperating with the DEA, the twins led a double life, arranging drug shipments and then feeding the information to their handlers, leading to the seizure of more than 250 kilos of cocaine and $4 million in cash. Pedro and Junior were forced to play a dangerous game as double agents: their handlers demanded total honesty, but if every one of their shipments ended up in the hands of federal agents, their suppliers in Mexico might start to wonder why the golden boys from Chicago were suddenly having such an unlucky streak. So, in an attempt to walk the tightrope, the brothers continued to distribute the cartel's kilos, neglecting now and again to tell their handlers.

"The whole timing of it was delicate," Pedro said. "The war kind of made things worse, and I felt like at any moment if I told El Chapo and Mayo that I wasn't going to receive drugs it would be weird to them. They would find that rare, because it never happened. I was afraid they might think I was choosing the other side."

As long as they remained in Mexico, with zero backup from the DEA, any suspicion on El Chapo's part would likely mean certain death. On several occasions, this led them to receive shipments of drugs whether they liked it or not. Once, Pedro said, after he accepted a load of heroin, he sold five kilos, and then threw another eight kilos, worth about $400,000, in the trash.

"I started having a little like, guilt about picking up these kilos, and I figured man, you know, if they would find them in my possession, I would be in more trouble," Pedro said. "I mean, it was me and my brother out there alone. We didn't have a DEA SWAT team in the next room, ready to come save us if something went wrong. We were forced to make these decisions split, at the moment."

. . .

Throughout the summer and into the fall of 2008, the DEA made bust after monumental bust based on the information that the twins were feeding them. But what their handlers at the DEA really wanted was hard evidence linking El Chapo and his partners to actual drug shipments in the United States. They needed information that could lead to a solid indictment in federal court so that, in the event that Mexican law enforcement captured El Chapo and the government agreed to extradite him, prosecutors could have more to convict him on than just the say-so of cooperating narcos. Now the final phase of Pedro and Junior's work as moles had begun, an attempt to get El Chapo himself on record. It was a daunting task, and some DEA agents expressed doubt that El Chapo would ever be dumb enough to get on the phone and discuss business. But the twins were trying nonetheless.

On November 9, 2008, just after 6 p.m., Junior Flores dialed a number into his phone, plugged an earpiece into a cheap voice recorder purchased at a Radio Shack in Mexico City, and hit the record button as Pedro stood by his side, listening nervously.

"*Adelante, diga*," Junior said. "Go ahead, tell me."

On the other end, Jesús Alfredo Guzmán Salazar—El Chapo's second son from his first marriage, better known as Alfredillo—answered. Junior was calling to discuss a shipment of heroin to Chicago, but Alfredillo seemed unprepared.

"Fuck, are you going to give it to me now, or, or, or, later?" Alfredillo stammered, a verbal tic that he shared with his father.

Before Junior and Alfredillo could get to the point, a cell phone started ringing in Pedro's pocket, as he listened to his brother speak. In a panic, Pedro realized who was calling: their DEA handler. He quickly silenced his phone. If you want to stay cool while your brother is recording incriminating phone calls from the son of the world's most wanted drug lord, it's best not to have the DEA calling you in the middle of it.

Without skipping a beat, Junior continued the conversation with

Alfredillo, exchanging the phone numbers for a pair of couriers who would complete the transaction in Chicago. In just one minute and fifteen seconds, they had recorded Alfredillo as he implicated himself in a million-dollar heroin deal.

On November 13, three days after the conversation between Junior and El Chapo's son, a courier working for Alfredillo drove out to a suburb of Chicago to deliver twenty kilos of heroin to an undercover DEA agent posing as a courier for the Flores brothers. Later that day, a runner working for El Mayo's son Vicente "Vicentillo" Zambada made another delivery, this one of eight kilos of heroin, to another undercover DEA agent. Over the next forty-eight hours, the twins pestered Alfredillo several times to remind his father to call them, and in the meantime complained to anyone who would listen that Vicentillo and El Mayo's dope was trash, only 40 percent pure, and that El Chapo's heroin was a bit better.

At 8:32 p.m. on November 15, El Chapo called Pedro Flores. After days of waiting for the call, Pedro found himself in a room full of people, unable to speak freely. He intentionally missed the call, stepped away from the group he was with for a more quiet spot, and two minutes after the first call, El Chapo rang again. This time, Pedro was ready with his recorder.

El Chapo greeted Pedro cheerfully and they made small talk for a bit, with Pedro at one point briefly correcting El Chapo when he got Pedro mixed up with his twin brother. Then they got down to business.

"Look, I'm bothering you because of what I picked up the other day," Pedro said. "I want to ask you for a favor."

"*Dime*," El Chapo replied. "Tell me."

"Do you think we can work something out where you deduct [$5,000 per kilo] from that for me?" Pedro asked

"What did we agree on?" El Chapo asked.

"You're giving it to me for 55 [$55,000 per kilo]," Pedro told him.

"How much are you going to pay for it?" El Chapo asked.

For about a minute, the two hashed out details, Pedro repeating himself multiple times for El Chapo, who seemed to be having a hard time hearing. After about half a minute of this, they came to an agreement when Pedro offered to pay up front the next day in exchange for a discount.

"All right, then, uh, I'll pick up the money tomorrow," El Chapo said. "That price is fine."

"Yeah? Okay," Pedro said. After a brief back-and-forth over logistics, El Chapo said he had to speak with someone, that he'd call back. In the next conversation, about ten minutes later, Pedro baited El Chapo into discussing business even more openly than in the previous call.

"I was going to ask you, I only have three [kilos] left," he said. "When do you think we can get more?"

This took El Chapo by surprise. In a recent conversation, the twins, caught between their suppliers and the DEA, had tried to reduce the amount of heroin they were receiving in Chicago, and had downplayed the number of kilos they could move. Now he was saying he had already run through most of what El Chapo had just sent him.

"What the fuck, man? Didn't you just say you could only get rid of a little bit?" El Chapo exclaimed.

"Ah, the truth is, these turned out good, I can't lie," Pedro said quickly, hoping to deflect suspicion with bemused confidence.

"How many [kilos] can you get rid of in a month?" El Chapo asked.

"If you want, right now we're doing about forty," Pedro replied.

"Oh, that's good," said El Chapo, pleasant as ever. "Hey, has anyone else sent you [a shipment]? Because this guy told me that they were going to send you."

Throughout the past couple of days, in multiple conversations, the twins had been laying the groundwork to not only get El Chapo discussing drug shipments but also to get him admitting to a larger conspiracy, one that included El Mayo. By acknowledging other traffickers, he'd walked right into their trap.

Over the next two weeks, the twins planned their escape, all while recording more and more phone calls with high-ranking traffickers. They got Vicentillo Zambada discussing the purchase of M16 rifles with grenade launchers; they got El Chapo's secretary discussing a shipment of hundreds of kilos of coke to Los Angeles; on one call, they managed to get their old friend Alfredo Vasquez, the train guru, to discuss at length El Chapo's use of planes and submarines to move drugs, while also negotiating a one-ton load of coke that the DEA would later seize in LA.

On November 30, 2008, Pedro and Junior finally escaped the nightmare balancing act, flew to the United States, and threw themselves at the mercy of the U.S. Department of Justice. Their wives, hip to the plot, piled into their SUVs and headed for the border, eventually crossing over safely into the United States.

They were now in for a new challenge: the lives of federal snitches. Again the DEA demanded total openness, requiring them to inform not just on El Chapo but also on longtime friends and accomplices with whom they'd worked in Chicago going back to their early days in the drug trade. If they wanted to avoid life in prison, it was their only option, and they cooperated willingly. But they also made serious missteps and tried to hide a bit of money on the side in case their families needed it; they didn't do a very good job of hiding it: shortly before he went to prison in the States, Pedro bought for his wife a parting gift in the form of a $200,000 Bentley. The DEA found out, confiscated the car, but would later downplay such transgressions. These were ethical lapses that might have sunk other informants, but when the DEA and federal prosecutors discovered the deception, they were willing to overlook it given the unparalleled amount of information they were getting from the brothers.

The Flores twins had escaped with their lives, and their wives and children were safe. But they didn't make it out of the drug trade unscathed. A few months after they turned themselves in, Pedro and Junior's father, Margarito Flores Sr., went to Mexico, against the advice of the brothers' DEA handlers. Within days, he vanished. The only trace of him was a note, affixed to his abandoned car, swearing revenge on the brothers for talking to the DEA.

But this revenge couldn't stop what the twins had set in motion. Less than a year later, a grand jury in Chicago issued an indictment—based largely on the recordings that the twins had made—charging El Chapo, El Mayo, Vicentillo Zambada, Alfredillo Guzmán, and more than half a dozen others with trafficking enough drugs and weapons to put them all behind bars in the United States for life. Now the authorities just needed to catch them.

When it finally came time for the Flores brothers to be sentenced in

2015, more than six years after they began cooperating, the twins each received fourteen years in prison. Not a bad sentence for a pair who personally oversaw the importation of sixty tons of cocaine into the United States.

. . .

As the Flores twins were making their getaway, the killings in Sinaloa continued.

Most of El Chapo's closest aides had stuck by his side, including the hit man Barbarino, the owner of the ranch where he had lain low after his escape in 2001; Dámaso López, the former prison official and now one of his most trusted aides; the security chief known as El Negro, whose team of ex-military sicarios now formed the core of El Chapo's armed forces; and Memín, the former special-forces soldier joined El Chapo's security detail back in 2004; they all stuck by El Chapo. Memín in particular was moving up in the world. He'd graduated from working security and been promoted again and again, working for a time to coordinate cocaine shipments from Honduras to Sinaloa, and then as the main bodyguard for Iván Archivaldo Guzmán Salazar and his brother Alfredillo, El Chapo's eldest sons. The two *Chapitos*, or Little El Chapos, now in their late twenties, had been actively involved in their father's business for several years, although they were more fond of partying and flaunting their wealth than their father ever had been, looking more like handsome young socialites than their father, who was still a highlander, a *serrano*, at heart.

But some high-ranking and formerly loyal men crossed over to the other side. The plaza boss in the northern Sinaloan cities of Guasave and Los Mochis, a longtime trafficker nicknamed El Chapo Isidro, sided with the Beltráns, killing or expelling El Chapo's men and ruling the city through cruelty and fear. In Navolato, the hometown of the Carrillo-Fuentes family, the Beltrán Leyvas struck an alliance with the remnants of El Viceroy's people, as well as with the Zetas, and the city became a home base for cells of Zetas hit men who began to recruit there.

When Memín wasn't overseeing security for the *Chapitos*, he was helping his boss, the hit man known as El Negro, wage war on El Chapo's enemies. Throughout 2008 and 2009, tit-for-tat murders and kidnappings occurred throughout the state as gunmen from each faction picked one another off on street corners and mountain roads, or kicked down one another's doors to spill blood where they lived. From time to time, however, the two sides would engage in brutal skirmishes, sustained gun battles in broad daylight that inflicted heavy casualties.

On December 8, 2009, Memín took part in a concerted attack on El Chapo Isidro's home base in the city of Guasave, riding along in a convoy of armored pickup trucks and luxury SUVs, each painted with an X to avoid friendly fire. As the convoy rolled through the town of El Burrión, just southeast of Guasave, they fell into a trap. Gunmen working for El Chapo Isidro had posted up at a gas station along the road and opened fire on Memín's convoy, raking the vehicles with machine-gun fire.

With bullets slamming into his windshield, Memín careened to the side of the road as his comrades jumped out of their vehicles armed to the teeth with AK-47s, AR-15s, grenade launchers, and a few Barrett .50-caliber sniper rifles, and returned fire. For about twenty minutes, the area echoed with the *rat-a-tat-tat* of automatic gunfire, bullets flying left and right, leaving cars and walls pockmarked. By the time the smoke cleared, two of Memín's gunmen were injured, although none seriously. On the other side, more than half a dozen of Isidro's men lay dead.

"Little by little, it died down," Memín recalled matter-of-factly. "We went back to Culiacán."

The other side had succeeded in stopping the attack on Guasave, but at a heavy cost. Later that day, bodies could still be seen splayed out on the ground, covered by tarps, while bullet-riddled trucks—some with a telltale X spray painted on the side—sat abandoned in the road, which was littered with broken glass and spent shell casings.

· · ·

On December 11, 2009, Arturo Beltrán Leyva threw a lavish Christmas party for himself at a mansion inside an elite, gated community outside Cuernavaca, the state capital of Morelos, in central Mexico. In the months leading up to that day, his group had been suffering losses at home in Sinaloa, while consolidating control farther afield, in strongholds in strategic areas of the Mexico-U.S areas close to the border. Recently, Arturo had been on the offensive, lashing out at El Chapo and El Mayo, and strengthening his control of trafficking routes through the states of Nayarit, Guerrero, and Morelos, where his hit men dumped bodies and severed heads affixed with *narcomantas* announcing the intentions of the self-titled "Jefe de Jefes."

But now it was time for a party, and Arturo spared no expense: dozens of escorts sashayed among the guests, while the Grammy Award–winning accordionist Ramón Ayala and his band crooned the night away. Like his brother Mochomo, Arturo apparently thought he was so above the law that he did not need to lie low.

He was wrong.

That evening, as the party raged, a unit of Mexican Marines operating on a tip from U.S. intelligence stormed the property, prompting a vicious gun battle with Arturo's bodyguards that left three gunmen dead, along with one innocent bystander. When the Marines finally took the house, they arrested eleven gunmen and found a stash of sixteen assault rifles, four pistols, and nearly two thousand rounds of ammunition, along with more than a quarter of a million dollars in cash.

Arturo slipped away, but he didn't make it far. Less than a week later, on December 16, the military cornered him once more at another luxury development outside of Cuernavaca, where more than four hundred Marines in face masks and full battle gear swarmed into the complex as a pair of attack helicopters circled overhead. In a desperate bid to keep the soldiers at bay, Arturo's men threw more than twenty fragmentation grenades. Amid the chaos, Melquisedet Angulo Córdova, a petty officer with the naval special forces, was mortally wounded.

This time, Arturo did not escape. When the shooting stopped, he lay dead, cut down in hails of gunfire along with six of his men. The triumphant Marines took their revenge on his mangled corpse, pulling his pants down to his calves to expose tighty whities and numerous bullet wounds. They plastered 500-peso notes to his bloody body and took gruesome photos later leaked to the press that showed his face destroyed by gunfire, both arms splayed out at grotesquely unnatural angles.

For more than a decade, there was speculation about how the Marines finally managed to locate Arturo. Had El Chapo learned of his location and sold him out? Had some party vendor or neighbor dropped a dime in hopes of cashing in on the reward for his capture? Had the Mexican government simply decided his time had come?

We know now. According to recently unsealed court documents, the information about Arturo's location came from none other than Édgar Valdez Villareal, La Barbie, the American cutthroat who had fought on behalf of the Beltrán Leyvas and El Chapo in Tamaulipas and Nuevo León in the early 2000s, before relocating to Acapulco, a resort town on the Pacific Coast in Guerrero. Like the Flores twins, La Barbie appears to have flipped around the time of the sudden explosion of violence between his bosses, and had begun talking to agents with the DEA. Perhaps he was hoping to find a way to negotiate surrender and stay alive, or perhaps he figured he could rise to take the place of the Beltrán Leyvas if he handed them over on a platter.

La Barbie's handlers eagerly passed the information to contacts in the Mexican Army, but for unexplained reasons, the Army failed to move quickly. So instead, they passed the tip along to the Mexican Marines, or SEMAR, a highly trained unit of special-operations troops who had begun carving out a role for themselves in the drug war. The Marines moved quickly and decisively, earning praise from U.S. diplomats, but raised an uncomfortable question: If the army had the tip before the Marines, why had its officers failed to act?

"Its success puts the Army (SEDENA) in the difficult position of explaining why it has been reluctant to act on good intelligence and conduct operations against high-level targets," an official wrote in a classified diplomatic cable a few days later.

In a meeting with U.S. officials weeks before the raid, Mexican defense secretary General Guillermo Galván Galván, the top army officer in the country, had acknowledged that the increased level of intel sharing between the two nations would be "worthless without a capable reaction force." Now it appeared the United States had found their capable reaction force, by sidestepping the army and giving the job to the Marines. Over the next few years, U.S. federal agents in Mexico would increasingly use the elite unit as their boots on the ground when they had actionable information and needed a partner who could get the job done, no matter who got in the way.

. . .

On December 21, four days after Arturo's death, the secretary of the navy stood at the grave of Ensign Melquisedet Angulo Córdova in Villahermosa, Tabasco, and with great solemnity presented a folded Mexican flag to his mother, Irma Córdova Palma. In the wake of the raid, Angulo was held up as a fallen martyr, a rare hero in a grimy war against a shadowy enemy marked by corruption, human rights abuses, and few victories. The government seemed aching to hold up an example of sacrifice, a model of iron-willed defiance of the criminals against whom President Calderón was supposedly waging war.

After laying Angulo to rest, the family of the martyr returned home to grieve in private. As they slept that night, a band of gunmen burst into the home and shot anything and anyone that moved, killing the dead man's mother, Irma; his aunt Josefa Angulo Flores; his sister Yolidabey Angulo Córdova; and his brother, Benito Angulo Córdova. The only survivor was a sister, whose name, prudently, was not released this time.

After the raid in Cuernavaca, President Calderón had hailed the death of Arturo Beltrán Leyva as a "convincing blow" to drug traffickers, the highest-ranking narco yet to fall in his campaign against the cartels. Days later, he spoke publicly one again, this time to condemn the slaughter of the family of the fallen officer.

"These contemptible events are proof of how unscrupulously organized crime operates, attacking innocent lives," Calderón thundered. "They can only strengthen us in our determination to banish this singular cancer."

Control of Arturo's faction passed to his brother, Héctor Beltrán Leyva, El Elegante. But their former network soon began to disintegrate and devour itself, a process that is still to this day in bloody fashion in Guerrero. But for the time being, El Elegante continued to wage war against his former compadre El Chapo.

Both factions still had a business to run, and profit prevailed over enmity in some areas of the country. This occurred most notably in the area around the lucrative border crossing in Nogales, Sonora, where in early 2010 crews loyal to both El Chapo and the Beltrán Leyvas appear to have struck an "unholy truce"—with the alleged help of the state attorney general of Sonora—in order to continue moving drugs across the border without attracting too much heat. But this was the exception: elsewhere, the war raged.

The killings in Tijuana continued.

The killings in Sinaloa continued.

The killings in Juárez continued.

11

A CITY BESIEGED

On a warm Wednesday evening in early September 2009, a team of gunmen calmly strode into Casa Aliviane, a rehab center located in the Bellavista neighborhood of Juárez, on a side street just a stone's throw from the Puente Internacional, the bridge spanning the Rio Grande and connecting Juárez to El Paso. Finding most of the residents in a meeting inside, the gunmen ushered them into a courtyard and ordered them to line up against a wall.

Casa Aliviane was home to some of the most desperate people in the city: addicts trying to get sober, alleged gang members trying to get off the streets, drug dealers who'd gotten hooked on their own product. Like many informal rehab centers in Mexico, it was a harsh, austere place, but for many who called it home it was a last hope. The outside walls were painted a vivid pink that belied the desperation inside.

Raising their automatic rifles, the gunmen took aim like a firing squad, and let loose. By the time the shooting subsided, eighteen people lay dead.

According to military officials, many of the victims of these attacks were members of Barrio Azteca, one of two major gangs banging it out on the city's streets on behalf of the Juárez Cartel. But as always, they offered no proof. For days, relatives of the murdered men stood vigil outside Casa Aliviane, weeping for their loved ones and demanding justice from President Calderón.

It was the fifth attack on a rehab center in a little over a year. The sixth attack came just two weeks later, on the eve of the 199th anniversary of Mexico's independence from Spain. As bells rang out across the country to mark "El Grito," the great cry of independence, a group of hit men strode into another rehab facility, Anexo de Vida—Annex of Life—and opened fire with automatic weapons. They tossed a grenade for good measure. According to varying accounts, between ten and thirteen people were slaughtered, including several staffers.

Even amid a tidal wave of violence, these brazen massacres at supposed safe havens marked a new level of brutality in Juárez. Some speculated that it was a concerted effort by street gangs to wipe out rival members or anyone who might be a potential recruit for their enemies. Others alleged that drug dealers had been using the centers as cover for illegal activities and made themselves targets. Still others, including Gustavo de la Rosa, a prominent local human rights activist, spoke darkly of a *limpieza social*, a social cleansing, being committed against poor, young, marginalized residents of the city. Many of these murders, de la Rosa told a reporter from the *Guardian*, were "planned assassinations of the unwanted."

"And if we look at exactly how they are done," de la Rosa said, "they are experts in killing characteristic of training by the army or police."

From the early days of Calderón's war on Juárez, government officials often did little to hide their disdain for murder victims. In a press conference in April 2008, as the violence was just revving up, General Jorge Juárez Loera, commander of the 11th Military Zone, scolded reporters for casting victims in an overly sympathetic light.

"I would like to see journalists change their stories and instead of 'one more murder victim' they should write 'one less criminal.'"

. . .

By late 2009, Juárez was in a state of heavily militarized anarchy, or as de la Rosa called it, "martial law without the law."

It would get worse. On January 31, 2010, a team of Barrio Azteca gunmen barged into a house in Villas de Salvárcar, a far-flung *colonia* clinging to the southeastern outskirts of Juárez, where the city's sprawl trails south along the border with Texas.

Informed by their boss that the party was a gathering of members of the *Artistas Asesinos*, sworn enemies of the Aztecas and allied with El Chapo, the gunmen screeched to a halt outside the party just after 11:30 p.m. As many as two dozen hit men poured out of the SUVs and dashed inside. At first there was confusion, as the gunmen looked upon the gathering. These were not the hardened gangsters of the Artist Assassins, but rather a group of teens, some of whom were members of a youth football team nicknamed the Double A's. Artist Assassins, Double A's. Someone had made a mistake.

"This isn't them," one of the gunmen cried. "It's a bunch of kids!"

"Fuck it," another replied. "We're here."

It was as simple as that. They'd already made the trip out there.

By the time the gunmen roared off in their SUVs, fifteen people lay dead or dying in the house that a neighbor had once described as the happiest home on the block. All but five of the victims were under the age of twenty.

·   ·   ·

Nacim Ortiz knew things had gotten bad the first time he saw a mutilated corpse hanging from a highway overpass.

Like so many residents of Juárez and El Paso, Ortiz remembers a time when the two cities functioned as one, residents paying little attention to the border as they made daily crossings back and forth. Born in El Paso in 1990, Ortiz grew up in his grandmother's house in Juárez, traveling there almost every day from his mom's house. His first language was Spanish, and in school he estimated that at least half of his classmates lived in Juárez and made the trip across the border each day to attend school in El Paso.

"Growing up there, you didn't think twice about the whole border difference," Ortiz said. "It was just one giant city."

Ortiz now works as a professional musician in Brooklyn, and has been living away from the border region for years, but like any good *fron-*

terizero, he was eager to discuss his hometown at the drop of a hat, even with a stranger like me.

Ortiz, whose mother is from the United States and whose father is Mexican, recalls fondly his youth spent at his grandmother's house, but even then, years before the war, there was a dangerous undercurrent in the city. When Ortiz was six or seven, his uncle, the youngest brother of his father, vanished one night without a trace.

"All we knew is that they found his truck at a bus station, door wide open, and he was, he just disappeared," Ortiz says.

Despite this, he recalls his adolescence as a happy one. Like many residents of the El Paso/Juárez area not actively involved in the drug trade, the sudden explosion of violence in late 2007 took him by surprise, particularly because El Paso remained quiet, safe, and largely untouched by the growing mayhem across the Rio Grande. In El Paso, which even throughout the war had one of the lowest murder rates in the country, news coverage of the fighting just over the border in Juárez was less visceral than the coverage in Mexico, with the most grisly images left out. But on visits to see his grandmother—she refused to relocate to El Paso—Ortiz recalls seeing horrific videos shown on the news, or passed around online, so-called *narcovideos* recorded by the killers and published for all to see.

"They wanted people to know what they were doing," he says.

El Chapo undoubtedly shares a hefty portion of blame for the conflagration that erupted in Juárez, but it is also too simple to say the war in Juárez was just the result of one greedy man in his mountain hideout sending young men to seize territory from other young men working for another greedy man. Widespread violence like this has no face, and to the residents of Juárez, it was never clear who was fighting whom. In the end, what does it matter if you're killed by people nominally allied with one narco boss or another? "Everybody else was just pawns," Ortiz says. "Amid all the chaos and the darkness, it was just utter confusion."

With gunmen belonging to this or that street gang or cartel faction simultaneously shooting it out with one another and with Calderón's troops, Juárez began to collapse in on itself. Many areas of Mexico were racked by spasms of violence, but Juárez stood out. Nowhere else was the killing so brutal for so long. In 2008, nearly half of the six thousand reported drug-linked killings in Mexico took place in Juárez. By 2010, the murder rate there was ten times higher than the national average, earning Juárez the dubious honor of being among the world's most dangerous cities. It became a common trope for reporters to liken the bloodshed to Baghdad, which may have sounded like an exaggeration until someone set off a car bomb.

More than 99 percent of murders went unsolved, and the city morgue became so overwhelmed that it began to dispose of bodies in mass graves. The narcos of every faction had their own secret sites for dumping bodies. Then again, so did the soldiers who, frustrated by the absence of a functioning judiciary or actively taking sides, were known to shoot suspects and bury them in the desert, just like the narcos, under a thin layer of soil, for their bones to be picked clean by carrion birds and coyotes. Not that they limited themselves to shooting suspected drug dealers and cartel gunmen. If someone ends up dead, the assumption goes, they probably did something to deserve it. Who's going to check twice when someone's guilt has already been decided in the morning newspaper? Or as the journalist Alfredo Corchado once put it: "In Mexico, they kill you twice. . . . The first time with a bullet and then by character assassination."

No one knows just how many innocents ended up out there in the desert. To this day, the families of the disappeared are still digging up graves. Just 3 percent of alleged crimes committed by the military against civilians are ever investigated.

With the number of homicides in Juárez climbing by the day, the beleaguered residents were also forced to deal with skyrocketing levels of other violent crime as the police force relocated their headquarters to hotels heavily reinforced with sandbags and blast barriers. There the cops remained, pinned down and unwilling to leave the safety of their makeshift bunkers. Gangs of kidnappers roamed the streets, picking off anyone who looked like they might have enough money to bring a quick payday and forcing them to either call their families for ransom or driving them from ATM to ATM withdrawing cash.

The soldiers patrolling the streets were of little help, and many of them joined in on the frenzy, muscling in on kidnapping and extortion rackets. The arrest of some prominent drug traffickers, heralded by Calderón and his supporters as a marker of the campaign's success, only muddied the water more, as criminal networks fractured and the battle lines grew ever more confusing.

As violence and economic collapse tore their city apart, the residents of Juárez learned how to survive. For Nacim Ortiz, that meant getting out of Dodge, off to college in Boston. Many of his family members left, too, escaping to a life somewhere farther from the border.

"When it really started getting heavy and all, I left," he says. "A lot of my uncles basically moved to Chihuahua, they just went further south, because a lot of this stuff was happening just mainly around the border."

As the violence, combined with the ravages of the 2008 global financial crisis, hollowed out the city's industrial sector, Juárez lost nearly 100,000 jobs by 2009, and the number of families dependent on welfare programs doubled. In the first half of 2008, the influx of people moving across the border to El Paso was such that the housing market there remained stable, even as foreclosures hit a record high nationwide. By 2011, 300,000 *juarenses* had fled for their lives—a displacement nearly equal to the entire population of Pittsburgh—and as many as a quarter of the city's homes were left abandoned.

Not everyone could relocate, and not everyone was willing to. Sandra Ramírez Chávez, a social worker and mother of two daughters, stayed here and did youth outreach work in some of the roughest *colonias* throughout the most chaotic years. The threat of violence, whether random or targeted, remained a constant worry, a dull hum that occupied her thoughts as she found herself endlessly strategizing how she might survive if they came for her.

"We got through them with a lot of fear, a lot of paranoia," she said nearly a decade later, sitting in the air-conditioned cool of her office. "It was truly a city besieged."

· · ·

In the wake of the massacre of high-school students in Villas de Salvárcar, it appeared as if finally the people of Juárez, huddled in their homes for so long, had awoken from their terrified stupor. At the time, President

Calderón was on a state visit to Japan, and from Tokyo he dashed off a hasty statement labeling the young victims as gang members. When it became increasingly clear that this was not the case, some of the relatives focused their fury on the president, standing in front of the bloodstained home with a banner laying the blame at Calderón's feet: "Until we find who is responsible, you Mr. President are the assassin."

Unlike in the vast majority of homicides, the police managed to track down the shooters (or so they claimed), three men said to belong to the Barrio Azteca gang who ultimately received a combined total of 240 years in prison. (A fifth man was released from prison years later after a judge ruled that police officers had tortured him and forced him to sign a false confession. When police are under pressure to solve cases in Mexico, they often find sudden motivation and investigative zeal to track down suspects. Wrongful convictions are rampant, and due process is often delayed, when available at all.)

Calderón, stung by the criticism he'd received for his initial response, traveled to the city ten days later to announce the launch of a program he dubbed *Todos Somos Juárez*, or "We Are Juárez," aimed at confronting the social problems that lay at the root of the violence. The government set about building parks and soccer fields in outlying neighborhoods, a drastically belated push to insert communal space and greenery into areas that had sprung up with no planning to house newly arrived factory workers. Residents of Juárez formed councils known as *mesas* aimed at tackling issues of quotidian municipal governance. The security *mesa* in particular took on a crucial role, as citizens leery of the police and afraid to report crimes could now turn to the council when they had a problem, trusting their fellow civilians to pass along the information to uncorrupted officials.

In April 2010, the army finally left Juárez. After two years and countless deaths, it had become increasingly clear that long-term anti-crime work was not in their wheelhouse, and Calderón decided it was time for the cops to make another go of policing Juárez. The Federal Police launched an aggressive campaign to retake the city, arresting hundreds of suspected cartel members and cracking down on other criminals involved in kidnapping and extortion rings—along with more minor infractions like driving illegal vehicles. In April, the same month the army withdrew, the Associated Press ran an article declaring "victory" for El Chapo, citing federal agents in the United States and Mexico, as well as sources within the drug trade, who said that El Chapo was now responsible for the majority of cocaine moving through the plaza. But all the arrests by the newly invigorated federal cops and El Chapo's "victory" had little effect on the daily lives of the people of Juárez: 2010 was the worst year yet, with more than three thousand murders on the books by the end of December. The mayor of Juárez blamed the ongoing violence on street gangs squabbling over the "crumbs" of domestic drug sales territory.

When a train is barrelling along at full speed, it can take up to a mile of squealing brakes and flying sparks before it comes to a halt.

The government did slowly began to chip away at the senior leadership of the Juárez Cartel: in July 2011, police arrested José Antonio Acosta Hernández, alias "El Diego," a former cop himself and a leading enforcer for El Viceroy, who claimed to have ordered or participated in more than 1,500 killings. A brutish killer whose dead eyes glared out from under a heavy brow and a high forehead, El Diego took responsibility for some of the worst terrors inflicted on the city, including a car bomb rigged with ten pounds of C-4 that killed a paramedic, a doctor, and two federal agents. He also took responsibility for the massacre in Villas de Salvárcar. For all the blood on his hands, he said he regretted ordering the birthday massacre. He felt "bad," he said in a low monotone, that he'd sent his men to gun down innocents, describing the slaughter as "not worth it."

The same month as El Diego's arrest, the *federales* left town and handed control back to the municipal police, now under the command of Julián Leyzaola, a tough-talking ex-military officer with a handsome mug and stoic gaze who had served as chief of police in Tijuana since 2008. Leyzaola, who retired from the army as a lieutenant colonel, was widely lauded at the time for drastically reducing the level of violence in Tijuana. He had braved repeated assassination attempts and nonstop death threats while transforming the city's police department from a corrupt and sidelined joke into a muscular and effective crime-fighting force. Brash and overflowing with macho scorn for the norms of civil society and the criminal underworld alike, Leyzaola liked to publicly thumb his nose at the powerful narcos who had, until his arrival, effectively run Tijuana. Leyzaola claimed to have once turned down an offer of $80,000 a week from an emissary of El Chapo. But staff at the U.S. consulate in Tijuana expressed concern at reports that the real secret behind Leyzaola's success in crushing one cartel faction was him making a "look the other way" deal with a rival group considered to be more discreet. (Leyzaola denied the allegations.)

He also had a penchant for torturing detainees, intimidating cops who didn't see eye to eye with his brutal methods, and was said to have once arrived at a murder scene and punched a dead narco's corpse in the face. Human rights advocates rightly protested such abuses (particularly the abuses of living prisoners), but many in Tijuana and Juárez saw this as a price to pay for the defeat of the drug traffickers who had been wreaking havoc, undeterred, in their cities for years. When Leyzaola arrived in Juárez, narcos greeted the new top cop by dumping in a city street a mangled corpse affixed with a note sarcastically welcoming him to town. He received a more sincere welcome from business leaders and some *juarenses* desperate for a change. Within days of his arrival, reports surfaced of illegal detentions, torture, and summary executions of drug suspects. But he also made the fight against crime a personal campaign, handing out his card to downtown business owners and encouraging them to call him if they faced threats of extortion; when they called the number on the card, it was none other than Leyzaola who picked up the phone, a striking gesture in a city where mistrust of officials ran deep and the police were seen as one predator among many.

Slowly but surely, the fighting started to die down. In 2012, Juárez recorded fewer than eight hundred murders. Life began to return to the city's streets.

· · ·

There are rarely clean, satisfactory answers in the world of drug trafficking, particularly when it comes to finding causes for the rise and fall of widespread violence. Some, like state prosecutor Jorge Arnaldo Nava Lopez, say the solution to the crisis lay in tough law enforcement and anticorruption measures within the police and military, combined with a coordinated focus on social programs and civil-society initiatives like the *mesa* councils. Now the lead prosecutor for the northern district of Chihuahua, Nava Lopez helped spearhead an anti-kidnapping initiative that helped bring the numbers plummeting, from 290 in 2009 to just three reported kidnappings in 2016. Both numbers are probably far lower than the true figures for those years, but still, it was a dramatic improvement. While focusing on rebuilding the population's trust in the authorities, he struck hard at kidnappers, sending dozens of convicted abductors to prison for life. It was trust, he said, along with a good deal of brute force, that was key to turning the tide.

Others, like the late journalist Julián Cardona, argue that the deaths fell largely due to the withdrawal of the army. Cardona covered the worst of the violence for Reuters and later collaborated with the legendary borderland writer Charles Bowden on a book about those years. In writing and in various interviews over the years, he made a convincing case: one less belligerent force, less chaos, fewer murders.

Still others argue that El Chapo won the war and cut a deal with the government, allowing the feds to pursue his enemies in the name of peace, a grim coexistence between the forces of the state and the forces of El Chapo. It's less of a conspiracy theory than it sounds: the majority of major traffickers arrested in Juárez during the violence belonged to factions under the umbrella of the Juárez Cartel, an onslaught that left them significantly weakened and gave El Chapo's guys more room to operate without fear of rival hit men. There's ample evidence that the Sinaloa faction had high-ranking cops on their payroll, and powerful allies of El Chapo had contact with the government at that time—including the DEA, to whom they fed information on their rivals. As of this writing, Genaro García Luna, the former head of the Federal Investigations Agency and architect of Calderón's crusade against organized crime, is sitting in a federal jail in Brooklyn on charges of colluding with El Chapo. Numerous cops who worked under García Luna in those years have been arrested for working with the Sinaloans. Hard evidence of El Chapo cutting a deal with the state to take over Juárez remains elusive, and likely always will.

When awful things happen on the scale of the horror that overtook Juárez, we crave explanations, we crave answers, in order to know why it happened, to know how to prevent it in the future, and if prevention fails, to know how to solve the problem should a similar crisis explode on the scene once more. But reality, particularly in the world of black-market businesses and drug-related ultraviolence, is messy. It is likely that some combination of these scenarios took place: El Chapo, with the implicit backing of federal cops and soldiers, won the war for the trafficking routes through Juárez, while tough policing and a focus on social welfare helped calm street violence, and the withdrawal of the army removed from the scene a major player in the chaos.

For several years, it seemed as if Juárez had really turned a corner. But in recent years, the fear and the violence have been stalking its streets once more. During a reporting trip I made to Juárez in June 2019, several plans to interview members of the drug trade fell through: an appointment at the local prison was canceled after an inmate was murdered and the facility went into lockdown, and another would-be source backed out at the last minute after he learned I was a gringo, for fear that being spotted with me would get him killed. While I waited to hear back from another former trafficker, I met with Oscar Maynez, a criminologist at the National Autonomous University of Ciudad Juárez. Maynez had been intimately acquainted with the brutal underbelly of his city: from 1999 to 2002, he'd worked as the city's chief of forensics, and it was during that time that hundreds of women went missing or turned up dead in the city, a rash of so-called femicides that reached stomach-turning proportions. Later, he'd worked in an advisory role for the mayor in the mid-2000s, but had thrown his hands up and left city government after one too many personality clashes with the chief of police, he said. As we sat in a crowded Starbucks, our discussion eventually made its way to the most brutal years of fighting, how it had appeared and how it had subsided. Maynez sighed.

"The violence in Juárez is going to be there always. It was like a river that overflows and eventually it's going to go back under," he said. "But it's not—it's never going to end."

Outside in the parking lot, my fixer, Miguel Perea, was busying himself by re-parking his car, backing into the spot so we could peel out quickly if need be.

. . .

Whatever the causes were, however, it was clear that El Chapo and his allies emerged from the war in Juárez largely in control of the trafficking routes through the city. Vicente Carrillo Fuentes and many of his high-ranking lieutenants were in prison, and La Linea and the gangs that had supported them were severely weakened. Of the major traffickers who had gone forth from Sinaloa in the 1980s, only El Chapo, El Mayo, and El Azul remained, directing their network from hideouts in the mountains of Sinaloa, where they remained firmly in control, as their enemies dropped one by one. They were survivors.

Most of the high-level traffickers arrested or killed during Calderón's *sexenio* hailed from networks actively opposed to the Sinaloa federation, leading to accusations that the state was favoring El Chapo over groups like the Zetas, the Gulf Cartel, and the Beltrán Leyvas—an accusation Calderón has repeatedly and forcefully denied.

But El Chapo and El Mayo did not go unscathed. On October 22, 2008, federal police clapped handcuffs on El Rey Zambada following a lengthy firefight in a residential area of Mexico City, a critical blow to their operations in the capital, where El Rey had specialized in bribing high-ranking officials and operating the distribution of cocaine along several crucial northbound smuggling routes.

Months later, El Mayo's eldest son and heir apparent, Vicente Zambada Niebla, went down, too, arrested on March 19, 2009, in the capital. Vicentillo was in Mexico City on an unusual mission: along with a longtime lawyer of El Chapo, he was meeting with DEA agents to provide information on enemies of his father, in exchange for a pledge of immunity from the feds, one they had given to the lawyer more than a decade ago. That was Vicente's story, anyway, detailed in an astonishing series of motions his lawyers filed after his arrest. The DEA, usually loath to reveal much about its dealings with informants, confirmed its agents had met with Vicentillo, but scoffed at the idea that it had provided any kind of get-out-of-supermax-free card to either the narco junior or to the lawyer. Whatever was discussed at that meeting, Vicentillo was arrested just hours later, much like El Pollo Guzmán had been arrested after his meeting with Joe Bond back in 2001. A year later, Vicentillo was extradited to the United States.

In 2010, El Chapo's longtime partner Ignacio "Nacho" Coronel Villarreal died in a shoot-out with the Mexican Army in Zapopan, Jalisco, a suburb of Guadalajara. The shoot-out left one soldier dead, and as troops swept into the home where Coronel died, they found a trove of luxury watches, jewelry, and $7 million in cash. Coronel had cultivated an image of himself as an old-school mafioso who respected tradition, and was said to have once kidnapped a sister of the Beltrán Leyva brothers, only to release her with a proclamation: "We are going to teach you to be a man. For us, family is sacred." But he was also something of a dark visionary, carving out a key role for himself as an innovator in the manufacture and trafficking of methamphetamine, earning himself the title "El Rey de Hielo," or the King of Ice. Cheap and relatively easy to manufacture in large quantities, meth proved a valuable new portfolio. Cocaine had been appealing to Mexican traffickers because they didn't need to grow it; with meth, traffickers didn't even need to worry about sourcing shipments from Colombia. Get their hands on the right chemicals, which moved easily across oceans and into ports, and they controlled nearly all of the supply chain from manufacturing to wholesale distribution. Meth flooded north, and cash flooded south. Coronel's death was a blow to El Chapo, but it didn't stop others under his umbrella from manufacturing the drug. It did, however, lead to one more eruption of little factions vying for supremacy in the areas where Coronel had once held things together. Death and mayhem followed in quick order. After Coronel's death, a faction of the men once loyal to him announced the formation of a new group, the Jalisco New Generation Cartel (CJNG), which a few years later would break away from El Chapo and become one of the most feared criminal organizations in the country under its leader, Nemesio Oseguera Cervantes, alias El Mencho.

• • •

As the presidency of Felipe Calderón drew to a close, it was clear that Mexican politics would continue to be defined by the drug war that he launched in his first days in office. And the dismal failure of his efforts to defeat organized crime with the military threatened not only Calderón's legacy, but the ability for his National Action Party (PAN) to hold on to the presidency and prevent the return to power of the PRI.

Ever since Calderón squeaked to victory in 2006, he had presided over a drastic and bloody reversal of the country's two-decade decline in homicides, as Mexico was plunged into the one of the most brutal spasms of violence since the Cristero War, in the wake of the revolution. Juárez and Tijuana had been gutted, and vast areas of the country had become hotbeds of kidnapping, extortion, and "unorganized crimes" like carjackings and armed robberies, a sign that the police could not meet the most basic needs of the country's citizens they were supposed to protect.

From the day Calderón took his oath of office to the day he passed the torch, violence linked to organized crime and drug trafficking took the lives of more than fifty thousand people. Tens of thousands more went missing; a huge number of those missing people had been forcibly disappeared, many of them by members of the police or the military.

Calderón's defenders sometimes argued that the rise in violence was a short-term result of a winning long-term strategy; a chicken with its head cut off, running like crazy before falling down and bleeding out on the ground. But the established groups that Calderón's troops beheaded refused to bleed out, as drug money and revenue from other simpler, more local, and more violent rackets kept them going. In Michoacán, where the president first deployed troops in 2006, armed criminal groups like La Familia Michoacana rose and fell, driving out other armed groups only to begin operating illegal rackets themselves, and giving birth to splinter factions like the bizarre, pseudo-religious Knights Templar. This gave rise to "self-defense" groups, who sometimes joined in the same cycle, replacing the armed groups against whom they had originally armed themselves. In Guerrero and Nayarit, several criminal groups once loyal to the Beltrán Leyvas broke off and began fighting with such reckless abandon that even once-safe resort towns like Acapulco became war zones, a stark departure from the times when the government had managed to keep such areas safe for tourists, by hook or by crook. Unlike previous generations of traffickers, many of these groups emerged in the

post-PRI, post-Zetas era, and developed a much more paramilitary structure and self-defined group identity than previous traffickers, as the need
to control territory and distinguish themselves from other newcomers
increased. In this landscape of atomized factions, an ever-larger number
of gangs fought one another for control of smuggling territory, human
trafficking, and the extortion of farmers and landowners growing cash
crops like avocados and limes.

· · ·

In the spring of 2012, twelve years after losing the presidency in 2000, the
formerly all-powerful PRI was poised to make a triumphant comeback,
fronted by Enrique Peña Nieto, the handsome young governor of Mexico
State frequently referred to by his initials, EPN. With his telegenic good
looks and his telenovela-actress wife, he and his backers in the PRI had
hoped that EPN could be passed off as the fresh new face that could
obscure the the dessicated fossil of the former ruling party. But EPN
had skeletons in his closet in addition to the skeleton of the PRI's past:
as governor, he had presided over a brutal police crackdown against a
protest in the town of Atenco, and accusations emerged of corruption,
including that he had purchased favorable coverage from the dominant
television news channel, Televisa. Many critics in Mexico alleged that he
was simply a puppet of Carlos Salinas de Gortari, the ruthless and deeply
corrupt president from 1988 to 1994 who'd overseen the implementation
of NAFTA. At what was supposed to be a friendly campaign stop at the
elite Universidad Iberoamericana in the capital, EPN was met with a sea
of students wearing Salinas masks. He and his security team were forced
to barricade themselves inside a second-floor bathroom after furious students crammed into the hallway outside and briefly prevented his exit.

The PRI's mask had slipped, but it wasn't enough to sink them. On
July 1, 2012, EPN beat out his opponents on the left and the right and
emerged victorious with just 38 percent of the vote. And on December 1,
the PRI returned to the presidential palace at Los Pinos, as EPN tried to
convince a wary country that his administration would not be a return
to the bad old days of one-party autocracy. His security strategy, he said,
would focus less on catching kingpins, and more on judicial reforms,

crime prevention, and programs addressing inequality—all issues that badly needed addressing but too often serve as buzzwords for neoliberal technocrats.

That lasted about a year; as oil prices began to plummet worldwide in 2014 and prompted a budget crunch at home, Peña Nieto slashed spending across the board. The austerity measures took a bite out of some of his more holistic crime prevention programs, leaving mostly the same brute-force tactics as before. He increasingly turned to the Mexican Marines for anti-drug operations, with enthusiastic support from the United States, and the Marines in turn became increasingly lethal against civilians.

Felipe Calderón, meanwhile, retreated to a teaching position at Harvard's Kennedy School of Government, his alma mater, where he penned an article citing Ciudad Juárez as a major success of his anti-drug policy.

12

THE INVISIBLES

B Y THE MID-2000S, Alex Cifuentes Villa and his siblings had done quite well for themselves. To the casual observer, the Cifuentes-Villa family had made great strides from their humble roots in Medellín, Colombia, where they'd been born into the home of a petty criminal. Jorge Cifuentes, a petite, bespectacled man with a receding hairline and downturned mouth, belonged to a country club in Bogotá that cost half a million dollars to join, where he rubbed elbows with the country's business and social elite. His older brother Francisco, the reputed head of the family until his death in 2007, had attended a military academy where he had forged long-lasting friendships with some of the most senior-ranking members of Colombia's armed forces. A younger brother, Alex, was overseeing the family's business interests in Mexico. And Dolly, Jorge and Francisco's sister, carried on a longtime affair and had two children with Jaime Uribe—the late brother of former Colombian president Álvaro Uribe. Another sister was dating a powerful colonel in the Colombian Army.

Alex Cifuentes and his siblings came of age when cocaine was synonymous with the so-called Medellín Cartel of Pablo Escobar, a period of intense conflict in Colombia, rife with car bombings, assassinations, and urban warfare between security forces and Escobar's hit men, along with guerrilla wars in the countryside and cities. One of Escobar's lieutenants lived in the same building as the brothers' mom, and as a boy

Alex frequented a bowling alley that the man had set up for the local kids. There, a young Alex hung around with bodyguards who worked for Escobar's man, and got a glimpse of the lives they led, of the life he wished to lead. When Alex was just fifteen, his mom sent him to live with an older brother named Fernando, where Alex took to driving around Cali in sports cars with a pistol tucked into his waistband.

While Alex tooled around Cali like a young playboy, his older brother Jorge headed to Mexico in the late 1980s as an envoy of Efraín "Don Efra" Hernández, a member of the smuggling network that would later split off from the so-called Cali Cartel and become known as the Norte del Valle cartel. In Mexico, Jorge was tasked with locating landing strips, keeping the makeshift airfields well stocked with fuel and food for incoming pilots, and, in Jorge's words, to "make sure the Mexicans weren't drunk." Jorge arrived in the chaotic years following the murder of Kiki Camarena and the breakup of the Guadalajara Cartel, when Don Efra and other Colombian kingpins were beginning to work with the new generation of traffickers, including the man who soon became one of Jorge's closest contacts in Sinaloa: El Mayo. And by extension, El Chapo.

Although he'd worked with El Mayo for years, it was not until 2003 that Jorge first met El Chapo. By this time, the Cifuentes-Villa business portfolio was a sprawling and diversified octopus, and they seemed to always be delving into new investments: a company specializing in instant coffee cubes, a hotel in Cartagena catering to scuba divers, a handful of environmental nonprofits, and various interests in mining, agriculture, construction, and Colombia's manufacturing sector.

The Cifuentes family were part of a new class of Colombian cocaine traffickers dubbed "the Invisibles." Unlike the flashy kingpins of the 1980s, the more business-minded dons of the Cali Cartel in the 1990s, or even the government-linked, far-right paramilitary traffickers of the late 1990s and early 2000s, the Invisibles prized discretion over ostentatious displays of wealth or public acts of drug-tainted philanthropy. They saw what had happened to those who came before them: Pablo Escobar hunted down and shot on a rooftop; the godfathers of Cali arrested and extradited to the United States; the leaders of the Norte del Valle Cartel dead, on the run, or in jail; even the legendary Don Berna—who survived years of chaos, joined up with a right-wing death squad, and ruled the underworld of Medellín as arguably the most powerful Colombian drug lord of all time—had been shipped off to federal prison in the United States.

For the Invisibles, anonymity meant survival, but perhaps more important, it meant the chance to enjoy their wealth, the ability to burrow their way into the elite strata of Colombia's neo-feudal upper class. So the Cifuentes siblings kept their heads down, posed as obscure but wealthy business owners, all while moving as much or more cocaine than many of the household names of days gone by. Unlike some of the more invisible Invisibles, there remained around the Cifuentes family a bit too strong a whiff of the blood and infamy of earlier eras for them to blend in completely, but thanks to well-connected friends and plenty of bribes, they operated their sham companies largely out in the open, while in the shadows they got rich from their true vocation.

In February 2003 Jorge headed to Sinaloa, and from Culiacán he flew out to the mountains to attend a party in honor of the second anniversary of El Chapo's escape. When Jorge landed, El Chapo was there to greet him, diamond-encrusted .38-caliber pistol tucked into his waistband and a shortened AK carbine slung over his shoulder. Jorge was so rattled by the flight to El Chapo's hideout that he greeted his host with a promise to buy him a helicopter, which he said would be much safer and more befitting El Chapo's status than the bumpy Cessnas the Sinaloans typically used. El Chapo was thrilled at the idea.

"Oh, he got very excited," Jorge said. "His little eyes were actually shining. He said thank you."

(Jorge followed through, too, and ended up gifting his new pal an MD 520 helicopter painted a vivid shade of blue. The little five-blade chopper was highly versatile, good for maneuvering through steep mountain passes, and proved a useful addition to El Chapo's fleet until some half-trained goon of a pilot crash-landed the thing. Jorge later claimed that he had the wreck pushed into a ravine in order to collect on the insurance.)

In a sit-down with El Chapo, his son Iván Archivaldo, and Dámaso López—the former prison official, by then a trusted lieutenant of

El Chapo—Jorge and the Sinaloans sipped mezcal and hashed out a plan to move coke from Colombia to Mexico using ultralight, carbon-fiber planes that could fly low enough to avoid radar detection. The first load of several hundred kilos was a success, and over the next several years the Cifuentes family became one of El Chapo's main cocaine conduits, routinely delivering hundreds of kilos by air.

The big break for the Cifuentes crew came in 2007, when cops in Brazil arrested another Colombian supplier of El Chapo, leaving El Chapo in the lurch at a moment when he needed consistent cash flow above all else. He was in the early stages of launching his all-out war for control of Juárez, the government of Mexican president Felipe Calderón was unleashing the army in what he claimed was an attempt to bring the country under control, and El Chapo's alliance with the Beltrán Leyva brothers was on the rocks. He needed money for weapons, he needed cash to put in the hands of the gangsters fighting on the streets of Juárez, and he needed to keep his smuggling routes running smoothly. He turned to the Cifuentes family.

The Cifuentes clan was in crisis mode as well. Francisco Cifuentes, the longtime leader of the sibling-run outfit, had recently been gunned down on his farm in Antioquia. He had died with bills to pay, among them a multimillion-dollar debt stemming from some prior unfinished deal between himself and El Chapo. Jorge decided to tap his little brother Alex to answer El Chapo's call. Alex, a longtime alcoholic, had seen better years, and was drying out in Cancún after surviving a bad bout of pancreatitis and steeling himself for another upcoming surgery. But when duty called, he answered, promising Jorge that, should he survive the surgery, he would do whatever it took to find their brother Francisco's killer and settle the debt with El Chapo.

After surviving his surgery, Alex took the typical bumpy-flight-and-breakneck-ATV-ride route to a mountain compound, where El Chapo greeted Alex with sympathy and gave his condolences for the loss of Francisco. El Chapo had never met the eldest Cifuentes brother in person, but they had worked with one another for years by now, and El Chapo had a suggestion for how to deal with the loss. The best thing to do, El Chapo said, would be to press on, keep working, and not let grief get in the way of business.

There was still the matter of the $10 million the family owed to El Chapo, but he had ideas for business in addition to stoical words of wisdom: Francisco had five widows, and one of them owned several farms, including one on Colombia's northern Pacific Coast, that would work nicely as staging areas for processing cocaine and moving it north, by air or by sea, to Mexico. Perhaps they could transfer some of those properties to El Chapo? To ensure everything went smoothly as they transferred the properties as part of their payment plan on Francisco's debt, Alex agreed to stay with El Chapo, part guest, part hostage.

At the time, El Chapo was splitting his time between more than half a dozen encampments and small homesteads scattered across a stretch of the Sierra Madre in Sinaloa and the neighboring state of Durango. The camps were simple affairs, usually a pine hut with tinted-glass windows for El Chapo, a small kitchen, and a small shed where the help could catch some shut-eye at the end of a long shift.

The camps were outfitted with a handful of modern conveniences, including a plasma-screen television stocked with DVDs, and a washer, a dryer, and refrigerator. Beyond that, they avoided luxuries that might draw attention. They weren't totally cut off; they had access to the internet via satellite, and used long-range, cordless telephones made by the Taiwanese telecoms giant Senao, as well as Motorola FX-2500 boxes they used to bounce a cell phone signal from the remote Sierra to the nearest area with cell service. But the internet was slow, and the phone often cut out when it rained.

El Chapo had been in hiding ever since his 2001 escape, and life had settled into a routine. After El Chapo woke at noon, a secretary would give him a list of calls and messages he had received, and after lunch he would grab a Senao cordless phone and take a walk, returning calls and involving himself in the minutiae of his international drug-trafficking operation, all the while armed with his trusty .38-caliber pistol and an AR-15 slung over his shoulder.

The staff typically consisted of a secretary and his assistant, two maids, and a security entourage of about fifty men, dispersed in three rings: one group of guards at the camp, another forming a perimeter on nearby roads, and a third ring farther afield to keep watch over military bases and cartel airfields. The guards worked twenty-day shifts before rotating out for some R&R in Culiacán, and typically started at about 2,000 pesos a week, which at the time was about $200. For the lower-ranking security personnel, it was a grueling existence, and the stress of keeping constant vigilance wore on some of them. One guard in particular, a guy named Toronjo, got so paranoid that El Chapo had to tell him to chill out, Alex recalled.

"Toronjo would wake us up like 30 minutes or 45 minutes before we even got an alert," Alex said. "And so Joaquín told him, well, you know, 'just call me five minutes before the army is close and even if I'm naked, I'll just run away just like that.'"

El Chapo may have been on the lam and at war, but that didn't mean he couldn't have a good time now and then. He received frequent visits from various girlfriends and wives, and threw a lavish party a few months after Alex's arrival. At that party, El Chapo's sons gifted him a camouflage Hummer, and Dámaso López gave the boss an armored pickup truck worth about $150,000.

Despite his initial role as a glorified hostage, Alex got along well with El Chapo, and the two would often blow off steam together. They frequently flew a rotating cast of escorts out to the mountains to entertain them. According to Alex, El Chapo liked his women underage, and referred to them as his "vitamins," boasting that his sexual conquests kept him young. (Later, through his lawyers, El Chapo would strongly deny this and other sordid allegations that Alex made.)

It must be said that Alex Cifuentes had some strange interests of his own. A hypochondriac who frequently claimed to be tormented by unexplained illnesses, he had become obsessed with astrology and the occult, and sought out the healing powers of witch doctors. He took "herbal baths to cleanse the soul," and would rant to anyone who would listen about the coming of the apocalypse, which he believed would occur in 2012 when the earth would collide with "Planet Niburu and Planet Oficuco." At some point, his personal email address was

"Illuminatixxx13@gmail.com. None of this appeared to be a deal breaker for his new friends in Mexico, however, and El Chapo even indulged the more unorthodox hobbies of his new hostage-lieutenant. They availed themselves of witch doctors on at least one occasion, and Alex once saw El Chapo buying snake oils.

Before long, Alex had earned himself a commanding role within the entourage that traveled with El Chapo from hideout to hideout. In late 2007, after Alex Cifuentes had been in Sinaloa for about four months, his brother Jorge came to visit. It had been about five years since his first audience with El Chapo, and in the intervening years, the operation had taken on a significantly more martial air.

"There was a lot of security, a lot of weaponry," Jorge recalled. "They had anti-air weaponry. It was a completely different organization than the one I had seen in 2003."

When Jorge arrived at El Chapo's mountain hideout after another dreadful, bone-rattling Cessna flight from Culiacán—too bad about the helicopter—the first thing he did was look for his brother Alex, and for a nervous moment Jorge didn't see his little brother anywhere. Suddenly, seemingly out of nowhere, a man in combat fatigues tapped him on the shoulder and greeted him with a cheerful "Hello, buddy!" Jorge was taken aback when he realized this paramilitary goon was Alex.

"He was like, in costume," Jorge said. "He looked like a mini-general."

There's a picture of them together in those days, El Chapo and Alex. On the right stands a young woman in low-rise jeans, a tight white crop top showing off her midriff, big hoop earrings, and lots of makeup, a not-quite smile playing around the corner of her lips as she splays an arm over the shoulder of Alex, crouching down so her head is level with his. Alex is decked out in military fatigues, jutting his chin and giving the camera a tough-guy look through heavy-lidded eyes. To his right, also wearing full camo, El Chapo stands straight, half a head taller and sporting his trademark mustache and a helmet of jet-black hair. He looks happier than the other two, staring dead ahead into the camera with a friendly, goofy-dad smile, not a care in the world.

• • •

El Chapo was not, however, living a carefree existence. In addition to the fighting in Juárez and the trouble brewing in Sinaloa between him and the Beltrán Leyvas, he had business to attend to, and he was attending to a lot of it with the Cifuentes family. In one meeting during Jorge's visit to Mexico in late 2007, Jorge and Alex, along with El Chapo, El Mayo, and their sons, sat down to hammer out a new routine of maritime smuggling. Working from his home base in Ecuador, Jorge would begin sending cocaine-laden speedboats to rendezvous with a fleet of Peruvian shark-fishing boats that El Chapo owned. After his workers had loaded the coke onto the shark boats, the fleet would head north into international waters off the coast of Mexico, where another flotilla of go-fast boats would zoom out to meet them, take the coke, and head to shore. It was a convoluted process that required a good deal of manpower and tight coordination, but by going so far out to sea and by keeping the main smuggling boats away from major ports, the traffickers hoped to avoid detection. On the first journey, they successfully managed to ship six tons of cocaine from Ecuador to Mexico.

Such a complex series of movements required smooth communication. And despite how well he'd taken to his life in the mountains, Alex had one major complaint: the internet sucked and the phones were unreliable. How could they coordinate the details of multimillion-dollar shipments if they could barely reach one another via inchworm internet and phones that acted up in the rain like an old knee injury? They needed a solution.

Luckily, Jorge knew just the man for the job.

13

THE IT *GÜEY*

PERCHED INSIDE THE cramped cabin of a twin-prop plane as it teetered its way off a runway on the outskirts of Culiacán and lifted up into the air, Christian Rodriguez peered out the porthole window and gazed down at the landscape as the agricultural fields and palm trees gave way to the parched, dry-season slopes of the foothills of the Sierra Madre Occidental. As the little plane chugged higher in altitude, he began for the first time to feel doubts settle in the pit of his stomach like a bag of rocks. He prayed that the pilot knew what he was doing.

It was 2008, and he had arrived in Culiacán two days earlier on orders from his boss. After he cooled his heels at a hotel in the city, some men had scooped Christian up and driven him out to the airstrip, a rough, makeshift affair, just a few hundred feet of flat ground cleared out of a field a few minutes outside the city.

Despite being a college dropout in his early twenties, Christian was doing well for himself. Business was booming for his fledgling cyber-security start-up, and in recent months, he had begun to work with an important new client: Jorge Cifuentes Villa. Christian's introduction to the Cifuentes empire had been through Jorge's sister Dolly, who had recommended him to Jorge to help with IT matters for the family's side businesses and money-laundering fronts. Once he had proved himself a capable and discreet expert, Jorge flew Christian to Ecuador, where Jorge was based. He wanted to know if Christian might be able to help with a little project: the family wanted to be able to communicate in real time, Jorge said, just like other business executives. And like many legal business executives, they needed to be able to keep their communications safe from snooping eyes and ears. Unlike legal businessmen, however, they needed to do this to keep their trade safe from cops and spies, rather than rival firms. Christian set about creating an encrypted network for them to use. The network was hosted on a virtual private network, or VPN, a tool that allows verified users to hook into the system and that anonymizes the location of the users by obscuring the origin point of the user's internet service protocol, or ISP address. By early 2008, Jorge, his siblings, and their top lieutenants were all communicating on the network, which they referred to as "the Spark."

Pleased with the network, Jorge thought that Christian might be able to help his brother up in Mexico. So like a boss dispatching his IT guy to a satellite office, he sent Christian up to Sinaloa to see if he could sell Alex and his Mexican friends on the wonders of encrypted messaging.

If Christian had felt any pangs of guilt about the illegal side of his business, he justified them to himself by pledging that he would get out as soon as he had enough capital to really get his legitimate business off the ground. But flying above the rugged badlands of the Sierra Madre, it started to dawn on him that it might not be that simple.

Christian's anxiety only increased when he spied the airstrip toward which the pilot was headed, carved at an incline into the top of a ridge, and even shorter than the one from which they had taken off. The whole thing had him spooked: he was much more comfortable at a business meeting in Bogotá or Mexico City, like any normal young entrepreneur; but here he was, sitting in a rickety little plane with a narco named El Gordo, making a heart-stopping landing in middle-of-nowhere opium country.

The pilot knew what he was doing, though, and nosed the Cessna down smoothly, rattling nothing more than his passenger's nerves as the plane finally taxied to a stop on the little airstrip. There a group of men in combat fatigues and toting assault rifles milled about awaiting their guest's arrival.

Christian squeezed himself out of the plane and strode toward the armed men, who ushered him onto the back of a four-wheeler, the vehicle of choice in these mountains where even the most determined off-road pickup truck has trouble navigating the glorified dirt tracks that pass for roads. With Christian holding on for dear life, his driver took off, zooming up the mountainside at a breakneck clip toward a small encampment near the top. It was not much more than a small house and a couple of sheds, where still more armed men in combat fatigues stood about awaiting the arrival of the pudgy IT guy.

Christian clambered off the back of the ATV and followed one of the guards into the little house. Inside stood a man who resembled Christian's boss, Jorge. Alex Cifuentes shook Christian's hand, then gestured to the man beside him, a stocky Mexican clad in fatigues and wearing a black baseball cap, who peered at Christian with an alert, intense gaze.

"This is my *socio*," Alex said.

Christian found himself face-to-face with El Chapo.

El Chapo extended a hand to Christian and greeted him warmly, making small talk about the young Colombian's trip, marveling with cheerful envy at his guest's ability to come and go as he pleased.

"You guys, professionals, you don't have any problem traveling," El Chapo said.

Like any good millennial tasked with explaining technology to an older colleague, Christian had arrived at El Chapo's encampment prepared to outline the basic concept of his encrypted network.

El Chapo was all ears.

"Joaquín was very active and very receptive," Alex recalled. "He would ask questions about the range that it would reach and the security that he would have with it."

The most pressing issue up in the mountains was the unreliable internet service; Christian proposed that they set up an internet cable starting in Culiacán, run it as far as possible toward the mountains, and then connect it wirelessly to the devices that El Chapo and his men were using at their encampments. El Chapo and Alex paid close attention throughout the demonstration, and pledged to have their technicians work on setting up the new wireless internet system as soon as possible.

Next, pulling up a digital slide show on a computer, complete with charts and illustrations, Christian explained the instant-messaging system that Alex was already using to communicate with his siblings. El Chapo was intrigued, but there was a catch: for a poor boy from the Sierra, running an international drug-smuggling operation is one thing; staying in school past third grade, learning to read, that's another. El Chapo could barely read or write, and preferred instead to speak about business in person or, when it was safe, on the phone. Could Christian rig up a system that would allow him to make secure phone calls? Christian could. He left the meeting with a handshake agreement and pledged to develop a network to El Chapo's liking for talking rather than texting.

. . .

Imagine you're sending a sensitive letter, and it's imperative that no one reads the contents of the letter apart from the intended recipient. You have to send it somehow, but what's to stop the mail carrier from opening it en route, or a thief from yanking the letter out of your friend's mailbox, or government censors steaming open the envelope and reading the contents, and sealing it before sending it on its way? If you could lock that letter in an impregnable box that could only be opened by a key hanging from a necklace around your neck and another key hanging on a necklace around your friend's neck, wouldn't you feel better about the safety of the letter as it crossed borders and passed through the hands of any number of mail carriers and other intermediaries?

End-to-end encryption essentially functions as that lockbox and key. Any data sent through an encrypted system requires one key—typically a long, gibberish string of numbers and letters—unique to the sender and one key unique to the recipient in order for the data, whether text message, email, or phone call, to be opened in a legible form. In a perfect world, end-to-end encryption allows the user to send data completely assured of its security until it's opened, and then to receive confirmation that the data was not tampered with along the way. The best platforms offer users the ability to read the key fingerprint of their intended recipient, in order to ensure that no interference has taken place. Aside from speaking face-to-face on the moon, end-to-end encryption offers some of the best privacy anyone can reasonably expect.

By the middle of the 2010s, a wide array of consumer-facing products and platforms like Signal offered robust end-to-end encryption and a pledge to not store user data or communications, allowing users to chat with one another with nearly complete assurance that their chats are protected from snooping governments. And in recent years, entire companies have sprung up around the need for secure smartphones— including one particularly rogue company that later did business with drug traffickers in Mexico.

But when Christian began designing encrypted comms for the Cifuentes family and El Chapo in 2008, the demand for encrypted communications was more niche, and such platforms were still a few years away. So with considerable creativity and foresight, Christian rigged a system from spare parts, building a network that even the most sophisticated hackers would later be unable to crack, even when they got their hands on a device that used the system. Looking back at the system a decade later, FBI agents familiar with the case told me they were impressed by what Christian managed to put together.

• • •

About a month and a half after Christian's first trip to the mountains, he returned to Sinaloa once more. In the interim, he had been busily working on the network used by the Cifuentes family, as well as designing a phone system for El Chapo.

The network, which was built on a system known as a voice over Internet protocol, functioned much like an office phone system would: each user would be given a phone with a unique, three-digit extension number that, when connected to the internet, could hook up to the network. If El Chapo wanted to reach one of his sons, or a lieutenant such as Dámaso López, all he had to do was dial the three-digit extension assigned to Dámaso and his call would be routed through a main internal server to Dámaso's phone. Any phone that could access the internet via Wi-Fi or cellular data could make calls on the server, but Christian went a step further and installed an adaptor that would allow an analog cordless phone to access the server as well. That would allow El Chapo to use a Senao phone and continue his leisurely midmorning walks through the woods, phone in hand.

After explaining this system to El Chapo, Christian decided it was time for a demonstration. Using a Senao cordless phone that he had configured on the VoIP network as a prototype, he dialed an extension and handed the phone to Alex. On the other end, Dolly Cifuentes picked up.

"Hi, can you hear me?" Alex asked his sister. She could.

Next, Christian showed El Chapo how to make a call to a cell phone. Holding the phone in one hand and the Senao cordless phone in the other, Christian dialed the three-digit extension number he had programmed to connect with the cell phone. After a moment's pause, the extension phone lit up with the incoming call.

El Chapo was sold. Without any further questions, he instructed Christian to build the network, and promised him $100,000 to get it up and running.

The crucial weakness of an encrypted comms systems like the one Christian built is the fact that all the data flowing through the system must pass through a central server; the data—a text about a coke shipment, a call to a buyer in the States—is only as safe as the server through which it flows. In some systems, including Christian's, the data becomes unencrypted while passing through the server before pinging out to the recipient, making it vulnerable to interception by a third party. So Christian had to be careful about where he set up his servers. After initially launching the system on servers based in Mexico, he read up a bit on server security and came to the conclusion that placing the servers in Canada would be a better bet, offering more reliable power at the server center and a government with more rigorous privacy laws than they might find in Mexico. He did not know that the Canadian government, along with other governments in places like the Netherlands, routinely cooperate with U.S. law enforcement under an agreement known as a mutual legal assistance treaty, or MLAT.

· · ·

The second order of business was hooking up more reliable internet in El Chapo's mountain hideouts. On Christian's orders, El Chapo's in-house IT man—a guy named El Gordo, or Fatty—set up a series of antennas to provide a better phone signal, and ran an internet cable as far out of Culiacán as they could, which, when relayed from antenna to antenna, allowed El Chapo and his men to access the Web without having to worry about inchworm speeds and service outages.

Within months, dozens of El Chapo's associates, family members, and underlings were chatting away on talk and text using the extension phones, allowing a new level of speedy communication that gave El Chapo instant access to all manner of associates across the globe without leaving his hideouts in the mountains. This was great for El Chapo, but was becoming a lot for the young Colombian hacker to manage, and his workload seemed to grow by the day. In addition to running comms for the Cifuentes family and looking after his legitimate business, he was now traveling to Sinaloa every other month in order to meet with El Chapo and help the boss's lieutenants set up new extensions and understand the software. Sometimes that meant sitting in an armored car on the outskirts of Culiacán, walking high-ranking traffickers through the finer points of end-to-end encryption, a grim parody of a normal IT worker's day-to-day work.

His headache was about to get worse. On one of Christian's routine trips to the mountains, after the usual hair-raising Cessna flight to a makeshift mountaintop airstrip, El Chapo had a new question: What did Christian know about spyware?

• • •

For El Chapo, the tech might have been new, but the desire to snoop was not. For nearly as long as he'd been in business, El Chapo had a history of spying on his friends, lovers, and underlings. Despite leaving his formal education behind as a child, El Chapo had always maintained a keen interest in technology, using the latest in gadgets and telecommunications to streamline his operation, as well as to protect himself from the government and to keep tabs on friends and enemies alike.

Back in the late 1980s, when El Chapo was running cocaine and marijuana across the border from Sonora into Arizona, El Chapo's engineers had introduced him to a device known as a "scrambler," which he would place on top of a phone to protect sensitive communications from government snooping, according to El Chapo's former lieutenant Miguel Ángel Martínez Martínez.

"[The scramblers] would be placed on top of the phones and then there would be tape and it would be placed on top of the phones and the person that you were speaking with had to have also another one," Martínez recalled. "So you would press a button, you would hear a noise, and the green lights would light up and that was when you could talk."

In order to ensure that the devices worked, El Chapo went to the source, confirming with corrupt Mexican cops on his payroll that his telephone conversations would really be protected. When he got the green light, as it were, he instructed Martínez and other top aides to never speak on the phone about business unless they were using the scramblers. (They might not have been as effective as the cop had said: El Chapo's 1993 arrest in Guatemala occurred in part thanks to a wiretap by Mexican cops that revealed his movements.)

Like his gadget-obsessed predecessor Miguel Ángel Félix Gallardo, El Chapo would often send the engineers to the United States, where they would embark on research missions and shopping sprees, ensuring that year after year he could improve his ability to stay in constant contact with his growing network of operatives. But it wasn't just the government that El Chapo had to worry about back then. As the war with the Arellano-Félix clan was heating up in the late 1980s and early 1990s, he became concerned about what people might be saying about him behind his back and began having his tech engineers wiretap everyone he could in order to find out.

"Mr. Guzmán has always liked communications, to be an expert in communications, to know what his people are thinking about him and what his enemies think of him," Martínez recalled. "[T]he most important thing in that environment was to know what everyone was thinking about, either your friends, your enemies, your compadres, your girlfriends, whomever."

During the time that Martínez was close with El Chapo, the former pilot recalled his boss using a variety of methods to spy on people that ranged from high-tech—a suitcase-borne device that could record up to five different phone lines at once—to low-tech spy-store gizmos, voice recorders hidden in pens and calculators that El Chapo's engineers would sneak into places that the boss wanted to bug. The things he heard on the wire helped give the diminutive El Chapo a leg up on the competition.

"Mr. Guzmán was one of the people with the most amount of information in the environment," Martínez said. "[T]hat's what allowed Mr. Guzmán to become really efficient in always knowing what was happening, who would leave, who would try to enter, who would try to hurt him."

El Chapo's obsession with spying on people in his circle continued after his 2001 escape from Puente Grande. In 2003, he and El Mayo coughed up more than half a million dollars to buy military-grade software that would allow them to intercept phone calls. At least one erstwhile ally met a grisly end for being unwise enough to disparage El Chapo and El Mayo on the phone. *"Pinche viejos,"* he called them, fucking old men. The fucking old men were listening, and they saw to it that the ornery young upstart didn't live much longer.

When Christian arrived in Sinaloa, a digital-age prophet of the new era of illicit corporate communications, El Chapo was embroiled in conflicts near and far, fighting for control of Juárez and struggling to maintain his control of Sinaloa against attacks by the Beltrán Leyvas, as some of his staunchest allies took sides with the enemy. Stung by such betrayals, he was more paranoid than ever. But with the increasing use of mobile phones, he saw an opportunity to keep tabs on those closest to him.

So, he asked, what did Christian know about spyware?

Not one to disappoint his boss, Christian did some research and soon settled on a program called FlexiSPY, which allowed the user to implant an invisible program on a particular telephone or computer that would then grant the user remote access. From afar, El Chapo would be able to read the text messages, emails, apps, and GPS location of any phone on which FlexiSPY was installed. He would even have the ability to turn an infected phone into a remote listening device, turning on the phone's microphone by calling a special phone number associated with the infected device.

Like the pens and calculators that El Chapo handed out in the 1980s and '90s, he began having Christian rig these "special phones" as he called them with FlexiSPY, before handing them out to girlfriends and his wife, underlings, and associates. On occasion, that required subterfuge on Christian's part, most of which played out like a bad spy novel. On one visit to the mountains, El Chapo asked Christian how long it would take for him to "make [a] computer special," explaining that he wanted the engineer to bug a computer belonging to one of his girlfriends, who happened to be visiting the mountain hideout at the same time as Christian. Three minutes, Christian told him. El Chapo's idea then was to distract the woman long enough for Christian to work his magic, and he managed to keep the woman occupied while Christian got hold of her computer and went to work.

The reports generated by the "special phones" were like candy for El Chapo, juicy little morsels that he couldn't stop devouring. He was hooked, and it soon developed into an obsession. If El Chapo had been a demanding client when Christian's work consisted only of maintaining the encrypted network—El Chapo calling frequently to ask questions and request that new extensions be added—he became a downright nuisance when he began using FlexiSPY. Christian was fielding calls from the boss nearly every day, helping him figure out why this special phone was not giving GPS location, or why that special phone hadn't sent information to the server in a few days.

"He liked it very much," Christian recalled later. "Alex Cifuentes and El Gordo told me it was like a toy for him."

El Chapo gleefully began to try to entrap the recipients of the phones. He became fond of calling up a girlfriend or lieutenant on their encrypted extension, to discuss whatever needed to be discussed, and then he would hang up and quickly activate the infected device's microphone and listen in on what the person had to say after getting off the phone with him.

Eventually, as the number of phones infected with FlexiSPY ballooned, it became too much for even the espionage-obsessed El Chapo to keep up with. To deal with the volume of information, Christian trained one of El Chapo's secretaries, Benjamín, to monitor the phones, tasking him with the job of pulling any relevant info and feeding it to the boss. Ever the strategist, El Chapo helpfully suggested that Benjamín wear headphones when listening to audio from the bugged phones and to tell any curious passersby that he was listening to music.

El Chapo may have found a way to spend less time on the spyware, but Christian was still being run ragged. Whenever El Chapo had a question that Benjamín couldn't answer, he'd order the secretary to call Christian, who was forced to pick up multiple calls a day from Benjamín, always with the same order:

"El Señor needs this fixed."

. . .

On February 3, 2010, Christian Rodriguez found himself in a hotel suite overlooking Times Square, as a tough-looking guy with a thick Russian accent explained why he was in the market for encrypted phones.

Christian was here on a referral. He had been working for El Chapo now for more than two years, and he was proud of the software he'd developed. He had not lost sight of the fact that the job had originally began as a sideline, a way to finance his legitimate cyber-security business, and he saw no reason why he shouldn't branch out a bit, offering the encryption to other clients who needed similar services. He didn't know much about the Russian, just that he was looking for a way to communicate without worrying about spies, and Christian didn't much care. If he could fly to the mountains of Sinaloa and offer his services to the most wanted man in the Western Hemisphere, why not sell the software in a quick, one-off deal to the Russian?

Between running the network for El Chapo and the Cifuentes family, catering to El Chapo's spyware obsession, running his legitimate business, and trying to carve out enough time for his both his young family and his mistress, Christian was under a tremendous amount of stress juggling the different parts of his life. He had no idea it was possible to be under even more stress. A lot more.

In the next room, a team of FBI agents were peering at a little monitor, watching and listening in as Christian, super-spy tech wizard that he was, talked himself straight into the steel jaws of the trap they'd set for him.

14

OPERATION SERVER JACK

UNBEKNOWNST TO CHRISTIAN Rodriguez and his clients in Mexico and Colombia, the FBI had been on his tail for more than half a year by the time he traveled to New York to meet with the man he believed to be a Russian mobster.

It all began on June 5, 2009. A uniformed FBI police officer was standing in his uniform outside 26 Federal Plaza in lower Manhattan, watching the flow of federal employees and other passersby swirl through Foley Square, when a man approached him out of the crowd. The man wanted to speak with an agent at the bureau, he said. He had information that they would find very interesting.

"Okay," the officer said. "What do you have?"

"I know about this guy," the tipster said, and went on to outline the basic story he'd heard, of an IT guy designing communications technology for drug traffickers.

Tips of all sorts land every day on the doorstep of federal law enforcement, delivered in person, online, or over the phone: suspicious homeowners ratting out their neighbor for dealing drugs, workers reporting their boss for fraud, people accusing a business of employing undocumented immigrants, and it can be a challenge to identify genuine intel amid all the bullshit conspiracies and petty attempts at revenge. But something about the composure of this tipster standing outside the federal building on that warm June day gave the FBI officer pause. The guy didn't seem like a wack job; it seemed like he knew what he was talking about.

The officer called up to Special Agent Sean McDermott, the boss of the FBI's C-23 Squad specializing in drug investigations, and asked McDermott to come downstairs with another agent to give the tipster a once-over. They didn't talk for long, just a few minutes, asking the guy the basics of what he knew. McDermott was impressed. He couldn't quite make heads or tails of what the tipster was telling him, something about computers, encrypted servers, messages between drug traffickers that the government couldn't access, but like the officer whom the tipster first approached, McDermott got the sense that the man was legit.

As soon as he was upstairs, he knew who might have a better understanding.

"There's all this technical computer stuff," McDermott said. "Let's go get Bobby, he knows that stuff."

"Bobby" was Robert Potash, a young agent relatively new to the squad. In another life, Potash had been an engineer, working for biomedical companies in the private sector. Like many FBI agents of his generation, Potash had heard the call to action in the wake of 9/11, when the bureau was on a hiring spree for people like Potash who had technical expertise. Potash signed up in 2005 and took the oath in 2007, and soon landed with C-23, one of two squads based out of the New York field office dedicated to investigating drug trafficking.

After 9/11, the FBI's focus had fallen squarely on counterterrorism. Think *The Sopranos*, in which the fictional Agent Harris is pulled off his surveillance of Tony Soprano's mafia crew (and yanked away from his habitual consumption of meatball subs from Satriale's) and is sent to get a gut parasite in Afghanistan. But by 2007, the bureau was increasingly looking at the possibility of a nexus between drug trafficking and terrorist outfits working with smugglers to finance their military operations against the West. The catchphrase motivating the agents was "transnational organized crime," a term that included drug traffickers all over the world and other underworld figures that the U.S. government might view as a threat—or hype as a threat when it came time to ask for a bigger budget each year.

When Potash arrived at C-23, the squad was doing some local investigations in New York but was largely focused on Colombia, where a small FBI outpost was dedicated to the Sisyphean task of disrupting the northern flow of cocaine at its source. He quickly earned a reputation on the floor as the brainy guy with a head for numbers, just the man to talk to about technical questions. Because Potash was relatively new, he wasn't yet neck-deep in investigative work like some of his colleagues. So when McDermott came to him with the tip about a mysterious cartel IT guy, Potash jumped at the opportunity to talk to the man himself.

The agents ushered the tipster upstairs to debrief him in earnest. He was a Colombian man who lived in Queens, and had heard tell of the cartel's IT guy through associates from back home. The agents were conscious of the fact that anyone who did a bit of research and knew how to frame it could appear to have real-life knowledge of drug trafficking: obscure names, references to events that few people would know about. More than once the agents had spoken with someone claiming to have information to report only to find that the tipster in question was a canny googler. The real test was to see if the tipster had knowledge of people, places, and events that were not public knowledge, not available in even the most far-flung newspaper or public database. As they questioned the man about his tip, they also asked for information that only a real insider—or at least someone with real inside knowledge—would know. And this guy knew. After establishing that this tip was worth following, they took the man's phone number and his address in Queens, promising to follow up soon, and sent him on his way.

They ran some checks on the new information and it began to look to Potash like this tipster could be the real deal. He looped in Stephen Marston, the agent on the squad who was training him. Marston, a big, jovial man who had the habit of cracking self-deprecating jokes and highlighting the work of others above his own, had joined the bureau in 2000 after a stint with the Coast Guard. The two agents shared an easy, affectionate rapport, due in part to the fact that they'd known each other before they started working alongside one another in the New York office. When Potash was considering joining the bureau, a mutual friend recommended he speak with Marston about his experience as a fed. It was only by chance that they were reunited when Potash was assigned to the drug squad in Manhattan.

The day after the tipster first arrived, Marston, Potash, and a translator went to speak with him again, this time in Jamaica, Queens, a sprawling, largely working-class and middle-class neighborhood north of John F. Kennedy International Airport that is home to immigrant communities from all over the world, including residents from Colombia and other Latin American nations. At the agreed-upon meeting spot, the tipster hopped into the car to talk. The agency car doubling as a makeshift mobile debriefing room must have made for an odd picture: five men sitting in a car parked on the side of a street in Queens, windows fogging up in the warm summer rain, and curious passersby occasionally peering in at them. But over the course of the two or so hours that the agents spent debriefing the man, they only became more convinced that he was onto something.

In Colombia, the tipster said, a young systems engineer named "Christian" was doing tech support for some major players in the cocaine trade, setting up computers and phones with an encrypted-messaging system that allowed traffickers to communicate with one another in real time. He didn't have a last name for the guy, but he knew Christian owned a legitimate cyber-security business and palled around with a loose network of like-minded hacker types. According to the source, Christian had begun working for traffickers in Colombia, but was also now doing work for an even bigger fish: El Chapo.

• • •

Over the next six months, Potash and Marston began working on what they called Operation Server Jack, and were soon traveling down to Colombia on a regular basis, working with locally based FBI and DEA agents to run down information on their mystery IT guy. By the end of 2009, they knew who Christian was, they knew of his connections to the Cifuentes family, and they knew of his frequent trips to Mexico. Through informants in the Colombian underworld, they had managed to get their hands on some encrypted phones, early smartphones by Nokia that Christian had given to a client. The technical team down at FBI headquarters in Quantico, Virginia, began trying every angle to engineer some kind of backdoor access to the network. If El Chapo had learned of this, it might have brought him comfort that the engineers were driving themselves crazy and finding the encryption too secure to crack. With only one side of the equation, only one encryption key and no access to the central server, they had no way of hacking into the larger system. They could see that the phone was bouncing off overseas servers, but they eventually deduced that this was just a function of the VPN it was using.

As it became apparent that brute force would not get them into the system, Potash and Marston decided they needed dirt on Christian, something solid that could be used to indict him in the United States. Something they could hold over his head to try to convince him his only option was to cooperate with them. They began laying the groundwork for a plan to lure Christian to U.S. soil and implicate himself on tape.

They had been careful about their choice of snitches. They didn't want Christian to think he was talking to a Latin American drug trafficker, lest he get spooked about word of this sideline work getting back to El Chapo or the Cifuentes family. It had to be someone with some distance. So they spoke with agents in other departments at the bureau who might have informants willing to do a bit of pinch hitting. One agent, who worked on Russian organized crime, said he had the perfect guy, straight out of central casting with a thick accent and a three-quarter-length leather coat to match.

An intermediary informant who knew Christian a bit from Colombia made the introduction, and now here they were in Manhattan. From the moment Christian arrived with the intermediary, the sting went perfectly. Sitting in the hotel suite, Christian chatted with his acquaintance about his work with El Chapo and his trips to the mountains, validating to the FBI that this was their man.

That was good, but it wasn't enough. While the bragging confirmed to the FBI that they had the right guy, it would never stand up as a confession in court, and it wasn't enough to charge Christian with a crime to secure his cooperation. In order to be able to back Christian into a corner and make clear to him that his only way out was cooperation, they would need to be able to hang serious felonies over his head.

Christian's chattiness had ceased when the supposed new client arrived. In clipped, accented English, the man explained to Christian that he needed secure phones, free from government interference.

Luckily, Christian had just the thing for this potential client. He explained to the Russian how this system could protect the man's communications from snooping governments or spying business rivals. The conversation was all business; just as he had done with El Chapo up in the mountains of Sinaloa, he patiently walked him through the basics of encryption and how to use the phones.

Christian was careful enough not to go around bragging to the Russian about his other clients. How would it look to this client if his new IT guy was talking about his existing clients to a stranger? This was a good move on his part, but in the other room the FBI agents were getting frustrated. This wasn't enough! The informant would have to draw him out in order to get him on tape incriminating himself enough for potential criminal charges that could be used to pressure him into cooperating. Setting up an encrypted network for a guy is not illegal, no matter how shady he seems; doing so with the knowledge that he plans to use it for illegal means makes the tech guy a co-conspirator. But the informant had to tread lightly: if he said anything to spook Christian, the agents would be back where they started, trying in vain to break into a system that appeared to be impenetrable.

The agents waited on tenterhooks in the room next door, listening in as Christian wrapped up his presentation. Time was running out for them to get dirt on him. Finally, the Russian made his move.

"Okay," he told the young Colombian. "I'm going to try them. I'm going to send one to Miami. I'm bringing a load of cocaine up to New York next week and I'm going to use the phones to coordinate the load."

Christian didn't bat an eye. They shook hands; Christian took the money and left with the go-between. In the room next door, Marston and Potash were elated. In that moment, Christian had signed his life away.

He was screwed: within forty-five minutes of meeting with the informant, Christian had implicated himself as a willing co-conspirator in what he had every reason to believe was a plot to move enough coke to put him away for life. In the end, Christian was so blasé about his client's motivations that the agents wondered if they could have just had him say "Hey, I'm here to buy the drugs!" all along.

15

WE NEED TO TALK

CHRISTIAN'S FINAL TRIP to the mountains came a little less than a year after his meeting in Manhattan. He had been working for El Chapo for nearly three years at this point, and although he had been making good money that he was funneling into his legitimate business, the stress of living a double life was beginning to wear on him. For the last several months, he had been doing everything he could to phase out his own day-to-day involvement in running the network and the spying program, handing off duties to El Chapo's in-house tech support crew.

As always, he arrived at El Chapo's encampment by plane, flying out of Culiacán and holding on for his life as the Cessna climbed into the mountains and landed at a death-defying angle on a makeshift ridgeline airstrip. He was there to discuss a new spyware system, one that would allow El Chapo to better intercept calls, text messages, and other activity on targeted devices. But when he arrived, El Chapo asked Christian a dumbfounding question: Would Christian be able to install spyware on every single public computer in Culiacán, a city of more than 800,000 residents?

Christian was gobsmacked. But, as always, he thought it over and prepared a demonstration for El Chapo to show how they might go about tapping every internet cafe in the city by strolling in, plugging in a USB device armed with the spyware, and infecting the cafes one by one. The main problem, besides the cloak-and-dagger antics required by such a plan, was that the antivirus software that the cafes used could block the spy program from embedding itself on the computers. With a wave of his hand, El Chapo instructed Christian to try to solve the problem.

As Christian was mulling over this new request, he was rudely reminded of who exactly he was working for, and where exactly he was, when a runner arrived in the encampment, sounding the alarm: the army was in the area, and headed their way.

At first, El Chapo remained even-keeled.

"Well, if they take this way up, let me know," he said, according to Christian. "If they take the other way up, then there's no problem."

When it became clear the soldiers were indeed on their way, El Chapo immediately gave the order to evacuate to another camp he had in the area that would be safer from any incursion by the soldiers. Everyone, including Christian and Alex Cifuentes, started packing in a hurry.

After so long living cheek by jowl with El Chapo, Alex had become used to this kind of thing; but he could see that the nebbishy young engineer was petrified, and ordered Christian to stay close by his side as they broke camp and fled the area on foot. In addition to El Chapo, Alex, and Christian, the group numbered nearly two dozen, including about fifteen guards, all armed to the teeth with AK-47s, AR-15s, and even a .50-caliber machine gun, in case a helicopter got within range.

"We walked and moved up the mountain further up, waiting to see what happened with the army," Christian recalled. "The army came up to the place that we were, so we started walking through the mountains to get away."

All night and into the predawn hours the posse hiked through the mountains, groping their way through the scrubby underbrush in near-total dark, barely able to see past their own noses. Eventually they arrived at a small house, where they slept for a few hours before taking off once more in the morning, trekking along as helicopters buzzed overhead and the dawn light began to shine over the horizon.

On the second day, the group linked up with a handful of El Chapo's men awaiting them with some mules, and trekked down a steep canyon. They spent that night sleeping rough, and in the morning continued on. On that third day, the little group finally reached a third safe house, where they were fed and bundled into a convoy of trucks that drove them out of the mountains to Culiacán.

Throughout the whole ordeal, El Chapo remained utterly composed.

"He was always very calm, very sure, and very tranquil," Christian said.

But Christian had had enough. They never met face-to-face again. And as far as Christian knows, El Chapo never did manage to hack every internet cafe in Culiacán.

. . .

Special Agent Bob Potash stood in the arrivals terminal of the El Dorado International Airport in Bogotá and tried to look inconspicuous. Loitering nearby, Special Agent Steve Marston kept an eye on the board announcing incoming flights. Amid the tumult of passengers arriving, families reuniting, they had their eyes peeled for a familiar face: Christian Rodriguez.

They were finally making their move on Christian. It was February 2011, more than a year since they had lured him to Manhattan for the sting operation. They still had made little headway toward cracking into the encrypted network that Christian had set up for El Chapo and his lieutenants, despite their best hackers down at Quantico trying from every angle. Word was getting around the bureau and other federal agencies about their investigation. They knew they were sitting on a major point of entry inside El Chapo's outfit, and they had run through a lot of resources by this point, between flights to Bogotá, man-hours spent trying to batter their way into the network, countless late nights puzzling over strategy, numerous meetings with other agencies where they found themselves promising a payoff . . . soon. By Christmastime, they were getting antsy. By February, when prosecutors in the United States unsealed an indictment against Jorge Cifuentes, they decided they had nothing to lose. They needed results, now.

Since the beginning of the investigation, in tandem with the Bogotá field office and various unspecified "partners" in Colombia, the agents had been building a profile of what the pros refer to as pattern of life:

where Christian slept, what he ate, when and where he traveled; now, thanks to that painstaking work, they knew Christian would be arriving sometime that day on an Avianca flight from Medellín. He was in town for business, and they wanted to grab him here, rather than on his home turf in Medellín, where anyone might spot him getting spirited away by cops and a pair of conspicuous gringos, potentially blowing his cover before he even needed cover.

FBI agents have no law enforcement powers in Colombia and are barred from making an arrest or detaining a potential informant, so Potash and Marston were working with a team of local law enforcement agents. As minutes ticked by, they began to wonder if they had missed him. A frequent flyer on the local airline, Christian was able to hop on whichever plane he wanted without a reservation, which only increased the agents' uncertainty. Did he opt for a later flight, or had they missed him in the throngs of travelers swarming through the terminal? After enough time had passed following the landing of the flight he was expected to be on, they checked the flight manifest and found to their relief that he had not yet arrived in Bogotá, and resumed the wait. It was among the longest hours of their lives.

Finally, their man arrived. Christian was dressed smart, like the young businessman he was, blue blazer over a white shirt tucked into jeans, strolling toward the terminal exit in nice shoes and carrying a leather satchel slung over his shoulder.

Two Colombian officials walked up to him discreetly and whispered in his ear, steered the surprised young man toward the curb, and ushered him into the backseat of the little Toyota waiting in the parking lot. Christian climbed in and scooted over to the far side of the backseat, but stopped as Potash opened the driver-side door and got in beside him. As he started to scoot back toward the passenger-side door, an FBI agent with the Bogotá office climbed in, boxing Christian into the middle seat of the increasingly claustrophobic little car. Marston scrambled into the front passenger seat as the Colombian driver took off.

Potash turned to Christian and greeted him in English.

"Hey, we're with the FBI," he said. "We need to talk."

The road leading into El Chapo's hometown of La Tuna, in the Mexican state of Sinaloa.

The evangelical Christian church in La Tuna that El Chapo
built for his mother in the late 1980s.

Juan Carlos Ramírez Abadía, alias
Chupeta, before plastic surgery.

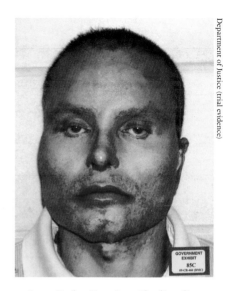

Juan Carlos Ramírez Abadía, alias
Chupeta, after plastic surgery.

Juan José Esparragoza Moreno,
aka El Azul.

Alfredo Beltrán Leyva, aka Mochomo.

Ismael "El Mayo" Zambada García.

Vicente Zambada Niebla, aka
Vicentillo. Son of Ismael "El Mayo"
Zambada García.

El Chapo after his arrest in 1993.

El Chapo after his arrest in 2016.

U.S. Customs agent Michael Humphries holds trash bags full of cash discovered
in a car driven by Arturo Guzmán Loera in Douglas, Arizona, in 1989.

A chile pepper can used by El Chapo's people to smuggle
cocaine into the United States in the early 1990s.

El Chapo (left) and Alex Cifuentes (center) in an undated picture likely taken between 2008 and 2012 with the daughter of a smuggler pilot.

GOVERNMENT
EXHIBIT
811-1
09 CR 466 (BMC)

A diamond-encrusted pistol bearing El Chapo's initials.

The exit of a drainage tunnel El Chapo used to escape
from a raid in Culiacán in February 2014.

The tunnel used to smuggle drugs between Agua Prieta, Sonora,
and Douglas, Arizona, discovered May 17, 1990.

Culiacán as seen from Mirador La Lomita, a scenic
lookout in the center of town.

A safe house known as "The Five" used by El Chapo to hide out in Culiacán
and raided by Mexican Marines and DEA in February 2014.

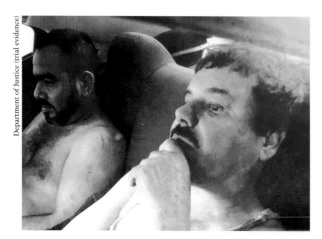

El Chapo and Orso Iván Gastellum Cruz, aka El Cholo Iván, shortly after their arrest near Los Mochis, Sinaloa, on January 8, 2016.

El Chapo's wife Emma Coronel Aispuro leaving the federal courthouse in Brooklyn on February 12, 2019, shortly after a jury found her husband guilty.

El Chapo's son Ovidio Guzmán López surrenders to Mexican troops during a raid in Culiacán on October 17, 2019. He would be released hours later amid heavy fighting.

"Yes, okay," Christian said, seeming stunned.

Turning to the driver, Potash asked if they could find someplace to talk, where the staff wouldn't ask too many questions.

"Take us to a hotel real quick," he said. "Real fast, no credit cards."

Nodding in assent, the driver headed to a love motel, an hourly hovel where the staff was used to accepting cash and would hand over the key without looking too closely at the odd group of guests. One of the Colombians went in to pay at the office, and the clerk guided the Toyota toward a little one-car garage designed to hide their car from passersby. A real classy affair.

Once they were in the motel room, they sat Christian down on a chair, while the agents shifted uncomfortably, perching themselves on a coffee table or leaning on the dresser, all of them avoiding the bed for fear of what fluids might have been spilled there.

Marston and Potash quickly cut to the chase: they knew who Christian was, and they knew who he worked for, and they wanted his help. At first, Christian tried his hand at minimizing his illegal work. Sure, he said, he knew the Cifuentes family, and he did some work for them. But El Chapo? Christian didn't know any El Chapo.

"I was frightened," Christian recalled later. "Admitting to the FBI agents that I worked for a public figure like El Chapo was very difficult."

It seemed to the agents that Christian still thought he might be able to get out of whatever jam he had found himself in, wake up from this nightmare, and go back to his life. But the FBI wasn't done with him. One of the local FBI guys began to say something to Christian, and as he leaned in, the Glock handgun in his shoulder holster started to hang out of his jacket. Christian stared at the weapon transfixed, hypnotized by what he took to be an implicit threat. He was petrified; for all he knew, these guys were hired by El Chapo to test his loyalty. In Colombia, as in Mexico, a police badge alone doesn't inspire much trust, and Christian couldn't be too careful as long as he had any doubts.

After an hour or two of this tiresome back-and-forth, the meter ran out on their motel room, and the agents decided to move the party to a less sordid locale, bundling Christian back into the little Toyota and driving to the Bogotá Marriott. If they were going to be there awhile, they didn't want to sit around breathing in the miasmic air of the hot-sheet motel.

As they settled into more comfortable digs in a large suite at the Marriott, more people began to arrive: two staffers from the embassy, a pair of DEA agents, and someone who came along with a platter of cold cuts, as Potash and Marston continued to chip away at Christian, talking in circles in an attempt to get him to see the light and start cooperating fully. One by one he gave up his denials, admitting that he did systems work, confessing that sure, he had a client in Mexico, but he was still denying any knowledge of the Mexican's name or business. Maybe they called him El Chapo, he said, but he didn't know the guy.

For hours, Christian sat there and deflected questions, as Potash and Marston took turns interrogating him and the Colombians and the other U.S. agents looked on. Christian remained composed, polite, but firm, like he was doing his best to endure a bad sales pitch.

Finally, reaching the eleventh hour—literally; they had been interviewing him for eleven hours at that point—the exasperated agents decided to play their trump card. The one they'd had in their back pocket for a year as they tried all other avenues to get into the system. This was their moment.

Potash stood up and grabbed a laptop.

"I'm going to play you this," he told Christian.

He placed the laptop on a chair facing the young engineer, pulled up a video file, and hit play. The room went silent as they watched the surveillance recording of Christian's meeting in Manhattan a year earlier, and out of the laptop speakers came Christian's voice telling his associate, the one who brokered the meeting, about his work for El Chapo, his trips to the mountains. As soon as Christian said the word "El Chapo," Potash hit pause. They didn't even need to play the rest.

Like a balloon deflating, Christian exhaled a long breath and sank back into his chair. Potash gently pounced.

"Okay," the agent said. "Do you know El Chapo?"

"Yes, I do," Christian murmured.

"Okay," Potash said. "Do you want to work with us?"

"Okay," replied Christian.

. . .

When Christian finally broke down, acknowledging his work for El Chapo and agreeing to work with the FBI, he had been in Bogotá for nearly twelve hours and had blown off the meeting that had brought him there in the first place. He was terrified that he was being watched, that staying in the capital any longer would expose him to El Chapo, or to the Cifuentes family, or to anyone whose suspicions could easily get him killed. He had to get back to Medellín, he told the agents. Christian was right to be fearful: just like any informant picked up in a drug case, any unexplained absence could lead to some uncomfortable questions.

Potash and Marston eyeballed their newly minted informant and made a judgment call: this guy was in their pocket now. They knew where he lived, knew his routine, and knew who he worked for, and Christian knew this. He wasn't going to do a disappearing act. And so they let him go.

The next time the agents met with Christian, it was in a fancy hotel in lower Manhattan, where they put him up on the FBI's dime. Christian had obviously traveled to New York before without raising suspicions with his employers, so they felt okay with another trip. Besides, being in the United States would allow them to speak with him in a more relaxed manner, far from prying eyes.

Over room service—Christian ordered a forty-dollar steak, an expense-account nightmare—he methodically walked the agents through the past few years of his life, describing his work for the narcos, explaining the tech, laying out the architecture of the encrypted networks, everything.

After nearly two years of trying to break into Christian's networks, piecing together information gleaned from other informants, it was thrilling for Potash and Marston to finally be able to get a walk-through from the architect himself. Christian delivered the presentation in a calm monotone, no bragging. They were impressed; this kid knew what he was doing.

They also began to get a sense of Christian's motivations for making a deal with the devil. He had always hoped that the ready cash coming in from his illegal work could jump-start his legitimate cyber-security business, and that once he had sufficient start-up capital, he would be able to go back to the white-hat work. But as he became more involved, it had become more and more apparent to Christian that one does not simply walk away from a job as El Chapo Guzmán's IT guy.

In one sense, the FBI had pounced on Christian at the exact right moment. It was only a few weeks after his terrifying escape from the army in the mountains, and the experience still had him rattled. This was not the kind of life Christian was capable of living, and he was more aware than ever of just how deep in over his head he had gotten, and he was ready to get out. But it was just that readiness to get out that made the agents wish they had jumped on him six months earlier. In the months leading up to the confrontation in Bogotá in February 2011, Christian had been working steadily to extricate himself from the day-to-day operation of running comms for El Chapo, training El Chapo's technicians Gordo and Benjamin to maintain the servers themselves. This posed a problem: if Christian had been the only one with access to the servers, he would be free to muck about on the network, setting it up to record calls and save data that would be useful to build a case against El Chapo. But now that there were other eyes peering in from El Chapo's side, they had to be much more careful about not carrying out any activity on the network that might raise eyebrows.

"They had access, as did Christian, and were aware, or could be aware of any of the activities that were happening in the servers," Marston said. "We did not want to leave a footprint from the FBI within those servers that could be found and essentially alert them to the presence of law enforcement."

After all the work Christian had put into distancing himself from El Chapo, he would now have to work his way back into the fold. He'd have to do it from afar. In the wake of the breakneck escape from the army, Christian had told El Chapo he was done with the mountains; he'd work remotely from now on. El Chapo, who had considered the escape one adventure in a lifetime of close calls, seemed insulted. He took it personally. They never spoke again.

For their part, Potash and Marston had no intention of sending

Christian back to Mexico, let alone trying to get him face-to-face with El Chapo. As professional and well-mannered as Christian was, the agents were certain he wasn't up to that kind of confrontation. They didn't want to be responsible for whatever grisly fate would almost certainly await him if he cracked or let his nervousness show.

Another problem that faced them: Christian had been too good at his job. Although he had pledged to help in any way he could, he actually could not access messages or phone calls between two extensions on the network, as only the owners of those extensions had keys to unscramble the messages. Like a systems engineer in an office who tells employees to change the preset password to ensure privacy, Christian had granted total security to the users of the network, even from the eyes of their trusty Colombian IT guy.

So they hatched a plan: if they couldn't access the servers in Canada without leaving footprints, they would move them to a friendly country, reconfigure them, and request permission from the host country to search the servers. They settled on the Netherlands.

This was not the first time Christian would be moving the servers, which would make it easier to sell the plan to El Chapo's in-house tech guys. In 2009, shortly after Christian had first set up the network, he had suggested moving the system onto servers based in Canada after reading on the internet that Canada provided a good deal more privacy and security than servers in the United States. So it was a relatively easy sell to convince El Chapo—through intermediaries—of the need to move the servers to Amsterdam, where Christian said drug laws were lax and American law enforcement had little presence.

This was a lie. United States agents maintain strong relationships with their counterparts in the Netherlands, and accessing the new servers would require little more than some paperwork, with the filing of warrant requests under the umbrella of the two countries' mutual legal assistance treaty, or MLAT agreement. As long as the agents made a compelling case to the Dutch that the information on the servers was subject to a criminal investigation, everything said on the network could potentially be up for grabs by the FBI.

So Christian set about moving the servers, with El Chapo convinced that they were making the servers more secure than ever. But there was a catch, Christian told his colleagues in Mexico: he was going to have to send out all new phones, each with a new key. And for each key he sent out, he kept a copy for himself, and for the FBI.

. . .

In early April 2011, Potash and Marston sat in the office of Special Agent Sean McDermott, their supervisor in the C-23 drug squad. With them was a translator, and sitting before them, on a computer, was an audio recording. They hit play, and strained to listen as the room filled with the sounds of two men speaking in thick Sinaloa accents. The translator described the conversation as it progressed: one person was speaking more quietly, almost deferentially, urging caution, while the other was speaking authoritatively, almost yelling.

Marston and McDermott spoke almost no Spanish, while Potash had some rudimentary Spanish under his belt, but from the tone of the conversation, they thought it was clear who was who. They were thrilled to finally hear El Chapo's voice, as domineering as they had imagined. It seemed like the other guy was in a lot of trouble, the agents joked among themselves. It was not until later, when Potash was discussing the recording with Christian, that they realized their mistake. They had it all wrong, Christian told them. The quiet guy? That was El Chapo.

In another call, recorded a few days later, they heard the same dynamic, one guy angry and full of bluster, while El Chapo tried to calm him down. On the call, recorded at 2:18 a.m. on April 9, 2011, the loud, domineering man they had mistaken for El Chapo was angrily venting about a recent police action that had interfered with operations. It was El Chapo, the quiet man, who was urging calm from his subordinate, a longtime servant of El Chapo named Cholo Iván.

"*Está cabrón*," Cholo yelled. "It's all fucked up."

"When you talk to them, you know they're policemen. It's better not to smack them around," El Chapo soothed. "Yeah, better not, better not, so we don't end up badly with them. Tell them that you're at their disposal."

"No, well, they were fucking watching me," Cholo replied. "They sicced the state, the *federales*, the municipals, even traffic, they sicced them on me, the sons of bitches. So right now I ran inland."

"Okay, Cholo, well, there, take it easy with the people," El Chapo interjected with a slight stutter. "If they stop somebody, don't curse them out or anything. You can get along respectfully."

The two men continued talking for some time about more mundane business matters, until El Chapo returned to the subject of the uncooperative cops.

"Listen, so then, did you beat up those policemen?" El Chapo asked.

"I kicked their asses, the *federales*, all of them," Cholo Iván boasted.

"And what did they tell you?" El Chapo asked.

"Well, what are they going to say?" Cholo said with a laugh. "Well, nothing, that they are fucked."

"Don't be so harsh, fucking Cholo, take it easy with the police," El Chapo cautioned once more.

"Well, you taught us to be a wolf," Cholo Iván said. "I'm remembering, and that is how I like to do it."

The agents sat back in amazement. After two years of chasing their tails trying to get into the network, here he was, at last: El Chapo Guzmán, speaking on the phone, clear as day. He spoke with a thick Sinaloa accent, with a distinct nasal twang to his voice and a singsong cadence, nothing like they had imagined. And to add to that, it appeared he was the one pushing reconciliation with the police, not the one thundering in anger at a perceived betrayal.

Day by day they heard more calls, more conversations that El Chapo had with various assistants, girlfriends, smugglers, and hit men. He'd call about daily life with business calls, sometimes leading the agents to confusion. They heard him ask for daily household supplies, sure, but now why was he asking someone about an order of two thousand cans of spray deodorant? And *cuernos de chivo*, goat horns: was he bootlegging ivory or something? It was not until they spoke with a linguist that they realized the "spray cans" were 40mm grenades, the kind you lob out of a grenade launcher, and the "goat horns," as anyone who's spent time in northern Mexico will tell you, are AK-47s.

The calls revealed something else: El Chapo appeared to be having trouble paying his men. In that April 9 call with Cholo Iván, they listened as El Chapo tried to reassure his lieutenant that payroll would be arriving soon.

CHOLO IVÁN: They don't even have any [money] to buy cigarettes over there in the jail because whatever I get here I keep investing it and well, I don't even have—

EL CHAPO: Soon—soon there's going to be something. Something is on the way already. Soon there's going to be some so you all can cover payroll and get some relief.

CHOLO IVÁN: You know that I never back out on you. Someone's ill, someone's mother or someone else, and the doctor Alan doesn't want to do anything over there. It's all messed up.

EL CHAPO: Soon there's going to be money for payroll, calm down. Soon, very soon. On Monday we have to start to give—

CHOLO IVÁN: That's why, like I tell you, if there is a way to at least go to the doctor, because you know that there may be—family gets sick, and well, we have to tend to them, but you get upset. That's why I'm asking if you can do that for me.

EL CHAPO: No, no, no, in case of an emergency it's right away.

CHOLO IVÁN: Yeah, a young man's mom is sick, or some guy's missus, and well, he wants me to do him a favor. Well, sometimes I don't have any money, so I send him to the hospital and there they refuse treatment. That's the thing.

EL CHAPO: All right, Cholo, coun-count on that and we'll be in touch.

El Chapo had indeed been having a rough couple of years. At the time of his conversation with Cholo Iván, fighting continued to rage in Juárez, and the war in Sinaloa against the Beltrán Leyvas carried on unabated. At the end of 2008, he had lost the Flores twins to the DEA (along with multiple major seizures of coke and heroin that they had facilitated as part of their cooperation) and had suffered several huge losses in Ecuador, including a six-ton seizure at sea in January 2009 and another seizure of nearly eight tons in October in Quito. Sure, there was always more where that came from, but from time to time, it seemed that El Chapo couldn't quite make ends meet. He was shelling out between $150,000 and $200,000 a month just to pay his direct employees in Sinaloa and keep his mountain hideouts supplied with food and the necessary creature comforts, but that was a pittance compared with the bill for bribery, which exceeded $1 million per month. At times it appeared he was spending money as fast as he could earn it.

· · ·

In the summer of 2011, just a few months after Christian began cooperating, El Chapo's extension went dark. Always paranoid, he seemed to have decided that he could no longer trust the network enough to conduct sensitive business on it. In a phone call to an associate, El Chapo explained that he didn't want to have his voice out there any longer, although he gave permission for his underlings to continue using the network to coordinate business.

Shortly before El Chapo stopped using the VoIP network, the FBI intercepted a phone call between El Chapo and his brother Aureleano, aka El Guano. Once again, it was El Chapo who came across as the voice of reason, talking his brother down from suspicions that a snitch in El Guano's group was giving information to the authorities. No, El Chapo said, if there was a snitch, they'd all be in handcuffs. It had to be the phones. At the end of the call, he instructed Guano to stick to BlackBerrys.

By this time, El Chapo was doing most of his communication using BlackBerry phones and the company's proprietary BlackBerry Messenger, or BBM. He was apparently under the assumption that because BlackBerry was a Canadian company, with servers located in Canada, his communications were safe from U.S. agents. El Chapo was right to be wary of voice calls: even as he told his associate that he would stop using the network, the FBI would soon be listening to the call. What he didn't know, however, was that the BlackBerrys he was using, set up by Christian, were operating on a server paid for by the FBI.

Despite his calm demeanor on the phone with El Guano, his unceasing paranoia about the motives of those around him led him toward a trap, and blinded him to the fact that he was essentially wiretapping himself, on behalf of the FBI, via the BlackBerrys and via his beloved "special phones."

With El Chapo no longer using the VoIP network, the agents began to focus instead on the reams of data coming in from the FlexiSPY reports generated from the "special phones" that El Chapo handed out.

Every FlexiSPY report that El Chapo or one of his minions read was managed by a Texas-based company called Cloudflare, which was contracted to handle data requests for FlexiSPY. The actual content of the reports was hosted on an Amazon Cloud server based in the United States, right under the noses of the FBI, the DEA, and anyone else who might have wanted to take a crack at El Chapo.

In December 2011, FBI agents approached representatives of Amazon and Cloudflare to see about the possibility of executing a search warrant in order to scoop up the data contained in the reports connected to accounts that Christian had purchased; Cloudflare kicked the can to Amazon, the actual holder of the data, but they didn't get much further there. In conversations with the FBI, a rep for Amazon shrugged ruefully and explained that it could be impossible for Amazon to locate the data. Once again, the agents faced technological difficulties that could have stymied them if not for their ace in the hole: Christian.

On December 22, 2011, Christian logged into his FlexiSPY account and downloaded every report that had been generated from the "special phones" El Chapo had handed out to his various lovers and lieutenants. Taking care not to review the information just yet—the FBI did not yet have a search warrant to comb through it—Christian copied the files onto a server owned by the FBI. The amount of information, and what it could tell the FBI, was staggering: text messages, call logs, all linking back to people closely associated with El Chapo. The reports even contained GPS locations for all the phones that El Chapo had given out, allowing them to plot the movements of the people possessing the phones—although not the phone El Chapo used for himself. He had no need to install spyware on his own phone.

· · ·

Peering into the FlexiSPY reports, the agents began to see the most inti-mate details of El Chapo's personal life, which often overlapped with his work. By the fall of 2011, El Chapo appeared to be increasingly relying on a handful of girlfriends to act on his behalf in business deals. One such girlfriend-lieutenant was a young woman from the mountains of southern Sinaloa and Durango named Lucero Sanchez López. Lucero and El Chapo had been seeing each other occasionally for about eight months when, that October, he asked her to go to the mountains and buy wholesale marijuana from farmers in the area.

Lucero's instructions were simple: head to the community where she had once lived, along with several others in Sinaloa and Durango, and begin procuring weed, packaged up in bundles of ten kilos each to be crammed into a plane, as much as it would hold. El Chapo sent her off with a reminder to pay attention to the "three Bs": *buena*, *bonita*, and *barato*; good, pretty, and cheap.

During her trips to the Sierra, El Chapo, who had previously been somewhat hard to pin down, became a model communicator, texting back and forth multiple times a day, a task that required her to climb a tall hill every morning and afternoon in order to get a signal on her BlackBerry. They discussed prices and quantities, and, ever the shrewd businessman, El Chapo asked her if she could get the kilos on credit. But at this she balked: she was of these small towns, and she knew the chances of the farmers getting paid back were slim. It didn't sit right with her. She ignored the request.

"I thought it was unfair that the people who had worked so hard knew that if it went out on credit that those people who had worked on it would not receive the money back," she recalled later.

In another instance, she said she bought lower-quality marijuana containing seeds from a buyer and former neighbor, in part because she felt bad for the man and his workers.

"I didn't want to leave it there, because I felt a pity for him. So I bought it from him. Those were people who were very low-income people and they worked way too much," she said.

The longer Lucero stayed in the mountains, the more paranoid she got about working for El Chapo, potentially being exposed to his enemies. When she told him this, she—and the FBI agents reading along—saw a more menacing side to him.

"Look, the mafia kills people who don't pay or people who snitch, but not if you are serious, love," El Chapo wrote.

Lucero scrambled to reassure El Chapo that she had no plans to rat him out. In fact, she said, she was proud of the work they were doing.

"I know that I'm not doing anything bad," Lucero wrote. "On the contrary, I think this is good for people, and even more so with you because you have helped the ranches a lot and I'm proud and hold my head up high guided by you, love."

"That's right, love," El Chapo replied. "Lies are what cause problems. Don't lie, and people will always see the good, love. Always remember that. I'm telling you this because I love you. Even if you make a mistake, don't deny it, and you will always be happy and people will appreciate you. I love you."

• • •

Another girlfriend, a Mexican woman named Agustina Cabanillas Acosta, appeared to have earned an especially high degree of trust from her fugitive lover. El Chapo had Agustina deal directly with suppliers, wholesale buyers, and other traffickers as far afield as Australia and China, and across the United States from San Diego, Los Angeles, and Nogales, Arizona, all the way to Detroit.

In one exchange, the agents read along as El Chapo messaged with Agustina as *she* messaged with an associate about the purchase of chemicals from China and Germany, two countries where the cartel is known to obtain precursor chemicals for the manufacture of meth and the synthetic opioid fentanyl. In another, El Chapo was seen giving his lover instructions for a trip by private jet—a "black flight," he said, no need for passports—to Ecuador, Venezuela, and Belize. He had so much faith in the security of his BBM communications that he hardly spoke in code anymore, as the FBI agents gleefully noted when reading a BBM with a wholesale buyer named "Güero" dated January 26, 2012, in which Agustina was trying to coordinate an offshore drug shipment to Güero's contact in Southern California.

"My friend here wants to know if you can start talking to the man," she told Güero. "If he would be willing to go fish in Los Angeles, and willing to receive 200 miles out from San Diego."

In response, Güero asked Agustina if she meant coke or weed, "small ones"—a reference to the more compact kilos of cocaine that he was expecting—or "grass." Agustina told him to hold on. Opening up her BBM chat with El Chapo, she relayed the question.

"The man is asking if you have there the material you told him about," she wrote.

"*Mota o perico?*" El Chapo asked. "Weed or coke?"

"The small ones," Agustina wrote.

"*Perico?*" El Chapo blithely confirmed.

"Yes," Agustina replied.

As an integral part of El Chapo's communication network, Agustina was in constant contact with various traffickers and associates about logistics, a feat that at times made her head spin.

"Yes, love," she replied to El Chapo in a conversation dated January 26, 2012. "If it takes a while to reply to you it's because I'm talking with four at the same time and I get really dizzy."

The associates that Agustina texted with appeared to view her as an authority figure, or at least the messenger of one, and at times spoke to her with deference as they sought permission to make this or that deal.

"So you can mention it, I have two clients, they want about 2,000 lbs; they want a price," the associate nicknamed "Güero" wrote to Agustina on January 12, 2012. "Do I have your authorization to reach an agreement with them?"

"Don't think about it," she responded curtly. "Just do it."

With El Chapo, on the other hand, as she relayed the messages she received in order to direct the others, she alternated between a businesslike tone and a saccharine sweetness that hinted at their intimate relationship.

"Tell [Güero] to get at least two houses which fit a van, love," El Chapo wrote.

"I already told him to get houses with garages, love," she replied.

"That's good," El Chapo said. "And how are the sales going?"

"Oh, like busy bees," Agustina wrote back. "Nonstop, love."

When speaking to a friend, however, Agustina revealed her deep suspicion of El Chapo. Her apparent animosity stemmed from an incident in
which she caught the technician El Gordo—who also worked with Christian on the FlexiSPY software and the encrypted network—hurriedly
closing browser tabs and images of security images on his computer,
arousing her distrust.

"He would want to do the same to me, to be spying on me. Fuck
that!" Agustina wrote to a friend on January 14, 2012. "Guess what? I'm
way smarter than him. . . . Besides, I don't trust these BlackBerrys, the
ones he gives me over here, because the bastard can locate them."

. . .

The FlexiSpy reports also gave the agents insight into El Chapo's family life, including his flirtatious relationship with his young wife, Emma
Coronel Aispuro. El Chapo first laid eyes on Emma in 2007 when she was
just seventeen, the newly crowned winner of a local beauty pageant. Born
in California and raised in Durango, Emma was the daughter of Ines Coronel Barreras, a cattle rancher and farmer of marijuana and opium, and
a niece of Ignacio "Nacho" Coronel Villarreal, the longtime partner of El
Chapo's who by the time he was killed in 2010 was the Sinaloa Cartel's
main man for meth manufacturing. Much of her early life is obscured,
but she has at least two brothers and a sister, and appears to have spent
most of her childhood and early life in Mexico, speaking little English
despite being born in the United States.

When the two met, El Chapo had been married three times and
fathered at least eight children by that point, although the number of
his children remains a bit fuzzy and the number is likely higher. His oldest children from his first marriage were already older than Emma and
beginning to involve themselves in his business, but El Chapo, like most
drug lords, never let a few previous marriages keep him from new love; as
an added bonus, a marriage to Emma would also help shore up his alliance with Nacho Coronel at a time that many of his other partnerships
were fractured or fraying.

In a 2019 interview with the *New York Times*, Emma described her early relationship with the drug lord thirty-two years her senior as chaste, a "lovely friendship" that after months of courtship bloomed into something more.

"With the passing of months we became girlfriend and boyfriend," she told the *Times*. "And when I turned 18 years old, we married in a very simple ceremony with family and only close friends."

The "simple ceremony with family and close friends" was, according to Mexican media reports, a massive party featuring an appearance by the popular *corrido* band Los Canelos de Durango and thronged by heavily armed guards (not to mention a heavily armed groom). The army showed up too, but by that time El Chapo had vanished.

El Chapo and Emma appear to never have had much time to enjoy domestic bliss. He was on the run constantly in the early years of their marriage, and according to Alex Cifuentes, she rarely visited El Chapo at his various hideouts in the Sierra Madre. They had been married several years when, in August 2011, she gave birth at a Los Angeles County hospital to twin girls, María Joaquina and Emali Guadalupe. The girls were U.S. citizens, just like their mother.

In text messages captured in the FBI's FlexiSpy reports, El Chapo and his young bride shared a flirty rapport, bantering over his love of her "enchiladas"—although she later told an interviewer that she is not the world's best cook. While he was directing his other lovers in their negotiations with weed farmers and wholesale buyers, he and Emma spoke lovingly about the minutiae of the twins' little lives: sleep schedules, plans for their six-month "birthday" party, and cutesy back-and-forths in which Emma sometimes texted as if it were the girls texting their daddy.

"I want my little princesses here to fix me my meals," El Chapo told Emma in a chat dated January 21, 2012.

"Yes daddy, what do you want us to make you?" Emma replied. "Enchiladas? Or maybe it's best if mommy makes them for you, after all, it was her enchiladas that made you fall in love with her."

In another conversation dated January 17, they discussed who the girls resembled most.

"Recently I've been told that Mali looks more like you, but she has a very sweet disposition," Emma wrote. "But Joaki has your mannerisms."

"Yes, the spitting image of Doña Consuelo," El Chapo said, referring to his mother.

Amid the lovey-dovey chitchat, the reality of El Chapo's work and lifestyle occasionally shone through.

"Our Kiki is fearless," El Chapo wrote on January 22. "I'm going to give her a *cuerno de chiva* [goat's horn, or AK-47] so she can hang with me."

16

CLOSE CALL IN CABO

O N FEBRUARY 22, 2012, FBI special agent José Moreno stood on the edge of a posh neighborhood in the Baja California resort town of Cabo San Lucas, all palm trees and green lawns and red-tile roofs, and watched the minutes go by. Along with a handful of DEA agents and United States marshals, he awaited the arrival of a team of Mexican special-forces agents.

Perched at the southern extreme of the Baja California peninsula, Cabo San Lucas—along with a few other towns collectively known as Los Cabos—has long been popular as a resort town for college students on spring break, and as a vacation spot for well-to-do and North American retirees. As much of the rest of northern Mexico went up in flames during Calderón's administration, the state of Baja California Sur, of which Los Cabos is part, had remained relatively calm. But the past few days had been hectic: the city had just hosted the G20 Summit, with visits from President Obama, then–secretary of state Hillary Clinton, and various heads of state, which brought with it myriad security headaches—for the local cops and the narcos lying low there alike.

El Chapo had been spending time in Los Cabos over the past several months, taking advantage of the relative peace and quiet there, more comfortable than the mountains and less pressure than Culiacán, where the bribes required to keep the cops off his back were adding up. In Cabo, he tended to travel around in a gold Suburban with dark tinted windows, and had traded his camo fatigues for jeans and long-sleeve T-shirts. Still, he usually had his trusty camouflage-print AR-15 within reach, and carried around a satchel full of grenades.

Alex Cifuentes had recently moved to Cabo as well. He had finally left the mountains in mid-2009 and worked down in Culiacán, but he had felt sidelined in the state capital, where Dámaso López was increasingly acting as El Chapo's right-hand man. After a close-call police raid in Culiacán, he decided to look out for himself for once, and headed to Cabo in mid-2011, staying in touch with El Chapo via BlackBerry, and with his family via an iPhone that Christian Rodriguez had told him was encrypted, totally safe.

In mid-February, El Chapo reached out to tell Alex that he was in town and wanted to see him, but Alex wasn't so sure. The city was still dotted with security checkpoints, and Alex brusquely told El Chapo that it wasn't a good idea to meet in person just yet.

"I told him to go elsewhere, that he shouldn't come close to there," Alex said. "He was going to bring all the heat on me."

Still, he left the gate to his condo garage open, "just in case [El Chapo] arrived in like, an emergency fashion."

• • •

Thanks to intel cobbled together from the FlexiSPY reports, along with a BlackBerry PIN linked to one of El Chapo's personal phones, Moreno and his team suspected that El Chapo was holed up in a tony section of Cabo called Hacienda Encantada. Over the past several days, Moreno and the rest of the agents overseeing the raid had been reading as El Chapo and his lover, Agustina Cabanillas Acosta, had spoken of plans to meet in Cabo, and along with data they were able to get from the phone associated with El Chapo, they had pinpointed his location in Hacienda Encantada, a gated cul-de-sac overlooking the sea where homes are routinely listed for north of $1 million.

Moreno, a ten-year veteran of the FBI at the time assigned to the bureau's Tijuana office, had intended to kick things off by 1:30 p.m., but the Mexican cops were late.

"They were supposed to be there in twenty minutes. Twenty minutes came and went, and they did not show up until almost an hour later," Moreno recalled. "By the time they showed up here to this target area, it was approximately three thirty-five in the afternoon."

While the SWAT team had been mustering nearby, El Chapo was texting with his wife. There had been some shooting in Culiacán that day, and she was concerned.

"Honey, some guys in La Guadalupe Victoria [neighborhood of Culiacán] were killed just now," she wrote at 2:40 p.m. "Was it any of your people?"

"No, darling," El Chapo responded.

"I love you love," Emma replied. "Talk to you soon."

As he texted with Emma, the federal agents began arriving at the rendezvous spot where Moreno was waiting. Upon the arrival of the agents—some members of an elite special-ops unit of the Policía Federal, others from an investigative team of the PGR—Moreno briefed them on the suspected location of their target, whom the U.S. agents believed to be in one of two homes on the cul-de-sac. But as the *federales* rolled into Hacienda Encantada, they immediately strayed from the plan, hitting each house one by one rather than going straight to the two that Moreno had highlighted.

When they finally hit the last house—a two-story villa with pastel adobe walls and an in-ground pool complete with a slide from the second floor into the water—they neglected to set up a perimeter in the rear of the home.

"I have no idea why they did that," Moreno said.

Huh.

Out on the street, Moreno and the other U.S. agents waited anxiously for about five minutes as the federal police secured the house. When members of the raiding party began to come out of the house toting various cell phones, ledgers, and assorted papers, the Americans entered, and Moreno spied Agustina Cabanillas along with another woman and two men detained by the Mexican police.

Moreno began to take stock of the place, strolling out back with a camcorder and walking forlornly around the yard. Scanning the patio with the video camera, he cursed under his breath in Spanish and walked past a wrought-iron spiral staircase through a sliding glass door into what appeared to have been the fugitive drug lord's bedroom.

The *federales* had already tossed the place, and clothes were piled on the king-sized bed, the only piece of furniture in the room apart from a knee-high bedside table and a dark, wooden wardrobe atop which sat a flat-screen television. The doors to the wardrobe were opened, askew.

In the papers recovered at the safe house, the agents found a ledger documenting drug sales, and a wish list for enough weaponry to equip a small army. They also recovered some clothing, including Nike sneakers (size 9), a few pairs of jeans (size 32x30), a receipt for a recent liposuction procedure that Agustina had undergone, and one of El Chapo's trademark black baseball caps. In one of the vehicles parked in the garage, they uncovered El Chapo's AR-15 in woodland camo skin with its M40 grenade launcher, along with a satchel full of grenades and a few other small arms.

As the Mexican feds and U.S. agents ransacked the house and interrogated the detainees, a force of about one hundred more Mexican agents backed by three Black Hawk helicopters deployed around Los Cabos in an effort to scour the city for El Chapo, in hopes of preventing an escape.

But El Chapo had vanished.

· · ·

When El Chapo had seen the cops barging into an adjacent house, he had only had a few moments to react. But that was enough. By the time the *federales* began battering down the door to his safe house, El Chapo was already dashing out the back door. Running past a series of square columns, he and his secretary known as Condor crossed the patio, scampered past the pool, dove through a screen of palm fronds and geraniums, and clambered down over a cement retaining wall to a culvert running behind the back of the property.

Less than two hours later, he called Alex to let him know he was already back in Culiacán.

"Joaquín just left," Alex Cifuentes recalled matter-of-factly. "He got in his car and he left and they didn't find him."

At 6:14 p.m., a few hours after the raid, Emma checked in on her husband, seemingly unaware of the drama unfolding in Cabo.

"Hello love, what are you up to?" Emma asked.

"All is well, love," El Chapo responded eight minutes later. "I'm on the road right now. I'll get back to you later. I love you all."

About three hours later, he texted her again, this time with a request. He had left in such a hurry that he and Condor had been forced to leave behind not only their weapons, but his clothes and toiletries as well. The shopping list he sent Emma included sweatpants, underwear, five shirts, shampoo, aftershave, a comb, a pair of small scissors, and black mustache dye. Just because you're the most wanted man in Mexico doesn't mean you can't stay fly. The next day, he added a couple of items to the list: jeans, size 32x30, and sneakers, size 8.5.

• • •

Back in Los Cabos, Alex Cifuentes watched with mounting dread as the Black Hawk helicopters swept across the southern tip of the peninsula from San José del Cabo in the east to Cabo San Lucas in the west, beaming their flashlights along the waterline, clearly visible from Alex's home in the neighborhood of Pedregal, a hilly maze of mansions on the southwest side of town overlooking the sea. Terrified that the choppers would descend on him at any minute, Alex closed the hurricane shutters, drew the blinds, turned off the lights, and waited out the storm. For a conspiracy theorist like Alex, this must have been his worst nightmare: black helicopters in the night sky, looking for him and his people.

About twenty-four hours later, he called his mom, using the iPhone Christian had provided him. If he was going to go down, he wanted to check in with her first. His mother, Carlina Villa, spoke frequently with her children about their business activities, providing advice and wisdom gleaned from a lifetime of living among Colombian drug traffickers. After a brief back-and-forth about whether they could hear one another—Carlina, then aged seventy-seven, had to put her glasses on, she said, then dropped her iPhone with a clatter, and wanted to know if her youngest son was sick—Alex gave his mother a quick update, speaking in code and almost cooing in a soft, loving voice.

"The mosquitoes have already arrived where I am," he said, referring to the helicopters. "The 'other one' managed to leave, but the thing is, it's quite possible something might happen tomorrow. So I call to say goodbye."

"Ay, *Dios mío*," Carlina sighed. "Are the others accompanying you, or did they dump you already?"

"Alone, alone," he said, still speaking in a calm, mellifluous voice. "But well, unexpectedly the other one rushed to see me. I warned him not to come over, the friend, and well, there was a commotion."

As his mother responded with various invocations of "*Dios mío*" and "Oh my Lord," Alex laid out his plan to stay off the grid and wait it out.

> ALEX: [unintelligible cross-talk] to wait, to wait for it to calm down, but that stubborn old man wanted to see me, to see me, to see me. And yes, such good luck that he managed to leave. Such good luck, otherwise he would be worse off.
>
> CARLINA: Mm-hmm.
>
> ALEX: Let's see if it comes. And well, so we're there—
>
> CARLINA: Ay, *Dios mío*.
>
> ALEX: On the lookout. You just give it your all, because that doesn't stop—
>
> CARLINA: Yes, by the hand of our Lord.
>
> ALEX: So that our Lord gives us the receiving.
>
> CARLINA: God bless you and keep you . . . and help you to be invisible so they don't come in wherever you are. . . . In the name of the Father, the Son, and the Holy Spirit. Amen.

With a string of pleas to the heavens and a recitation of a narco-matriarch's prayer, Carlina bid farewell to her son. Thanks to Christian, the FBI had it all on tape.

• • •

In the wake of the raid in Los Cabos, Special Agents Steve Marston and Bob Potash decided they needed to take a different tack. El Chapo had been badly spooked, and seemed to be back to his old ways of hiding out in Sinaloa, either just outside of Culiacán or in the mountains. So that spring and summer, they began to use the GPS location available through FlexiSPY to chart the movements of his various lovers, particularly when El Chapo summoned them for a tryst. The way it typically worked was that El Chapo would text one of his girlfriends and tell them to meet one of his secretaries—usually Condor, or a guy named *"Nariz,"* or the Nose—in a public place in Culiacán. From there, they would head off to the rendezvous location, but El Chapo knew better than to put that in writing, and on his instruction, they would turn their phones off en route. The agents had a map of the women's movements in the city, but they always went off the grid before their movements provided any useful hint as to the location of El Chapo or his hideouts. They had a local team on the ground in Culiacán attempting to trail the girlfriends, but thanks to the five-minute delay in obtaining GPS location, they were never able to stick a tail on the women after Nariz or Condor picked them up.

El Chapo had been off the VoIP telecom system for more than six months now, and most of Christian's interactions with him were regarding FlexiSPY, and conducted through El Chapo's in-house IT guys. The various members of the Cifuentes family, on the other hand, were merrily chatting away on "encrypted" iPhones that Christian had provided them, paid for by the FBI. Thanks to the intel from these conversations, the FBI managed to get a bead on Jorge Cifuentes, who had been on the run since 2011, when the Department of the Treasury had officially sanctioned him and his family, effectively freezing their ability to use the banking system. Armed with that information, the Colombian government pounced, seizing more than three hundred assets belonging to the family, including cars, businesses, and private islands in the Caribbean.

So Jorge headed for the hills, literally, taking cover in a slum on the outskirts of Caracas, where he shacked up with a nineteen-year-old indigenous woman. His only contact with the larger world was conversations with his siblings, Alex and Dolly Cifuentes, in which he often raved about how obedient his new bride was, how she cooked and cleaned for him, and how he read the Bible to her at night.

Relations between Washington and Caracas were tense at the time, thanks to the anti-imperialist bluster of President Hugo Chávez and the efforts by the United States to undermine his administration. Law enforcement sources who described the operation to me were cagey about how exactly they coordinated it, but working with their Colombian counterparts, they said they were able to feed information about Jorge to the Venezuelans. On November 8, 2012, armed with that information, Venezuelan authorities tracked him down, arrested him, and paraded him in front of the cameras—looking like a mousy little businessman on a bad day, hairline receding, mouth downturned, sad eyes peering out from behind rectangular glasses, his little frame swimming in an oversized ballistic vest—before extraditing him to Colombia.

• • •

As the months crept by, Christian had been slowly but surely extricating himself from El Chapo's orbit. His role by this point was mostly to provide support for the "special" FlexiSPY devices and the BlackBerrys. He and the fugitive drug lord had not spoken directly since the escape from the mountains, and during the time that he was working for the FBI, his handlers had no intention of putting him in a room with El Chapo; they didn't think he could stay cool under that kind of pressure.

He continued to field questions from El Chapo's in-house IT team, Gordo and Benjamin, and was running the FlexiSPY system on the FBI's servers in the Netherlands, along with the iPhones on the Cifuentes family plan, but his direct involvement was nearing an end, and the agents were beginning to look for new ways to access El Chapo's inner circle.

The double—or triple—life was beginning to wear on Christian. He was still making decent money working for El Chapo and for the Cifuentes family, and the FBI was giving him a steady stream of cash to keep the systems running. But he had been under terrific pressure for years now, and the stress was beginning to show. On top of all that, he had a lot to worry about at home. In addition to his girlfriend and their young children, he had a secret family as well with another girlfriend with whom he had also conceived children. A quintuple life—that's a lot to manage.

Then, on January 7, 2013, the FBI intercepted a phone call that brought everything to a halt. In a phone call with his mother, Alex got to discussing the arrest of his brother Jorge several months earlier. Carlina Villa was going to visit Jorge in jail, and Alex wanted her to pass along a message.

"Send my regards," Alex told Carlina. "And tell him that Christian was the one who blew the whistle."

On the same day that he told his mother that they suspected Christian of cooperating, Alex was texting with his secretary, a woman named Andrea Fernández Velez, in which he asked her to dig up information on Christian in order to track him down.

"Send someone to go there tomorrow and see if they see Christian, among others," Alex wrote.

"They might have to ask for him. I don't know him," Andrea responded. "Give me his last name, he must have Facebook."

"I don't know his last name," Alex responded.

When Christian saw those two exchanges, he was terrified. Finally, after all the stress of being a double agent, he'd been outed. He was done. He and his family had already relocated to the United States, and now it became permanent. But still Christian couldn't relax, and he went days on end without sleep. Within months of learning he'd been burned, Christian suffered what he described as a "nervous breakdown," which was so severe that he ended up in the hospital for weeks, where he had electric pulses zapped into his brain to treat acute anxiety and depression. That was followed by another nervous breakdown, and more shock treatment.

In the years that he had been working as an informant, the FBI paid Christian more than half a million dollars in expenses and compensation, for which he failed to pay taxes even after his arrival in the United States, because he "didn't want to." Despite his tax dodge, his laundering of ill-gotten money in Colombia, and the immense help he provided to two of the most prolific drug-trafficking organizations in the world, he was never charged with a crime.

As of January 10, 2019, he was still in therapy.

17

THE DRAGNET

IN THE FALL of 2012, as Christian's involvement with the Sinaloans was waning, his handlers at the FBI realized they would soon need a new mole inside El Chapo's crew. They needed someone who, like Christian, was a bit of an outsider, not a narco lifer, someone in over their head, someone who could be flipped with the right mix of motivation and fear.

They settled on Andrea Fernández Velez, the personal secretary to Alex Cifuentes, who was frequently just a step removed from El Chapo. Andrea, a pretty Colombian woman in her early thirties, had met Alex some years before. Her employment with Alex began informally, doing odd jobs for him and the family, picking up clothing or pricey household items for him, including a set of five-hundred-dollar sheets. Like Alex, she was born in Medellín, and when she first moved to Mexico, he let her live in a home he owned in Cancún. As she gained his trust, the odd jobs became more regular, more important, until she had become one of his closest aides. Eventually her duties included coordinating drug shipments, meeting with buyers and sellers, even running a modeling agency that she used as a cover to send girls to El Chapo's hideout and to parties thrown for corrupt politicos and military officers. She found it intoxicating at first, that kind of trust and power bestowed upon her by some of the heaviest drug traffickers in the Western Hemisphere. As Alex's assistant, Andrea was a conduit through whom many of the boss's decisions flowed and that meant, by proxy, she was involved at virtually every step it took for a kilo of cocaine (or several thousand kilos) to get from a production lab in Colombia to a smuggling hub in Mexico to distributors and wholesale buyers in North America.

Thanks to the wiretaps they had on the Cifuentes family's iPhones and the info they had gotten from FlexiSPY, Special Agents Potash and Marston had plenty of dirt on Andrea, enough that a grand jury in the United States had secretly indicted her on drug charges severe enough to put her away for life. But they didn't want to arrest her; they wanted to scare the daylights out of her in order to turn her, as they had with Christian.

Although Colombian by birth, Andrea had been living in Mexico to work for Alex. This was an issue for Potash and Martson; they wanted to confront her in Colombia, as far away from El Chapo's eyes and ears as possible. So they waited until September 2012, when she went to Bogotá on business, to make their approach. They knew she had tickets to fly back to Mexico, so they set up shop at the Bogotá airport hoping to snag her in transit, as they had nearly two years earlier with Christian.

On the first day of their stakeout, Andrea canceled her flight and rebooked for the next day, so Potash, Marston, and their team of local FBI and Colombian law enforcement turned up the next day, hoping to catch her before one of the three flights a day to Mexico City. They waited all day, but she never showed. For a full week they staked out the Bogotá airport, growing increasingly frustrated, coming up with theories about why she hadn't turned up. Had something happened to her? Was she going into hiding? As they waited, they went for walks through the airport, practicing their pitch, going back and forth on the best way to try to win her over.

Finally, on the seventh day, Andrea strolled into the terminal. In the week that Potash and Marston had been haunting the departures terminal, they had seen a couple of Andrea look-alikes, false alarms, so when the real Andrea walked in, they blinked a few times and squinted. It had to be her. Several Colombian members of the team approached Andrea and steered her to a quiet corner of the terminal, where Potash and Marston were waiting.

"We're with the FBI," they told her. "You really need to talk to us."

Andrea said okay, and they led her toward a waiting car outside the terminal.

After driving Andrea to a secure location, they showed her the indictment against her. Almost immediately, she agreed to help. Pressing the issue, Potash told Andrea she was in a lot of trouble, stressing that it was best if she came with them somewhere they could talk.

Again, Andrea said okay.

Not quite getting the memo, Potash reiterated that speaking with them was Andrea's only real option.

"Okay!" she replied, exasperated.

Marston gave Potash a nudge, a nonverbal cue along the lines of "I think you've made your point."

By the time the agents approached her in Bogotá, Andrea had already begun having doubts about her career. She had seen the potential harm that could come to people in El Chapo's orbit and had had her own close calls as well. In one memorable incident, Alex had sent her to Ecuador to meet with a corrupt army captain whom El Chapo wanted kidnapped for supposedly stealing from him. Unaware that Alex and El Chapo were using her as bait, Andrea met the officer in a restaurant. When a group of kidnappers dressed as police burst into the restaurant to seize the officer, Andrea fled to the kitchen and hid in terror, convinced that she was a target as well. She was furious with Alex for putting her in danger when she found out later that she had been an unwitting part of the ruse.

She needed a way out, and now, sitting face-to-face with the FBI agents, a path to freedom had dropped in her lap.

Andrea was a more traditional mole than Christian had been, providing more human intel and less of the high-tech spying that Christian's cooperation had allowed. As Alex's eyes and ears, she was empowered to represent him at meetings throughout the Americas, from Quito to Bogotá to Mexico City to Toronto. Soon she was feeding information to Marston: phone numbers, the identities of various associates, intel to help them build a coherent portrait of the operations of El Chapo and Alex, which they in turn fed to their counterparts at other federal agencies.

. . .

While the FBI agents were working the human-intel angle, agents with Homeland Security Investigations, or HSI, were beginning to set up a series of wiretaps on the BlackBerry devices that El Chapo and his lieutenants used under the mistaken assumption that they were secure from interception. BlackBerry Messenger, or BBM, can be quite secure, if a company (or the members of an illegal conspiracy) sets up its own servers, but El Chapo and his pals were basically using store-bought BlackBerrys on the company's main servers, so all investigators needed was a BBM PIN and they could get a wiretap warrant on it. Even without Christian's help, the feds were soon gathering reams of evidence.

Investigators had begun to get a glimpse into how El Chapo was communicating via BBM in June 2012, following a raid on a suspected safe house in Tepic, the state capital of Nayarit. They had kicked down the doors hoping to find the fugitive drug lord himself, but when Mexican agents raided the safe house, all they found was a lackey and a few dozen BlackBerrys, which he had been using to communicate with all the operatives below him in the communication chain. Unwittingly, they had uncovered the physical location of one node, one "office," from which workers sent and received messages.

This discovery revealed the lengths El Chapo was going to insulate himself from detection. In the wake of the Cabo raid, El Chapo, ever paranoid about his communications, devised this new system to swiftly relay messages and communicate with his underlings without ever having to personally get near a BlackBerry. The agents referred to El Chapo's new system as the "fat-finger router," and it worked like a more sophisticated version of how El Chapo had previously been communicating through girlfriends like Agustina Cabanillas Acosta and Lucero Sanchez Lopez. Another term the agents tracking the communications used to refer to this strategy of anonymized communication was a "mirror system."

El Chapo's mirror system was based on a series of levels, or tiers. At the bottom were the far-flung field operatives and associates, who would send messages to tier one, the so-called office phones. Each office phone had several field operatives reporting in and would relay these messages up to tier-two devices, in the hands of higher-ranking lieutenants. They would in turn copy and paste the message—along with the nickname of the original sender—and send it up to the top tier, the secretary in direct contact with El Chapo. Once El Chapo had a response, the secretaries would tap it out to the tier-two phones, and the information would flow back down the chain. So when a wholesaler in Canada or a cocaine producer in Ecuador received instructions from El Chapo, it would have filtered through a minimum of three phones.

It was far less high-tech than Christian's system, but a hell of a lot harder to infiltrate; even if the feds managed to flip one person on the network, they'd have an extremely limited amount of info, and nothing tied directly to El Chapo. Still, the BlackBerrys were far from secure, and in February 2013, with phone numbers provided by Andrea and other sources, HSI agents based in Nogales, Arizona, began to get wiretaps on BlackBerrys used by cartel associates. Slowly, painstakingly, they began mapping out the network. As the HSI team began to tug at the thread, they were amazed at what the cartel managed with such rudimentary technology, according to John Zappone, a special agent with the HSI field office in Nogales.

"It was a very unique method of communication that we basically hadn't seen before," Zappone recalled.

As the agents pulled in more communications, they slowly began to illuminate portions of El Chapo's network. They read along as a buyer in Central America planned a shipment of coke from the mountainous border between Colombia and Ecuador to a town on the coast of Ecuador to a landing strip in Belize; as a cartel guy in Guatemala was coordinating with El Chapo's pilots to get coke into Mexico; as a lieutenant of El Chapo discussed a plot to murder a cop in Baja California who was making trouble for a corrupt politician; as an operative way down in the jungles of Colombia discussed the purchase of cocaine base, and then as he made sure it got onto boats on the Pacific Coast, sending updates through the mirror system the whole time.

• • •

In November 2013, a team of Mexican agents raided a small ranch on the outskirts of Culiacán, overwhelming the security guards, who belonged to a team of hit men calling themselves "Los Ántrax." One of the men swept up in the raid was a portly, middle-aged man who gave his name as Enrique Rodríguez García, who seemed to have been in the wrong place at the wrong time. It was not until days later that the authorities realized that the prisoner was actually a high-ranking lieutenant of El Chapo and in his own right one of the most wanted drug traffickers in the Western Hemisphere: Alex Cifuentes.

Even after the arrest of Alex, Andrea continued to pass information to the FBI: a phone number here, a name there, helping to fill in the gaps in the agents' understanding of the people close to El Chapo and the people he did business with on the wholesale side in the United States and Canada. But that part of the investigation had largely run its course. The focus shifted to the wiretaps on El Chapo's BlackBerrys, an effort largely run by HSI and the DEA.

· · ·

In the Mexico City field office of the DEA, Special Agent Drew Hogan coordinated with the HSI agents as more and more texts came in; they were trying to get closer to El Chapo. Hogan had arrived in Mexico in 2012, after assignments chasing money launderers from Tijuana to Bolivia. He was well suited to this kind of painstaking detective work, piecing together text messages and putting together a picture of the larger operation. By identifying the BBM numbers that received the most messages, Hogan and the other investigators were able to pinpoint which device was an "office," and then map out the layered tiers, before deducing based on the nicknames included in each text who might be who. It was starting to make sense: "*Tocayo*," or "Namesake," was Iván Archivaldo, El Chapo's eldest son; "*Suegro*," or "Father-in-Law," had to be Inés Coronel, father of Emma Coronel; then there was Picudo, the secretary who had helped El Chapo escape in Los Cabos, and Cholo Iván, the shooter whom El Chapo had once cautioned against excess violence, and Condor, a secretary who was one of El Chapo's most loyal servants. As they gained intel on those closest to El Chapo, the likelihood of locating the boss himself increased.

But El Chapo's paranoia, which unbeknownst to him had been his undoing with the FlexiSPY intel, was now serving him well. Every thirty days or so, or every time El Chapo's people got spooked, many of the devices would drop off the map, and the investigators would have to get new warrants on the BlackBerrys that some lackey would buy in bulk. They continued to stay up on the wiretaps, continued to read through countless texts going up and down the mirror system, and by the beginning of 2014, they were finally zeroing in on El Chapo. The mission was twofold: they needed to find him and capture him, and they needed to build a case against him for when they did. As a result, they were careful to get warrants for their wiretaps, go through all the proper channels, and clear things with the U.S. attorneys in the jurisdictions in which El Chapo might find himself on trial. They didn't want to give his lawyers anything they could use in the future to have the case thrown out. That had happened before: in 1992, a Pennsylvania bounty hunter working for the DEA had kidnapped a doctor accused of taking part in the 1985 torture and murder of Kiki Camarena in Guadalajara. A grand jury indicted the doctor on charges related to Camarena's abduction and murder, but his lawyers successfully argued that the process by which the doctor ended up in U.S. custody had poisoned the case against him. He walked free and returned to Mexico. Thirty years later, rather than whiling away his days in a prison cell, the doctor now runs a taco restaurant in Guadalajara. The U.S. government knew it couldn't make the same mistake with El Chapo.

• • •

While the agents were closing in, El Chapo continued to run his operation remotely, amazing the snooping investigators with his obsession with minutiae, just as he had when negotiating the price per kilo of heroin with the Flores twins back in 2008.

Despite some major setbacks—the arrest of Ines Coronel Barreras in Agua Prieta, Sonora, on April 30, 2013, or the arrest of Alex Cifuentes that November—El Chapo continued to play a major role in the global drug trade. He and El Mayo and their allies were still moving multiple tons of coke, heroin, and meth—and, at an increasing rate, the powerful, synthetic opioid fentanyl—into the United States each year, all while also shipping loads of drugs as far afield as Australia and Europe.

El Chapo and El Mayo also continued to hold tremendous power in Sinaloa, where several different factions loyal to them ran security, domestic drug sales, and coordinated smuggling operations. Hit squads like Los Antrax, overseen by an ostentatious, social-media-loving killer nicknamed Chino Antrax, enforced the cartel's will. Unlike areas of Mexico in which organized-crime groups were splintering into countless warring factions, Sinaloa had returned to some degree of stability as El Chapo and El Mayo emerged largely victorious over the Beltrán Leyvas. For anyone who violated the traffickers' mandates against crimes like car theft or kidnapping, "justice" was swift and brutal; car thieves who refused to heed warnings sometimes turned up dead, with toy cars displayed on their bodies as a message to anyone else who failed to fall in line. For civilians in Culiacán, years of coexistence with violent crime had led them to develop daily strategies to avoid violence: they knew not to honk at fancy cars that cut them off in traffic, to avoid discussing certain topics and mentioning certain names, and for many it worked. Daily life continued, as it almost always had.

El Chapo, meanwhile, was spending much of his time in the city. Perhaps he had grown overconfident, or perhaps he had grown tired of mountain life. He still moved around on a nearly daily basis, shuffling between a series of safe houses referred to by numerical code names: The One, The Two, The Three, and so on. In nondescript homes scattered through upscale neighborhoods across town, El Chapo kept sparsely decorated digs where he and his closest aides could lie low, receiving visitors who included Emma Coronel, various girlfriends, and others who needed an appointment with the boss.

At each safe house, El Chapo's interior decorators had rigged up elaborate escape hatches hidden beneath the bathtub, which led to tunnels connecting to the city's sewer system. El Chapo had never lost his faith in the value of tunnels. Just in case.

18

THE LION'S DEN

ON THE AFTERNOON of February 13, 2014, four Black Hawk helicopters carrying a strike team of Mexican Marines lifted off from their base in La Paz, Baja California Sur, and swung to the east, four-blade rotors chopping the salty sea air as the convoy cruised low over the Sea of Cortez.

Sitting with his back to the cockpit, the starboard gunner to his left, DEA special agent Victor Vazquez could hardly hear himself think, let alone shout into his helmet mic loud enough to communicate with the Marines on board his helicopter. Born in the state of Durango, he had served in the U.S. Marine Corps and as a San Diego sheriff's deputy before joining the DEA, and he had spent the last five years with the DEA chasing narcos in Mexico. He had mostly been focusing on La Familia Michoacana in Guerrero and its splinter group the Knights Templar, a bizarre, cultlike militia infamous for its messianic leader known as "El Más Loco," or the Craziest One. But now he was on the trail of one of Mexico's true players, the shadowy kingpin thought by many to be the true power behind the Sinaloa Cartel, perhaps more so even than El Chapo: Ismael "El Mayo" Zambada. Vazquez was hoping to score big.

Vazquez, along with fellow DEA agent Drew Hogan, had arrived in La Paz a month earlier with this group of Mexican Marines, and spent the intervening weeks running training exercises, a cover for their true mission. These elite troops, along with their DEA advisors, were stationed in Baja California for one purpose: to capture the leaders of the Sinaloa Cartel. For years, the DEA, HSI, and FBI had been using informants and wiretaps to construct a detailed picture of the cartel's communications networks and trying to decipher the movements of its leaders, and now, finally, they had a bead on them.

They were there for three men: El Chapo, El Mayo, and Rafael Caro Quintero, the former Guadalajara Cartel leader who'd been in prison since his arrest in 1985, just after the kidnapping and murder of DEA agent Enrique "Kiki" Camarena. Or rather, he'd been in prison very recently. Six months earlier, a state judge had ordered that Caro Quintero be released on a technicality, and he was now rumored to be lying low in the mountains of Sinaloa near where he was born. It was unclear to what extent Caro Quintero was involved in drug trafficking following his release, but the DEA has a long memory, and it was not about to let Caro Quintero, the man they held responsible for Agent Camarena's brutal murder nearly three decades earlier, live out the rest of his days a free man.

Aside from Vazquez, Hogan, and the SEMAR unit from Mexico City, no one knew the real reason for their presence in Baja. Even among the other Mexican Marines, widely viewed as the least corrupt branch of Mexican law enforcement or military, it was crucial to keep the true mission a secret. Their instructions were to move on whoever "jumped" first. When they got intel that El Mayo had been spotted at a ranch on the outskirts of Culiacán, they got ready to move.

The force was small for the task at hand, about one hundred men in total, with about forty-five arriving by chopper and the rest rolling in by land in pickup trucks marked with the Spanish acronym for the Marines, SEMAR. Considering the potential danger, and the fact that they'd be on El Mayo's home turf, it was a smaller group than Vazquez would have liked.

"I'm in there with a hundred Marines, yes, well-trained, trusted Marines," Vazquez recalled. "Still, one hundred Marines is still not enough for that state."

They had to tread lightly, even if there was little chance that the Marines could maintain the element of surprise when the choppers made landfall in Sinaloa. Drug traffickers here, as in other parts of Mexico, rely on a vast army of *halcones*, or falcons, lookouts paid to keep tabs on a given street corner, intersection, hotel, or country road and feed information up the chain, granting the traffickers a sprawling intelligence network.

"It's any corner, a specific location, and their job is to look out all day," Vazquez said. "A taco guy, a vendor working on the gas station, they look and they're looking at law enforcement, military, enemy cartel coming in their area and their job is to report it via phone or handheld; whatever device is given to them."

If a gringo gets off the plane in Culiacán, chances are someone at the airport is making a phone call. If a soldier takes a piss, someone in the hills is going to know about it. So when four Black Hawk helicopters come roaring over Sinaloa off the Sea of Cortez, those phones are going to light up, and the whole state is going to be on alert. They'd probably lost the element of surprise the moment they landed in La Paz—forget arriving in Sinaloa unnoticed.

The choppers flew low as they made landfall, sweeping above the scrubby Sinaloa countryside at just a few hundred feet, the machine gunners scanning the ground for anything that looked like a lookout, or a gunman aiming to take a potshot at the helicopters, or a convoy racing to escape. As they approached the ranch, on the eastern outskirts of Culiacán, the winter sun was beginning to inch below the horizon, and apart from a pair of trucks cruising on a road below, there appeared to be few people out and about in the patchwork farmland they passed.

The Black Hawks' rotors kicked up dust as the pilots touched down in a field about one hundred yards from the ranch's main house, and Vazquez, dressed in full camo and toting an assault rifle, jogged toward the house as the Marines ahead of him began to methodically search the building for any sign of Mayo or his associates.

They swept into the house, checking it once, twice, three times for any signs of recent life, anything that suggested the drug lord had left in a hurry: food on the stove, plates in the sink, even a warm toilet seat. But El Mayo was nowhere to be found.

Night had fallen save for a sliver of light shining from behind the foothills of the Sierra Madre that separated the ranch from the sea to the west, turning the sky a deep purple as the Marines headed for the property's second building, their flashlights cutting beams of light through the darkness as they crossed the back patio and entered the building, holding their weapons at their sides, alert. Vazquez, his sleeves rolled up in a futile effort to beat the heavy Sinaloa heat, followed a Marine into the building, peering cautiously around each corner as he made his way through the house to the bedroom. The house was neat, looked barely lived in, a painting here and there on the walls and the living room arranged tidily with a couch and two armchairs around a coffee table. In the bedroom, the bed was made, and a chest of drawers revealed a few personal items as the Marines rifled through it looking for clues. A small television set sat facing the bed, switched off.

As Vazquez and his comrades searched the house, a pair of Marines stood on the front patio guarding the caretaker, a middle-aged man with jet-black hair and a mustache wearing a striped dress shirt and white jeans, sitting calmly in a rocking chair. One of the Marines, his face covered by a keffiyeh, scrolled through a BlackBerry. Nearby, the raiders found two other men, known associates of El Mayo, hiding in some bushes.

Although there was no sign of El Mayo, the raid wasn't a total bust. With information extracted from the detainees, the Marines located and unearthed a handful of blue plastic barrels, inside which they found about a hundred assault rifles. They spent the next two days searching the nearby hills, but they came no closer to finding El Mayo.

• • •

Back in La Paz, Special Agent Drew Hogan was pissed. He thought they should have been looking for El Chapo. Blowing their cover on this hunt for El Mayo would make the search for El Chapo that much harder.

Part of it, of course, was the competitive nature of federal agents. Hogan saw El Chapo as his guy, the case he had been living and breathing since arriving in Mexico two years prior. So to focus on the other two targets felt to him like a distraction. But he also had a good case to make: the capture operation in Sinaloa was based largely around intelligence work that focused on El Chapo's network, El Chapo's lieutenants, and El Chapo's secretaries, and the Marines were much more likely to succeed if they didn't ransack every ranch in the state looking for other fugitives.

As for Caro Quintero, that just seemed like overkill to Hogan. He understood the symbolic significance Caro Quintero had to the DEA; but Hogan felt he was at war with El Chapo, and wars are not won by making sentimental decisions. Compared to El Chapo, Hogan considered Caro Quintero a nobody, a has-been with little to suggest that he had returned to the drug game.

"They didn't have shit on him, but they threw him into the mix, like, 'Yeah he's up here on a mountain somewhere,'" Hogan said. "We had worked all this time to really bring the Marines in for El Chapo, and here are these guys trying to piggyback on our op."

But El Chapo? They had a sprawling surveillance operation against him, and based on their wiretaps they knew he was lying low in Culiacán. When the Marines and their DEA "advisors" first headed to La Paz, Hogan had had his eyes set on a ranch outside of Culiacán where El Chapo sometimes met with his sons and senior lieutenants. For Hogan, the ideal plan had been to wait for El Chapo to take a trip to the ranch and nab him there, as far away as possible from the crowded streets of Culiacán, where a wrong move could result in an urban battle in the heart of El Chapo's fiefdom.

The February 13 raid on the ranch associated with El Mayo had put a stop to that. Now the chances of El Chapo leaving the city for some fresh air down at his ranch had dropped to zero, and pressure was mounting for the Marines to pack up and head back to the capital. The unit in La Paz was mainly focused on organized crime groups in other regions of Mexico. Their higher-ups were growing weary of this diversion from normal duty, and pressure was mounting. If they were going to hit El Chapo, they'd now have to nab him in Culiacán.

On February 16, the Marines, with Vazquez still in tow, headed to a field on the north side of Culiacán where they set up a command post, for what was now turning into an extended search of the city for El Chapo or any associate who might lead them to him. They began by looking for the secretary known as Condor, who they knew to be spending the most face time with El Chapo. If they could find Condor, it was certain that El Chapo would be nearby.

Thanks to wiretap information from HSI, the Marines knew the approximate area of two houses that Condor had frequented in recent weeks, using the "ping" from his BlackBerry to pinpoint his physical location each time he used the phone. But any hope for a quick in-and-out began to fade as soon as the Marines and Vazquez began searching Culiacán. The first location was a dud, no trace of the secretary or any indication of where he might be. On the way to the second location, they met resistance from cop cars, who pulled Vazquez and the Marines over in the unmarked vehicle the team was using to cruise around town. Everyone was on edge.

"Drew, the fuckin' cops won't leave us alone; they're all over us," Vazquez texted Hogan. "They've tried stopping us multiple times. This entire city knows we're here."

Hogan, who had moved to a SEMAR base in the port of Topolobampo, more than 150 miles northwest, decided it was time to shift gears. There was another secretary named Mario Hidalgo Arguello, a former special-forces soldier nicknamed El Nariz—Spanish for "the Nose"—whom they knew to be in frequent contact with El Chapo.

"Fuck it," Hogan texted back. "Nariz is our next best option. Find him and he'll tell us exactly where El Chapo is at."

"So go after Nariz?" Vazquez asked.

"Yeah," Hogan replied. "Follow the Nose."

Pacing the helicopter pad at Topolobampo and pleading silently for a break in the search that would allow him to head to Culiacán and put his own boots on the ground, Hogan couldn't shake the sense of dread he felt as his fellow agent and the Marines rolled through the city. He had reason to be concerned. The local cops in Culiacán were seen as compromised, and the soldiers at the local garrison could not be trusted much more than the cops. Vazquez and the Marines were surrounded by possible enemies, a little net trying to catch a big fish. At any moment they risked being stymied by local authorities or, worse, overwhelmed by gunmen who they feared could pour out of the woodwork at the drop of a hat—or with a few taps of a BlackBerry keypad. All El Chapo had to do was put out a call for backup and he could have who-knows-how-many fiercely loyal shooters on the street turning the mission into a bloody fiasco of *Black Hawk Down* proportions.

Criminals less powerful than El Chapo had certainly put up a bloody fight when cornered. One recent engagement weighed particularly heavily on their minds. Just two months before, on December 18, a simple pre-dawn raid on the condominium of a high-ranking lieutenant of El Mayo in a beachside Sonora town an hour's drive from the border with Arizona had turned into one of the deadliest battles the DEA had ever "advised" on foreign soil. The DEA agents, embedded that morning with a team of federal police, had just rolled up to the condo parking lot when they were greeted by a hail of withering gunfire from a belt-fed machine gun overlooking the lot. They returned fire, but remained pinned down as the traffickers' reinforcements—including local cops coming to scoop up wounded hit men—poured into the area and opened up on the *federales* and the DEA agents. The firefight only subsided when bodyguards for the mortally wounded narco lieutenant dragged him out the back door, leaving a trail of blood smeared across the floor and out the door into the parking lot. In total, five gunmen were killed and two federal police-men were badly wounded. The area was so hostile that the DEA agents embedded with the Mexican feds had no choice but to haul ass north to a hospital more than two hundred miles away in Tucson, Arizona, fleeing as Sonora became a beehive of crooked cops and hostile gunmen.

The target in Sonora had been a violent man, but in terms of clout, he was no El Chapo Guzmán, no Mayo Zambada. Now, as Vazquez and the Marines headed onto their target's home base—the "lion's den," as both Vazquez and Hogan would later call it—the full-scale combat that their colleagues had survived in Sonora was never far off their minds. Especially because they knew the raiding party was being watched: over the last twenty-four hours, Hogan and the HSI team in Nogales, Arizona, had been reading in real time as El Chapo's people texted one another with updates on the movements of the Marines. Hogan had been feel-ing a mounting sense of frustration ever since the attempt to capture El Mayo several days earlier, and now it only increased.

. . .

While the drama was unfolding elsewhere in Culiacán, El Chapo's former lover Lucero Sanchez López had a drama of her own to deal with. The same day that the Marines had arrived in town, El Chapo had spotted her, and reached out to her for the first time in a while. Her attempts to pull away seemed to have been in vain.

After she stopped going to the mountains to buy weed for him in early 2012, Lucero had begun working with El Chapo and his associates to set up front companies, fake businesses that they could use to import chemicals, disguise drug shipments, and launder drug proceeds. One company based in Ecuador, where El Chapo was sourcing much of his cocaine, was set up under the pretense of exporting ground-up fish meal; another, a juice company based in Mexico City, did not export a single gallon of juice nor a single bushel of fruit, but did help launder around $5 million for El Chapo. The businesses were typically registered in the name of some poor, uneducated sap who could be paid a pittance and knew how to take orders. Lucero would help recruit people she knew from the countryside, and explain the basics to them, showing them how to set up bank accounts, where to register the companies. In her spare time, she saw to El Chapo's domestic needs.

"I would just be there in the house, living there with him," she said. "I would make his purchases, his personal clothing, his lotions, everything that deals with his own personal care. I was like his housewife."

She wasn't always comfortable with El Chapo. One incident, early in the relationship, weighed on her when she contemplated how easily her lover ordered the deaths of people who had once been close to him. In December 2011, she and El Chapo were sitting together and eating dinner at a safe house in Culiacán when El Chapo's secretary, Condor, burst into the room with an urgent message.

"Tio, [Juancho] died," Condor said, referring to Juan Guzmán Rocha, a nephew of El Chapo's who had long served as one of his closest aides.

At first, Lucero had thought that perhaps he had died of an illness, or that rivals had gotten to him. What Lucero did not know then was that Juancho had been murdered because El Chapo suspected that his nephew had been lying to him. Juancho committed the fatal sin of telling El Chapo he was out of town, only to be spotted soon after in Culiacán by an employee of Dámaso López—a minor fib in most walks of life, but to El Chapo the lie was evidence that Juancho could no longer be trusted. On El Chapo's orders, a group of hit men led by the security chief El Negro snatched Juancho and his bodyguard off the street, tortured them both, and dumped their bodies on the outskirts of town.

When Condor arrived that night with the news, Lucero saw El Chapo go silent, and a momentary look of uncertainty passed over his face. But when he turned to look at Lucero, he had a steely look in his eyes. From El Chapo's reaction, it became clear: her boyfriend had ordered the murder.

"He said from that point on, whoever betrayed him was going to die regardless of whether they were family, or women," Lucero recalled. "If people ratted him out that they were going to die."

Lucero continued to see El Chapo for more than a year after that, working as a go-between for marijuana purchases and setting up front companies on his behalf. But by the beginning of 2013, Lucero had had enough. Between her growing paranoia about being arrested or killed for her connection to the fugitive drug lord, and the growing darkness she felt radiating from him in their personal interactions, she started looking for a way out of the relationship.

But when you're the lover of a man like El Chapo, such things rarely have a clean finale.

"The relationship had ended, but it seemed that it actually would never end," she said.

Finally, on February 16, 2014, three days after Vazquez and the Marines had raided El Mayo's ranch, Lucero got the call. Skulking from one safe house to another in Culiacán, El Chapo had spotted Lucero on the street, and now he wanted her to come to him. It had been more than a year since they had last seen one another, but his sexual appetite was as insatiable as ever, and seeing Lucero reminded him of the times they had shared. He sent her a message on her BlackBerry, summoning her to his safe house in La Libertad, a middle-class neighborhood of Culiacán a kilometer or two from the center of town.

The Marines' presence in Culiacán did not seem to be a concern at first. But they had barely had more than a chance to say hello and sit down for a bite to eat when Condor came into the room to tell them that El Chapo had to move locations. As he gathered his things to hop into the truck with Condor, El Chapo told Lucero to sit tight and wait; he would send word to her when it was safe for her to come find him. So she waited. And waited. For hours, Lucero sat in the safe house, awaiting word from her lover, until finally, a maid who worked for El Chapo called Lucero and told her to head to an address in Guadalupe, another nice middle-class neighborhood not far from downtown. She found him there, lying low in a two-story home. Inside, it was sparsely decorated, with a table in the main living room, and an indoor pool, along with a bank of security monitors.

From the time she arrived at the backup safe house, they spent hours together. Lucero did not go into detail about how they spent this time, but they were up late. Finally, around 3 or 4 a.m., he drifted off to sleep, but Lucero lay awake, unable to doze off after this reunion with the most wanted man in Mexico, from whom she had tried so hard to move on.

. . .

Victor Vazquez, meanwhile, was still on the hunt for Nariz. It was late now, almost midnight, and thanks to chatter over the BlackBerry wiretaps they knew Nariz was planning a party, and they knew where. Arriving at the neighborhood where Nariz was supposed to be hanging out, they found a pair of Chevy Suburbans parked in the street, blocking access to anyone not on the guest list. Vazquez was with a small team, so he radioed for backup and asked the other Marines to surround the area, fanning out to form a perimeter and prevent anyone from leaving or entering. Then they invited themselves into the party.

Rolling up to the gathering, Vazquez hopped out of his car and hung back as a group of Marines ran toward the group of about fifteen men and ten women who were gathered outside on the street, drinking and listening to music. On Vazquez's orders, the Marines lined the men up and commanded them to empty their pockets, on the lookout for a telltale BlackBerry. Any one of these men could be their target. Vazquez had no idea what Nariz looked like, but he had a guess.

"I knew that it had something to do with his nose. He had a big nose, small nose, no nose, something," he recalled. "Something told me to focus on the nose."

Any one of these men could be Nariz. Armed with his quarry's BlackBerry PIN, Vazquez began to go down the line, eyeing the snout of each man and, when they found a BlackBerry, checking the phone's PIN against the number associated with Nariz. As he worked his way through the group, Vazquez could feel his heart pounding. He knew he'd arrived at a critical moment in the search for El Chapo. This was his shot, and he had to proceed carefully.

"This is it, this is our moment," Vazquez thought to himself as he approached the last three men in line. "One of these guys has to be it."

While Vazquez and the Marines searched the men, the women were left to their own devices, idling restlessly nearby, watching the search, complaining to anyone who would listen about the interruption of the festivities. As Vazquez arrived at the third-to-last man, one of the women suddenly stood up.

"I have to go check on my baby," she said, to no one in particular.

Vazquez felt a jolt. Years spent in the military and law enforcement had trained him to trust his gut, and this sudden declaration seemed off to him. Without taking his attention from the men in front of him, he watched as the woman walked a few paces down the block and turned to enter the nicest house on the street, complete with a brand-new car in the driveway.

"He's in there, he's in that house!" Vazquez thought to himself.

The DEA agent signaled to the two female Marines on the team, a doctor and a nurse, and together the three of them strolled over to the house and walked inside. The jumpy woman was in the living room, cradling her baby tightly, and began yelling at the Marines.

"Get out of my house!" the woman cried. "You're corrupt, get out of here."

Vazquez didn't buy it. If she was so concerned about the Marines upsetting the baby, why was she also yelling at the top of her lungs?

The woman refused to budge. Holding the baby to her chest and keeping her elbows pinned to her side, she struggled with the two female

Marines as they tried to wrestle the baby out of the woman's arms and drag her out of the house. As they tussled, a phone dropped from her armpit and clattered to the floor.

"Check that phone," Vazquez barked at the Marines. "He's in the house."

As one of the Marines scooped up the phone, several others began to search the house in earnest, and before long they found a man cowering in a closet in the master bedroom. They marched the man up to Vazquez so they stood face-to-face. The man peered back at Vazquez over a big, honking schnozz.

"*Tu eres Nariz*," Vazquez said. "You're Nariz."

He wasn't asking. Nariz, dressed in a red and black polo shirt, nodded morosely, his bulbous nose bobbing up and down.

As they had pieced together the movements of El Chapo and his henchmen, they'd discerned that they referred to their safe houses by numbers. And earlier that day, HSI had intercepted a text between Nariz and another henchman in which he ordered the other man to pick up some birria goat stew and some bottles of water and bring them to the house labeled "the Five." But that only gave them the approximate location, narrowed down to a few city blocks. They knew if they swarmed the block without knowing which house to hit, they'd never find El Chapo in time. They needed the exact location.

"Where is he?" Vazquez demanded. "I want to know where he's at right now."

Nariz didn't have to ask Vazquez whom he meant.

"He's at the Three," Nariz replied.

Vazquez called bullshit.

"No. He's not," he told Nariz. "Where are you bringing the birria tomorrow?"

With a look of shocked resignation, Nariz's eyes went wide and he dropped his head, exhaling like he'd taken a punch to the gut.

"He's at the Five," Nariz acknowledged.

Soon, Vazquez said, Nariz had supplied the location of the safe house.

It's very possible Nariz *did* get a punch in the gut, or worse. In the accounts given by Vazquez and Hogan, Nariz simply folded and gave up the boss. But there exist more than enough accusations of the use of torture by Mexican security forces, including the supposedly saintly SEMAR, to wonder if they harmed him in order to make him so forthcoming. Later, official sources would categorically deny that the Marines had mistreated Nariz or any of the other traffickers captured that day, but others speaking on background scoffed at that. One former Mexican official later mused to a *New Yorker* reporter that it would be more unusual if Nariz had *not* suffered torture at the hands of his captors.

However they managed to cajole, convince, or coerce Nariz into giving them the exact location of the safe house, they now had it. Leaving a crew of Marines to maintain a perimeter at the cul-de-sac, Vazquez passed along the location of the safe house to the rest of the team and climbed into an unmarked car with Nariz to drive over to "the Five" as stealthily as they could manage. He told the Marine behind the wheel to follow the directions of the captured gofer.

"Listen, when [Nariz] tells you to make a left, make a left," Vazquez told the Marine behind the wheel. "When he makes a right, make a right. Once you reach the last turn before the house in the street, you stop, you don't go."

Vazquez wanted them close to the safe house, as close as possible without raising any alarms. They knew they were likely being watched regardless: news of the raid on El Mayo's ranch had already broken in local papers, and now, for the past twenty-four hours, SEMAR trucks had been rolling through town, choppers hovering overhead, causing great alarm and apprehension among residents of the city. Ever since the Marines had arrived in Culiacán, HSI investigators in Nogales had been picking up chatter on the wiretaps and intercepted two-way radios making it clear that El Chapo's men knew their movements, trading reports gleaned from *halcones* phoning in tips from around the city. HSI fed the intel to Vazquez, giving him a glimpse into the reactions by El Chapo's people.

Climbing into his own car and turning the ignition, Vazquez pulled behind the car with Nariz inside, and for the next fifteen minutes, they drove under his instructions of their newly pliant guide, turning this way and that as they wound through the streets of Culiacán, until finally the Marine driver pulled to a stop and radioed to Vazquez.

"Nariz told me that once I make this right the house is on this street," the driver said.

"Good," Vazquez replied. "Don't park your car there."

Vazquez turned to the Marine sergeant driving with him and asked the sergeant to call in backup and surround the neighborhood, nobody in, nobody out.

"Once we make that turn it's going to be a go, and we need to have a good perimeter," he said.

Quietly, the backup Marines crept into position, blocking traffic with their marked SEMAR trucks and laying spike strips across the streets to prevent a runaway car from breaking out of the perimeter or barreling its way in. As he waited for the Marines to set up, Vazquez was in constant contact with Nogales, and the texts they were intercepting allowed the agents to zero in on El Chapo's exact location inside the house.

"Don't waste your time with the upstairs, go straight to the master bathroom," he called to the Marines, as they marched up to the front door, hoisted a battering ram, and gave it their all.

They heave-hoed and smashed the steel ram into the door once, twice, three times, but it refused to give. For nine long minutes the men smashed away at the door, unable to break through. As one man tired, he handed the battering ram to another Marine, who continued to bash away. Vazquez had never seen anything like it: he'd kicked plenty of doors in his day, and they typically gave way after a couple good bashes, but this door would not budge. All the while, he stood anxiously behind the Marines, reminding them of their objective.

"Don't waste your time upstairs," he repeated. "Straight to the master bathroom!"

. . .

As Lucero finally started to drift off around 3 or 4 a.m., she heard a commotion outside, shouting voices, a helicopter buzzing overhead, and a repeated bang! bang! bang! on the door. Condor dashed into the hallway outside El Chapo's room and rapped sharply on the door.

"*Tio, tio*, open up, they're on us, they're on us!" he cried.

Lucero was terrified, and felt like she was in shock, but the other oc-

cupants of the house—El Chapo, Condor, and a maid named Chaparra—
sprang into action.

El Chapo leapt out of bed, stark naked, and ran toward the bathroom.
"Love, come, come with me, come in here," he cried to Lucero.

Lucero dashed toward the sound of El Chapo's voice, pausing just
a moment to glance up at the television monitors, where she spied the
chilling image of a large group of uniformed men in helmets smashing
a battering ram against the door. With no time to linger, she continued
on to the bathroom, where she found the three of them standing around
a yawning opening in the floor. The entire bathtub had risen up toward
the ceiling, and in the space that had once held the tub, a set of wooden
steps led into the dark. El Chapo went in first, then Lucero, then the others, and as Condor filed in after them, he pulled the bathtub back down,
sealing them in.

Lucero now found herself in what appeared to be a crawl space beneath the bathtub that led about five yards toward a reinforced metal
door with a wheel, similar to a large safe door. Condor and El Chapo were
struggling to turn the wheel, and when they finally forced the door open,
all four of them took off running through the tunnel, with a buck-naked
El Chapo leading the charge, followed by Lucero, Condor, and finally the
maid.

"It was horrible," Lucero recalled. "I had never been in a place like
that. It was a humid place filled with water, with mud."

Groping her way along the side of the tunnel that stretched before
them, Lucero tried not to be left behind by her fleeing beau.

. . .

Vazquez was still standing outside when the door to the safe house gave
way. Standing in the entryway, Vazquez heard the Marines storm inside
as he waited. As an "advisor" on the mission, he had to hold back until
the Marines gave the all-clear. But it was agonizing to stand still at what
could be the moment of truth. Finally, after what felt like an eternity but
was likely just a few seconds, his radio crackled to life.

"*Túnel, túnel, túnel!*" the raiders cried, from the bathroom. In the
garage, Vazquez heard the loud bang of a concussion grenade, tossed by

one of the Marines into the hole underneath the bathtub. He waited for the sound of gunfire, but it never came. Still unable to enter the house, Vazquez turned his attention to the perimeter, dashing about to make sure the area was secure, calling to one team of men to release a man they had detained.

"That's not him," he cried, as more and more Marines arrived on the scene, the unit captain barking out orders over the radio.

Inside the house, the Marines were so close to their prey that they could hear footsteps as El Chapo, Lucero, Condor, and the maid dashed away through the tunnel. But fearing that El Chapo could have booby-trapped the tunnel or might let off a burst of gunfire at anyone following him, the men were forced to cool their heels in the bathroom, listening helplessly as El Chapo made his escape.

• • •

Once she caught a second to take in her surroundings, Lucero found to her dismay that she, El Chapo, Condor, and the maid were in a sewer. The architect of El Chapo's escape hatch had connected the bathroom crawl space to the city's subterranean drainage system, and while it was perfect for a quick escape perhaps, but it did not make for the most pleasant walk. For more than an hour the four escapees sloshed through thigh-high sewage water as they made their way toward a drainage outlet that flowed into the Humaya River, about a kilometer northwest of the safe house. They were engulfed in darkness as they inched their way toward the river, save for the occasional street grate that would throw a few bars of light to guide them.

Finally, the little group emerged from the drainage tunnel and found themselves overlooking a canal, perched on a shrubby ledge about six feet below the level of the road that ran alongside the river. In the night sky above them military helicopters crisscrossed the sky in an increasingly frantic attempt to locate the fugitive. By this time the soldiers had surely discovered the entrance to the tunnel, and El Chapo was getting desperate. As Condor tried to get another secretary on the phone, El Chapo suggested carjacking the next unlucky driver to come along the road, much like he had done all those years ago when he escaped the assassins at the

Guadalajara airport in 1993. But this time it didn't come to that: Condor finally managed to raise a lieutenant named Picudo on the radio, and the henchman soon arrived in a car, scooped them up, and took them to another safe house nearby, where the still-nude kingpin put on a change of clothes.

They had little time to waste. Nariz had already given up the one safe house, so any location that the compromised secretary knew about was no longer safe. They had to get out of Culiacán. As day broke, they ventured out into the streets of a city under siege, slipped through the military cordon, and left Culiacán behind as the sun began to rise over Sinaloa.

. . .

After about an hour of scouring the safe house and the tunnel, Vazquez and a group of Marines left a few men standing guard and moved on, with Nariz guiding them to the next location, another nondescript house with a bare-bones interior, and then on to the next house. This third safe house was empty of people, and the raiders headed straight to the bath-room, where a handcuffed Nariz plugged a small, pronged device into an outlet next to the sink mirror. With a crackling sound the grout sealing the tub to the black wall tiles broke free and the shell of the tub lifted up on pneumatic risers, revealing an escape hatch nearly identical to the one at the first house.

This time, however, they didn't linger. Vazquez knew word would be out that the Marines were hitting the safe houses, and wanted to raid as many locations as possible before El Chapo's men could scatter with whatever evidence—drugs, weapons, phones—might be there. With Nariz and some more Marines, they continued on, hitting one safe house after another, along with warehouses and a home that belonged to Con-dor. It was daylight now, and at each safe house, the Marines blocked off streets with white pickup trucks marked with the SEMAR logo, heavily armed troops standing in the streets with assault rifles and black face masks. El Chapo was long gone, but over the next four days, the sweeps did turn up some good evidence, including 2,800 packages of metham-phetamine, dozens of plastic bananas stuffed with cocaine, a weapons cache with ammo, handguns, and rocket-propelled grenades, and a family photo of El Chapo with his sons Ovidio and Joaquín.

That evening, the Marines arrested Picudo, the lieutenant who had picked up El Chapo, Condor, Lucero, and the maid just hours before. Like Nariz, Picudo soon began blabbing—possibly after being tortured—and informed the Marines that he had driven El Chapo to the coastal resort town of Mazatlán, about two hours southeast of Culiacán. As the main SEMAR force continued to roll around town to give the impression that they were still searching for the fugitive drug lord there, Vazquez, Hogan, and a small crew of Marines changed into tourist clothes, board shorts, and sandals, and drove to the beach.

As they headed to Mazatlán, driving just two or three to a car, HSI began picking up chatter on BBM wiretaps as *halcones* along the route sent word up the mirror system that Marines were headed south dressed like tourists. Nothing escaped the eyes and ears of El Chapo's people. In order to allay suspicion, Vazquez ordered the cars to keep even more space between them, turning a loose convoy into a long train of isolated vehicles.

"Instead of traveling two vehicles together, I decided to have the first vehicle go even farther away," Vazquez said. "Which made us, in a way, more vulnerable."

Despite the nerve-racking drive, in which an ambush could have caught any of the vehicles alone and outgunned, the Marine unit, along with Vazquez and Hogan, arrived in Mazatlán in one piece, regrouped at a safe house command post in the city, and got some rest. They had an early morning ahead of them.

• • •

Standing outside the Hotel Miramar, a twelve-story hotel and condo building overlooking the *malecón*, the boardwalk that stretches the length of Mazatlán, Victor Vazquez was a bundle of nerves as he waited to hear the all-clear over the radio. He, Drew Hogan, and the Marines had awoken at 4 a.m. on the morning of February 22, armed with seemingly ironclad intel from HSI that El Chapo was holed up at the Miramar, and now the Marines were inside, going floor by floor.

Finally, Vazquez heard his radio crackle to life, and it chirped the words he had been waiting for, the code signaling that they had secured the target.

"Siete, siete, siete!" a Marine cried. "Seven, seven, seven."

In the end, El Chapo went down easily. After he had spent years in the mountains surrounded by dozens of heavily armed guards, the Marines cornered him in a bedroom on the fourth floor of the Hotel Miramar. It was just him, Condor, Emma Coronel, and their twin girls. In a last-ditch attempt to forestall the inevitable, he had grabbed an assault rifle and barricaded himself in the bedroom, but as Emma pleaded with the Marines not to harm their daughters, El Chapo surrendered.

Vazquez raced into the parking garage, where vehicles were waiting to whisk the captive away. When the men hustled the diminutive prisoner toward the cars, Vazquez finally found himself staring down the most wanted man in Mexico.

"Eres tu," Vazquez said. "It's you, Chapo."

19

DÉJÀ VU

Hours after the arrest in Mazatlán, news of El Chapo's capture began to filter out to Mexico, and to the world. To prove it, the government released a photo showing the captured kingpin on his knees in what appeared to be a parking lot, shirtless and sporting a small cut beneath his left eye. Staring at a point beyond the camera, his eyes were dark, and showed little emotion. Much later, another picture emerged, showing El Chapo sitting on a couch in a bright white room, sun pouring through the blinds. His hands are trussed in front of him with bandages, and another bandage is wrapped around his head to cover his eyes. To El Chapo's left, wearing camo fatigues, a black balaclava, and a ballistic vest with a handgun holstered on the front, DEA Special Agent Victor Vazquez is kneeling, with his right arm resting casually on the sofa. Standing behind El Chapo is Special Agent Drew Hogan, cutting a slimmer figure than Vazquez but clad in a similar military getup and balaclava. On his head, he wears one of El Chapo's famous black baseball caps.

The afternoon after El Chapo's capture, a team of Marines in black face masks paraded him in front of news cameras in Mexico City—cleaned up a bit, dressed in black jeans and a white dress shirt. As they crossed the tarmac, one of the Marines grabbed him by the back of the neck and pushed his head so he was facing the cameras. Then they spirited him away to the Federal Social Readaptation Center #1, a maximum-security prison on the outskirts of the city of Almoloya de Juárez, better known as Altiplano.

El Chapo's new home was a forbidding place. Perched on hilly grassland northwest of Mexico City, Altiplano is all beige walls and high mesh fencing topped with razor wire, surrounded by guard towers. The prison's outer perimeter forms a square, with a bit of no-man's-land between the fence and the prison itself, a cluster of tightly packed cell blocks inside another square. The airspace around Altiplano is a no-fly zone, and the government is said to use frequency jammers that make it impossible for anyone inside the prison to use a cell phone or radio. At various times it's been home to an all-star cast of Mexico's most notorious criminals, including old associates of El Chapo like Miguel Ángel Félix Gallardo, Héctor "El Güero" Palma, enemies from the Gulf cartel, the Zetas, and the Arellano-Félix organization, along with assorted kidnappers, extortionists, and assassins. When El Chapo arrived, Mexican security forces could boast that no one had ever escaped, not even close, and they scoffed at the idea of El Chapo slipping away as he had done from Puente Grande thirteen years prior.

So El Chapo was in prison again. But what did that mean for Sinaloa, or for Mexico? While federal agents from both the United States and Mexico patted one another on the back, observers cautioned that El Chapo's organization, with its numerous subsidiaries, franchises, and factions, was likely to keep chugging along with or without its infamous leader. Still, the capture was a major coup for President Enrique Peña Nieto, who had campaigned on an image of technocratic competence but found himself dragged down in the polls by an economic crisis and by corruption scandals that reminded many Mexicans all too much of the PRI's long history of skullduggery and graft. So now he seized the opportunity to capitalize on El Chapo's downfall. In a statement shortly after El Chapo's arrest, Peña Nieto reassured a wary nation that the slippery drug lord was going to stay behind bars this time. To let him escape once more, the president said, would be "unforgivable."

But El Chapo was already planning his next moves.

Among his first orders of business was a bloody bit of house cleaning. In messages smuggled out to Dámaso López, El Chapo ordered the murder of his chief of security, Manuel Alejandro Aponte Gómez, better known as El Negro. A former soldier, El Negro had arrived in Sinaloa in 2003 on antinarcotics duty but soon deserted to work for El Chapo. Over time, he had risen through the ranks to command a fearsome band of killers and had fought in some of the most notable skirmishes during the war with the Beltrán Leyva clan. But his failure to protect his boss from capture made him deeply suspect, and El Chapo had become convinced that it was El Negro who had given his location to the Marines. El Negro had had a hand in numerous kidnappings and murders on El Chapo's orders; now it was his turn. Dámaso dutifully relayed the order to El Mayo, and a few months later, El Negro's body, showing signs of torture and riddled with bullet wounds, turned up on the edge of town.

Observers at the time speculated that the murder of El Negro was a power play by Dámaso, who by the spring of 2014 had been working for El Chapo for more than a decade. And indeed, El Chapo had come to view Dámaso as something of a second-in-command, equal only to El Chapo's blood kin. In letters that El Chapo wrote from his cell at Altiplano and smuggled out via his attorney, he appeared to consider Dámaso in the same management class as his own sons, and obsessed over the possibility that an informant would drop the dime on Alfredo, Iván, Ovidio, or Dámaso, cautioning them to be wary of everyone in their immediate orbit. Writing to them in April, he shared a bit of fatherly advice that he himself had once followed, although he had clearly gotten a bit lax in recent years. "There are two things that must be done: no one should know where you all sleep except yourselves, and don't go to public places, and nothing will ever happen," he wrote. "The danger is the people from the company, because they're the ones that can set you up. The five of you should talk about what I'm telling you and like I say, without a [snitch], they will never find you all, and a snitch will always be someone close to us."

Even from prison, communicating with Dámaso through letters written in his spidery, barely legible scrawl, El Chapo took a keen interest in the details of his faction's finances. He ordered Dámaso to contact various cocaine traffickers in Mexico and Colombia who owed them kilos, reminded his lieutenant to pay for rental properties that far-flung operatives were using in Europe, urged him to file a claim for a property that the government had seized, instructed Dámaso on how to split up drug proceeds between families of fallen henchmen, and dictated how much Dámason and El Chapo's four eldest sons should take for themselves as payment.

"Hire accountants throughout the state and pay the widows from there," he wrote. "Whatever is left per month, half is for you and half is for the four of them."

At El Chapo's urging, Dámaso dispatched a worker to Toluca, a few miles southeast of the prison, in order to manage the flow of bribes to guards and administrators at Altiplano. El Chapo was up to the old tricks that he had learned years ago during his incarceration at Puente Grande prison in the 1990s, and already they were bearing fruit.

"I wanted to tell you that although nothing here is easy, in a way I have gotten lucky because the director has been very kind to me," El Chapo wrote in a letter to Dámaso. "He has helped me when I asked."

Still, he didn't intend to stick around for long. In another letter to Dámaso, he instructed his lieutenant to gather his three eldest sons and meet up with Emma Coronel, as she had something important to tell them. At a get-together in April in Culiacán, Emma—who had visited her husband in prison—gave them a message, Dámaso recalled.

"My compadre was sending the message that he was thinking of taking the risk again and escape from the prison," Dámaso said. "And he wanted to know whether I could help him with that."

· · ·

El Chapo bided his time. He stayed busy by writing love letters to former girlfriends and by teaming up with his former rival, the drug trafficker known as La Barbie, to organize a hunger strike—one in which he apparently did not personally participate. In addition to his wife and lawyer, he took visits from Lucero Sánchez López, whose seemingly endless relationship with El Chapo refused to die despite the fact—or due to the fact—that she was now an elected state deputy of the PRI.

El Chapo was in constant contact with his people on the outside, largely through his lawyers and Emma, and they kept him up to date on the comings and goings in Sinaloa. Despite the fact that El Chapo's communications with his lieutenants flowed freely, Mexican authorities insisted that El Chapo was being held "in isolation." For good measure, they rigged up a camera and trained it on the cell, making him visible twenty-four hours a day to guards monitoring his every move.

At 8:52 p.m. on July 11, 2015, a year and a half after his capture, an overhead camera peeked down as El Chapo paced the length of his cell, a spartan affair with three concrete walls and one of metal bars, furnished with a cot, a bedside table, and a shower stall with a waist-high partition that gave a modicum of privacy. On the bedside table sat a roll of toilet paper and what appeared to be a smartphone. El Chapo was dressed in prison beige, and a spare shirt hung on the wall opposite his bed. After pacing a couple of times, from the shower stall to the bedside table and back, he stepped into the stall and bent over as if to fuss with something on the floor of the shower, the one part of the cell not visible to the camera's perch in the corner above the bed. Then he took a couple of steps to the bed, sat down, and removed his shoes. He sat for one beat, then two, then stood up. In four steps, he walked to the shower, and vanished from sight.

Lowering himself through a twenty-inch-by-twenty-inch hole in the bottom of the shower, El Chapo dropped three feet below the floor of his cell and found his footing on a ladder made of PVC piping, before climbing thirty feet down the shaft to the tunnel below, where a rescuer—Emma Coronel's brother, according to Dámaso—awaited him by a motorcycle that had been rigged to run on a crude track laid along the tunnel floor. With El Chapo safely on the back of the bike, they zoomed a kilometer and a half to the other end of the tunnel, and climbed through the exit shaft, emerging through a square hole cut in the floor of an unfinished house. Boarding an ATV, the pair rode a short distance to a warehouse, where they switched to a waiting SUV and drove about two hours north to an airstrip in the state of Querétaro, where a pilot was waiting to fly him to safety in Sinaloa.

When guards finally came to check on him, the only living thing that remained in the cell was a sparrow that El Chapo's men had used to test the tunnel's air quality.

. . .

The escape was more than a year in the making, hatched in meetings between Dámaso and El Chapo's sons, who looped in El Chapo using Emma as an emissary. Starting in April 2014, Dámaso López and El Chapo's sons began laying the groundwork; they bought the property about a kilometer away from the prison, where workers began to dig, and they bought the warehouse nearby, where they stored some weapons and an armored pickup truck. Next they smuggled a GPS watch into the prison, allowing them to pinpoint the location of El Chapo's cell so the tunnel crew could dig in the right direction.

It was one of the most well-worn tricks in El Chapo's book. He made his name by digging tunnels in Agua Prieta and Tijuana, he fled from the Marines in Culiacán through a tunnel, and now, once more, he was using a tunnel to bend the world to his will. The tunnel was another architectural marvel, running more than a kilometer from the sham work site, under the prison walls, and directly into the stall of El Chapo's shower, with lights and ventilation strung up all the way. The walls were dug to a uniform height and width from entrance to exit, with spare oxygen supplies placed at strategic intervals, just in case. The tunnel, which one retired DEA agent guessed cost $5 million to build, required the removal of more than three thousand tons of dirt, according to one estimate.

By the spring of 2015, El Chapo's rescuers grew so close that he could hear as they tried to break through the concrete, and he wasn't the only one. They were making so much noise as they got closer that other inmates began to complain of the racket. Their complaints fell on deaf ears.

When El Chapo finally squeezed his way down the tunnel shaft and made his way to freedom, it took eighteen long minutes for prison guards to check on his cell and find the escape route, a delay that led to speculation that they'd been on the take. In the immediate aftermath, the attorney general's office interrogated more than two dozen guards and arrested seven of them in connection with the jailbreak. President Enrique Peña Nieto was on a state visit to France when the news broke, and was already dealing with a PR snafu stemming from the size and cost of his swollen entourage of three hundred aides, security guards, and hangers-on. As with Vicente Fox back in 2001, the reputation of Peña Nieto's administration, already bruised, trembled in the storm of of anger and incredulity that arose from El Chapo's ability to vanish from inside a facility that was supposed to be the country's most secure prison.

While Peña Nieto continued his visit to France, El Chapo was already safely back in his hometown of La Tuna, staying at his mountaintop home overlooking the village, El Cielo, and holding court with family and friends.

A cousin who greeted El Chapo upon his return later recalled the moment fondly.

"He would come back when you least expected it, and there he was," the cousin told me. "Everyone came to see him, and he asked to see his friends, and asked for the people he trusts to come by, they go and talk with him."

About a week after the jailbreak, El Chapo summoned his partners and lieutenants, including El Mayo, Dámaso, and Dámaso's son, to his mountaintop home overlooking the village. Over breakfast they toasted his escape and, just as they had thirteen years before, began planning for the future.

• • •

Less than six months later, in predawn gloom, a team of heavily armed soldiers dressed in SEMAR uniforms of camo fatigues, face masks, and black ballistic vests gathered outside the door of a two-story home in the northern Sinaloa city of Los Mochis. Most of the soldiers fanned out along an exterior wall, while two men stood in front of the entryway and began to swing a battering ram against the door with a metal-on-metal clang that echoed into the darkness.

Bang. Bang. Bang.

"*Vamos, vamos, vamos,*" one of the gunmen cried. "Let's go, let's go, let's go."

Bang. Bang. Bang.

With the seventh swing, the door gave way. The breach men threw the battering ram to the ground with a metallic echo and the troops poured inside and hell opened up as soldiers and gunmen alike opened fire. Taking cover in the corner of an entryway, the soldiers fired their assault rifles in quick bursts at the hit men defending the home, and tossed grenades inside. Plaster fell to the floor as deafening gunfire and explosions shook the house. One of the Marines fell to the ground wounded.

"They got me!" he cried.

• • •

After his first escape, El Chapo had remained free for more than a decade, reaching new heights of power, influence, and wealth despite being one of the most wanted fugitives in the world. And from the outside, there was little to suggest that the second time would be any different. But the Marines and the DEA, FBI, and HSI agents tracking him knew it would only be a matter of time before they cornered him once more.

For one thing, the interagency cooperation that had helped the U.S. feds and Mexican Marines track him down in 2014 remained largely intact, so the team hunting him was miles ahead of where the authorities had been back in 2001. For another thing, it never seemed to get through to El Chapo that he should stop using his beloved BlackBerrys. So dedicated was he to the devices, a retired DEA agent once told me with a laugh, that El Chapo had single-handedly kept the company in business even as their market share waned.

Throughout the summer and into the fall, federal agents had continued to track El Chapo's possible location, tapped his lawyer's phones, and kept tabs on the people near him. They had come close to capturing him on at least one occasion, when El Chapo fled an approaching chopper by scrambling into a gully with a child in his arms, reportedly using the baby as a human shield. He got away, but the noose was tightening. In October, the authorities laid siege to Culiacán and remote areas in the highlands of Sinaloa and Durango, displacing hundreds of ranchers and *campesinos* in the process, a grim replay of the upheaval so many generations of cops and soldiers have wrought upon the people of these mountains.

Then, finally, in early January 2016, the hunters zeroed in on the home in Los Mochis, Sinaloa's northernmost urban center, where work crews were seen going to and from some mysterious interior renovation, and cartel associates were chattering on intercepted BBMs about the imminent arrival of *"Abuela,"* or Grandma, an obvious code name for an important guest.

After months of tracking, early on the morning of January 8, 2016, a team surveilling the house spotted a white van picking up a large carry-out order of tacos and heading back to the house. A few hours later, at about 4:30 a.m., the raiders swooped in, guns blazing.

Under intense fire from the Marines, the surviving cartel gunmen pulled back, retreating to the roof, as the soldiers moved into a large living room and kitchen area, filled with smoke and debris. In one corner, a man lay on his side, dead or mortally wounded, blood pooling on the floor around him. In another, a gunman was sprawled on the floor, a bullet hole in his temple. Yelling to one another, the Marines secured the room and began heading up to the second floor, and eventually to the roof. By the time the house was secure, five gunmen lay dead and the soldiers had two women and two men handcuffed in white plastic flexi-cuffs. But their target, *Abuela*, a short, stocky man with a mustache and alert, beady little eyes that peered out from wanted posters across the world, had long since ducked into a closet, descended into a tunnel dug in the floor, and made his escape.

Emerging from a drainage tunnel, El Chapo and his faithful servant Cholo Iván found themselves standing across from a Walmart. They hijacked a car, a white Volkswagen, but in just a few blocks the vehicle conked out, so they abandoned it and commandeered the next car that drove down the road. For a moment, perhaps, the fugitives thought they had gotten away. After so many close calls, so many near misses, so many breakneck escapes, why not? But fate did not side with El Chapo on this early winter morning as it had so many times before. About twelve miles southeast of the city a team of federal police halted the car at a checkpoint and detained them long enough for a Marine unit to come scoop them up. Sitting side by side in the backseat, disheveled in undershirts and handcuffs, El Chapo and Cholo Iván slumped down in defeat.

Less than forty-eight hours later, a sprawling, at times rambling article by the actor Sean Penn appeared on the website of *Rolling Stone*, in which Penn described a daredevil meeting he and the telenovela star Kate del Castillo arranged with El Chapo in the mountains of Sinaloa a few months earlier. Following the meeting, which ended abruptly when Mexican troops were spotted nearby El Chapo's hideout, Penn wrote that El Chapo had agreed to appear on camera and answer pre-written questions—which Penn submitted via BBM, of course.

The video is a curious artifact. In a nondescript location, mountains in the far background under an overcast sky, he sits and stares at the camera, his ample stomach stretching against a blue and white paisley shirt with the collar splayed open. El Chapo's mustache is gone, but atop his head, as always, is a black baseball cap.

He's not the most articulate person, and he's not a natural in front of the camera. In response to maddeningly general questions, he describes in maddeningly general terms his childhood, growing up in poverty, leaving at eighteen for Culiacán and then Guadalajara—and quickly clarifies that he never went long without going back to see his mom in La Tuna. He says he's not a violent man, he simply defends himself when he has to. As his cameraman, also not a natural, zooms in and out, a rooster crows in the background and some kind of motor throbs off camera. Now and then, men in camouflage fatigues walk through the frame behind him carrying assault rifles. Freedom, he says, is "very nice."

As he responds to the questions, written by Penn, translated, and posed to him by the cameraman—who, to his credit, pushes his subject at times to answer in greater depth—El Chapo seems a bit bored, like he's doing a pointless chore. He becomes most animated when his cameraman asks him if he bears responsibility for the damage done by the drugs he moves.

"Do you think it's true that you are responsible for the high level of drug addiction, for the fact that there are so many drugs in the world?" the man asks.

"The day that I don't exist, it's not going to decrease at all. Drug trafficking? That's false," El Chapo replies, sucking his teeth slightly in disapproval and shifting in his seat.

"This will never end."

. . .

When El Chapo was arrested the first time, the possibility of extradition seemed remote. In the early years of Peña Nieto's *sexenio*, the cooperation between Mexican and U.S. agencies that had flourished under Calderón had screeched to a halt, as the resurgent *PRIista* administration was reportedly aghast at the level to which Calderón had allowed the United States to operate on Mexican soil. As part of the new administration's effort to publicly distance itself from such cooperation, Peña Nieto's attorney general swore in the wake of the 2014 arrest that Mexico would hold El Chapo in prison for "300, 400 years" before handing him over to the United States for trial. But now, after another deeply embarrassing escape, Mexico City was singing another tune. Within days of the raid in Los Mochis, Mexican officials were already moving to clear the way for El Chapo's transfer to the United States.

But even then El Chapo wasn't ready to call it quits. About a month after his latest arrest, Dámaso met yet again with Emma Coronel to discuss plans to spring her husband.

"[Emma] told me that my compadre sent his regards and that he would send word to say that he was going to make a huge effort to escape again and that he would also send word to ask me if I could help him," Dámaso recalled.

By now they had it down to a formula. With $100,000 of El Chapo's money, Dámaso began looking for a new plot of land within tunneling distance of Altiplano, where workers would once again begin digging toward El Chapo's cell.

This time, however, El Chapo wasn't in one place for long. A month or two after Dámaso met with Emma, the authorities moved him to a prison on the outskirts of Ciudad Juárez. El Chapo's people tried to lean on their government contacts to get him moved back, sending a whopping $2 million bribe to a top prison official, who promised to try to get El Chapo back to Altiplano. It was for naught.

On the evening of January 19, 2017, Mexican agents hustled the king-pin out of his cell and bundled him onto a private jet, which flew him and a team of U.S. marshals to Long Island MacArthur Airport in Islip, New York. As the plane landed, a horrified El Chapo, his eyes welling with tears, could be seen peering out of his porthole window as he arrived to confront his greatest fear: custody in the hands of the merciless gringos.

EPILOGUE

EL CHAPO ALWAYS wanted to make a movie.

Picture this: The most wanted man in Mexico has clawed his way back to power after escaping from what was supposed to be the most secure prison in the country. He has rebuilt his empire, and is moving more coke, weed, heroin, and meth into the United States than ever before. Then, after being captured again, he escapes again! He's back in the mountains, no prison can hold him! His name is synonymous with drug trafficking. He's the most famous capo in a generation, having risen from a crowded field of fellow smugglers to be the most recognizable brand-name drug lord since Pablo Escobar. He's outlived most of his enemies, only to see them replaced by new enemies.

As El Chapo consolidated his position in the decade following his escape, he was never the only kingpin in town, nor even the most powerful; he was just one powerful leader in a federation of several powerful leaders. The Beltrán Leyvas, his allies-turned-enemies, had more friends in high places, and more sway with local proxies in areas outside of Sinaloa; El Mayo had probably wielded more power at home in Sinaloa—albeit behind the scenes. But El Chapo, with his prison break and his decade-plus track record of making fools of the cops and soldiers and gringos chasing him, was the lightning rod, the face of it all.

North of the border rappers pay homage to El Chapo, and in Mexico, folk troubadours like Los Canelos de Durango pen *narcocorridos* in El Chapo's honor, belting out his exploits over the clamor of guitar and accordion.

El Chapo wanted a movie. Ballads were one thing, but the narrative was out of his hands, and other people were profiting off his hard work, his well-earned fame. Books, television shows, songs, all making money for other people. Already basking in an infamy that eclipsed his real-world power and wealth, El Chapo had held multiple meetings over the years with producers and movie stars in a bid to put himself on-screen.

The idea for a movie about El Chapo first came to the wife of Alex Cifuentes, El Chapo's Colombian hostage-turned-lieutenant, in early 2008, shortly after Alex went to join El Chapo in the mountains as human collateral.

"She recommended to Señor Joaquín that he do that because he was always on the news and in the newspapers and everywhere," Alex recalled later. "So she said he should do a movie about his life so he could make the money because the money was being made by all the papers."

In the world of Mexican narcos, this wasn't that unusual: the movie industry in Mexico is awash with low-budget, direct-to-DVD action films, so-called *narcopelículas* glorifying the lifestyles and exploits of drug traffickers, some of them absurd fever-dream villains, others thinly fictionalized. Generally speaking, these are not the best movies. Still, they sell, and one can find innumerable *narcopelícula* DVDs sold at markets across Mexico. They are sometimes financed with drug money from narcos looking to launder a bit of cash and make a cool movie in the process, or by prominent criminals hoping to put out an idealized depiction of their life's work. In the wake of the 2009 arrest of Edgar Villarreal, the American-born Beltrán Leyva ally known as La Barbie, the captured narco told police he had forked over $200,000 to a movie producer for a film about his life, although he never followed through to make the movie.

When Alex brought the movie idea to El Chapo, he loved it, and they hatched a plan: with the help of a ghostwriter, El Chapo would draft his life story, while Alex would find a producer to turn the manuscript into a movie. With the help of one of his men in Colombia, Alex eventually settled on a Colombian producer named Javier Rey, a onetime documentary maker who shifted from making films about human rights issues in the 1980s to making feature films in the mid-2000s, including the 2007 joint Mexican-Colombian production *Polvo de Ángel* (Angel Dust).

A few months after Alex's wife first suggested making a movie, Rey journeyed to Sinaloa and flew out to one of El Chapo's mountain hideouts in order to interview the kingpin. Over a series of interview sessions, El Chapo held forth on his life, regaling the producer with epic tales of his life and work, his escape from Puente Grande, confrontations with enemies, even an incident in which he claimed to have been detained by soldiers and hung upside down by a helicopter. To underscore his claim that the troops had tortured him, El Chapo showed the producer his hands, which he said bore the marks of the rifle butts the soldiers had used to smash his fingers. (Alex did not recall seeing any visible scars.)

To facilitate the project, El Chapo instructed various relatives to sit down with Rey and give the producer additional info on his life. Out of these efforts emerged a manuscript, a biography of sorts with the working title "El Señor de la Montaña," or "The Lord of the Mountain," according to one law enforcement agent who has seen the manuscript. A copy was sent to one of El Chapo's lawyers, and another is sitting somewhere on an FBI server, given to the agents a few years later by an informant.

Over the next several years, the movie project inched along, even as El Chapo steadily became bogged down in fratricidal wars with former allies. He met with Rey once more in 2012, but this time it didn't go so well; at a final meeting in Mexico, Rey told Alex that he was looking to receive 35 percent of any profits from the book and movie. When El Chapo heard that, he exploded. He had been planning to give the producer a much smaller lump sum, but now this request, which he perceived as abject greed on Rey's part, got him thinking about this stranger to whom he had opened up, had told about his life, introduced to his wives and children. Brooding about Rey's perceived treachery, El Chapo became convinced that the producer was an informant who had come to collect information and give it to the authorities to help capture El Chapo and build a case against him. He decided the producer had to die, and told Alex to make sure it happened.

Alex began plotting to have one of his men in Colombia murder Rey, just as he had attempted (however sloppily or half-heartedly) to locate Christian Rodriguez. Before he could put the plan in motion, however, Alex was arrested outside of Culiacán in 2013, and from jail sent word to his wife telling her to warn the producer of the danger he was in. Rey survived.

El Chapo never lost his interest in making a movie. It seems his meeting with Kate del Castillo and Sean Penn was done in the interest of getting a movie made, and his lawyers even reached out to a *New Yorker* writer to see if he'd like to help with such a project. In the end, it was El Chapo's criminal trial that delivered the dramatic showcase that he had long sought. But once again, the narrative was out of his hands. Beginning in November 2018 in the federal courthouse of the Eastern District of New York in downtown Brooklyn, the trial was a three-month slide show of greatest hits, featuring an all-star cast from his past, including the cartoonishly disfigured mass murderer, Chupeta; Lucero, the tearful ex-lover; Miguel Ángel Martínez Martínez, the former cocaine addict and onetime close friend harboring a twenty-year-old grudge against the defendant; Dámaso López, the treacherous lieutenant who still swore love and loyalty; Christian Rodriguez, the young outsider whom El Chapo had trusted with his life and who in the end helped tie the whole case together.

But what was the point of it all? For prosecutors, and the government they served, the point of this case it was clear: putting El Chapo away sent an "unmistakable message." What that message was depends on who you talk to. According to the Justice Department, the message was that no drug lord was untouchable. To El Chapo's defense team, the message was that El Chapo was stitched up, doomed from the start. To many Mexicans, dismayed at the lack of testimony about actual crimes in Mexico, the message was that selling drugs to willing buyers in the States is worse than murdering tens of thousands of people in Mexico. With some exceptions, such as the discussion of the bribery allegations against Genaro García Luna and Enrique Peña Nieto (which both deny), prosecutors were largely successful in keeping the proceedings laser focused on the testimony against El Chapo and in barring any discussion of anything that would cause embarrassment to unnamed "individuals and entities" not directly tied to the El Chapo case.

As if to underscore the folly of the whole affair, news broke the same week that jury deliberations began that officials in Arizona had made the largest-ever seizure of fentanyl along the border. Days before the verdict arrived, the DEA announced the seizure of fifty pounds of fentanyl in Chicago (destined for the Bronx). El Chapo was newly convicted, but he'd already been in the United States for more than two years. Any notion that his absence from Mexico would put a dent in the drug trade was a fantasy. It always had been.

On July 17, 2019, months after being found guilty, El Chapo appeared in public for the last time to hear his sentence, and to make one final statement to the public. Apart from a few quiet yes-and-no answers during the trial, it was the first time he'd spoken publicly since appearing on video for Sean Penn back in 2015. As the trial had wound down, there had been great speculation as to whether El Chapo would take the stand, and some disappointment when he had sensibly chosen not to. Now was the chance, however, to hear his last words.

Standing up at the defense table, El Chapo greeted Judge Brian M. Cogan and launched into a muted diatribe against his treatment in the United States.

"They say they are sending me to a prison where my name will never be heard again," El Chapo said, pausing for his translator to repeat in English. "I take this opportunity to say there was no justice here."

Stumbling a bit as he read his prepared remarks, he cataloged the indignities he had faced during his incarceration in Manhattan.

"I have been forced to drink unsanitary water, denied access to air and sunlight," he said. "It has been psychological, emotional, mental torture twenty-four hours a day."

Up next was Gina Parlovecchio, one of the lead prosecutors, who lambasted El Chapo for his apparent lack of remorse.

"Throughout his criminal career, this defendant has not shown one shred of remorse for his crimes," Parlovecchio said. "You heard that again today."

The final word came from Andrea Fernández Velez, the former assistant to Alex Cifuentes turned FBI informant who had escaped a contract on her life, apparently the only person willing to read a so-called victim impact statement at the hearing. Breaking down in tears several times as she read her own prepared remarks in Spanish, Andrea apologized for her mistakes, and laid out the psychological toll she had suffered when she realized that the people she had worked with so closely wanted her dead.

"When we started to develop the movie project, I came to view him as a good person, with great kindness and charisma," she said. "When I saw the reality and wanted to distance myself, my friends turned out to be . . . captors.

"When I tried to leave the organization, I was told I could only do it one way: in a plastic bag, feetfirst," she continued, as El Chapo ignored the scene completely and turned to blow a kiss to his wife. "I lost my family, my friends. . . . I became a shadow without a name. I had everything, I lost everything, even my identity."

Then she turned away from the man who had wanted her dead, and walked through a side door toward the rest of her life, looking back over her shoulder just once.

Finally, with Andrea gone, it was time for the sentencing, although due to federal guidelines and the charges of which El Chapo had been found guilty, it was always a foregone conclusion. After so much anticipation, it was almost anticlimactic to hear the judge read out the sentence: life in prison plus thirty years.

In the final moments of the spectacle of El Chapo, the ending he never would have written for himself, the Lord of the Mountains turned around, craning his neck for one last glimpse at his wife. It was likely to be the last time he would ever lay eyes on her.

He gave her a thumbs-up, smiled, and turned his head to walk toward his grim fate. The marshals led him through the door and he disappeared forever into the black hole of the United States federal prison system.

His final act is playing out now, in a tiny cell in ADX Florence, a supermax prison on the windswept high desert plains of Colorado.

In Mexico, the story goes on without him.

. . .

Just after 3 p.m. on October 17, 2019, a group of Mexican National Guard soldiers stood in the car bay of a stately modernist mansion, angular walls gleaming a brilliant white as the afternoon sun beat down on this part of the ritzy neighborhood of Tres Ríos, Culiacán, their assault rifles trained on a black door that led into the building. The poorly planned and hastily executed operation was intended to be a quick snatch-and-grab extraction; they were supposed to be at the airport by now. But for forty-five minutes the soldiers had found themselves in a stalemate, unable to enter the home, the inhabitants unwilling to exit.

A short distance away, gunfire echoed out, the staccato burst of automatic weapons, about nine shots, *ta ta tatatatatatata!*

The whole thing had already gone sideways.

On the other side of the wall, from the direction of the first burst of gunshots, came the sound of multiple weapons firing, too many to count. The unmistakable sound of an honest-to-God firefight. Still more shots echoed out, these from farther away, a hint that the chaos outside had begun to spread across the city. The first soldier made another plaintive motion with his hand, as if to ask "What are you waiting for?" as the soldier opposite him lowered into a crouch.

Suddenly the door opened inward slightly, and everything happened fast, everyone was shouting, "Hey hey hey, come out, put your hands up, come out!"

The first person to come out was a woman, clad in a black and white striped shirt; she put her hands up in surrender, but yanked them away as one soldier tried to grab her wrist. Behind her, looking scared, stood two young men, one pudgy and wearing a white polo shirt, the other slimmer, handsome, clad in a white dress shirt and a black baseball cap. This young man was who the soldiers came for, and everyone knew it. Ovidio Guzmán López, the twenty-nine-year-old son of El Chapo.

Everyone began shouting at once. "Calm down, calm down!" a soldier yelled, and the woman tugged at Ovidio's arm as three more men walked out the door behind him with their hands raised. Seemingly concerned for their well-being, Ovidio frowned as soldiers grabbed the men. "Hey, no, he has nothing to do with it!" he pleaded.

Ovidio took his cap off, put it back on, and peered back inside the house, until finally a soldier roughly forced him to his knees, facing the wall, hands up. As he turned his head, at a certain angle, the way his jet-black hair sprouted from under the baseball cap, the shape of his head, the resemblance was striking: he is his father's son.

The woman, hands outstretched, continued pleading with the soldiers, trying to put herself between them and the young men facing the wall. The troops appeared hesitant to touch her as they attempted to stabilize the situation. "Hey, help me," they begged her, "*no pasa nada*, don't worry!"

Ovidio got back on his feet now, phone in hand, as the soldiers ordered him to make a call to his people to ask them to stand down.

"Listen, stop everything," he said. "I don't want chaos."

Ovidio's people did not listen.

• • •

Outside the walls of the mansion in Tres Ríos, nobody knew what was going on. It started off just before 3 p.m., just a few gunshots at first, scattered fighting, not necessarily an everyday occurrence in Culiacán but not unheard-of. Sergio,* a college student, had just gotten out of class that afternoon at the University City campus of the Autonomous University of Sinaloa when his phone began to light up with messages. First one video, then more, and more, all showing chaotic scenes of shoot-outs. Sergio, twenty-three, is a native of Culiacán, and like all *culichis* he'd learned to live with violence.

"Usually a shooting lasts half an hour, an hour, and it's over," Sergio told me later.

But this time the shooting did not stop.

It soon became clear that the seemingly random outbursts of violence across Culiacán were all part of the same incident. It was a coordinated effort to surround the soldiers who had seized Ovidio, blockade highways in and out of the city, seal off the bridges that connect various sectors of Culiacán, and sow general chaos across the city. A video soon emerged of gunmen, having seized a toll plaza south of the city, chatting and shaking hands with soldiers, who apparently had chosen detente over a deadly firefight.

The troops appeared unprepared for such an uprising. During one heavy exchange of gunfire, a soldier ran out of ammunition and turned to a nearby reporter, at a loss.

"What should I do?" the soldier asked.

"Take off your uniform!" the reporter said, recalling the incident later to the *New York Times*. "You're a target, take it off!"

Appearing as if from nowhere, armed men in tactical vests began racing around the city as gunmen blocked off bridges, hijacked buses, and set them ablaze across major avenues. They engaged soldiers in running street battles. In videos that were circulating on social media and via WhatsApp, heavily armed gunmen in pickup trucks raced toward Culiacán, whooping with unbridled joy.

"We're in charge now," one gunman cheered, as he and his compatriots sped down a highway.

Later, there were reports that the gunmen were offering 20,000 pesos (a little over $1,000) and a rifle to anyone who joined them.

At a prison on the western outskirts of Culiacán, gunmen stormed the gates and released dozens of inmates, who promptly began hijacking passing cars; at a housing complex for military families in southwestern Culiacán, gunmen laid siege to the place, taking the families inside hostage and threatening to burn the buildings down unless Ovidio was released. Driving in flatbed trucks with high siding and mounted with .50-caliber machine guns, armed men fought running battles with army and National Guard soldiers, as well as municipal police.

As security forces struggled for control of Culiacán, this city of nearly one million people froze. Untold numbers of civilians huddled for cover wherever they found themselves, ducking behind the tires and engine blocks of their cars, or crouching in restaurants. Videos began to appear on social media of fierce firefights between soldiers and cartel gunmen, heavy weapons firing full auto, snipers lying prone in the street and taking careful aim with giant .50-caliber rifles. Disturbing videos of carnage emerged: a soldier lying in the bed of a truck, his leg nearly severed below the knee; a fallen soldier sprawled on the pavement clad in camo pants and black T-shirt, shoeless, as a gunman loops a noose around his neck and drags his body across the ground; a mother running across the street, her terrified child flopping in her arms; a father huddling behind a car with his small daughter.

"Daddy, can we get up?" she asks.

"No, my love," he responds softly, breathing heavily and trying to keep his voice level. You can hear the fear in his voice, and the struggle to keep his baby girl calm. "We have to stay here. On the ground."

"Why on the ground?" she asks, her little voice quizzical but seeming not to grasp the danger they are in.

In the parking lot of the City Club supermarket, where Ovidio's brother Édgar Guzmán López had been gunned down more than eleven years before, a shoot-out left several children trapped as bullets cracked through the air.

Among the civilians caught by the gunfire were two young laborers, José Arturo, twenty-three, and Nicolás, thirty-two, who were gunned down as they tried to make it back to their workshop in what they mistakenly believed was a moment of calm.

About five weeks later, on November 28, 2019, I found myself in the office of a furniture store, speaking with the owner, Miguel.* He had sent the two workers out that morning to the Centro de Ciencias museum, a little more than a mile down the road from the City Club grocery store. By the time they finished the job, gunfire had begun to ring out in the streets, and when they called the boss as he himself huddled in his workshop, he told them to stay put until it was over.

Miguel didn't know the two men well. They were contract laborers, and had only been with him about a month, but he helped pay the cost of their burial. He seemed tired, weighed down by the whole thing.

"[They were] young, young," he said wearily. "They were very hard workers, very responsible."

At some point, apparently thinking the fighting had died down, they left the science museum and headed back to the shop. He didn't hear from them again. The next day, Miguel received a phone call from a friend of his son, who'd seen the company truck in Tres Ríos, riddled with bullets.

More than a year later, the circumstances of their deaths remain murky; it's unclear whether the bullets that killed them came from soldiers or criminals, but one theory is that as they drove near the Tres Ríos neighborhood, where the worst fighting took place, they were mistaken for gunmen. In a photo taken that day, the bodies of José Arturo and Nicolás can be seen lying on the ground next to the truck, which with its high white siding bears a distinct resemblance to many of the vehicles that gunmen had used that day to race around the city as they fought running battles with security forces. In that photo, an army truck painted in black and green digital camouflage sits just a few feet away, its doors thrown open, its back tires flattened.

"The most likely thing is that [the soldiers] confused them," Miguel told me. "That's all we can say."

According to officials in Sinaloa, a total of fourteen people died on the day that many now refer to as "Black Thursday." Almost everyone I spoke to believes the number was much higher.

• • •

You may know the rest. After hours of heavy fighting, orders came in from Mexico City: the soldiers were to release Ovidio. So they let him go, he disappeared, and the hundreds of gunmen who had paralyzed the city melted away into the night. It quickly emerged that the order to release Ovidio had come from on high, and later, President Andres Manuel López Obrador announced that he had personally given the order, a desperate concession that successfully brought the fighting to a halt. The operation had been on the behalf of the DEA, in order to arrest Ovidio and extradite him; but it was Mexicans, *culichis* who died that day, as it almost always is. So he made the call, he said, to prevent any more deaths.

In the immediate aftermath of Black Thursday, barrels of ink were spilled by pundits who wondered if López Obrador had surrendered to organized crime, and what that might mean for the future of Sinaloa, and for Mexico. To be sure, the fact that an army of civilians with guns could go head-to-head with government armed forces and win its main objective—the release of Ovidio—told a troubling story about the Mexican government's ability to command a monopoly on violence, which most scholars see as a key element of state control.

The controversial decision to release Ovidio drew scrutiny to the security strategy of López Obrador, who campaigned as a left-wing anti-corruption reformer and pledged to confront organized crime with "hugs, not bullets." The controversy obscured a larger issue, however: despite pledging a less militaristic solution to the country's soaring murder rates and entrenched criminal violence, López Obrador has leaned on the military even more than his predecessors, creating a new wing of the military, the National Guard, which he has used to block Central American migrants at Mexico's southern border and in anti-drug operations like the one in Culiacán.

But it must be said: in the case of Black Thursday, as has virtually always been the case in Mexican drug violence, the gunmen who came out into the street and fought against the army and the National Guard had no intention of overthrowing the state. Despite the language of some news outlets describing a "takeover" of the city, it was more of an armed strike aimed at *paralyzing* the city for a period of time, rather than a bid for outright control of Culiacán. The city was a battleground that day, but gunmen did not seize city hall, did not raise their own flag above the city or declare territorial control of the city itself. This has never been the goal of drug traffickers in Mexico; their aim is profit, and they have much more efficient and subtle ways of ensuring that local governments and law enforcement agencies look the other way when need be.

Nor was the confrontation unprecedented. There have been other armed strikes by organized crime groups in Mexico, most notably an attack in 2015 by the Cártel de Jalisco Nuevo Generación, when gunmen burned vehicles in the streets of Guadalajara and brought the city to a standstill to prevent the capture of their reputed leader. This is not to downplay the horror of that day, but to say that any discussion of Black Thursday that examines it in a vacuum is missing crucial aspects of what took place, and what it means for Mexico, while overblown rhetoric can easily lead to the same brute-force tactics that have only made the violence in Mexico worse.

For the residents of Culiacán I spoke with a month after the events of Black Thursday, the citywide battle had indeed felt like something apart from the usual violence they lived with. As with the violence that broke out in May 2008, amid the rupture between El Chapo and the Beltrán Leyvas and the death of Édgar Guzmán López, Black Thursday represented for the people of Culiacán a temporary fracture in the order with which they have learned to negotiate daily life amid a low-intensity war. In the hours after Ovidio's release, the city settled into an uneasy, unnatural calm. But within a few days, the rhythms of everyday life resumed.

A measure of local feelings about safety that is perhaps better than anecdotal interviews lies in the National Urban Security Survey (known by the Spanish acronym ENSU), which is conducted on a quarterly basis by Mexico's National Institute of Statistics and Geography (INEGI). According to that survey, the reported percentage of *culichis* who felt that life in Culiacán was unsafe actually went *down* that fall, from 66.6 percent in September 2019 to 66.2 percent that December. By March 2020, that number had leapt up to 77.8 percent, although it dropped back down to 65.1 percent by September, nearly a year after the gun battles of October 17, 2019. By and large, that day, as traumatic as it was, does not appear to have had a lasting impact on how *culichis* view their city.

What Black Thursday *did* represent was a demonstration of force, and one that El Chapo may have been unwilling to condone when he was still at large. During the operation to capture El Chapo in 2014, DEA agents on the ground were constantly on guard for some kind of mass uprising, an attack by El Chapo's men aimed at obstructing their movements, or at rescuing their leader upon his eventual capture. This did not happen. We may never know why: perhaps El Chapo laid out plans for such an operation, but the Marines and their advisors in the DEA moved too quickly. But perhaps El Chapo never made any such plans.

The uprising to rescue Ovidio, with all its indications of premeditation and well-thought-out strategy, marked a new willingness by Sinaloan gangsters to use force openly, to roam the streets of Culiacán in broad daylight, displaying their weapons. It said more about the style of El Chapo's sons than it did about the balance of power between organized crime and law enforcement in the state.

Iván, Alfredillo, Ovidio, and their brother Joaquín have always done things differently than their father. They're of a new generation, the so-called narco juniors, raised amid wealth and privilege that their fathers did not have as young men. El Chapo and El Mayo grew up in harsh conditions and fought tooth and nail for their status and territory. Their sons, on the other hand, have been powerful since a young age, with money and influence at their fingertips. They're city boys, raised in luxury, and they love to show it off. They're also less willing to make the sacrifices their fathers did, hiding out in the mountains, living on the run. They want to live in opulence, and they want everyone to see it.

Whatever lack of discretion El Chapo showed in his flirtation with fame and his attempts to make a movie, his children and other narco juniors put that to shame, flaunting their wealth in public and on social media. The sons of men who grew up with nothing, and who spent their lives speaking in code and using the latest in encrypted technology, were blithely bragging about their lifestyles on Twitter and Instagram.

Even hard men like Chino Ántrax, whose hit squad was one of the main sources of muscle for El Chapo in Culiacán, caught the social media bug, posting gold-plated AKs and photos of his girlfriends to Instagram. So too did El Mayo's son Ismael Zambada Imperial, aka Mayito Gordo, or Fat Little Mayo, who prior to his arrest in 2014 had become such an avid poster that El Mayo is rumored to have put his foot down and banned his children and subordinates from using social media.

One can only imagine how such tomfoolery appeared to a man like El Mayo, who survived as long as he did by not tempting fate, staying up in the hills rather than pulling stunts or causing problems that might force his friends in the military to come find him on behalf of the United States. Whereas El Chapo's legend rested on his escapes, El Mayo's legend is that of a man who has no need to escape because he's never been locked up in the first place, never seen the inside of a jail cell—or at least not on the government's terms. Unlike El Chapo, who made repeated ventures down to urban centers such as Culiacán, Mazatlán, Los Cabos, and Los Mochis, El Mayo was content to stick to the hills, administering power from afar. In the only interview he's ever given, a conversation held with *Proceso* founder Julio Scherer, El Mayo waxed poetic about the solace and safety he finds in his highland hideouts.

"The mountain is my home, my family, my protection, my land, the water that I drink," he told Scherer during the meeting, which took place under such strict secrecy that many of Scherer's colleagues at *Proceso* did not know of it until the issue was going to print. "The land is always good."

That lesson apparently didn't make its way to Mayito Gordo, who was arrested in 2014 and extradited to the United States in January 2020, the third son of El Mayo to end up in the hands of the gringos. Mayo's one remaining son not in prison, Mayito Flaco (Skinny Little Mayo), is the exception. Like his father, he keeps a low profile and stays out of trouble, according to Antonio,* a drug trafficker I spoke with in Culiacán who told me he works closely with El Mayo's faction.

"Mayito Flaco, they say, that kid stays in the mountains, sending his workers to do this or that," Manuel said. "He doesn't mess with people, contrary to the ones who went bad, like Mayito Gordo, who's always going around with his corridos, having parties. . . . Mayito Flaco, he has no *corridos* to be heard."

On the day that federal troops embarked on their ill-fated mission to arrest Ovidio, it had been nearly three years since El Chapo's final arrest outside of Los Mochis, almost two years since his extradition to the United States, and just three months since he had been officially sentenced to spend the rest of his life in a North American prison cell.

In the months after his extradition in 2017, bloodshed had broken out in Sinaloa, as the factions controlled by El Chapo's sons, often referred to as the Chapitos, struggled for control of their father's empire against a faction overseen by Dámaso López and his son, known by the nickname "Mini-Lic."

Violence surged in Culiacán that spring, but it was short-lived: in April 2017, police arrested Dámaso López in Mexico City. According to Ismael Bojórquez, editor of the scrappy and fiercely independent weekly newspaper *Riodoce*, Dámaso never had a chance.

"Dámaso was a lawyer, wrapped up with the narcos, but he was not a man of arms. The war was already lost for that *pendejo*," Bojórquez told me. "He should have understood that, and didn't. That El Chapo, no matter how much he wanted to, was not going to leave it to him. He was going to leave it to his sons."

Javier Valdez, a fellow editor and cofounder of *Riodoce*, had even more contempt for Mini-Lic. In an article published in April 2017, Valdez examined the rise and fall of El Chapo's once-loyal lieutenant. He also turned an eye to the future—or lack of a future—of Mini-Lic, whom he described as a "weekend gunman," all show with nothing to back it up, unfit to take the place of his father, let alone El Chapo. In a play on the term *narcocorridos*, the songs lauding the exploits of traffickers, he described Mini-Lic as a *"narco de corridos."*

"He likes to show off gold and jewelry," Valdez sneered. "Nothing to see as a budding capo, or a successor of El Chapo or his father. Nothing."

A few months later, Dámaso's son appeared at a border crossing and turned himself in to federal agents in the United States. Both father and son were soon offering full cooperation with North American prosecutors and investigators.

Amid the last spasms of fighting between the Chapitos and Mini-Lic, a pair of hit men cornered Javier Valdez as he drove near the *Riodoce* offices and gunned him down in the street, an atrocity for which all sides denied responsibility. The assassination sparked a groundswell of revulsion toward organized crime, and against the impunity that killers enjoy in Mexico, as thousands marched demanding "not one more." But little changed. On a visit to Culiacán in August 2019, I met up with Bojórquez at El Guayabo, a cantina where Valdez had always held court and where the *Riodoce* crew still have their own table. After a round of Tecates, we headed back to the office a block away. When the conversation turned to the murder of his friend, I asked Bojórquez about that chant, "not one more."

"Yes, yes, but that didn't happen. That was just a slogan," Bojórquez said with a sigh. "Actually, since that happened, I told myself that unfortunately things here were not going to change. That there was a context of violence that was not going to change. And a context of impunity. And almost a system of impunity that also was not going to change. And look, [López Obrador] came along, and absolutely nothing has changed."

When Dámaso testified at the trial of El Chapo, he emphatically denied that he or his son had anything to do with the murder of Javier Valdez. Prosecutors in Mexico are currently seeking the extradition of Mini-Lic to stand trial as the "intellectual author" of the assassination plot, but some people familiar with the case suspect the possible involvement of some faction within the security forces.

The Chapitos, at any rate, seemed to have won the power struggle for

Culiacán. They now appear to run their father's business in an uneasy alliance with El Mayo; but ask anyone here who the real power is in Sinaloa and it's no question. The Chapitos might share their father's name, but El Mayo is the man.

. . .

The arrest and sentencing of El Chapo, the defeat of Dámaso, any number of drug seizures and kingpin takedowns—nothing has put a dent in the amount of drugs pouring into the United States or the guns pouring into Mexico. It is beyond dispute that the ideology of prohibition, which supposedly undergirds the war on drugs, is a hopelessly utopian project. This sentiment regarding the futility of prohibition and the inevitability of legalization of at least marijuana is gaining more traction each year, and it is growing more common to hear such arguments from unlikely sources. Take for example Ruben Castillo, the federal judge in the Northern District of Illinois who presided over the guilty plea of El Mayo's son Vicente "Vicentillo" Zambada. In an impassioned monologue delivered at Vicentillo's sentencing hearing in May 2019, Castillo decried the futility of an endless war of attrition against a rotating cast of narco villains with no meaningful attempts to stanch the appetite for illegal drugs in the United States.

"I would be the first one to admit here in open court on the record after twenty-five years of being a federal judge that if there is a so-called drug war, we have lost it," Castillo said. "We have lost it. And it's time for this country to think about doing something different."

I was stunned that day, sitting in his courtroom in downtown Chicago, to hear these words coming out of the mouth of a federal judge. At the time, I found it exciting to hear someone like Castillo admit that the drug war is a dead end. But the more I've reflected on this idea of failure, the more I wonder if that is true. Castillo's earnest lament brings to my mind an episode from the early days of the war on drugs that completely rewrote the book on U.S.-Mexico relations, despite being publicly viewed as a failure: Operation Intercept.

In 1969, under the guise of counternarcotics work, the Nixon administration launched Intercept, a massive security operation along the entire length of the border with Mexico in which every vehicle entering the United States from Mexico would be thoroughly searched for drugs and other contraband. Over the next twenty days, traffic backed up for hours at ports of entry, and cross-border trade ground to a halt. It was a gut punch to border communities from Tijuana to Matamoros, and knocked the wind out of the Mexican government, as well—a swift and brutal demonstration of the pain that could be inflicted on Mexico if it refused to bend the knee to Washington's demands.

At its conclusion on October 11, Operation Intercept was widely derided as an embarrassing debacle, a stunt that was as inept and heavy-handed as it was ineffective. In a brief, finger-wagging editorial published on October 12, the *New York Times* lambasted the operation as "clumsy," a "total fiasco" that could only harm U.S.-Mexico relations.

But the people who planned the operation didn't agree. Just ask G. Gordon Liddy, the dirty trickster of the Nixon administration who would later become famous for his role in the Watergate scandal. In his post-prison memoir, Liddy looked back on Operation Intercept—and the reaction to it—with glib satisfaction.

"Operation Intercept has been called a failure—but only by those who never knew its objective. It was actually a great success," Liddy wrote. "It was an exercise in international extortion, pure and simple, and effective, designed to bend Mexico to our will."

Taken at face value, the current iteration of the war on drugs launched in 2006 by Felipe Calderón has been an abject failure. Nearly fifteen years on, hundreds of thousands of Mexicans have been murdered and tens of thousands more have been forcibly disappeared; organized-crime groups that were once largely focused on drug trafficking have branched out and diversified, making them more difficult to combat and often employing ever-greater violence and exploitation on local populations in Mexico; access to illicit drugs in the United States has never waned, but rather increased, particularly synthetic drugs like fentanyl and its analogues and methamphetamine, which have driven a crisis of overdose deaths to epidemic proportions.

So yes, at face value the war on drugs is an obvious, calamitous failure. But just as it was naive of the *Times* to declare Operation Intercept a failure, it is also a mistake to view the current war on drugs as a failure. And as much as it might sound like radical common sense, perhaps this narrative of a failed—but noble—crusade only serves to obscure the larger picture.

If you look past the stated goals of the war on drugs, the question of "failure" becomes murkier. This is not a grand conspiracy, but rather the logical result of many overlapping and competing interests, which can be made sense of with the simple question of *"Cui bono?"* Who benefits?

The unpleasant answer to this unpleasant question: the war on drugs works out great for a lot of people and a lot of institutions. It's not just drug traffickers who've gotten rich off the inflated wages of drug trafficking. So much illegal drug money flows through big banks that it may have been drug money alone, a great source of liquid capital, that kept the global financial system from fully collapsing in 2008.

From the moment the passage of the Harrison Narcotics Act of 1914 set the framework for modern drug regulation, the prohibition of drugs has provided valuable ammunition to bureaucratic warriors looking to protect their agency's budget and increase its operational mandate. Take the prohibition of marijuana: in the early 1930s, amid the ravages of the Great Depression, the Federal Bureau of Narcotics saw repeated budget cuts and staff reductions, to the horror of its director Harry Anslinger, the founding father of North America's modern war on drugs. So what did Anslinger do? He began beating the drum against the perils of marijuana; by 1937, the United States had banned cannabis, and Anslinger's newly empowered FBN had control over the bulk of the federal antinarcotics effort. This budgetary and operational zeal for expansion continues in the modern era, too. When Nixon formed the DEA in 1972, its budget was just $65 million; in 2019, the agency's budget was $3.1 billion.

Mexico has undergone a dramatic militarization in which security forces, most notably the Marines (SEMAR) and the army and President López Obrador's new National Guard, have gained tremendous increases in power within Mexico, in terms of operational capacity, budget increases, and political influence; the "national security threat" of organized crime demands it.

Politicians in both countries have won elections and maintained their positions in office through fearmongering messaging and "tough-on-crime" stances; the perpetual "threat" of uber-powerful drug cartels demands that our leaders be men of action. And it has proved a useful cudgel in foreign policy: the United States has found ample opportunity to accuse its foes in countries like Venezuela, Ecuador, Bolivia, and Nicaragua of links to drug trafficking while looking the other way for allies such as Juan Orlando Hernández, the repressive president of Honduras whose direct ties in drug trafficking is a matter of public record. Without an urgent and ongoing "war on drugs," the U.S. State Department would have one less arrow in its quiver.

Not everyone engaged in anti-drug efforts is in it for cynical, power-hungry motives, of course; many of the law enforcement agents I've spoken with on both sides of the border have struck me as sincere, true believers that their admittedly quixotic mission is making the world a better place. But the drug war has been immensely profitable on a personal level, as well as institutional, to many of the people tasked with pursuing it: the first federal anti-drug force in the United States, a division of the Internal Revenue Service, was eventually disbanded due to comically rampant levels of corruption. And while corruption within U.S. federal law enforcement agencies has rarely, if ever, risen to the institutionalized levels often found in Mexico, there has been a steady occurrence of agents of the DEA, Customs and Border Protection, and other federal outfits found to be collaborating with drug traffickers. At a local level, the problem is even more severe: the drug war was working out great, for example, for the mayor and chief of police of Columbus, New Mexico, a tiny border town in which both men and others were involved in a scheme to sell weapons in Mexico—a scheme that, when uncovered, led to the dissolution of the town's police force.

Arms manufacturers in the United States and gun stores along the border do a booming business selling to anyone who's buying. Law enforcement agencies and military branches in the United States have also used the logic of antinarcotics forever war to win consistent, year-over-year budget increases; as long as they can make the case that the drug trade poses a national security threat, how can lawmakers deny much-needed funds to protect the homeland?

This forever war has proved convenient in other ways: in Mexico, a heavily militarized country with significant natural resources, the overwhelming violence of the drug war provides a useful smoke screen for unrelated atrocities when people get in the way of "progress." Human rights workers, environmental activists, and journalists face immense personal risk in Mexico, and are murdered at an alarming rate, with near universal impunity. And with so much existing violence occurring in the areas where these brave souls often work and often die, or when entire communities are displaced from resource-rich land, it is an easy narrative to link the violence and displacement to bogeymen like Los Zetas or the Cártel de Jalisco Nuevo Generación, while deflecting attention away from large-scale mining or timber interests, say, or the vicious corruption of local authorities. If not for the mind-numbing violence of the ongoing war on drugs, the murder of activists and journalists would be considerably more difficult to obscure or ignore. Nowhere was this more clear than the botched cover-up following the 2014 mass kidnapping of forty-three young students in Iguala, Guerrero. In the wake of that crime against humanity, which even amid so much daily bloodshed shook Mexico to its foundation, the narrative immediately centered on the presence of a single organized crime group in the area, Guerreros Unidos, and its alleged links to local police forces. Thanks to tireless advocacy by the families of the disappeared and extremely courageous reporting by a number of Mexican journalists, we now are more certain than ever that, whatever role the Guerreros and their allies in local law enforcement did have in this mind-bendingly horrific crime, it was likely done in concert with elements of the federal police and the Mexican Army. That cover-up may have failed, but it's easy to see how focusing solely on name-brand criminal outfits, outlandish crime bosses, and expendable local authorities helps to obscure the role of powerful state forces in crimes against humanity.

So again, *cui bono?*

• • •

It's been more than two years since I first laid eyes on El Chapo in Judge Brian Cogan's courtroom in Brooklyn, and by the time this book is published it will have been more than two years since El Chapo was finally sentenced to life in prison. In the time since I began working on this book, tens of thousands of people have been murdered in the homicide epidemic that continues to wreak havoc in Mexico, a direct result of the ongoing war on drugs and the chaos and violence that ripple out from it. Often the violence hit hard in places that I had just recently gotten to know a bit.

Less than two weeks after I walked through downtown Agua Prieta after dark with Keoki Skinner, enjoying the pleasant hubbub of the city's first street festival in recent memory, Agua Prieta descended into chaos as rival gunmen opened fire on one another, and by the time it was over nearly a dozen people were dead.

The week I spent in Juárez took place during a quietly mounting tide of violence, approaching homicide numbers that rivaled the years of war. In November 2019, the city exploded into a frenzy of violence; a seemingly coordinated series of bus burnings lit up the night and a wave of murders shook to the core a populace that had only just begun to feel stable again, finally allowing itself to hope that the worst years were behind them. By the end of 2019, Juárez had recorded more than 1,500 homicides.

In the mountains of Sinaloa, life has gotten steadily worse in the years since El Chapo was captured, and many people I spoke to there and in Culiacán look back on his tenure as a time of relative prosperity. This is likely in part due to the instability caused by his capture, but the trend had begun well before he was removed from the equation. The price of marijuana has been crashing for years, and the price of opium has cratered, too, in part thanks to the introduction of synthetic opioids like fentanyl. The "iron law of prohibition" states that efforts to disrupt drug supply will necessarily result in the use of increasingly compact substitutes. Just as cocaine made sense in the 1980s to drug traffickers who could make astronomical profit without having to worry about growing drugs themselves, fentanyl is easy to smuggle and does not require the labor and land that opium does. One trafficker whom I spoke with told me that a kilo of raw opium gum he would have bought a few years ago for 25,000 or 30,000 pesos (about $1,200 to $1,500) is now selling for 10,000 pesos.

"In the mountains, the producers are earning less profit, and product is going to waste," he said.

Attempts at crop substitution in the Sierra have largely failed, thanks to poor planning and not enough consultation with the farmers who know what grows in the area. As a result, farmers who could once count on a decent income growing opium or marijuana can no longer make a living, legally or illegally. Entire families are being driven out of the Sierra by hardship, drought, and violence—fighting between armed groups and persecution by the army and Marines—and many of them have ended up at the margins of Culiacán, swelling the ranks of the newly urbanized poor. And where there are large numbers of poor young men, there is often violence.

In August 2019, I drove to the outskirts of Culiacán to speak with a family of seven living in a tin-roof shack on the edge of town, several hundred feet from a massive garbage dump. A few months earlier, in June, intense fighting suddenly broke out in their home village in the mountains of Badiraguato, and they'd been forced to flee within hours. When I met the family, they'd been living in the little shack for a weeks, they said, and it was not easy to adjust. Fanning herself in the evening heat, the mother lamented the situation she found herself in after being so suddenly uprooted.

"Life is different [in the mountains]," she said. "There you work and you buy what you need for a certain amount of time and here you have to be working daily to be able to eat. Because if you don't work, you don't eat."

In their home in the mountains they grew corn and beans, and raised chickens and pigs. Mango trees provided fruit and shade. Last they heard, whatever armed group had seized their village had razed all the buildings, apparently in order to grow poppies. Here on the outskirts of Culiacán, what little furniture they had they'd picked out of the dump. There was no respite from the heat.

"I feel like the sun burns hotter here," she said.

For all the discussion of the fighting in Mexico from 2007 to 2012 as the Bad Years, the years that came after have been just as bad in many ways, perhaps worse. The number of homicides reached a record 27,213 in

2011, and from there dipped down for a few years, reaching a relative low of 20,010 in 2014; then the number started climbing. It hasn't stopped. Each year since has marked a grim uptick in the number of souls lost to violence: 24,559 in 2016; 32,079 in 2017; 36,685 in 2018; 2019 came in at a slight, statistically meaningless downturn of 36,661 murders. The new normal is four times worse than the number of homicides in 2007, the year that Calderón sent in the military. Vast swaths of the country are essentially in a constant state of low-intensity warfare, a war where the belligerents are cloaked in shadow, security forces are at deadly odds with the populace, and the victims are systematically dismissed and defamed, assumed to be guilty for the crime of being overwhelmingly young men with few job prospects.

Some journalists and researchers make an effort to identify the number of homicides in Mexico that are "related to organized crime"; I am not convinced that this is useful, or even possible. Many reports cling to thinly sourced explanations for this or that surge in violence: the CJNG is fighting the Sinaloa Cartel for control of Zacatecas; the Cartel del Noreste is fighting the Gulf Cartel for control of Tamaulipas; the Santa Rosa de Lima Cartel is fighting the CJNG for control of Guanajuato; El Chapo's sons, Los Chapitos, are fighting El Mayo for control of Sinaloa. Perhaps there is some truth to some of these tales, but at this point I don't know what we stand to gain from analyzing violence from this perspective. The country is militarized; the violence is generalized; arresting this "capo" or that "lieutenant" is not going to stop the bloodshed. It can also make things worse: when the journalistic narrative accepts as fact that a certain area is a "stronghold" of a given "cartel" or is known to be the site of fighting between organized-crime groups, it can be used to deter further questioning in the event of an atrocity linked to state security forces.

Of course it is important to understand violence on a local level, and this requires an understanding of the players; but it is as important or more so to understand the local dynamics that are driving violence. We can no longer lean on cinematic, interpersonal stories to explain the fighting. This is a systemic issue and must be analyzed as such.

The story of organized crime in Mexico has always been inseparable from the story of state power. Even those like El Chapo, the high-level traffickers, have always been expendable; with a few notable exceptions, the powerful people protecting the expendable drug traffickers have remained untouchable.

In 2018, more than a year after El Chapo was extradited, Iván Archivaldo Guzmán Salazar gave an interview to a Belgian magazine. As far as I know it is the only interview he's ever given, but it received little attention in the English and Spanish-language press. Iván addressed the extradition of his father, the "tremendous pain" it caused him, and the betrayal he felt that the Mexican government had carried out when it allowed his father to be sent to the United States, likely never to return. In that interview, the journalist, an Ecuadorian named Ernesto Rodríguez Amari, asked Iván what he made of allegations that the Mexican government was involved in organized crime.

"I don't know if they are the most organized, but at least they represent the most legitimate mafia," Iván said. "This mob has the real power. I can confirm that Mexican politicians use that power for their own interest."

The best way of understanding the drug trade is this: it is a capitalist enterprise in Mexico, and as such it has always had a corrupt and fuzzy relationship with the state—and has always been subject to the coercive demands and fickle priorities of U.S. foreign policy. Prohibition increases the risks, the frequency of violence, and the profit margins, but does not inherently separate the drug trade from the state. Many early drug traffickers were cops, and many early cops were drug traffickers, and the line has never gotten much more clear.

El Chapo, like many other men in his profession, was born poor, with few options, and rose in a world that demanded violence and rewarded ruthless ambition. As he gained power, wealth, and influence, he also took on a role as something of an intermediary between the state and the people who lived in areas where he held sway. He was no rebel, no Jesús Malverde. He wasn't the first, and it is already clear that he wasn't the last.

ACKNOWLEDGMENTS

THIS BOOK IS built from tens of thousands of pages of court documents, trial transcripts, and hard evidence submitted in court; hundreds of books, newspaper stories, and scholarly articles; and dozens of interviews with current and former agents of the DEA, FBI, HSI, and law enforcement agencies in Mexico, prosecutors, journalists, hit men, heroin cooks, smugglers, and civilians in the areas of Mexico that for decades have been at the epicenter of a deadly conflict euphemistically known as the "war on drugs." I hope this book honors those who came before me, and adds to the broader understanding of El Chapo, the region that created him, and the systems that encouraged him.

I give my deepest thanks to everyone who spoke to me for this book, whether as a source or in giving crucial context and guidance, whether on the record or off. Some asked to remain nameless, and some I was not able to include, but the information they gave, sometimes at great personal risk, made this book what it was.

Tremendous and eternal gratitude to Liz Garber-Paul and everyone else at *Rolling Stone*. This book exists because Matthew Benjamin believed in it and because Peter Borland, Sean Delone, and everyone else at Atria Books and Simon & Schuster helped get me to the finish line. Thank you also to the team at 3Arts, particularly Richard Abate and—most of all—Rachel Kim, who had my back every step of the way. And of course, my great friend and even better lawyer, Sam Light. I'm lucky to know you.

I would be nothing without my family. Thank you to my mom, Nancy Strong, for taking me in over several extended "writing retreats" and for putting up with my frustration and angst. Mom, I'm sorry about lying to you about spending Thanksgiving in Mexico City when I was really in Culiacán. Didn't want you to worry. Big thanks to my dad, Don Hurowitz, and stepmom, Betsy Hurowitz, for supporting me through it all. To my lifelong partners in crime, Mike, Dan, Katie, and Big Noah, SCZ forever. Shout-out to Spencer, the first of the new generation. Thanks for letting me crash on the couch for so many months in my nomad days.

To all my friends who kept me safe and sane, you know who you are.

Mi jefa de investigación, Jimena Lascuraín, *gracias por todo.* Conal Darcy and Kate Reistenberg transcribed most of my interviews; Martha Pskowski and Ethan Harfenist pitched in on research; and Frankie gave me the keys to the library. To *mi compa* Miguel Ángel Vega, thank you for lending many hands and for your excellent driving through that fucking thunderstorm. Thank you to Miguel Perea for help in Juárez, and to Keoki Skinner for showing me around Agua Prieta. Thank you to Isaac Scher and Natalie Schachar for fact-checking help. Any mistakes are my fault and mine alone.

Thank you to Jan-Albert Hootsen, the Mexico representative of the Committee to Protect Journalists, for fielding early questions, immediately offering me a place to stay, and acting as my check-in man whenever I was in dodgy areas.

To the El Chapo trial crew, I couldn't have asked for a more cooperatively competitive group of aces with whom to spend three months through freezing wind, bitter cold, and delirious exhaustion. In particular: Keegan Hamilton, Alejandra Ibarra, Molly Crane-Newman, Emily Saul, Sonia Moghe, Sonja Sharpe, Irene Plagianos, Jesús García, Victor Sanchez, David Brooks, Rebeka Smyth, Alan Feuer, and *La Reina de la Lista*, Marisa Cespedes.

To my roommates in New York and Mexico, thank you for putting up with my insane hours, and days of cranky silence followed by manic chattiness. And eternal thanks as well to Anthony Smith for giving me a place to crash time and again, and for nonstop support and friendship.

I am deeply and fundamentally indebted to the work of scholars, journalists, and others who came before me and whose work helped me make sense of things. In particular I'd like to thank Jesús Esquivel,

Alexander Aviña, Benjamin T. Smith, Adela Cedillo, Malcolm Beith, Ismael Bojórquez, Oscar Loza Ochoa, Patrick Timmons, Jayson Maurice Porter, and Ioan Grillo.

To Javier Valdez, whom I wish I'd met, and to Julián Cardona, whom I wish I'd gotten to know better.

Finally, to Stella, I owe you everything. I wrote and rewrote much of this book amid the dread and uncertainty of the COVID pandemic, as our world shrank to a few walls and daily walks through silent streets. You made it all bearable somehow. Throughout everything, you had my back, and I could only do my best to have yours. The love and support you showed, and your immense grace in the face of so many ups and downs, showed me a glimpse of the life we will share, and it is bright and full of joy. You are my light in the dark.

BIBLIOGRAPHY

BOOKS AND BOOK CHAPTERS

Ard, Michael J. "Mexico's Democratic Transition." Essay. In *An Eternal Struggle: How the National Action Party Transformed Mexican Politics*, 1–19. Westport, CT: Praeger, 2003.

Astorga, Luís. "Cocaine in Mexico: A Prelude to 'Los Narcos.'" Essay. In *Cocaine: Global Histories*, edited by Paul Gootenberg, 183–91. London, etc.: Routledge, 1999.

Astorga, Luís. *Drogas Sin Fronteras*. México, D.F.: Debolsillo, 2015.

———. *El Siglo De Las Drogas: Del Porfiriato Al Nuevo Milenio*. México, D.F: Debolsillo, 2016.

———. Essay. In *Organized Crime and Democratic Governability: Mexico and the U.S.-Mexican Borderlands*, edited by Roy Goodson and John Bailey, 58–82. Pittsburgh, PA: University of Pittsburgh, 2000. https://www.jstor.org/stable/j.ctt9qh7d4.7.

Aviña, Alexander. "A War Against Poor People: Dirty Wars and Drug Wars in 1970s Mexico." Essay. In *México Beyond 1968: Revolutionaries, Radicals, and Repression during the Global Sixties and Subversive Seventies*, edited by Enrique Ochoa and Jaime M. Pensado, 134–52. Tucson, AZ: University of Arizona Press, 2018. https://www.jstor.org/stable/j.ctv2t4cp8.12.

Bartley, Russell H., and Sylvia E. Bartley. *Eclipse of the Assassins: The CIA, Imperial Politics, and the Slaying of Mexican Journalist Manuel Buendía*. Madison, WI: The University of Wisconsin Press, 2015.

Beith, Malcolm. *The Last Narco: Inside the Hunt for El Chapo, the World's Most Notorious Drug Lord*. New York: Penguin, 2010.

Bender, Steven. *Run for the Border: Vice and Virtue in U.S.-Mexico Border Crossings*. New York: New York University Press, 2016.

Benítez Manaut, Raúl. "Containing Armed Groups, Drug Trafficking, and Organized Crime in Mexico: The Role of the Military." Essay. In *Organized Crime and Democratic Governability: Mexico and the U.S.-Mexican Borderlands*, edited by John Bailey and Roy Goodson, 126–58. Pittsburgh, PA: University of Pittsburgh, 2000. https://www.jstor.org/stable/j.ctt9qh7d4.10.

Boullosa, Carmen, and Mike Wallace. *A Narco History: How the United States and Mexico Jointly Created the "Mexican Drug War."* New York: OR Books in partnership with Counterpoint Press, 2016.

Castañeda Rodríguez Rafael, ed. *Esplendor y caída De El Chapo: El Fin Del Narcotraficante más Poderoso Del Mundo*. Ciudad de México: Editorial Planeta Mexicana, 2019.

Castillo, Elias, and Peter Unsinger. Essay. In *Organized Crime and Democratic Governability: Mexico and the U.S.-Mexican Borderlands*, edited by John J. Bailey and Roy Goodson, 199–216. Pittsburgh, PA: University of Pittsburgh, 2000. https://www.jstor.org/stable/j.ctt9qh7d4.13.

Cedillo, Juan Alberto. *La Cosa Nostra En México (1938–1950): Los Negocios De Lucky Luciano y La Mujer Que corrompió Al Gobierno Mexicano*. México, D.F.: Grijalbo, 2011.

Corchado, Alfredo. *Midnight in Mexico: A Reporter's Journey through a Country's Descent into the Darkness*. New York: The Penguin Press, 2014.

Curzio, Leonard. "Organized Crime and Political Campaign Finance in Mexico." Essay. In *Organized Crime and Democratic Governability: Mexico and the U.S.-Mexican Borderlands*, edited by John Bailey and Roy Goodson, 83–102. Pittsburgh, PA: University of Pittsburgh, 2000. https://www.jstor.org/stable/j.ctt9qh7d4.8.

Dale, Peter Scott. "Drugs, Anti-Communism and Extra-Legal Repression in Mexico." Essay. In *Government of the Shadows: Parapolitics and Criminal Sovereignty*, edited by Eric Michael Wilson, 173–94. New York, NY: Pluto Press, 2009. https://www.jstor.org/stable/j.ctt183p870.13.

Debord, Guy. *Society of the Spectacle*. Detroit, MI: Black & Red, 1983.

Dueñas Gabriela Polit. "Dealing with Everyday Violence: The Journalist and the Painter." Essay. In *Narrating Narcos: Stories from Culiacan and Medellin*, 79–101. Pittsburgh, PA: University of Pittsburgh Press, 2013. https://www.jstor.org/stable/j.ctt5hjr76.9.

Enciso Froylán. *Nuestra Historia Narcótica: Pasajes Para (Re)Legalizar Las Drogas En México*. México, D.F.: Debate, 2015.

Esquivel J. Jesús. *La CIA, Camarena y Caro Quintero: La Historia Secreta*. México, D.F.: Penguin Random House Grupo Editorial, 2014.

Esquivel, J. Jesús. *EL JUICIO: Crónica De La Caída Del Chapo.* México, D.F.: Penguin Random House Grupo Editorial, 2019.

Flores Pérez, Carlos. "Political Protection and the Origins of the Gulf Cartel." Essay. In *A War That Can't Be Won: Binational Perspectives on the War on Drugs,* edited by Kathleen Staudt, Z. Anthony Kruszewski, and Tony Payan, 119–48. Tucson, AZ: University of Arizona Press, 2013. https://www.jstor.org/stable/j.ctt16xwbq2.9.

Fuentes, Carlos. *The Death of Artemio Cruz.* Translated by Sam Hileman. New York: Farrar, Straus and Giroux, 1986.

Gibler, John. *To Die in Mexico: Dispatches from Inside the Drug War.* San Francisco: City Lights Books, 2011.

Goldman, Francisco. *The Interior Circuit: A Mexico City Chronicle.* New York: Grove Press, 2016.

González Fredy. "Mexico for the Mexicans, China for the Chinese: Political Upheaval and the Anti-Chinese Campaigns in Postrevolutionary Sonora and Sinaloa." Essay. In *Paisanos Chinos: Transpacific Politics among Chinese Immigrants in Mexico,* 15–42. Oakland, CA: University of California Press, 2017. https://www.jstor.org/stable/10.1525/j.ctt1p0vkf0.7.

Grayson, George W., ed. *Mexico: Narco-Violence and a Failed State?* New Brunswick, NJ: Transaction Publishers, 2017.

Grillo, Ioan. *El Narco: Inside Mexico's Criminal Insurgency.* London: Bloomsbury Publishing, 2014.

Hernández Anabel. *Narcoland: The Mexican Drug Lords and Their Godfathers.* Translated by Iain Bruce. London: Verso, 2014.

Hogan, Andrew. *Hunting El Chapo: The Inside Story of the American Lawman Who Captured the World's Most-Wanted Drug Lord.* New York: Harper, 2019.

Jones, Nathan P. *Mexico's Illicit Drug Networks and the State Reaction.* Washington, DC: Georgetown University Press, 2016.

Linnemann, Travis. "Drug War, Terror War, Street Corner, Battlefield." Essay. In *Meth Wars: Police, Media, Power,* 176–211. New York: New York University Press, 2016. https://www.jstor.org/stable/j.ctt1bj4rft.10.

Lazcano, Manuel. *Vida en la Vida Sinaloense,* ed. Nery Cordova Culiacán, Mexico: self-published, 1992.

Martin, William C. "Cartels, Corruption, Carnage, and Cooperation." Essay. In *A War That Can't Be Won: Binational Perspectives on the War on Drugs,* edited by Tony Payan, Kathleen Staudt, and Z. Anthony Kruszewski, 33–64. Tucson: University of Arizona Press, 2013.

Martínez Oscar J. *Ciudad Juárez: Saga of a Legendary Border City.* Tucson: University of Arizona Press, 2018.

McCormick, Gladys. "A Laboratory for State-Sponsored Violence, 1952–1958." Essay. In *The Logic of Compromise in Mexico: How the Countryside Was Key to the Emergence of Authoritarianism*, 133–61. Chapel Hill, NC: The University of North Carolina Press, 2016. https://www.jstor.org/stable/10.5149 /9781469627755_mccormick.10.

McCoy, Alfred W. *The Politics of Heroin: CIA Complicity in the Global Drug Trade, Afghanistan, Southeast Asia, Central America, Columbia.* Chicago: Lawrence Hill Books, 2003.

Ortiz Sarkis, Miguel. "Orígenes y Tendencias Del Narcotráfico En México." Essay. In *Gobernabilidad y Seguridad En América Latina: Desafíos Del Sector Defensa*, edited by Cristian Garay Vera, Luís Pérez Gil, and Valeska Troncosa Zuñiga, 200–20. Santiago: Instituto de Estudios Avanzados de la Universidad de Santiago de Chile, 2014. https://www.jstor.org/stable /j.ctt14jxsgv.14.

Osorno, Diego Enrique. *El cártel De Sinaloa: Una Historia Del Uso Politco Del Narco/ a History . . . of the Political Use of the Narco.* Grijalbo Mondadori, 2009.

Paley, Dawn. *Drug War Capitalism.* Edinburgh: AK Press, 2015.

Pansters, Wil. "Zones and Languages of State Making: From Pax PRIista to Dirty War." Essay. In *México Beyond 1968: Revolutionaries, Radicals, and Repression During the Global Sixties and Subversive Seventies*, edited by Jaime M. Pensado and Enrique Ochoa, 33–50. Tucson, AZ: University of Arizona Press, 2018. Project MUSE.muse.jhu.edu/book/59522.

Payan, Tony, Kathleen Staudt, and Z. Anthony Kruszewski. *A War That Can't Be Won: Binational Perspectives on the War on Drugs.* Tucson, AZ: University of Arizona Press, 2013.

Pimentel, Stanley A. "The Nexus of Organized Crime and Politics in Mexico." Essay. In *Organized Crime and Democratic Governability: Mexico and the U.S.-Mexican Borderlands*, edited by John Bailey and Roy Goodson, 33–57. Pittsburgh, PA: University of Pittsburgh, 2000. https://www.jstor.org/sta ble/j.ctt9qh7d4.6.

Poppa, Terrence E. *Drug Lord: A True Story. The Life & Death of a Mexican Kingpin.* El Paso, TX: Cinco Puntos Press, 2010.

Reveles José. *El Chapo: Entrega y traición.* México, D.F.: Debolsillo, 2014.

———. *Las Historias más Negras De Narco, Impunidad y corrupción En México.* México, D.F.: Grijalbo, 2012.

Ríos, Viridiana. "How Government Coordination Controlled Organized Crime: The Case of Mexico's Cocaine Markets." Essay. *In The Journal of Conflict Resolutions*, Special Issue: Drug Violence in Mexico, 59, no. 8 (December 2015): 1433–54. https://www.jstor.org /stable /24546349.

Romero, Robert Chao. "Mexican Sinophobia and the Anti-Chinese Campaigns." Essay. In *The Chinese in Mexico: 1882–1940*, 145–90. Tucson, AZ: University of Arizona Press, 2010. https://www.jstor.org/stable/j.ctt1814j07.11.

Schiavone Camacho, Julia Marie. "The Expulsion of Chinese Men and Chinese Mexican Families from Sonora and Sinaloa, Early 1930s." Essay. In *Chinese Mexicans: Transpacific Migration and the Search for a Homeland, 1910–1960*, 65–80. Chapel Hill: University of North Carolina Press, 2012. https://www .jstor.org/stable/10.5149/9780807882597_schiavone_camacho.8.

Scott, Peter Dale, and Jonathan Marshall. *Cocaine Politics: Drugs, Armies, and the CIA in Central America*. Berkeley and Los Angeles: University of California Press, 1991.

Shannon, Elaine. *Desperados: Latin Drug Lords, U.S. Lawmen, and the War America Can't Win*. Bloomington, IN: iUniverse, Inc., 2015.

Shirk, David A., Duncan R. Wood, and Eric L. Olson. *Building Resilient Communities in Mexico: Civic Responses to Crime and Violence*. Washington, DC: Mexico Institute, Woodrow Wilson Center for International Scholars, 2014.

Sontag, Susan. *Regarding the Pain of Others*. New York, NY: Farrar, Straus and Giroux, 2003.

Zavala, Oswaldo. *Los Cárteles No Existen: Narcotráfico y Cultura En México*. Barcelona: Malpaso Ediciones, S.L.U., 2018.

JOURNAL ARTICLES

Astorga, Luís. "Los Corridos de Traficantes de Drogas en México y Colombia." *Revistas Sociales* 59, no. 4 (October 1997): 245–61. https://www.jstor.org /stable/3541131.

———. Working paper. *Drug Trafficking in Mexico: A First General Assessment*. Paris: Management of Social Transformations (UNESCO), 1999. https:// unesdoc.unesco.org/ark:/48223/pf0000117644.

Atuesta, Laura H., and Aldo F. Ponce. "Meet the Narco: Increased Competition among Criminal Organisations and the Explosion of Violence in Mexico." *Global Crime* 18, no. 4 (2017): 375–402. https://doi.org/10.1080 /17440572.2017.1354520.

Camilo Castilo, Juan, Daniel Mejía, and Pascual Restrepo. Working paper.

Scarcity Without Leviathan: The Violent Effects of Cocaine Supply Shortages in the Mexican Drug War. Center for Global Development, February 26, 2014. https://www.cgdev.org/publication/scarcity-without-leviathan-violent -effects-cocaine-supply-shortages-mexican-drug-war.

Campbell, Howard. "Female Drug Smugglers on the U-S.-Mexico Border: Gender, Crime, and Empowerment." *Anthropological Quarterly* 81, no. 1 (2008): 233–67. https://www.jstor.org/stable/30052745.

Craig, Richard B. "Human Rights and Mexico's Antidrug Campaign." *Social Science Quarterly* 60, no. 4 (March 1980): 691–701. https://www.jstor.org /stable/42860645.

———. "Operation Condor: Mexico's Antidrug Campaign Enters a New Era." *Journal of Interamerican Studies and World Affairs* 22, no. 3 (August 1980): 345–63. https://www.jstor.org/stable/165493.

Esparza, Adrian X., Brigitte S. Waldorf, and Javier Chavez. "Localized Effects of Globalization: The Case of Ciudad Juárez, Chihuahua, Mexico." *Urban Geography* 25, no. 2 (2004): 120–38.

Gootenberg, Paul. "Cocaine's Long March North, 1900–2010." *Latin American Politics and Society* 54, no. 1 (2012): 159–80. https://www.jstor.org/stable /41485345.

Grillo, Ioan. "Mexican Cartels: A Century of Defying U.S. Drug Policy." *The Brown Journal of World Affairs* 20, no. 1 (2013): 253–65. https://www.jstor .org/stable/24590897.

Knight, Alan, "The Myth of the Mexican Revolution," *Past & Present* 209, no. 1 (November 2010), 223–73.

Lupsha, Peter A. "Drug Trafficking: Mexico and Colombia in Comparative Perspective." *Journal of International Affairs*, International Underground Economic Systems (Spring/Summer 1981) 35, no. 1 (1981): 95–115. https:// www.jstor.org/stable/24357005.

Mariñez Navarro, Freddy, and Leonardo Vivas. "Violence, Governance, and Economic Development at the U.S.-Mexico Border: The Case of Nuevo Laredo and Its Lessons." *Mexican Studies/Estudos Mexicanos* 28, no. 2 (2012): 377–416. https://www.jstor.org/stable/10.1525/msem.2012.28.2.377.

Meyer, Maureen, Stephanie Brewer, and Carlos Cepeda. "Abused and Afraid in Ciudad Juárez." *Washington Office on Latin America*, September 2010. https://www.wola.org/analysis/abused-and-afraid-in-ciudad-juarez/.

Mottier, Nicole. "Drug Gangs and Politics in Ciudad Juárez: 1928–1936." *Mexican Studies/Estudios Mexicanos* 25, no. 1 (2009): 19–46. https://www.jstor .org/stable/10.1525/msem.2009.25.1.19.

Open Society Justice Initiative. *Undeniable Atrocities: Confronting Crimes against Humanity in Mexico.* Open Society Foundations, 2016. https://www .justiceinitiative.org/uploads/7dc9f3b9-21dc-4d14-90fd-aaa29ff12cc3 /undenialble-atrocities-2nd-edition-20160808.pdf.

Paley, Dawn. "Cold War, Neoliberal War, and Disappearance: Observations from Mexico." *Latin American Perspectives,* 2020. https://www.academia.edu /44843066/Cold_War_Neoliberal_War_and_Disappearance_Observations _from_Mexico.

Paley, Dawn. "Drug War as Neoliberal Trojan Horse." *Latin American Perspectives,* Environmental Violence in Mexico (September 2015) 42, no. 5 (September 2015): 109–32. https://www.jstor.org/stable/24574871.

Ríos, Viridiana. "How Government Coordination Controlled Organized Crime: The Case of Mexico's Cocaine Markets." Essay. In *The Journal of Conflict Resolutions,* Special Issue: Drug Violence in Mexico, 59, no. 8 (December 2015): 1433–54. https://www.jstor.org/stable/24546349.

Rodríguez Ulloa, Carlos. *Sinaloa: Fin De La Hegemonía y Epicentro De La Guerra Que Comienza (In: Atlas De La Seguridad y La Defensa De México 2016).* Casa de Análisis de Seguridad con Democracia (CASEDE), February 2017. https://www.casede.org/PublicacionesCasede/Atlas2016/Carlos _Rodr%C3%ADguez_Ulloa.pdf.

Shirk, David A. *The Drug War in Mexico: Confronting a Shared Threat.* Washington, DC: Council on Foreign Relations, 2011. https://www.jstor.org /stable/resrep05747.8.

Smith, Benjamin T. "The Rise and Fall of Narcopopulism: Drugs, Politics, and Society in Sinaloa, 1930–1980." *Journal for the Study of Radicalism* 7, no. 2 (2013): 125–65. https://doi.org/10.14321/jstudradi.7.2.0125.

Timmons, Patrick. "Trump's Wall at Nixon's Border." *NACLA Report on the Americas* 49, no. 1 (March 14, 2017): 15–24. https://nacla.org/news/2017/03 /27/trump%27s-wall-nixon%27s-border.

Trejo, Guillermo, and Sandra Ley. "Why Did Drug Cartels Go to War in Mexico? Subnational Party Alternation, the Breakdown of Criminal Protection, and the Onset of Large-Scale Violence." *Comparative Political Studies* 51, no. 7 (2018): 900–937. https://journals.sagepub.com/doi/abs/10.1177 /0010414017720703?journalCode=cpsa.

Turbiville Jr., Graham H. "Silver over the Border: US Law Enforcement Corruption on the Southwest Border." *Small Wars and Insurgencies* 22, no. 5 (November 29, 2011): 835–59. https://doi.org/10.1080/09592318.2011.620811.

NOTES

INTRODUCTION

1 *scattered communities that grew into a society calling itself the Rarámuri:* Ryan Goldberg, "The Drug Runners," *Texas Monthly,* July 2017, https://features.texasmonthly.com/editorial/the-drug-runners/.

2 *Culiacán now boasts a population of nearly a million people:* The population in 2015, the most recent available year, was 905,265, according to the *Instituto Nacional de Estadística y Geografía (INEGI);* http://cuentame.inegi.org.mx/monografias/informacion/sin/poblacion/default.aspx?tema=me&e=25.

3 *The story goes that Jesús Malverde:* Esquivel (2015) and Grillo (2014).

3 *Malverde is said to have met his end in 1909:* Ibid.

4 *The rank given to El Chapo by* Forbes *magazine in 2009:* According to *Forbes,* El Chapo's net worth in 2009 was somewhere around $1 billion. Prosecutors later estimated he raked in at least $12.6 billion over the years—and demanded forfeiture of all of it—but we will likely never know El Chapo's true net worth. *Order of Forfeiture in United States vs. Joaquin Archivaldo Guzmán Loera,* 09-CR-466.

5 *He even showed up at El Chapo's trial:* Emily Saul, "El Chapo's Lawyers Are Literally Praying for Acquittal," *New York Post,* November 20, 2018. https://nypost.com/2018/11/20/el-chapos-lawyers-are-literally-praying-for-an-acquittal/.

6 Joaquin lo era lo es y será: "El Señor de la Montaña," by Canelos de Durango. From the album of the same name released April 23, 2015. Pegasus Records LLC, lyrics via Musica.com, https://www.musica.com/letras.asp?letra=1119301.

6 *They were singing narcocorridos:* For a thorough discussion of *narcocorridos,* see Chapter 10 of *El Narco* by Ioan Grillo, or "Los Corridos de Traficantes de Drogas en México y Colombia" by Luís Astorga, 1997.

7 *The Mexican sociologist Luís Astorga:* I, along with every other scholar of organized crime in Mexico, am deeply indebted to the work of Astorga, whose meticulously researched work in books like *El Siglo de las Drogas* is founda-

tional to existing critical understandings of the history and landscape of the drug trade and its relationship with the state.

8 *These traffickers and the men like El Chapo:* This is based on "Narcopopulism," by Benjamin T. Smith (2013), "A War Against Poor People: Dirty Wars and Drug Wars in 1970s Mexico," by Alexander Aviña (2018), as well as the work of Luís Astorga and interviews with Aviña and the scholar Nathaniel Morris in the fall of 2020 and with journalist Jesús Esquivel in the summer of 2019.

8 *The breakdown began in the 1990s:* See Trejo and Ley, "Why Did Drug Cartels Go to War in Mexico?"

9 *In the decade and a half since the current drug war began in Mexico:* The statistics for deaths and disappearances vary. According to a government report issued in January 2021, more than 82,000 people have disappeared in Mexico, with the overwhelming majority of those occurring since 2006. According to a recently updated report by the Congressional Research Service, the number of homicides linked to organized crime stands at around 150,000 since 2006. The number is likely substantially higher: https://www.gob.mx/cnb/es/docu mentos/informe-cnb-29-de-enero-2021?state=published https://fas.org/sgp/crs /row/R41576.pdf.

9 *Nationwide, in 2018, 90 percent of homicides went unsolved:* Mexico Violence Project, statistics via the National Institute of Statistics and Geography (INEGI), Encuesta Nacional de Victimización y Percepción sobre Seguridad Pública (ENVIPE), 2019. Released September 2019, https://www.inegi.org.mx /contenidos/programas/envipe/2019/doc/envipe2019_presentacion_nacio nal.pdf, accessed January 12, 2021.

9 *civilians have a fundamental distrust of the authorities:* According to INEGI statistics from 2019 on perception of corruption by police agency, 58.2 percent of Mexicans consider the Policía Federal to be corrupt; Fiscalía General de la República (Attorney General's office), 56.9 percent; State Police, 65.7 percent; judges, 70.1 percent; transit police, 77.3 percent. Only the Mexican Marines (18.2 percent), the newly created National Guard (23 percent), and the Army (24.4 percent) are believed by a majority of Mexicans to be free of corruption. From the National Institute of Statistics and Geography (INEGI), Encuesta Nacional de Victimización y Percepción sobre Seguridad Pública (ENVIPE), 2020. Released December 2020, https://www.inegi.org.mx/contenidos/programas/envipe /2020/doc/envipe2020_presentacion_nacional.pdf, accessed January 12, 2021.

9 *the overwhelming majority of crimes are never reported:* Ibid. The most common explanation by those surveyed for not reporting a crime is "perdido de tiempo"—considering it a waste of time—while 15 percent reported the reason as a lack of trust in authorities. I consider these to be twin problems, however: if people trusted the authorities to solve a crime, they would not consider it a waste of time to report that crime.

9 *between 2008 and 2019, under an accord known as the Mérida Initiative:* Con-

gressional Research Service, "Mexico: Evolution of the Mérida Initiative, 2007–2020," updated July 20, 2020, accessed January 12, 2021, available at https://fas.org/sgp/crs/row/IF10578.pdf.

10 *direct commercial arms sales to Mexico:* Tally by Mexico Violence Project, statistics via Security Assistance Monitor and the Center for International Policy, accessed January 12, 2021. MVP figures: https://www.mexicoviolence .org/essential-numbers; SAM/CIP: https://securityassistance.org/security-sector -assistance/.

10 *ongoing human rights abuses:* For more on human rights abuses by the Mexican military, see "Undeniable Atrocities: Confronting Crimes Against Humanity in Mexico," Open Society Justice Initiative, 2016, https://www.justice initiative.org/uploads/7dc9f3b9-21dc-4d14-90fd-aaa29ff12cc3/undenialble -atrocities-2nd-edition-20160808.pdf, accessed January 12, 2021.

10 *Scary words have been thrown around like "insurgency":* For a more thorough critique of how dominant media narratives of the drug war overstate the capability and aims of organized crime groups, see *Los Cárteles No Existen* by Oswaldo Zavala (2018).

11 *"It was the city that the police had assigned to Mr. Guzmán":* Testimony of Miguel Ángel Martínez Martínez on November 27, 2019, pp. 1407–8.

12 *In one memorable exchange, defense attorney John Lichtman:* I should note here that Lichtman had a point. Why believe the words of a convicted criminal? This book, like the case prosecutors built against El Chapo, relies extensively on the testimony of men like Cifuentes, but I have weeded out the obvious falsehoods and use only the information corroborated elsewhere. Testimony of Alex Cifuentes on January 15, 2019, pp. 5230–31.

14 *Alex Cifuentes had moments ago accused:* This exchange is from my own reporting and from the testimony of Alex Cifuentes on January 15, 2019, pp. 5289–5305.

17 *I found myself in a half-empty coffee shop in Culiacán:* Author interview with "Beto," May 14, 2019, in Culiacán.

17 *When word of Beto's death reached him, the reporter all but bragged:* Matthew Campbell, "Drug Baron's Last Supper With Me," *Sunday Times,* August 3, 2019, https://www.thetimes.co.uk/article/drug-baron-s-last-supper-with-me-rzjjfztg2.

CHAPTER 1: THE BOY FROM LA TUNA

27 *Joaquín Archivaldo Guzmán Loera was born on April 4, 1957:* For many years El Chapo's birthdate was something of a mystery. Some put the year as 1954, others as 1957, and the exact day was also fuzzy. I base this in part on the testimony of Lucero López Sánchez, who made reference to his birthday in an intercepted text message, and on a warrant filed by the FBI as part of a Mutual Legal Assistance Treaty (MLAT) request that gave his birthday as I have it here.

27 *"Ever since he was a child, he was a talented and bright kid":* Author interview with relative of El Chapo, May 17, 2019, in La Tuna.

28 *"Just like in any big family":* Ibid.

28 *"Ever since he was little, he always had hopes":* Maria Consuelo Loera Pérez speaking with Guillermo Galdos in "The Legend of Shorty," a film by Angus McQueen and Guillermo Galdos for PBS *Frontline*, Film4, Channel 4, and BFI, 2014, https://www.pbs.org/wgbh/frontline/film/drug-lord/transcript/.

28 *On Sundays, his sister has said: El Chapo: Kingpin on Trial*, by Keegan Hamilton and Miguel Ángel Vega for *Vice News*.

28 *In his only known interview:* Sean Penn, "Watch El Chapo's Exclusive Interview in Its 17-Minute Entirety," *Rolling Stone*, January 12, 2016, https://www.rollingstone.com/politics/politics-news/watch-el-chapos-exclusive-interview-in-its-17-minute-entirety-35543/.

29 *The hemp plant arrived in Mexico in the Sixteenth Century:* Ernest L. Abel, *Marihuana: The First Twelve Thousand Years* (New York: Plenum, 1980), 100.

29 *but over time the plant's flowers and the THC they contained:* "The Origin of Contemporary Drug Contraband: A Global Interpretation From Sinaloa," dissertation by Froylán Enciso (2015).

29 *government officials first made note of the presence of the plant:* Tommy E. Murphy and Martín A. Rossi, "Following the Poppy Trail Origins and Consequences of Mexican Drug Cartels," March 2019, https://sistemas.colmex.mx/Reportes/LACEALAMES/LACEA-LAMES2019_paper_128.pdf.

29 *Many local farmers started to augment their subsistence crops:* Smith (2013).

29 *a brisk trade grew between the Sinaloan port city of Mazatlán and merchants in San Francisco:* In his excellent 2015 doctoral thesis, Froylán Enciso makes a convincing case that the dominance of Chinese merchants in the early drug trade has been overstated, obscuring the role of the transnational pharmaceutical trade. Enciso (2015), p. 13.

29 *With the prohibition of opium in the United States in 1914, and in Mexico in 1920:* Mexico banned the growth of opium in 1916, and its importation in 1920: Ibid.

30 *The early drug trade in Sinaloa:* For more on the trade between Mazatlán and California, see Enciso (2015) and Grillo (2011).

30 *The early state builders and founding intellectuals of post-revolution Mexico:* Robert Chao Romero, *The Chinese in Mexico, 1882–1940* (Tucson: University of Arizona Press, 2010), 180–83.

30 *Throughout the 1920s, anti-Chinese propagandists churned out newspapers:* This passage detailing the anti-Chinese pogroms of the 1930s are based on the scholarship of Gonzalez (2017), Chao Romero (2010), and Schiavone Camacho (2012), as well as the self-published memoirs of Manuel Lazcano (1992).

31 *Between 1926 and 1940, more than two thirds:* Between 1926 and 1930,

the population dropped from 24,218 to around 18,000. By 1940, Chinese-Mexicans numbered 4,856: Chao Romero (2010), p. 175.

31 *In Sonora, just 92 people remained:* These figures come from Schiavone Camacho (2012), p. 70.

31 *Sensing an opportunity, Mexican smugglers leapt into the fray:* Grillo (2011), pp. 64–67.

31 *forging ties with American mafiosi:* For more on the relationship between Mexican traffickers and Italian and Italian-American organized crime figures, see *La Cosa Nostra en México 1938–1950: Los negocios de Lucky Luciano y la mujer que corruptió al gobierno mexicano,* by Juan Alberto Cedillo. Cedillo writes: "Since the Chinese were expelled from the region, the business of opium had been controlled by governors, mayors, police chiefs, big businessmen, and landowners," [translation by this author] and describes the efforts of Bugsy Siegel and Max Cossman to develop a credit system that enabled small-time farmers to grow poppies: pp. 378–79 of 1994 in the 2011 ebook version published by Grijalbo.

31 *Many of its sons fought in the Revolution:* My understanding of this period and its effects on Sinaloa and in particular Badiraguato come from interviews with the historian Nathaniel Morris, Badiraguato native Pacha Fernández, and Carlos Manuel Aguirre's 1975 book, *Los Caribaneros de Santiago de los Caballeros,* available online at: https://ahgs.gob.mx/los-carabineros-de-santiago/.

31 *Drug trafficking was essentially a state-controlled industry:* Smith (2013).

32 *The very existence of anti-drug laws made control over rural areas a more manageable task:* Author interview with Nathaniel Morris, December 1, 2020.

32 *"If the soldiers knew":* Ibid.

33 *Once labeled "the perfect dictatorship":* This term was coined in 1990 by the Peruvian novelist Mario Vargas Llosa and, despite being referred to ad nauseam, remains a potent and in my mind accurate description. "Vargas Llosa: Mexico es la dictadura perfecta," *El Pais,* September 1, 1990, https://elpais.com/diario/1990/09/01/cultura/652140001_850215.html.

33 *On February 8, 1975, Enciso writes, three army helicopters descended:* This passage is based on the work of Froylán Enciso in *Nuestra Historia Narcótica* (Mexico City: Penguin Random House Grupo Editorial, 2015), pp. 119–22.

33 *In a 2018 interview, El Chapo's sister Bernarda:* Keegan Hamilton and Miguel Ángel Vega, *El Chapo: Kingpin on Trial.*

34 *In Sinaloa, the cultivation and trafficking of opium and marijuana emerged as a key pillar of stability:* See "The Rise and Fall of Narcopopulism" by Benjamin T. Smith (2013) and "Serrano Communities and Subaltern Negotiation Strategies," by Nathaniel Morris (2020). My understanding of this dynamic is deeply indebted to these works, as well as interviews with both Smith and Morris that corroborated information gleaned from my own interviews in Badiraguato in 2019.

34 *gomeros passed the tradition from father to son:* Author interview with "José"in Badiraguato, April 2019.

34 *letters penned by El Chapo in later years show a spidery, uneven handwriting full of spelling mistakes:* Several letters written by El Chapo were entered into evidence at trial on January 23, 2019, during the testimony of Dámaso López Nuñez. For what it's worth, he could be seen taking notes most days during the trial.

35 *According to a former lover:* Julio Scherer García, *"De 'El Chapo' a Zulema: 'Cuando yo me vaya . . . ,"* *Proceso,* February 22, 2014, https://www.proceso.com.mx /reportajes/2014/2/22/de-el-chapo-zulema-cuando-yo-me-vaya-129465.html.

35 *When El Chapo married his first wife:* My understanding of El Chapo's early family life comes largely from Beith (2012), as well as extensive subsequent news coverage of his sons.

36 *According to a psychological profile:* Malcolm Beith, *The Last Narco,* p. 58.

36 *"Chapo always talks about drug business":* Testimony of Miguel Ángel Martínez Martínez on March 21, 2006, in *USA v. Corona Verbera.* Accessed via Pacer.

CHAPTER 2: EXODUS

38 *President Richard Nixon ordered a dramatic show of force along the entire length of the U.S.-Mexican border:* For a detailed look at how Intercept altered the trajectory of history along the border see Timmons (2017).

39 *Mexico City likely saw a way to placate their neighbor and seize control of local protection rackets:* This analysis of anti-drug efforts in Sinaloa in the late 1970s is based in part on the work of Adela Cedillo, who was kind enough to provide me with a copy of her chapter on Operation Condor in *Histories of Drug Trafficking in Twentieth Century Mexico,* a forthcoming book edited by Benjamin T. Smith and Will Pansters. In the following notes I will cite it as "Cedillo (2019)".

39 *"To stay in the good graces of his patrons in power, the plaza holder had a dual obligation":* Poppa (2010), pp. 42–43.

39 *Local authorities tolerated, protected, and even participated in the drug trade:* Smith (2013): pp. 125–66.

40 *a pro-legalization author even offered a fig leaf:* Like earlier flirtations with drug legalization, this effort was a dead end. The power brokers in the capital knew the United States would never allow it: Luis Astorga. "Drug Trafficking in Mexico: A First General Assessment," United Nations Educational, Scientific and Cultural Organization, 1999.

40 *Murders soared:* "Heroin Traffic in Mexican City Brings Violence," Alan Riding, *New York Times,* December 28, 1976, https://www.nytimes.com/1976/12 /28/archives/heroin-traffic-in-mexican-city-brings-violence.htm.

40 *The state saw a resurgence in left-wing agitation:* Author interview with Oscar Loza Ochoa, August 19, 2019, in Culiacán.

41 *PJF agents earned such a reputation:* La Voz de Sinaloa, January 16, 1969, cited in Astorga, "First General Assessment."

41 *on-the-ground support from advisors with the fledgling DEA:* Richard Craig, "Operation Condor: Mexico's Antidrug Campaign Enters a New Era," *Journal of Interamerican Studies and World Affairs* 22, no. 3 (August 1980): pp. 345–63.

41 *"In this respect it's a new and much better ball game":* Ibid.

41 *People who lived through those years:* Author interview with Pacha Fernandez, May, 2019.

42 *The army's tactics took on a similarly brutal form during Operation Condor:* Richard Craig, "Human Rights and Mexico's Antidrug Campaign," *Social Science Quarterly* 60, no. 4 (1980): pp. 696–98. And Aviña (2018).

42 *These scorched-earth tactics mostly fell on the heads of poor farmers:* while the leading traffickers often managed to avoid losses: Cedillo (2019), p. 20.

43 *Over the course of the operation:* Ibid.

44 *The third relationship that helped catapult Félix Gallardo above the shoulders of lesser narcos:* Félix Gallardo and Matta Ballesteros would later be identified as partners by numerous witnesses in the aftermath of the murder of DEA Agent Enrique Camarena. As with El Chapo, however, it's good to take with a grain of salt information that comes out *after* a given trafficker becomes infamous. In this case, I base this information not only on the statements of witnesses in later years but also on internal DEA reports filed by Camarena himself in 1984, in which an informant placed Félix Gallardo and Matta Ballesteros (as well as a top DFS commander) in the same room in late April 1984. Internal DEA investigative report filed by Special Agent Enrique Camarena, May 3, 1984.

45 *Obsessed with gadgets, he dropped tens of thousands of dollars at a time on the latest radio equipment:* Details on Félix Gallardo's use of radio equipment come from the testimony of his cousin, Frank Retamoza, during the trial of Matta Ballesteros in the Southern District of California, December 7, 1990.

45 *He had a stingy side, too:* Testimony of Frank Retamoza, December 7, 1990.

46 *The area emerged in Spanish colonial times as a center of Mexico's mining industry:* P.J. Bakewell, *Silver Mining and Society in Colonial Mexico: Zacatecas, 1546–1700* (Cambridge, UK: Cambridge University Press, 1971), pp. 29–30, 114, 190.

46 *El Chapo arrived in Zacatecas in 1984:* My conclusion that El Chapo was in Zacatecas at this time is based on two sources: contemporaneous DEA reports and an interview with a relative of El Chapo who recalled working in Zacatecas with El Chapo and El Azul in 1984. There's scant documentation of El Chapo's movements during this time period, but the investigative reports filed by DEA agents at the time confirm that El Azul was active in the area; combined with recollection by El Chapo's relative of the year and location, that's far better confirmation than what's available for many of the fables of

what El Chapo was doing at this time. Interview with confidential source, May 17, 2019, in La Tuna, Badiraguato. DEA reports filed by Special Agent Enrique Camarena, 1984.

46 *There was occasional infighting among the crews:* According to one of Camarena's informants, two groups of marijuana growers got into a shootout on May 5, 1984, after one crew stole a water pump from the other's field, resulting in four injured. Report of Investigation filed by Special Agent Enrique Camarena, May 7, 1984.

46 *the largest operations were directly financed by members of the Sinaloa diaspora:* Report of Investigation by Special Agent Enrique Camarena, January 13, 1984.

46 *A few miles northeast of Fresnillo:* Report of Investigation by Special Agent Enrique Camarena, December 12, 1983.

47 *It was under his wing that El Chapo:* Author interview with El Chapo relative, May 17, 2019, in La Tuna, Badiraguato, Sinaloa.

47 *In Zacatecas, this required armies of laborers:* Details on Sinaloan laborers bussed in for grow operations and details of their wages come from reports filed by Camarena on March 19, April 17, and May 7, 1984.

47 *From 1960 to 1970, officials in Mexico:* Figures for cocaine seizures come from Astorga (2016), p. 153.

47 *Traffickers like Carlos Lehder . . . began shipping it in ever larger quantities:* "Drugs, Law Enforcement and Foreign Policy," Senate Committee on Foreign Relations Report (Dec. 1988), 14-6 (AKA the "Kerry Report").

48 *By the time it reached the streets of Chicago or New York:* These figures come from testimony of cooperating witnesses during the trial of El Chapo, as well as Government Exhibit 508-2, entered into evidence in the Eastern District of New York, November 14, 2018.

48 *As far as they were concerned, Operation Condor had been a success:* "Narcotics— Meeting with Attorney General on DEA Participation in GOM Eradication Campaign," Wikileaks cable 1978STATE063482_d, March 13, 1978, https://wikileaks.org/plusd/cables/1978STATE063482_d.html.

49 *"[The DFS] became involved in drug trafficking":* Interview with confidential former DEA source, October 2019.

49 *the agency expanded exponentially:* Camilo Vicente Ovalle [*Tiempo suspendido*], *Una historia de la desaparición forzada en México, 1940–1980* (Ciudad de México: Bonilla Artigas Editores, 2019), p. 86.

49 *Matta Ballesteros's SETCO airline was a veritable Contra Airways:* Scott-Dale, "Drugs, Anti-Communism and Extra-Legal Repression," pp. 176, 184.

50 *Félix Gallardo was described as a "big supporter" of the Contras:* This description, via Félix Gallardo's pilot Werner Lotz, comes from Peter Scott Dale and Jonathan Marshall's *Cocaine Politics* (1991), p. 41.

50 *Neto Fonseca was seen in the company of CIA pilots:* Lawrence Victor Harrison interview with DEA Special Agent Hector Berrellez, transcribed in Report of Investigation by S/A Manuel Martínez, September 25, 1989.

50 *the CIA saw the DFS as essential to its interests:* In 1981, then-DFS director Miguel Nazar Haro was arrested in San Diego on allegations of running a cross-border car-theft ring (an international top cop chop shop, if you will). In response, the FBI's legal attaché for Mexico City called the car-thief spy chief "an essential repeat essential contact for the CIA station in Mexico City." In a cable to Washington, the attaché warned that Washington's security and counterintelligence priorities in Mexico would "suffer a disastrous blow if [Nazar Haro] were forced to resign." Sure enough, when the U.S. Attorney prosecuting the case in San Diego complained to reporters that the DFS chief had vanished back to Mexico, President Ronald Reagan fired him. After returning to Mexico, Nazar Haro remained in his position until the end of the term of President López Portillo, despite the indictment. So confident was he in his U.S. backing that he even sued *Time* magazine for defamation, seeking $11 million in damages: Elaine Shannon, *Desperados: Latin Drug Lords, U.S. Lawmen, and the War America Can't Win.*

50 *Félix Gallardo was a shareholder of the state-owned investment bank SOMEX:* Astorga (1999), p. 22.

51 *At a rotating series of headquarters:* Testimony of Frank Retamozza Gallardo, on May 18, 1990, *USA v. Caro Quintero.*

51 *The traffickers had the run of the city, sometimes carrying military-grade weapons:* Testimony of Lawrence Victor Harrison on June 6, 1990, *USA v. Matta Ballesteros.*

52 *on most days was teeming:* DEA interview with Lawrence Harrison, September 25, 1989. DEA-6 report filed by Special Agent Manuel R. Martínez, entered into evidence in *USA v. Caro Quintero et al.*

52 *He also began to see some internal divisions:* Testimony of Victor Lawrence Harrison on June 6, 1990, *USA v. Matta Ballesteros et al.*

52 *In one instance, an informant told the DEA:* DEA-6 report filed by Special Agent Enrique "Kiki" Camarena on May 7, 1984. Entered into evidence in *USA v. Caro Quintero et al.*

53 *"He had a great sense of humor":* Author interview with Mike Vigil, October 29, 2019.

54 *Camarena was a regular visitor to the local office of the Federal Judicial Police:* Testimony of Virginia Reynoso Martínez on May 17, 1990.

54 *He and the other DEA agents in Guadalajara had followed the money:* This account is via Shannon (2015).

54 *A cousin of Félix Gallardo:* Testimony of Frank Retamoza on December 7, 1990.

55 *in 1978 the Mexican government revoked access:* Embassy Mexico, "Press Guidance on Withdrawal of DEA from GOM Eradication Program," WikiLeaks Cable: 1978MEXICO04410_d, dated March 16, 1978, https://wikileaks.org /plusd/cables/1978MEXICO04410_d.html.

55 *employing hundreds of workers:* In news coverage of the raids, journalists cited reports that some workers had claimed that they had been "enslaved" at Rancho Búfalo, working twelve-hour days with no pay, and that some workers were executed when they grew too ill to work. While this is possible, it conflicts with other sources, including reports by Camarena, which show that working on marijuana farms was a considerably more attractive job than other harvest jobs around at the time, raising the possibility that some workers exaggerated the coercion involved in order to avoid punishment. Similar claims have arisen regarding workers executed after digging tunnels for El Chapo in the 1990s, but I have never found evidence supporting these claims beyond oft-repeated myths coming from law-enforcement sources. Claims of mistreatment: Joel Brinkley, "Vast, Undreamed-of Drug Use Feared," *New York Times,* November 23, 1984, https://www.nytimes.com/1984/11/23/world /vast-undreamed-of-drug-use-feared.html. Contradictory information on work conditions: DEA reports filed by Enrique Camarena and entered into evidence in *USA v. Caro Quintero et al.*

55 *Government agencies in the United States had previously estimated:* Ibid.

56 *Camarena told them what he knew:* Details on the torture and murder of Camarena are reconstructed from the transcript of his interrogation, entered into evidence in *USA v. Caro Quintero et al.*

57 *the brother-in-law of a former Mexican president:* Ruben Zuno Arce was a longtime smuggler of heroin and later cocaine who was married to the sister of José Luis Escheverría, president from 1970 to 1976. At trial in 1992, prosecutors described Zuno Arce's role as "greas[ing] the wheels for political protection." William Yardley, "Ruben Zuno Arce, Guilty in Drug Killing, Dies at 82," *Washington Post,* September 19, 2012.

57 *some critics have questioned the validity of the testimony:* For a detailed analysis of the irregularities in the Camarena case, see Bartley and Bartley, *Eclipse of the Assassins.*

57 *convictions against at least three of the plotters:* Matta Ballesteros and another man, René Verdugo, had their convictions overturned in 2018 after it emerged that an FBI "hair analyst" had presented fraudulent testimony claiming to place them in the house at 881 Lope de Vega. Matta Ballesteros remains imprisoned on separate drug charges, and Verdugo was released and deported to Mexico. Interview with Martin Stolar, May 10, 2020; and *"Después de 33 años en prisión liberaron a uno de los presuntos asesinos del agente de la DEA Enrique Camarena,"* Infobae.com, May 31, 2019, accessed May 11, 2020.

58 *Félix Gallardo went underground:* Diego Osorno, "El Cartel de Sinaloa," p. 231.

59 *he was the first Mexican president to label organized crime a national security threat:* David Shirk, Drug Violence and State Responses in Mexico, https:// fliphtml5.com/pudz/gldr/basic.

59 *The military arrested more than six hundred members:* This information is via a declassified diplomatic cable on April 10, 1989 and accessed via the U.S. Department of State's online Freedom of Information Act reading room. "Mexican Authorities Arrest Major Trafficker Miguel Ángel Félix Gallardo," Embassy Mexico, April 10, 1989, Department of State case No. F-2013-02102, Doc No. C05417938. Accessed May 23, 2020.

59 *Among those arrested:* Ibid. The local cops arrested that day were later released by a federal court for lack of evidence, a move then-governor Francisco Labastida Ochoa said was *itself* a ploy to protect other officials on Félix Gallardo's payroll. In an interview with the *Los Angeles Times* in the run-up to the 2000 presidential election, Labastida's former top prosecutor Manuel Lazcano Ochoa accused federal police commanders of working to protect the faction of Héctor "El Güero" Palma, which by that time had fallen out with Félix Gallardo's crew. Labastida himself was later accused in a secret CIA report of protecting drug traffickers, specifically allying with Félix Gallardo against El Güero: Mary Beth Sheridan, "PRI Candidate's Drug Stance Draws Doubts," *Los Angeles Times,* April 30, 2000, accessed May 23, 2020; Bill Gertz, "Mexico: CIA Links Interior Minister to Drug Lords," *Washington Times,* February 5, 1998, accessed via Media Awareness Project, May 23, 2020.

59 *An initial tally:* Embassy Mexico, "Mexican Authorities Arrest Major Trafficker Miguel Ángel Félix Gallardo."

CHAPTER 3: SINALOA COWBOYS

61 *as Keoki Skinner drives me through town:* I visited Agua Prieta on May 30 and June 1, 2019. Much of the first portion of this chapter is based on my first-hand observations and reporting during that trip, as well as my interview with Skinner. Unless otherwise noted, direct quotes by Skinner are from author interviews with him on those dates.

62 *Douglas has never been the same since the closure in the 1980s of a pollution-spewing copper smelter:* Author interview with Keoki Skinner, May 30, 2019, in Agua Prieta; "Clean Air Costly for Arizona Town: Closure of Copper Smelter Will Slash Jobs, Tax Revenue," Associated Press, January 5, 1987, https://www .latimes.com/archives/la-xpm-1987-01-05-fi-2300-story.html.

62 *"This doesn't exactly look like a town built by* maquilas": Author interview with Keoki Skinner, May 30, 2019.

63 *A young cameraman from a Phoenix TV station:* Author interview with Keoki

Skinner; "American TV Cameraman Rescued in Mexico," UPI, September 18, 1985, https://www.upi.com/Archives/1985/09/18/American-TV-camerman-rescued-in-Mexico/7559495864000/.

65 *He told folks he was a lawyer, up from Guadalajara:* Author interview with Keoki Skinner.

65 *He snapped up a vacant lot for $90,000 in cash:* Details of Francisco Camarena Macias's arrival in Agua Prieta are via Keoki Skinner.

66 *Camarena Macias . . . worked out of an office secretly tucked in the second story of a supermarket:* Testimony of Miguel Ángel Martínez Martínez on March 21, 2006.

67 *When he got to Agua Prieta in the late 1980s, he had a new task:* Ibid.

67 *El Chapo allowed him to use the informal pronoun:* Ibid., p. 62.

67 *The tunnel became the primary route through which El Chapo sent cocaine into the United States:* Testimony of Miguel Ángel Martínez Martínez on November 27, 2018, p. 1410, and March 21, 2006, p. 34.

67 *"fucking cool tunnel":* Ibid., p 75.

68 *Between 1988 and 1991, El Chapo and his crew smuggled thirty-five tons of cocaine:* United States of America, Plaintiff-appellee, v. Arlene Newland, Antonio Hernández-Menendez, Santos Hernández-Menendez, Nick Newland, Defendants-appellants, 69 F.3d 545 (9th Cir. 1995).

68 *In order to get drugs to the border, the gang opened an airstrip in Cumpas, Sonora:* Testimony of Miguel Ángel Martínez on March 21, 2006, pp. 15–16.

68 *"Mr. Guzmán told me I was a really bad pilot":* Testimony of Miguel Ángel Martínez Martínez on November 26, 2018, p. 1340.

69 *They spoke in code over high-frequency radio:* Ibid., 1342–43.

69 *"Compadre . . . Now it's a great party":* Ibid., 1362–63.

69 *occasionally he would test his lieutenant's integrity:* Testimony of Miguel Ángel Martínez Martínez on March 21, 2006, USA v. Corona Verbera, pp. 46–47.

69 *"I wasn't the right hand of El Chapo Guzmán":* Testimony of Miguel Ángel Martínez Martínez on March 21, 2006, p. 119.

70 *their main connections in Colombia were members with Pablo Escobar's Medellín Cartel:* Testimony of Miguel Ángel Martínez Martínez on November 26, 2018, pp. 1349–50.

70 *Gacha, who was gunned down alongside his son:* Joseph B. Treaster, "A Top Medellin Drug Trafficker Dies in a Shootout in Colombia," special to the *New York Times*, December 16, 1989, https://www.nytimes.com/1989/12/16/world/a-top-medellin-drug-trafficker-dies-in-a-shootout-in-colombia.html.

70 *His new contact was a young Colombian trafficker named Juan Carlos Ramírez Abadía:* Testimony of Juan Carlos Ramírez Abadía on November 29, 2018, pp. 1820–22; Testimony of Miguel Ángel Martínez Martínez on November 26, 2018.

70 *The prevailing rate most Mexican smugglers charged:* From the testimony of Miguel Ángel Martínez Martínez. Previous estimates by scholars and law enforcement sources have put this figure as high as 50 percent, but here I defer to the expert.

70 *"I'm a lot faster," El Chapo told Chupeta:* Testimony of Chupeta on November 29, 2018, pp. 1856–57.

70 *In under a week, El Chapo's men moved the first load of 4,000 kilos:* Ibid., pp. 1865–67.

70 *From then on, the Colombians had a new name for the young capo from Sinaloa:* Testimony of Miguel Ángel Martínez Martínez on November 27, 2018, p. 1406.

71 *"With him, in Mexico, you seldom lost":* Testimony of Chupeta on November 29, 2018.

71 *The absurd profits from cocaine had sent the amount of bribe money paid by Mexican traffickers skyrocketing:* Paul Gootenburg, "Blowback: The Mexican Drug Crisis," NACLA, November 18, 2010, https://nacla.org/article/blow back-mexican-drug-crisis.

71 *That was more than the annual budget of the Mexican attorney general's office:* Ibid.

71 *more than half the annual budget allocation of the entire U.S. Drug Enforcement Administration:* The DEA budget in 1993 was $853.7 million: https://www .justice.gov/archive/jmd/1975_2002/2002/html/page100-103.htm#footnote1.

71 *They would hand over the bribe money to the officials overseeing a given area:* This passage on the mechanics of corruption in Mexico is based on a variety of sources, including the testimony of numerous witnesses at the trial of El Chapo, the testimony of witnesses during the Kiki Camarena trials in 1990, and the description of the Plaza System by Terrence Poppa in "Drug Lord."

72 *"You work for Joaquín?":* Testimony of Miguel Ángel Martínez Martínez on November 27, 2018, pp. 1465–66.

72 *The domestic market for drugs in Mexico has dramatically expanded:* "Mexico: systems for the epidemiological diagnosis of drug abuse, by Medina-Mora et al. (2003); Joshua Partlow, "Mexico's Drug Use Hits Home," *Washington Post*, December 21, 2017.

72 *a kilo of cocaine in those years cost between $2,000 and $3,000:* This paragraph on cocaine prices in various markets is based on the testimony of Jesús Reynaldo Zambada García on November 14, 2018; the testimony of Miguel Ángel Martínez Martínez on November 26, 2018; and on figures introduced by prosecutors as "Government Exhibit 508-2" in *USA vs. Guzmán Loera.*

72 *Once a month, Learjets loaded with as much as $10 million in drug money:* Testimony of Miguel Ángel Martínez Martínez on November 27, 2018, pp. 1469–72.

72 *he said he imported tomatoes:* Ibid., p. 1472.

73 *On November 10, 1989, a United States Customs agent named Michael Humphries:* Testimony of Michael Humphries on November 20, 2018, 1351–52.

73 *In a photo taken that day, Humphries can be seen grinning:* Government Exhibit 214-6, *USA vs. Guzmán Loera.*

73 *The seizure smashed the record at the time:* Testimony of Michael Humphries, November 20, 2018, p. 1216.

73 *"Compadre, they already set Arturo free":* Testimony of Miguel Ángel Martínez Martínez on November 27, 2018, pp. 1422–23.

73 *As yet unencumbered by infamy:* This paragraph on El Chapo living it up is based on the testimony of Miguel Ángel Martínez Martínez on November 26 and November 27, 2018.

74 *El Chapo even got a California driver's license under the name Max Aragon:* "EU dio a 'El Chapo licencia de conducir,'" Univision, November 4, 2013, https://archivo.eluniversal.com.mx/nacion-mexico/2013/eu-dio-a-34el-chapo-34-licencia-de-conducir-962866.html.

75 *On May 9, federal agents . . . busted a truck:* Testimony of Carlos Salazar on November 14, 2018, pp. 638–54.

75 *"This is fucking over":* Testimony of Miguel Ángel Martínez Martínez on March 21, 2006, p. 89.

75 *As angry as El Chapo was with Camarena Macias:* Ibid., pp. 89–90.

75 *In Agua Prieta, not all was lost:* Ibid.

75 *The federal agents who discovered the tunnel were shocked by its sophistication:* Testimony of Carlos Salazar, November 14, 2018; "Agents Find Drug Tunnel to U.S.," Associated Press, May 19, 1990; https://www.nytimes.com/1990/05/19/us/agents-find-drug-tunnel-to-us.html.

76 *They'd have to start calling him* "El Lento": Testimony of Miguel Ángel Martínez Martínez on November 27, 2018, p. 1414.

CHAPTER 4: THINGS FALL APART

77 *On April 21, 1993, a team of Federal Judicial Police stopped a tractor trailer in Tecate:* Testimony of Thomas Lenox on November 20, 2018, pp. 1120–22.

77 *At the time, it was one of the largest seizures:* "Record Seizure of Cocaine Is Reported in Mexico," Associated Press, April 23, 1993, https://www.latimes.com/archives/la-xpm-1993-04-23-mn-26350-story.html.

78 *"Fuck it, compadre":* Testimony of Miguel Ángel Martínez Martínez on November 27, 2018, p. 1435.

78 *It had began in early 1990:* Ibid., p. 1413.

78 *After some brainstorming, one of El Chapo's lieutenants had an idea:* Ibid., p. 1425.

78 *As early as 1984:* According to an informant of DEA Special Agent Enrique "Kiki Camarena," DEA-6 report filed by DEA Special Agent Enrique "Kiki"

Camarena on May 15, 1984. Entered into evidence in *USA v. Caro Quintero et al.*

78 *At first El Chapo considered buying a pepper factory:* Testimony of Miguel Ángel Martínez Martínez on November 27, 2018, pp. 1426–33.

79 *"If you picked up a can from the top part of it":* Ibid., p. 1433.

79 *The chile idea was such a smash hit that others seem to have copied it:* Testimony of Miguel Ángel Martínez Martínez on November 28, 2018, pp. 1564–66.

79 *packed to the brim with dummy chile cans:* Ibid., pp. 1432–34.

79 *But he did so without paying the taxes:* Testimony of Jesús Reynaldo Zambada García on November 15, 2018, pp. 825–26.

79 *they had begun their career smuggling clothes and consumer electronics:* George W. Grayson, *Mexico: Narco-Violence and a Failed State?* (New Brunswick, N.J.: Transaction, 2010), 81.

80 *The youngest of the three, Ramón was the muscle:* Indictment in *USA v. Arellano Félix et al,* filed October 8, 1998.

80 *stories abound of Ramón attacking strangers at the slightest provocation:* David Epstein, "Devils, Deals and the DEA," *ProPublica* (co-published with *The Atlantic*), December 17, 2015.

80 *The brains of the operation was baby-faced Benjamín:* Indictment in *USA v. Arellano Félix et al,* filed October 8, 1998

80 *Benjamín had the unnerving habit:* Kevin Sullivan and Mary Jordan, "U.S. Called the Loser in War on Drugs," *Washington Post,* October 31, 2002, https://www.washingtonpost.com/archive/politics/2002/10/31/us-called-the-loser-in-war-on-drugs/93152081-dd77-4ad2-82e9-add85f310b8d/.

80 *The Arellano-Félixes were deeply embedded in Tijuana:* Beith (2010), pp. 135–37.

81 *One DEA informant:* David Epstein, "Devils, Deals and the DEA."

81 *by the very cops they thought would be their saviors:* Ibid.

81 *When they began working in Tijuana:* Testimony of Testimony of Miguel Ángel Martínez Martínez on November 26, 2018, p. 1495, *USA v. Joaquin Archivaldo Guzman Loera.*

81 *The local representative for El Chapo and his allies:* Testimony of Jesús Reynaldo Zambada García on November 15, 2018, pp. 791–92.

81 *According to Luís Astorga: Siglo de las Drogas,* p. 188.

81 *Güero—whose nickname, meaning "Blondie":* E. Eduardo Castillo and Mark Stevenson, "Drug lord Palma arrested in Mexico on return from US," Associated Press, June 17, 2016, https://apnews.com/article/977755c892af4cdd aff89a20a1d9a303.

81 *A Venezuelan trafficker connected with the Arellano Félixes:* Sebastian Rotella, "Mexico's Cartels Sow Seeds of Corruption, Destruction: Crime: Fight for control of U.S.-bound drug trade is deadly competition. Gangs enlist police and politicians," *Los Angeles Times,* June 16, 1995, https://www.latimes.com /archives/la-xpm-1995-06-16-mn-13754-story.html.

82 *Other stories trace the feud back to a birthday party:* Testimony of Vicente Zambada Niebla on January 3, 2019, p. 3999, *USA v. Joaquin Guzman Loera.*

82 *El Chapo and the brothers came together for a sit-down:* Ibid., pp. 4000–4001.

82 *It was the beginning of the end of the days in which:* Guillermo Trejo and Sandra Ley, "Why Did Drug Cartels Go to War in Mexico? Subnational Party Alternation, the Breakdown of Criminal Protection, and the Onset of Large-Scale Violence," *Comparative Political Studies* 51, no. 7 (2018): pp. 900–937.

82 *To control the plaza, Ramón began recruiting foot soldiers:* Jones, *Mexico's Illicit Drug Networks,* 51. Indictment in *USA v. Arellano Félix et al,* filed October 8, 1998.

83 *To get the men in fighting shape:* David Epstein, "Devils, Deals and the DEA"; Hugh Dellios, "U.S. Street Gangs Serving as Mercenaries for Mexico's Drug Lords," *Chicago Tribune,* July 11, 1993, https://www.chicagotribune.com/news/ct-xpm-1993-07-11-9307110350-story.html.

83 *El Mayo and his brother El Rey managed for several years to maintain cordial relations with the brothers:* Testimony of Vicente Zambada Niebla on January 3, 2019, p. 3959.

83 *"The Arellano-Félixes thought they were the kings, the owners of Tijuana":* Testimony of Jesús Reynaldo Zambada García on November 15, p. 825.

83 *Buried sixty-five feet below ground, the tunnel:* Joseph B. Treaster, "Huge Drug Tunnel from Mexico into U.S. Is Found," *New York Times,* June 3, 1993, https://www.nytimes.com/1993/06/03/world/huge-drug-tunnel-from-mexico-into-us-is-found.html.

83 *One Customs official later quipped:* "U.S. Seizes Land at Border Near Unfinished Drug Tunnel."

84 *El Chapo and his allies made it clear to their suppliers that no one was to do business with Tijuana:* Testimony of Juan Carlos Ramírez Abadía on December 3, 2018, p. 1887–88.

84 *"I saw that the Sinaloa Cartel people were stronger":* Ibid.

84 *This was bound to end in bloodshed:* A sudden drop in available supply of cocaine has been shown to closely correlate with a rise in homicides as traffickers fight more for less. See Camilo Castilo, Mejía, and Restrepo, "Scarcity without Leviathan: The Violent Effects of Cocaine Supply Shortages in the Mexican Drug War," Center for Global Development Working Paper 356, February 2014.

84 *In September 1992, in Iguala, Guerrero:* "'El Güero' Palma, una historia de una carrera criminal," *Proceso,* June 10, 2016, https://www.proceso.com.mx/reportajes/2016/6/10/el-gero-palma-historia-de-una-carrera-criminal-165647.html.

84 *months later, a group of Ramón's shooters abducted six of El Chapo's men:* Beith (2010), pp. 179–80; Cayteno Frías and Javier Valdez, "Buscará la DEA extradición de Arellano Félix," *La Jornada,* March 10, 2002, https://www.jornada.com.mx/2002/03/10/004n1pol.php?origen=politica.html; Marjorie Miller

and Sebastian Rotella, "Barons of a Bloody Turf War : Rich and ruthless, the Arellano Felix brothers reportedly control narcotics traffic on the Baja border. Their battle to fend off Mexico's biggest drug kingpin may have cost a cardinal his life," *Los Angeles Times*, June 4, 1993, https://www.latimes.com/archives /la-xpm-1993-06-04-mn-43299-story.html.

84 *In Culiacán, a car bomb blew up:* Casto Ocando and María Antonieta Collins, "The Eternal Fugitive: Leap to Fame," Univisión, November 8, 2013, https:// web.archive.org/web/20140123015240/http://www.univision.com/la-huella-digi tal/openpage/2013-11-08/el-chapo-special-ch-2-eng.

84 *The final straw came in 1992:* Testimony of Vicente Zambada Niebla on January 3, 2019, pp. 4001-2.

84 *Martínez tried to offer words of caution:* Testimony of Miguel Ángel Martínez Martínez on November 27, 2018, p. 1515.

84 *"Either your mom is going to cry, or their mom is going to cry":* Ibid.

85 *on the night of November 7, 1992:* Ibid., pp. 1518–22.

85 *Piling out of the truck, El Chapo's men made a frontal assault on the club:* Ibid., pp. 1521–22; Beith (2010), p. 154.

85 *someone had also tipped off Ramón:* Testimony of Miguel Ángel Martínez Martínez on November 27, 2018, p. 1522.

85 *When the smoke cleared, six people were dead:* Ibid.; "Six killed in Mexico disco shootout," United Press International, November 9, 1992, https://www.upi.com /Archives/1992/11/09/Six-killed-in-Mexico-disco-shootout/5689721285200/.

85 *Two months after the debacle in Puerto Vallarta:* This passage is reconstructed from the testimony of Vicente Zambada Niebla on January 3, 2019, pp. 4002–6.

87 *the number of murders skyrocketed:* Tim Golden, "Violently, Drug Trafficking in Mexico Rebounds," *New York Times*, March 8, 1993, https://www.nytimes .com/1993/03/08/world/violently-drug-trafficking-in-mexico-rebounds.html.

87 *El Chapo was traveling light that day:* Testimony of Miguel Ángel Martínez Martínez on November 27, 2018, pp. 1526–27.

87 *a bullet slammed into his foot:* Testimony of Miguel Ángel Martínez Martínez on November 27, 2018, p. 1531.

87 *he desperately sought cover inside the terminal:* Testimony of Miguel Ángel Martínez Martínez on November 27, 2018, pp. 1528–29.

87 *Frantically stuffing cash back into the suitcase:* Ibid.

88 *For some reason, it had waited at the gate:* Statement of Senator Christopher H. Smith before the House Committee on International Relations, April 6, 2006, https://www.hsdl.org/?view&did=743365.

88 *Back in the parking lot, a white Mercury Grand Marquis:* Testimony of Miguel Ángel Martínez Martínez Martínez on November 27, 2018, p. 1528.

88 *He had made the mistake of arriving at the airport at the wrong time:* Ibid.

88 *fourteen bullet holes:* Statement of Senator Christopher H. Smith before the

House Committee on International Relations, April 6, 2006; https://www
.hsdl.org/?view&did=743365.

88 *The Mexican government announced a $5 million bounty:* Anita Snow, "Mexican
Government Offers $5 Million Reward in Bishop's Killing," Associated Press,
May 27, 1993, https://apnews.com/article/fea3f76c463c1d70c6766000fb189505.

88 *"It was too much pressure," Martínez recalled:* Testimony of Miguel Ángel Martínez Martínez on November 27, 2018, p. 1532.

88 *The murder of a high-ranking official in the Catholic Church:* "An End to Impunity: Investigating the 1993 Killing of Mexican Archbishop Juan Jesús Posadas Ocampo," Hearing Before the Subcommittee on Africa, Global Human
Rights, and International Operations, House Committee on International
Relations, April 6, 2006.

89 *In one of the strangest episodes:* Chris Kraul and Sebastian Rotella, "Cartel
Used Papal Envoy, Book Relates," *Los Angeles Times,* April 30, 2002, https://
www.latimes.com/archives/la-xpm-2002-apr-30-fg-mexdrug30-story.html.

89 *El Chapo lay low for two days:* Testimony of Miguel Ángel Martínez Martínez
on November 27, 2018, p. 1532.

89 *he was arrested shortly after his arrival:* Ibid.

89 *A few days later, a team of Guatemalan soldiers:* Juanita Darling, "Mexico Arrests Reputed Top Drug Kingpin," *Los Angeles Times,* June 11, 1993, https://
www.latimes.com/archives/la-xpm-1993-06-11-mn-2027-story.html.

90 *Flanked by a pair of prison guards in black uniforms:* This scene is reconstructed from archival footage via the AP. Translation is my own: https://www
.youtube.com/watch?v=fYM1x0vxQHI.

90 *This was all a stark departure from the conversation he'd had with interrogators
on the flight to Mexico City:* Anabel Hernández (2013), pp. 30–32.

91 *A judge did not agree:* Tim Weiner, "Mexican Jail Easy to Flee: Just Pay Up,"
New York Times, January 29, 2001, https://www.nytimes.com/2001/01/29/world
/mexican-jail-easy-to-flee-just-pay-up.html.

91 *A year later, he was also convicted in the murder of the archbishop, although
another judge later threw that ruling out:* Beith (2010), pp. 66–67.

91 *With the exception of Francisco Rafael, who was arrested in December 1993:*
Margarita Rojas, "Francisco Rafael Arellano Félix (perfil)," Milenio, October 19, 2013, https://www.webcitation.org/6KV2NUYut?url=http://www.milenio
.com/cdb/doc/noticias2011/21e40cd6434b1983cd2f4ec1602d2557.

91 *The next time Ramón was seen in public:* Footage via YouTube, https://www
.youtube.com/watch?v=E6lPE5BqFL4; David Epstein, "Devils, Deals, and
the DEA," *ProPublica,* December 17, 2015, https://www.propublica.org/article
/devils-deals-and-the-dea.

91 *El Chapo's side took hits, too:* Testimony of Jesus Reynaldo Zambada Garcia
on November 15, 2018, pp. 826–28.

CHAPTER 5: I AM TITO

92 *It paid to do El Chapo's bidding:* The figures for cooks and custodial supervisors is via Hernández (2013), pp. 118, while the figure for the warden is via the testimony of Miguel Ángel Martínez Martínez on November 27, 2018, p. 1540.

92 *When El Chapo wanted lobster:* Hernández (2013), p. 140.

92 *When he wanted new shoes, a change of clothes, a cell phone, he got them:* Testimony of Miguel Ángel Martínez Martínez on November 27, 2018, p. 1402.

92 *where he arranged for conjugal visits with his wives:* Ibid. pp. 1540–41.

92 *In the immediate aftermath of the shoot-out at the Guadalajara airport:* Ibid., pp. 1530–36.

93 *El Azul was taken aback by the huge quantity of drugs:* Ibid., p. 1537.

94 *the DEA seized it at the border crossing in Mexicali:* Ibid., p. 1538.

94 *Chupeta, the North Valley Cartel kingpin, was furious:* Ibid., p. 1538.

94 *Chupeta agreed to continue sending coke:* Ibid., p. 1539.

94 *He largely handled the money-laundering side of things:* "'El Chapo' rival Héctor Beltrán Leyva dies in jail," BBC, November 19, 2019, https://www.bbc.com /news/world-latin-america-46261159.

95 *"It looked like a beer can that had been run over by a semi":* Author interview with Mike Vigil on October 29, 2019.

95 *they came across the injured El Güero and uniformed* federales *acting as his bodyguards:* Ginger Thompson, "A Drug War informant in No Man's Land," *New York Times,* April 28, 2013, https://www.nytimes.com/2013/04/29/us/us -mexico-dea-informant.html.

95 *a .38 super with a palm tree on the handle:* "'El Güero' Palma, historia de una carrera criminal," *Proceso,* June 10, 2016, https://www.proceso.com.mx/reportajes /2016/6/10/el-gero-palma-historia-de-una-carrera-criminal-165647.html.

95 *Amado had originally arrived in the state of Chihuahua:* Terrence E. Poppa, *Drug Lord: The Life and Death of a Mexican Kingpin: A True Story* (El Paso, Texas: Cinco Puntos Press, 2010), pp. 428, 440, 448.

95 *By the mid-1990s:* Ibid., p. 450.

95 *many journalists in Mexico did not even dare print his name:* Charles Bowden, *Down by the River: Drugs, Money, Murder and Family* (New York: Simon & Schuster, 2004) p. 77.

95 *The only major faction that didn't originate in Sinaloa:* Carlos Antonio Flores Pérez (2013) "Political Protection and the Origins of the Gulf Cartel," in Payan, Tony, et al. (ed.), *A War that Can't Be Won,* p. 120.

96 *He decided he would talk to the DEA:* Author interview with Joe Bond on September 26 and October 3, 2019; "Memorandum of Law in Support of Government's Second Motions In Limine," aka Document 326 in *USA v. Guzmán Loera,* originally filed on September 21, 2018, and unsealed on May 5, 2019.

96 *The Mexican economy had long been undergoing a steady trend of liberalization:*

Jorge Máttar, Juan Carlos Moreno-Brid, and Wilson Peres, *Foreign Investment in Mexico after Economic Reform* (Mexico City: CEPAL, 2002).

96 *but under President Salinas de Gortari, this had leapt into overdrive:* Alberto Chong and Florencio López de Silanes, "Privatization in Mexico," Inter-American Development Bank, August 2004, https://publications.iadb.org/pu blications/english/document/Privatization-in-Mexico.pdf.

96 *Mexico had just two billionaires:* Joel Millman, "Mexico's Billionaire Boom," *Washington Post*, November 27, 1994, https://www.washingtonpost.com/ar chive/opinions/1994/11/27/mexicos-billionaire-boom/fe100dbb-20aa-44a1-9 e11-726c1a046a36/.

96 *At one supposedly confidential gathering:* Andres Oppenheimer, *Bordering on Chaos: Guerillas, Stockbrokers, Politicians and Mexico's Road to Prosperity* (Boston: Little, Brown, 1996). Excerpted on PBS.org, retrieved April 16, 2020.

97 *For the poor in both countries, it was a nightmare:* "Did NAFTA Help Mexico? An Assessment After 20 Years," by Mark Weisbrot, Stephen Lefebvre, and Joseph Sammut, Center for Economic and Policy Research, February 2014.

97 *He gave speeches:* "Discurso de Luis Donaldo Colosio," March 6, 1994, www .bibliotecas.tv/colosio/discursos/candidato06mar94.htm.

97 *Then, on March 23, 1994, a gunman with ties to the local branch of the PRI gunned him down:* "1994: Colosio Assassination Was Start of Mexico's Catastrophic Year," NPR, March 23, 2014, https://www.npr.org/2014/03/23 /293255136/1994-colosio-assasination-was-start-of-mexicos-catastrophic-year.

98 *The assassination opened up the race:* Tim Golden, "The Case of the Murdered Candidate," *New York Times*, August 21, 1994, https://www.nytimes.com/1994 /08/21/magazine/the-case-of-the-murdered-candidate.html.

98 *Zedillo, a relatively low-ranking party member:* Tim Golden, "Election Aide May Succeed Slain Mexican," *New York Times*, March 26, 1994, https://www .nytimes.com/1994/03/26/world/election-aide-may-succeed-slain-mexican.html.

98 *As a parting gift:* Daniel Yergin and Joseph Stanislaw, *The Commanding Heights: The Battle for the World Economy* (New York: Free Press, 2002), pp. 260–65.

98 *This began in February 1995 with a bang:* Julia Preston, "Raul Salinas Guilty in Killing and Is Sentenced to 50 Years," *New York Times*, January 22, 1999, https://www.nytimes.com/1999/01/22/world/raul-salinas-guilty-in-killing-and-is -sentenced-to-50-years.html.

98 *allegedly used his proximity:* Sam Dillon, "A Fugitive Lawman Speaks: How Mexico Mixes Narcotics and Politics," *New York Times*, December 23, 1996.

98 *both judgments were later tossed out:* Carlos Antonio Flores Pérez (2013) "Political Protection and the Origins of the Gulf Cartel," in Payan, Tony, et al. (ed.), *A War that Can't Be Won*, p. 131.

98 *"Back in 1993, it was very unpopular":* Tim Golden, "Mexico and Drugs: Was

U.S. Napping?" *New York Times*, July 11, 1997, https://www.nytimes.com/1997/07/11/world/mexico-and-drugs-was-us-napping.html.

99 *Ruíz Massieu died by suicide:* Tim Golden, "Mexican, in U.S. Suicide Note, Blames Zedillo for His Death," *New York Times*, September 9, 1999. When Calderoni himself fled Mexico under accusations that he'd tortured prisoners and taken bribes, he retaliated against his former bosses by giving a series of tell-all interviews to American reporters, detailing a slew of sordid ties between the Salinas brothers and drug traffickers. Among those were accusations that the Salinas brothers had arranged for the assassination of the brother of Ruíz Massieu, who was married to the Salinases' sister. After Mexico tried to demand his extradition, Calderoni hired the same lawyer who had represented both García Ábrego and Ruíz Massieu.

100 *The agency had grown more muscular, better funded:* In 1985, the DEA's budget was $362 million. In 1994, it had grown to $970 million. For more information see "DEA Staffing and Budget," https://www.DEA.gov/staffing-and-budget.

100 *"They don't give a damn":* Jaime Kuykendal quoted by Elaine Shannon in *Desperadoes.*

100 *the agency requested nearly $3 billion for the 2020 fiscal year:* FY 2020 Budget Request, https://www.justice.gov/jmd/page/file/1142431/download.

101 *"With peace breaking out all over the place":* Douglas Jehl and Melissa Healy, "In Reversal, Military Seeks Drug War Role," *Los Angeles Times*, December 15, 1989, https://www.latimes.com/archives/la-xpm-1989-12-15-mn-177-story.html.

101 *The new budget assigned the Pentagon to take the lead on all aerial and maritime monitoring of suspected drug routes:* Bryna Brennan, "Military Moving Ahead with Plans for Drug War," Associated Press, December 16, 1989.

101 *Navy budget planners recommended:* Jehl and Healy, "In Reversal, Military Seeks Drug War Role."

101 *Then–defense secretary Dick Cheney assigned a new group called Task Force 6:* Ibid.

101 *The Pentagon authorized Delta Force hostage-rescue teams to capture drug traffickers abroad:* Michael Isikoff and Patrick E. Tyler, "U.S. Military Given Foreign Arrest Powers," *Washington Post*, December 16, 1989, https://www.washingtonpost.com/archive/politics/1989/12/16/us-military-given-foreign-arrest-powers/9ff56a09-9271-4778-ae99-03c60b3b1f0b/.

101 *"Getting help from the military on drugs used to be like pulling teeth":* Jehl and Healy, "In Reversal, Military Seeks Drug War Role."

101 *As Washington began to take a national security approach:* Even with the surge in funding for the DEA and the use of military equipment and tactics, drug enforcement still had a tendency to take a backseat to other national priorities. During the Salinas administration, some drug enforcement agents working in Mexico spoke of political pressure from officials in Washington who did not want to jeopardize NAFTA and other policy issues that required

cooperation from Mexico City. Tim Golden, "Mexico and Drugs: Was U.S. Napping?" *New York Times,* July 11, 1997.

101 *One of the DEA agents taking part in these special-ops missions was a young Mexican American agent named Joe Bond:* Author interviews with Joe Bond on September 26 and October 3, 2019.

102 *Joe Bond was born in Mexico City:* All biographical details via ibid.

103 *This cost the anesthesiologist his life:* Molly Moore, "Drug Lord's Doctors Found Embedded in Cement," *Washington Post,* November 7, 1997, https://www.washingtonpost.com/archive/politics/1997/11/07/dead-drug-lords-doc tors-found-embedded-in-cement/58c01706-a852-4def-981f-9ba649d4429e/.

103 *He even has a photo of the dead drug baron, his face bloated but still recognizable:* Author interview with Joe Bond on October 3, 2019.

103 *On November 7, 1997:* Author interviews with Joe Bond and Motion to Admit Defendant's Voluntary Statements to U.S. Law Enforcement as filed on May 5, 2019, pp. 46–49.

104 *As Joe Bond, Larry Villalobos, and Pepe Patiño pulled up to the outer perimeter of Puente Grande:* All details of the meeting at Puente Grande via author interviews with Joe Bond on September 26 and October 3, 2019, as well as an internal DEA report of the interview that I viewed.

109 *"They're territorial, these fucking U.S. attorneys":* Author interview with Joe Bond on October 3, 2019.

110 *"If you needed any kind of help, he was there":* Tim Golden, "Killing Raises Doubts on Mexico's War on Drugs," *New York Times,* June 5, 2000.

110 *Video cameras at the border crossing:* "The Arellano-Félix Tijuana Cartel: A Family Affair," PBS, https://www.pbs.org/wgbh/pages/frontline/shows/drugs/business/afo/afosummary.html.

110 *Two days later, the men were found in their car:* "Forum on Crime and Society," UNODC Centre for International Crime Prevention, December 2001, https://www.unodc.org/pdf/crime/publications/forum1vol2.pdf.

111 *"They found out through the warden that Pepe Patiño was there with the DEA":* Author interview with Joe Bond on October 3, 2019.

111 *Fox won the election:* Julia Preston, "Challenger in Mexico Wins; Governing Party Concedes," *New York Times,* July 3, 2000, https://archive.nytimes.com/www.nytimes.com/library/world/americas/070300mexico-election.html.

111 *he once sparked controversy among Mexico's hyperliterate elite:* Aquiles Siller, "Cuando Vicente Fox creó en 2001 al escritor 'José Luis Borgues'" October 15, 2019, https://politico.mx/minuta-politica/minuta-politica-gobierno-federal/cuando-vicente-fox-creó-en-2001-al-escritor-josé-luis-borgues/.

111 *It helped that his opponent was Francisco Labastida Ochoa:* Mary Beth Sheridan, "PRI Candidate's Drug Stance Stirs Debate," *Los Angeles Times,* April 30, 2000, https://www.latimes.com/archives/la-xpm-2000-apr-30-mn-25039-story.html.

112 *The work of containing the communists fell to the PRI:* Peter Dale Scott, "Anti-

communism and Extra-legal Repression in Mexico," in *Government of the Shadows: Parapolitics and Criminal Sovereignty,* eds. Eric Wilson and Tim Lindsey (London: Pluto Press, 2009), pp. 175–76, 178.

112 *Fox's victory seemed to promise a new era:* Kevin Sullivan and Mary Jordan, "Fox Inauguration Ends Mexico's One-Party Rule," December 2, 2000, https://www.washingtonpost.com/archive/politics/2000/12/02/fox-inauguration -ends-mexicos-one-party-rule/c2251362-e51a-4932-8263-c2dd001659c6/.

112 *the drug trade was entering a new phase:* Much of this paragraph is based on the quantitative and qualitative analysis of Trejo and Ley, as well as on the work of Astorga and Shirk (2010). Guillermo Trejo and Sandra Ley. "Why Did Drug Cartels Go to War in Mexico? Subnational Party Alternation, the Breakdown of Criminal Protection, and the Onset of Large-Scale Violence," *Comparative Political Studies* 5, no. 7 (2018): pp. 900–37.

CHAPTER 6: AN EXCELLENT SURPRISE

114 *he took a particular liking to 23-year-old Zumela Yulia Hernández:* This account of El Chapo's relationship with Zulema is based largely on passages from *Narcoland,* by Anabel Hernández, and Zulema's interview with Julio Scherer, of the monthly news magazine *Proceso.* Julio Scherer García, *"De 'El Chapo' a Zulema: 'Cuando Yo Me Vaya . . .'" Proceso,* February 22, 2014.

115 *According to Hernández:* While Zulema Hernández spoke fondly of El Chapo, it should be stressed that he took part in a sexually abusive system that made the few women prisoners at Puente Grande uncomfortable. After El Chapo's escape, when he was no longer around to protect Zulema, the guards repeatedly raped her or pimped her out to other inmates, according to Hernández. Complaints from prison employees and female inmates mostly fell on deaf ears, and the human rights officials who did try to raise the issue found their supervisors unwilling to listen.

115 *"When I needed anything, I would ask, and he would give it to me":* Testimony of Dámaso López Nuñez on January 22, 2019, p. 5832.

115 *"[Rumors that] Mr. Guzmán Loera could soon gain his freedom":* Beith, "The Last Narco," p. 68.

115 *In fact, El Chapo didn't need help from the legal system:* This account of El Chapo's escape is built largely from the testimony of Jesús Reynaldo "El Rey" Zambada García, Vicente "Vicentillo" Zambada Niebla, and Dámaso López Nuñez in Brooklyn federal court in November of 2018 and January 2019.

116 *In a letter to Zulema Hernandez:* Julio Scherer García, *"De 'El Chapo 'a Zulema: 'Cuando Yo Me Vaya . . .'" Proceso,* February 22, 2014, https://www.proceso .com.mx/reportajes/2014/2/22/de-el-chapo-zulema-cuando-yo-me-vaya-129 465.html.

116 *In September 2000, Dámaso López had resigned:* Testimony of Dámaso López Nuñez, January 22, 2019. According to an article in El Universal, the exact

date was September 30: Zorayda Gallegos and Silber Meza, "El Chapo had a prison expert on the Sinaloa Cartel's payroll," *El Universal,* July 21, 2015, https://www.eluniversal.com.mx/articulo/english/2015/07/21/el-chapo-had -prison-expert-sinaloa-cartels-payroll.

116 *Then, in early January, newly sworn-in president Vicente Fox:* Hernandez (2013), pp. 141–46.

116 *the Supreme Court of Mexico ruled that extradition of inmates such as El Chapo could proceed:* Vanessa Maaskamp, Extradition and Life Imprisonment, 25 Loy. L.A. Int'l & Comp. L. Rev. 741 (2003). Available at: http://digitalcommons .lmu.edu/ilr/vol25/iss3/12.

117 *Puente Grande is divided into eight different security units:* Testimony of Dámaso López on January 22, 2019, pp. 5829–31.

118 *At each diamond, El Chapo heard the muffled click:* Testimony of Vicente Zambada Niebla on January 3, 2019, pp. 3966–69.

118 *The guard did a cursory search of the interior of the vehicle:* Testimony of Dámaso López on January 22, 2019, p. 5837.

118 *In Narcoland, Anabel Hernandez:* Hernandez (2013), chapters 6 and 7.

119 *More than five hundred cops fanned out across the state of Jalisco:* Beith (2012), p. 72.

119 *"Today, I reaffirm our war without mercy":* Ken Ellingwood, "Mexican President Reaffirms War on Crime," *Los Angeles Times,* February 1, 2001, https:// www.latimes.com/archives/la-xpm-2001-feb-01-mn-19793-story.html.

119 *Mexican government officials pointed fingers angrily in all directions:* Beith (2012), pp. 72–81.

119 *"What happened in Jalisco is evidence of the capacity of corruption":* Ibid.

120 *A few days after the escape, Jesús Reynaldo Zambada García, aka El Rey:* Testimony of Jesús Reynaldo Zambada on November 15, 2019, p. 850. The following passage is based on Zambada's testimony from page 850 to page 866.

120 *"Don't worry about it":* Ibid., p. 856.

121 *When the news broke of El Chapo's escape, Special Agent Joe Bond was in his office:* This passage, including all quotes, are based on the recollections of Joe Bond. Author interview with Joe Bond in Washington, D.C., October 2, 2019.

122 *He enjoyed a good relationship with much of the U.S. diplomatic community:* Embassy Mexico, "Calderón's Security Cabinet," Wikileaks Cable: 06MEX ICO6871_a, December 11, 2006, https://wikileaks.org/plusd/cables/06MEX ICO6871_a.html.

123 *García Luna had a reputation for being territorial:* Author interview with Joe Bond, Oct. 2, 2019.

123 *speaking with me in early October 2019, Bond:* I conducted a phone interview with Bond on September 25, 2019 and an in-person interview in the Washington, D.C., area on October 2.

123 *"I had to dance with the devil":* Author interview with Joe Bond on October 2, 2019.

124 *Bond told them he thought this was absurd:* Ibid.

124 Arturo was arrested September 6, according to this *Jornada* piece.

124 *El Pollo was even smaller than his brother:* Details on Arturo Guzmán's physical appearance are from Bond's recollections and from images of Arturo entered into evidence in the trial of El Chapo and made public during a press conference September of 2001: Gustavo Castillo García, *"Captura la PGR a Arturo Guzmán Loera, líder del Cártel de Sinaloa," La Jornada,* September 8, 2001.

125 *"Joe, we had to pick him up":* Author interview with Joe Bond on October 2, 2019.

126 *"It felt really bad":* Ibid.

126 *In El Chapo Land, the natural response to the arrest of El Pollo was to try to break him out:* Testimony of Vicente Zambada Niebla on January 3, 2019, p. 3996.

126 *Three years later . . . El Pollo was murdered in prison:* The murder of Arturo Guzmán Loera was discussed in detail during the testimony of Vicentillo, and corroborated by contemporaneous news accounts in *Proceso,* the *Los Angeles Times,* and others. *"Trasladan a reos peligrosos de La Palma a otros penales," Proceso,* January 18, 2005; Chris Kraul, "Slaying Points Up Mexico's Weak Grip," *Los Angeles Times,* January 6, 2005.

126 *El Chapo held a series of meetings with his allies:* Testimony of Jesús Zambada García on November 15, 2018, and Vicente Zambada Niebla on January 3, 2019.

127 *"I'm with you one hundred percent":* Testimony of Vicente Zambada on January 3, 2019, pp. 3996–97.

127 *"Let's go to Sinaloa":* Testimony of Jesús Zambada García on November 15, 2018, pp. 863–64.

CHAPTER 7: LET'S GO TO SINALOA

128 *It was to el Cielo that El Chapo returned:* Testimony of Jesús Reynald Zambada García on November 19, 2018. Corroborated in interviews with residents of La Tuna conducted in April and May of 2019.

129 *Among the farmers El Chapo bought from in those days:* Author interview with "José," April 16, 2019, in Badiraguato, Sinaloa.

130 *"He was a very simple man, and very natural":* Ibid. This interview was conducted and transcribed in Spanish, all translations my own.

130 *The relationship between local trafficker-strongmen:* For more on the negotiation between local farmers and wholesale drug buyers, see Nathaniel Morris, "Serrano Communities and Subaltern Negotiation Strategies: The Local Politics of Opium Production in Mexico, 1940–2020," in *Social History of Alcohol and Drugs* 34, no. 1 (Spring 2020), accessed May 12, 2020.

130 *When El Chapo was operating out of a series of hideouts in the mountains of the Golden Triangle:* Testimony of Alex Cifuentes on January 14, 2019, pp. 5085–86.

130 *"Well, if it was a small group of about twenty-five men":* Ibid., p. 5086.

130 *small-time, self-employed farmers like José formed the backbone:* Ibid.

130 *This status quo has been upended in recent years:* Author interviews with drug traffickers and cultivators in Sinaloa in 2019. Romain LeCour, Nathaniel Morris, and Benjamin Smith, "No More Opium for the Masses: From US Fentanyl Boom to the Mexican Opium Crisis, Opportunities Amidst Violence?," Wilson Center, February 2019, https://www.noria-research.com/maps-no-more -opium-for-the-masses/.

130 *by the time a stamp of heroin or a dime bag of weed has been sold:* LeCour, Smith, and Morris estimate that opium production in Mexico in 2017 generated around $1 billion in profits for peasant growers. That's a tidy sum, but a tiny fraction of the $100 billion potentially generated by street sales of heroin, according to the DEA's estimate.

131 *"He is a legend, truly, a legend":* Author interview with "José," April 16, 2019.

131 *Cops on the payroll of El Mayo cornered the notorious butcher in Mazatlán:* Testimony of Jesús Reynaldo Zambada on November 15, 2018, pp. 865–67.

131 *Ramón's identity was only confirmed:* "Mexican Tests Confirm Dead Man was Drug Fugitive," Associated Press, March 14, 2002.

132 *"On occasion, up in the mountains, we would talk about that":* Testimony of Jesús Reynaldo Zambada García on November 15, 2018, p. 866.

132 *On March 9, 2002:* Deborah Amos, "How Officials Jolted a Cocaine Cartel," ABC News, January 6, 2006, https://abcnews.go.com/Nightline/story ?id=128536; "DEA Confirms Capture of Benjamin Arellano Felix," news release by the DOJ on March 9, 2002, https://web.archive.org/web/2012080903 0526/http://www.justice.gov/dea/pubs/pressrel/pr030902.html.

133 *According to recent court documents . . . the rot began at the very top:* See 1:2019cr00576 *USA v. Garcia Luna et al.*

133 *According to El Mayo's brother El Rey:* Testimony of Jesús Reynaldo Zambada García on November 20, 2018, pp. 1104–6.

133 *the various kingpins . . . gathered at a meeting in Mexico City:* Author interview with Mike Vigil, October 28, 2019.

133 *many of the midlevel operatives working for one or the other leader considered it to be a single organization:* Testimony of Tirso Martínez Sánchez on December 10, 2018, p. 2542.

133 *At a meeting held in early 2002:* Testimony of Vicente Zambada Niebla on January 3, 2019, pp. 3978–82.

134 *In about 1997, El Mayo and the Carrillo-Fuentes family gave control of the route:* Testimony of Tirso Martínez Sánchez on December 10, 2018, p. 2554.

134 *Born in Guadalajara in 1967, Tirso grew up destitute:* Ibid.

135 *Working out of warehouses in Mexico City:* Ibid., pp. 2618–19.

135 *The workers would then pack the compartments with as much as 1,800 kilos:* Ibid., 2578–79.

135 *In doing so, he flouted the power of the so-called Gulf Cartel:* Ibid., 2619–20.

136 *cultivated deep ties with the* PRIista *elite:* For a discussion of the Gulf Cartel's ties to the *PRIista* elite, see Carlos Antonio Flores Perez, "Political Protection and the Origins of the Gulf Cartel," in *A War That Can't Be Won: Binational Perspectives on the War on Drugs*, edited by Tony Payan et al. (Phoenix: University of Arizona Press, 2013), pp. 119–48, www.jstor.org/stable/j.ctt16xwbq2.9, accessed April 20, 2020.

136 *García Ábrego's principal lieutenant was a man named Osiel Cárdenas Guillen:* William C. Martin (2013), p. 35.

137 *His initial recruits were fellow soldiers:* "Evolution of Los Zetas in Mexico and Central America: Sadism as an Instrument of Cartel Warfare," by George Grayson (2014).

138 *In time, the Zetas would eventually split off from the Gulf Cartel:* Ibid.

138 *The old order of the drug trade in Mexico . . . was coming to an end:* See Trejo and Ley, "Why Did Drug Cartels Go to War in Mexico?"

138 *traffickers had been incentivized:* Angélica Duran-Martínez, "To Kill and Tell? State Power, Criminal Competition, and Drug Violence," *Journal of Conflict Resolution* 59, no. 8, Special Issue: Drug Violence in Mexico (December 2015): 1377–1402, accessed July 25, 2019.

138 *On November 9, 1999, a pair of U.S. agents:* Tim Golden, "Head to Head: D.E.A. Agents and Suspects," *New York Times*, November 24, 1999, https://www.nytimes.com/1999/11/24/world/head-to-head-in-mexico-dea-agents-and-suspects.html.

139 *"This was very, very close," one U.S. official said at the time:* Ibid.

139 *As late as 2002, El Chapo, El Mayo, and the other Sinaloa capos:* Testimony of Jesús Reynaldo Zambada García on November 19, 2018, pp. 902–4.

140 *Some, like El Rey Zambada, say the conflict began:* Testimony of Jesús Reynaldo Zambada García on November 15, 2018, pp. 902–3.

140 *Mexican soldiers in Matamoros arrested the Friend Killer:* Gustavo Castillo García, Armando Torres Barbos, and Martín Sánchez Treviño, *"Bajo fuego, la captura del capo Osiel Cárdenas,"* La Jornada, March 15, 2003, https://www.jornada.com.mx/2003/03/15/048n1con.php.

140 *On August 1, a heavily armed convoy of La Barbie's men:* Cecilia Ballí, "Borderline Insanity," *Texas Monthly*, August 2005, https://www.texasmonthly.com/articles/borderline-insanity/.

141 *One new hire who fit the bill:* Testimony of Isaias Valdez Ríos on January 24, 2019.

142 *El Chapo summoned the new hire over:* Ibid.

143 *They continued to work closely with cocaine producers in Colombia:* Testimony

of Germán Rosero on December 5, 2019. *USA v. Guzmán Loera et al.*, 09-CR-00466. pp. 2203–15.

144 *One exception, however, was the operation at Benito Juárez International Airport:* Testimony of Jesús Reynaldo Zambada García, November 15, 2019, p. 773.

CHAPTER 8: THE FLORES TWINS

145 *Pedro and Margarito "Junior" Flores got an early start in the drug game:* Much of this chapter is based on the testimony of Pedro Flores in *USA v. Guzmán Loera et al*, along with court documents related to the case against Pedro and his brother Margarito, aka Junior.

145 *Adrian ordered a young Junior . . . to get the keys from the car:* This anecdote is from *Cartel Wives*, the "as-told-to" memoir penned by Pedro and Juniors' wives. In a comically similar mix-up, Pedro made the same mistake about keys and kilos during his testimony against El Chapo:

> Q: What would you do with the keys?
> A: I would unload them in my own stash house.
> Q: I'm sorry. I didn't mean the kilograms—
> A: I'm sorry.
> Q: —I meant the actual keys.
> A: Put the key back where I found them.
> Q: And just for the jury's benefit and everyone else's, when I say keys—
> A: I thought—thought you meant kilos, I'm sorry. The car keys.

Testimony of Pedro Flores on December 18, 2018, p. 3437.

145 *The big break for the brothers Flores came in 1998:* Ibid., pp. 3430–32.

145 *The supplier who began working with them after the arrest of their father was a man they called "El Profe":* Ibid., p. 3435.

146 *"pretty hectic day":* Ibid., p. 3439.

147 *They soon caught the eye of a Mexican trafficker named Lupe Ledezma:* Ibid., p. 3432.

147 *they sometimes caused local produce prices to crash:* Ibid., p. 3438.

148 *"There was about 150 heads of sheep":* Ibid., p. 3505. Unless otherwise stated, all quotes by Pedro Flores are from his testimony on December 18 and December 19, 2018.

148 *with nearly $1 trillion in freight passing through it each year:* Judith Crown, "As the Nation's Rail Hub, Chicago Is an Expensive and Dangerous Bottleneck," *Crain's Chicago Business*, August 23, 2017.

156 *The Zetas brand spread quickly:* Grillo (2011), Chapter 6.

157 *On January 7, 2007:* "Mexican President takes a hard stance on crime," *The New York Times*, January 7, 2007.

157 *In Tijuana, troops and* federales *would replace the city's 2,320 municipal cops:* William Finnegan, "In the Name of the Law," *New Yorker,* October 18, 2010.

158 *Mexico as a whole was actually getting less violent:* World Bank data via macro trends.net, https://www.macrotrends.net/countries/MEX/mexico/murder-homicide-rate.

159 *At the time Calderón took office, journalists in Mexico and U.S. diplomats in the State Department noted:* Embassy Mexico, "Ambassador's Meeting with Presumed President Elect Calderon," Wikileaks Cable: 06MEXICO4310_a, August 4, 2006, wikileaks.org/plusd/cables/06MEXICO4310_a.html.

CHAPTER 9: JUÁREZ

161 *The city had a startlingly high rate of murders of women:* "Crying out for Justice: Murders of Women in Ciudad Juárez, Mexico," Washington Office on Latin America, Latin America Working Group, March 2005, https://www.wola.org/sites/default/files/downloadable/Mexico/past/crying_out_for_justice.pdf.

162 *In 2007, there were 336 murders reported in Ciudad Juárez:* Lorena Figueroa, "Homicides in Juárez drop to '07 levels," *El Paso Times,* January 4, 2016, accessed January 18, 2021, https://elpasotimes.com/story/news/world/Juárez/2016/01/04/homicides-jurez-2015-drop-07-levels/78280942/.

162 *By the end of 2008, the city had recorded at least 1,578 murders:* "Ciudad Juárez Registers Record Murder Rate," InsightCrime.org, January 5, 2011, accessed July 21, 2020.

162 *Tens of thousands of residents in Juárez became refugees:* Damien Cave, "A Mexican City's Troubles Reshape Its Families," *New York Times,* February 9, 2011, https://www.nytimes.com/2011/02/09/world/americas/09juarez.html.

163 *many of whom lived for years under a self-imposed curfew, rarely venturing out after dark if they didn't have to:* Author interview with Sandra Ramírez Chavez on June 5, 2019, in Juárez.

163 *In 2018, there were 1,259 murders in the city:* Rick Jervis, "As Trump Demands a Wall, Violence Returns to Texas Border in Ciudad Juárez," *USA Today,* February 15, 2019, accessed July 21, 2020.

163 *including the massacre of eleven people:* Byline redacted, "Compitieron narcos con masacres antes de 'firmar' la supuesta tregua," *El Diario de Juárez,* September 18, 2018, accessed July 21, 2020.

163 *"Not everyone's talking about crime":* Jervis, "As Trump Demands a Wall."

163 *He still caries a bullet in his body:* Interview with Carlos Sánchez on June 3, 2019, in Juárez.

164 *"What do you want from us?": ¿Qué quieren de nosotros?" El Diario de Juárez,* September 19, 2010, https://web.archive.org/web/20110722223358/http://www.diario.com.mx/notas.php?f=2010/09/19&id=ce557112f34b187454d7b6d117a76cb5.

164 *A cottage industry bloomed here:* Oscar J. Martínez, *Ciudad Juárez: Saga of a Legendary Border City* (Tucson: University of Arizona Press, 2018), 34.

164 *eagerly tied fact-free horror stories of marijuana use to racist stereotypes of the Mexican workers they sought to eject:* Olivia B. Waxman, "The Surprising Link Between U.S. Marijuana Law and the History of Immigration," *Time*, April 19, 2019, https://time.com/5572691/420-marijuana-mexican-immigration/.

164 *the United States and Mexico launched the Bracero Program:* Martínez, *Ciudad Juárez*, pp. 128–30.

164 *President Nixon brought the border to a standstill for weeks:* Patrick Timmons, "Trump's Wall on Nixon's Border," NACLA, March 27, 2017, https://nacla.org /news/2017/03/27/trump%27s-wall-nixon%27s-border.

165 *Making matters worse:* J. Martínez, *Ciudad Juárez: Saga of a Legendary Border City* (Tucson: University of Arizona Press, 2018), pp. 184–89.

165 *the issue of drug trafficking and cultivation has largely concerned the smuggling of drugs to the United States:* June S. Beittel, "Mexico: Organized Crime and Drug Trafficking Organizations," Congressional Research Service, July 28, 2020, https://fas.org/sgp/crs/row/R41576.pdf.

166 *border cities like Juárez and Tijuana:* Patricia Case et al., "At the Borders, on the Edge: Use of Injected Methamphetamine in Tijuana and Ciudad Juárez, Mexico," *Journal of Immigrant and Minority Health* 10, no. 1 (2008): pp. 23–33. doi:10.1007/s10903-007-9051-0, accessed July 29, 2020.

166 *"Workers in this model were not viewed as human beings":* Tony Payan, "Ciudad Juárez: A Perfect Storm on the US-Mexico Border," *Journal of Borderlands Studies*, November 26, 2014.

166 *El Chapo and his allies made a concerted push:* George W. Grayson, "The Evolution of Los Zetas in Mexico and Central America: Sadism as an Instrument of Cartel Warfare," April 2014; Testimony of Édgar Iván Galván on January 7, 2019, pp. 4371–73.

166 *For most of El Chapo's career:* The links between Amado Carrillo Fuentes and El Chapo and El Mayo were discussed at trial by Jesús Reynaldo Zambada García, Vicente Zambada Niebla, Tirso Martínez Sánchez, and others.

167 *His initial introduction to El Chapo took place sometime in mid-2001:* Testimony of Tirso Martínez Sánchez on December 10, 2018, pp. 2601–10.

168 *"I was in between a rock and a hard place":* Ibid., p. 2634.

168 *El Chapo's people murdered El Viceroy's brother, Rodolfo Carrillo Fuentes:* This murder was discussed in detail at trial by Jesús Reynaldo Zambada García on November 19, 2018, and by Vicente Zambada Niebla on January 3, 2019.

168 *El Viceroy on New Year's Eve of that year arranged the murder of El Chapo's brother Arturo in prison:* This murder was discussed in detail by Vicente Zambada Niebla on January 3, 2019.

168 *with the help of an enforcement gang known as La Línea:* "Mexican police arrest drug boss 'El Brad Pitt,'" Reuters, March 16, 2011, https://www.reuters .com/article/us-mexico-drugs/mexican-police-arrest-drug-boss-el-brad-pitt-idUS

TRE75F54N20110616. For more on La Linea, Barrio Azteca, and other gangs active in Juárez, see Chapter 9 of Martínez (2018) and N. Jones, "Understanding and Addressing Youth in 'Gangs' in Mexico," in *Building Resilient Communities in Mexico: Civic Responses to Crime and Violence*, ed. David Shirk, Duncan Wood, and Eric Olson (Washington, DC: Woodrow Wilson International Center and Justice in Mexico, 2014), pp. 89–118.

168 *La Linea had built up a fearsome reputation, but existed as a whisper:* Charles Bowden, "Teachings of Don Fernando," pp. 73–91, in *Submersion Journalism: Reporting in the Radical First Person from Harper's Magazine* (New York: The New Press, 2008), p. 89.

168 *Cops on the cartel payroll made sure:* Parker James Asmann, "How Mexico's 'Small Armies' Came to Commit a Massacre," *InSight Crime*, November 15, 2019, https://insightcrime.org/news/analysis/how-mexico-small-armies-commit-massacre/.

169 *one former government official recalled:* Interview with Oscar Maynez in Ciudad Juárez, June 4, 2019.

169 *One such crew was Barrio Azteca:* Martínez (2018), p. 190.

169 *Meza, who went by the alias M-10, was a former Juárez municipal policeman:* Testimony of Vicente Zambada Niebla on January 3, 2019, pp. 4065–66.

169 *In late 2005 or early 2006, he traveled to the mountains of Sinaloa:* Ibid.

169 *Jaguar had previously been closely allied with La Linea:* Testimony of Édgar Iván Galván on January 7, 2019, pp. 4371–72.

170 *Jaguar turned to . . . an El Paso–based drug smuggler named Edgar Iván Galván:* Ibid., pp. 4379–90.

170 *"Jaguar is the type of person who does not questions":* Ibid. p. 4388.

170 *"He told me I shouldn't go to Juárez for a while":* Ibid., pp. 4372–73.

171 *Over the next few years, Galván handled about four or five major shipments of weapons to Jaguar:* Ibid., pp. 4400–4401.

171 *One haul included a monstrous .50-caliber rifle:* Ibid., p. 4399.

171 *"That's a .50-caliber," Jaguar replied:* Ibid.

171 *one that directly supports the bottom line of United States gun dealers:* McDougal et al., "The Way of the Gun: Estimating Firearms Traffic Across the U.S.-Mexico Border," https://igarape.org.br/wp-content/uploads/2013/03/Paper_The_Way_of_the_Gun_web2.pdf.

171 *On paper, Mexico has quite restrictive gun laws:* John Burnett, "Law-Abiding Mexicans Taking Up Illegal Guns," NPR, January 28, 2012, https://www.npr.org/2012/01/28/145996427/mexican-community-takes-taboo-stance-on-guns.

171 *Only the police and military are allowed to carry assault weapons:* Tim Johnson, "Mexico, awash in weapons, has just one legal gun store," McClatchy Newspapers, February 5, 2014, https://www.mcclatchydc.com/news/nation-world/world/article24726304.html.

171 *But in practice, it's illegal to own anything more powerful than a .22:* Kate Lin-

thicum, "There is only one gun store in all of Mexico. So why is gun violence soaring?" *Los Angeles Times*, May 24, 2018, https://www.latimes.com/world/la -fg-mexico-guns-20180524-story.html.

171 *Of the estimated 15.5 million illegal guns in Mexico:* Arindrajit Dube, Oeindrila Dube, and Omar García-Ponce, "Cross-Border Spillover: U.S. Gun Laws and Violence in Mexico," *American Political Science Review*, August 2013.

172 *Estimates vary, but anywhere from 80 percent to 90 percent:* McDougal et al (2013).

172 *The rate of violent deaths by soon followed:* One study estimated that the ban's expiration was responsible for 16.4 percent of the increase in the homicide rate in Mexico between 2004 and 2008. Luke Chicoine, "Exporting the Second Amendment: U.S. Assault Weapons and the Homicide Rate in Mexico," University of Notre Dame Department of Economics, https://www.econ-jobs .com/research/32941-Exporting-the-Second-Amendment-US-Assault-Weapons -and-the-Homicide-Rate-in-Mexico.pdf.

172 *"We seized more than 90,000 weapons":* "Mexico Wants to Sue U.S. Gun Makers," CBS News, April 21, 2011, accessed July 21, 2020.

172 *the U.S. government committed hundreds of millions of dollars:* "Mexico: Evolution of the Mérida Initiative, 2007–2021," Congressional Research Service, January 13, 2021, https://fas.org/sgp/crs/row/IF10578.pdf.

173 *the United States always found "progress":* "Mexico-Merida Initiative Report (15% Report)," U.S. Department of State, 2012, accessed October 12, 2020.

173 *only once withheld the 15 percent:* The decision to withhold the funds came in the wake of the mass kidnapping of 43 students in Iguala, Guerrero. It's worth mentioning that Congress put temporary holds on funds in 2010 and 2012, but the aid eventually found its way to Mexico. Joshua Partlow, "U.S. blocks some anti-drug funds for Mexico over human rights concerns," *Washington Post*, October 18, 2015, https://www.washingtonpost.com/world/the_americas /us-blocks-some-anti-drug-funds-for-mexico-over-human-rights-concerns/2015 /10/18/8fa3925e-710b-11e5-ba14-318f8e87a2fc_story.html.

173 *video emerged that appeared to show police:* The videos were originally published by the newspaper *El Heraldo de Leon* and by the television station Televisa. Carlos Tornero, the police chief for the city of Leon, claimed that the exercises were designed for withstanding, rather than practicing, torture. La Raza Blog, "Police Videos Cause a Stir in Mexico," *Los Ángeles Times,* July 2, 2008, accessed October 12, 2020.

173 *The Mérida money arrived:* Information up to March 2017, including dollar amounts and details of the Mérida Initiative, come from Clare Ribando Seelke and Kristin Finklea, "U.S.-Mexican Security Cooperation: The Mérida Initiative and Beyond," Congressional Research Service, June 29, 2017, accessed October 12, 2020.

173 *As the author Dawn Paley points out:* See Chapter 5: "Plan Mexico and Militarization," in Dawn Paley, *Drug War Capitalism* (Edinburgh: AK Press, 2015).

174 *most notably with the Mexican Marines:* For more on human rights violations by the Mexican Marines: Arturo Ángel, "Con Peña aumentó la letalidad en operativos de la Marina: por cada herido hubo 20 muertos," *Animál Político,* March 11, 2019, accessed January 18, 2021, https://www.animalpolitico.com /2019/03/marina-letalidad-enfrentamientos-fallecidos-heridos/; Camilo Carranza, "Killings by Mexican Marines Underscore Lack of Oversight." InSight Crime, March 27, 2019, accessed January 18, 2021, https://www.insightcrime .org/news/analysis/killings-mexican-marines-underscore-lack-oversight/.

174 *One summer day in 2008:* Marc Lacey, "Hospitals Now a Theater in Mexico's Drug War," *New York Times,* December 5, 2008, accessed April 20, 2020.

174 *"I'm not going to give in":* Marc Lacey, "The Violent Battle for Control of a Border City," *New York Times,* March 1, 2009, accessed April 20, 2020.

CHAPTER 10: THE YEAR OF SKINNY COWS

176 *One former federal cop:* Testimony of Sergio Villarreal Barragán, *USA v. Iván Reyes Arzate,* November 8, 2018.

176 *Mochomo had been raising a ruckus of late:* According to Alexander Cifuentes, El Chapo had "warned Muchomo to go live in the mountains, that he should be either a quieter man and he shouldn't have those kinds of parties in such a small city . . . that Mochomo had been arrested because he had thrown a scandal on his birthday." Testimony of Alex Cifuentes on January 14, 2019, pp. 5080–81.

176 *When the cops cornered Mochomo:* "Key Lieutenant to Boss of Drug Cartel Caught," Associated Press, January 22, 2008, https://www.seattletimes.com /nation-world/key-lieutenant-to-boss-of-drug-cartel-caught/.

176 *The next day, police in Mexico City raided a safe house:* "Mexico Captures 11 Alleged to be Cartel Hit Men," Associated Press, January 23, 2008, https:// www.nbcnews.com/id/wbna22793072.

176 *"Arturo Beltrán was blaming my compadre":* Testimony of Dámaso López, January 22, 2019, p. 5877.

177 *he had, through a lawyer, been in intermittent contact with the DEA:* For more on the relationship between the lawyer—Humberto Loya Castro—and the DEA, see David Epstein, "Devils, Deals, and the DEA," *ProPublica,* December 17, 2015, https://www.propublica.org/article/devils-deals-and-the-dea.

177 *Pretty much everyone assumed that El Chapo had been behind Mochomo's arrest:* Embassy Mexico, "Weakening of Gulf, Sinaloa Cartels Generates Mexico's Spike in Violence," Wikileaks Cable: 08MEXICO1766_a, June 9, 2008, https:// wikileaks.org/plusd/cables/08MEXICO1766_a.html.

177 *"my compadre was trying for there not to be any shoot-outs or confrontations":*

Testimony of Dámaso López Nuñez, January 22, 2019, *USA v. Guzmán Loera*, p. 5877.

177 *On April 30, three months after Mochomo's arrest:* Ibid.

178 *In the first eleven days of May:* This list is drawn from one printed on May 12, 2008, in the daily newspaper *Noroeste,* accessed August 22, 2019, at the Archivo Histórico General del Estado de Sinaloa.

178 *On May 8, just after 8:30 p.m., El Chapo's son Édgar:* "Matan a hijo de 'El Chapo,'" *Noroeste*, May 10, 2008.

179 *In a photo taken of the crime scene that night:* Ibid.

179 *The killings continued:* "50 asesinatos en el 11 días del Mayo," *Noroeste*, May 12, 2008, accessed August 22, 2019 at the Archivo Histórico General del Estado de Sinaloa.

180 *On May 11, a team of* federales *cornered a cousin of El Chapo:* "Arraigan a supuesto primo de 'El Chapo,'" *Noroeste*, May 16, 2008. Accessed August 22, 2019 at the Archivo Histórico General del Estado de Sinaloa. And online at: https://www.noroeste.com.mx/publicaciones/view/arraigan-a-supuesto-primo-de -el-chapo-36207.

180 *the federal police and the army launched a joint operation:* Javier Valdez Cárdenas and Gustavo Castillo, *"El ejército ocupa Culiacán y Navolato, en un intento por abatir ola de violencia,"* La Jornada, May 14, 2008, https://www.jornada .com.mx/2008/05/14/index.php?section=politica&article=012n1pol.

180 *In the city of Guamúchil:* "Atacan una base de la Ministerial," *Noroeste*, May 14, 2008. Accessed August 22, 2019 at the Archivo Histórico General del Estado de Sinaloa. And online at https://www.noroeste.com.mx/publicaciones/view/ ataca-comando-base-de-la-pme-en-guamuchil-35848.

181 *Splashed across the front page:* "Es la Guerra," *El Debate de Sinaloa*, May 13, 2008, accessed at El Archivo Histórico General del Estado de Sinaloa, August 22, 2019.

181 *The bloodshed continued across the state:* "Otros 19 asesinatos en cuarta semana del mes," *Noroeste,* May 26, 2008, accessed at El Archivo Histórico General del Estado de Sinaloa, August 22, 2019.

182 *On the opinion page of* El Debate de Sinaloa: "Bienvenidos a Culiacán," *El Debate de Sinaloa,* May 13, 2008, accessed at El Archivo Histórico General del Estado de Sinaloa, August 22, 2019.

183 *It got to the point where if you saw a police officer:* Interview with Fernando Brito, August 19, 2019, in Culiacán, Sinaloa.

183 *"I didn't realize what was happening in Culiacán":* This quote and the rest of the information about Fernando Brito comes from the author's interview with Brito on August 19, 2019.

184 *This is life in a low-intensity war:* This passage is informed by my own interviews with residents of Culiacán about life during this period, as "The Two Black

Thursdays in Culiacán and the Challenge to the Codes of Urban Space," by Iliana del Rocío Padilla Reyes, Mexico Violence Research Project, October 2020.

184 *according to one trafficker:* All quotes by "Antonio" are from an interview I conducted with him on May 15, 2019, in Culiacán.

185 *But for Pedro and Junior Flores . . . the war was the final straw:* Testimony of Pedro Flores on December 18, 2018.

186 *Until this point they had been allowed to operate in a "sweet spot":* Ibid., p. 3530.

186 *"My wife became pregnant in 2008, and I began to think about our future":* Testimony of Pedro Flores on December 18, 2018, pp. 3529–32.

186 *Over the decade in which the twins had run their business:* Testimony of Pedro Flores on December 18, 2018, p. 3428, and Government's Sentencing Memorandum, Document #353 in *USA v. Pedro and Margarito Flores.* Accessed via Pacer.

187 *The brothers had been on the DEA's radar for several years:* Testimony of Pedro Flores, December 19, 2018, pp. 3664–65; *USA v. Flores et al.*, 05-CR033, Eastern District of Wisconsin.

187 *the DEA had been in the dark:* Frank J. Main, "How a West Side Drug Bust Led the Feds to 'El Chapo,'" *Chicago Tribune*, January 26, 2018, https://chicago.suntimes.com/2018/1/26/18527622/el-chapo-west-side-bust-dea-sinaloa-cartel-chapo.

187 *a lawyer for the brothers based in Chicago knocked on the DEA's door:* Pedro Flores, December 18, 2018, p. 3430.

188 *"The whole timing of it was delicate":* Testimony of Pedro Flores, December 12, 2018, pp. 3534–37.

188 *"I started having a little like, guilt about picking up these kilos":* Testimony of Pedro Flores, December 18, 3535–40.

189 *Throughout the summer and into the fall:* Information on seizures related to the Flores twins comes from document 383 "Exhibit B" in *USA v. Guzmán Loera et al.* Accessed via Pacer.

189 *Junior Flores dialed a number into his phone:* The transcript and translation of this call is that of the prosecution, entered into evidence as "Government Exhibit 609A-1T" in *USA v. Guzmán Loera et al.*

190 *On November 13 . . . a courier working for Alfredillo*: Testimony of Pedro Flores on December 19, 2018, p. 3591, and testimony of Mario Elias on December 19, 2018, pp. 3764–69.

190 *El Chapo greeted Pedro cheerfully:* The transcript and translation of this call is that of the prosecution, entered into evidence as "Government Exhibit 609A-6T" in *USA v. Guzmán Loera et al.*

191 *They got Vincentillo Zambada discussing the purchase of M16 rifles:* Testimony of Vicente Zambada Niebla on January 1, 2019, pp. 4036–38.

192 *Their wives, hip to the plot, piled into their SUVs:* This detail comes from *Cartel*

Wives. Despite containing myriad details about the lives of Pedro and Junior, I've relied on this source as little as possible in favor of sworn testimony by Pedro and other court documents.

192 *But they also made serious missteps and tried to hide a bit of money:* Testimony of Pedro Flores on December 18, 2018, p. 3539.

192 *Within days, he vanished:* Details of the kidnapping of Margarito Flores Sr. come from the prosecution's sentencing memorandum, aka Document 373, filed in the Northern District of Illinois on January 14, 2015.

193 *When it finally came time for the Flores brothers to be sentenced:* Sentencing order as to Pedro Flores and Margarito Flores Jr. Filed on January 27, 2015, in the Northern District of Illinois.

193 *Most of El Chapo's closest aides had stuck by his side:* This passage draws on the testimony of Alex Cifuentes, Dámaso López, and Isaias Valdez Ríos in *USA v. Guzmán Loera.*

193 *the city became a home base for cells of Zetas hit men:* Testimony of Alex Cifuentes on January 14, 2019, pp. 5085–86.

194 *On December 8, 2009, Memín took part in a concerted attack:* This passage is based largely on the testimony of Isaias Valdez Ríos on January 24, 2019, pp. 6194–97, as well as a video of the aftermath entered into evidence as Government Exhibit 701-A.

195 *In the months leading up to that day:* Embassy Mexico. "Casino Ties to PAN Candidates," Wikileaks Cable: 09MONTERREY259_a, July 2, 2009, https://wikileaks.org/plusd/cables/09MONTERREY259_a.html.

195 *Arturo had been on the offensive:* Messages included threats to "kidnappers" and anyone who betrayed the Beltrán Leyvas: Héctor de Mauleón, *"La ruta de sangre de Beltrán Leyva,"* Nexos, February 1, 2010, https://www.nexos.com.mx/?p=13503, accessed January 17, 2021.

195 *That evening, as the party raged:* Adam Gabbatt, "Grammy-winning star caught up in raid at Mexico drug cartel party," *Guardian,* December 15, 2009, https://www.theguardian.com/world/2009/dec/15/ramon-ayala-mexico-raid.

195 *Less than a week later, on December 16:* Embassy Mexico, "Mexican Navy Operations Nets Drug Kingpin Arturo Beltrán Leyva," Wikileaks Cable: 09MEXICO3573_a, December 17, 2009, https://wikileaks.org/plusd/cables/09MEXICO3573_a.html.

195 *The triumphant Marines took their revenge:* In the wake of the operation and the leaking of the photos of Arturo's corpse, some in Mexico saw an uncomfortable parallel with the increasingly graphic way in which armed groups— many of which included ex-soldiers—were displaying the bodies of their victims. I would note, however, that given the prevalence of military-linked death squads operating in Mexico in those years and in the years since (see *Undeniable Atrocities*), the photos hint at something more sinister than a mere mimicry of drug gang tactics. Ken Ellingwood, "Staged Photos of Slain Drug

Lord Stir Controversy," *Los Angeles Times,* December 22, 2009, https://www
.latimes.com/archives/la-xpm-2009-dec-22-la-fg-mexico-druglord22-2009dec
22-story.html, accessed January 17, 2021.

196 *According to recently unsealed court documents:* The information on La Barbie's cooperation is gleaned from a transcript of his sentencing hearing, held
June 11, 2018, in the Northern District of Georgia. The court documents,
which I accessed June 11, 2020, were first reported by Anabel Hernández, *"Valdez Villarreal: el narco testigo de la corrupción de García Luna era informante de
la DEA y el FBI,"* *Arestegui Noticias,* June 11, 2020, accessed June 11, 2020.

196 *The Marines moved quickly and decisively:* Embassy Mexico City, "Mexican
Navy Operation Nets Drug Kingpin Arturo Beltran Leyva," WikiLeaks Cable:
09MEXICO3573_a, December 17, 2009, https://wikileaks.org/plusd/cables
/09MEXICO3573_a.html, accessed January 17, 2021.

196 *Mexican defense secretary General Guillermo Galván Galván:* Embassy Mexico
City, "Director of National Intelligence Dennis Blair's Meeting with General
Galvan Galvan, October 19," WikiLeaks Cable: 09MEXICO3077_a, October
26, 2009, https://wikileaks.org/plusd/cables/09MEXICO3077_a.html, accessed
January 17, 2021.

197 *The only survivor was a sister, whose name, prudently, was not released this time:*
Elizabeth Malkin, "Revenge in Drug War Chills Mexico," *New York Times,*
December 22, 2009, https://www.nytimes.com/2009/12/23/world/americas
/23mexico.html.

197 *After the raid in Cuernavaca, President Calderón:* Ibid.

198 *"unholy truce":* In the words of a U.S. diplomatic cable: "An unholy truce be-
tween two of the largest cartels in Northern Mexico, Beltran [*sic*] Leyva and
Guzman [*sic*] Loera, holds violence at bay along the railroad tracks in Nogales,
Sonora which skirts the U.S. border." "SONORA, MX - UNHOLY TRUCE
AT THE BREAKING POINT?" WikiLeaks Cable: 10MEXICO93_a, February
4, 2010, https://wikileaks.org/plusd/cables/10MEXICO93_a.html, accessed
January 18, 2021.

CHAPTER 11: A CITY BESIEGED

199 *On a warm Wednesday evening in early September:* Details of the Casa Aliviane
attack and its aftermath are drawn from a number of contemporaneous news
articles, including National Public Radio, "Gunmen Kill 18 at Drug Rehab
Center in Mexico," September 3, 2009, https://www.npr.org/templates/story
/story.php?storyId=112503893&t=1610907797374, accessed January 17, 2021;
Ken Ellingwood, "18 Killed in Juárez Clinic for Addicts," *Los Angeles Times,*
September 16, 2009, https://www.latimes.com/la-fg-mexico-rehab-attack4
-2009sep04-story.html, accessed January 17, 2021; BBC, "Gunmen Target
Mexico Rehab Centre," September 3, 2009, accessed January 17, 2021, http://
news.bbc.co.uk/2/hi/americas/8235101.stm.

200 *Gustavo de la Rosa, a prominent local human rights activist:* Ed Vulliamy, "Life and Death in Juárez, the World's Murder Capital," *Guardian,* October 4, 2009, https://www.theguardian.com/world/2009/oct/04/mexico-drugs-death -squads-Juárez, accessed January 18, 2021.

200 *government officials did little to hide their disdain:* Comments by General Jorge Juárez Loera are drawn from Melissa del Bosque, "The Deadliest Place in Mexico," *Texas Observer,* February 29, 2012, https://www.texasobserver.org/ the-deadliest-place-in-mexico/, accessed January 17, 2021.

200 *"martial law without the law":* Ed Vulliamy, "Life and death in Juárez, the world's murder capital," *Guardian,* October 3, 2009, https://www.theguard ian.com/world/2009/oct/04/mexico-drugs-death-squads-juarez.

200 *On January 31, 2010, a team of Barrio Azteca gunmen:* Details of the Villas de Salvárcar massacre are primarily drawn from Ricardo C. Ainslie, "Villas de Salvárcar," chapter 23 in *The Fight to Save Juárez: Life in the Heart of Mexico's Drug War* (Austin: University of Texas Press, 2013).

201 *Nacim Ortiz knew things had gotten bad:* I met Ortiz by chance, at a dog park in Brooklyn on a sunny day in late April 2019. When he heard me discussing with a friend my upcoming reporting trip to the border, Ortiz came over to chat. I asked him if he could tell me about his youth there, and a while later I called him from Mexico City. All quotes and biographical details come from author interview with Nacim Ortiz, July 29, 2019.

202 *El Paso, which even throughout the war:* Susannah Jacob, "El Paso Is Tops Again on Low-Crime Cities List," *Texas Tribune,* December 8, 2011, https:// www.texastribune.org/2011/12/08/el-paso-tops-lowest-crime-rate-list-second-time/, accessed January 17, 2021.

202 *news coverage of the fighting:* Author interview with Nacim Ortiz, July 29, 2019.

203 *In 2008, nearly half of the six thousand reported drug-linked killings:* Marc Lacey, "Hospitals Now a Theater in Mexico's Drug War," *New York Times,* December 5, 2008, accessed April 20, 2020.

203 *until someone set off a car bomb:* The first car bombing recorded in Ciudad Juárez occurred on July 15, 2010, when a car exploded near a federal police building. According to news reports at the time, the perpetrators dressed up a man in a police uniform to lure in victims before setting off the explosives remotely, killing a doctor, a cop, and a passing musician, along with the un- fortunate man used as bait. Despite frantic speculation that the fighting had entered a new phase of indiscriminate violence, and despite a note left at the scene threatening further bombings, this appeared to be an isolated use of the tactic. Tracy Wilkinson, "Mexico Cartel Kills Four in Car Bombing," *Los Angeles Times,* July 17, 2010, https://www.latimes.com/archives/la-xpm-2010 -jul-17-la-fg-mexico-car-bomb-20100717-story.html, accessed January 19, 2021.

203 *"In Mexico, they kill you twice":* Monica Campbell, "Despite Violence, Journal-

ists in Mexico Innovate to Report," NiemanReports.org, accessed April 20, 2020.

203 *Just 3 percent of alleged crimes:* Kate Linthicum, "Soldiers took them in the night. Now Mexico's drug war strategy is on trial," *Los Angeles Times,* April 25, 2018, accessed April 20, 2020.

204 *the housing market there remained stable:* Ignacio Alvarado, "Mexicans Fleeing Drug War Help El Paso Housing Market," Reuters, September 10, 2008, accessed April 22, 2020.

204 *By 2011, 300,000* juarenses *had fled:* Tony Payan, "Ciudad Juárez: A Perfect Storm on the US–Mexico Border," *Journal of Borderlands Studies,* 29 no. 4 (2014): pp. 435–47.

204 *the entire population of Pittsburgh:* U.S. Census data, 2018 estimate.

205 *"Until we find who is responsible":* Julián Cardona, "Families Blame Mexico's Calderon over Massacre," Reuters, February 2, 2010, accessed April 22, 2020.

205 *Residents of Juárez formed councils:* Steven Dudley, "Police Use Brute Force to Break Crime's Hold on Juárez," InSight Crime, February 13, 2013, accessed April 29, 2020.

205 *The Federal Police launched an aggressive campaign:* Calderón appears to have explicitly modeled this strategy after the "Broken Windows" theory made famous in the 1990s by former NYPD commissioner William Bratton, who later took his strategy to Boston, and then to LA. In a February 17, 2010, meeting with then–DHS secretary Janet Napolitano, Calderón suggested that only by using what he called "the Bratton Approach" and taking a zero-tolerance stance on crimes large and small could they establish the rule of law in Juárez. Embassy Mexico, "DHS Sec Napolitano's Meeting with President Calderon, February 17," WikiLeaks cable: 10MEXICO111_a, dated February 18, 2010, accessed January 20, 2021, https://wikileaks.org/plusd/cables/10MEXICO111 _a.html.

206 *In April, the same month the army withdrew:* Alicia Caldwell and Mark Stevenson, "AP Exclusive: Sinaloa Cartel Takes Ciudad Juárez," *San Diego Tribune,* April 9, 2010, accessed April 23, 2020.

206 *The mayor of Juárez blamed the ongoing violence:* Ibid.

206 *El Diego . . . also took responsibility for the massacre in Villas de Salvárcar:* "Capturan 'El Diego,' Lider de La Linea," *Reforma,* August 1, 2011, accessed April 30, 2020.

206 *For all the blood on his hands:* El Diego was later extradited to the United States, where he pleaded guilty to the murder of an employee of the U.S. consulate in Juárez, among other crimes. A judge sentenced him to seven concurrent terms of life in prison, an additional three concurrent life terms, and, for good measure, tacked on an extra twenty years.

207 *But staff at the U.S. consulate:* U.S. Department of State diplomatic cable, "POLICE MURDERS SHOW THE DIFFICULTY OF BRINGING DOWN

THE DRUG CARTELS IN TIJUANA," July 14, 2009, published by WikiLeaks, accessed April 23, 2020.

208 *Nava Lopez helped spearhead an anti-kidnapping initiative:* Interview with Jorge Arnaldo Nava Lopez, June 4, 2019.

208 *Others, like the late journalist Julián Cardona*: Julián Cardona died suddenly in October 2020. I spoke with Julián twice during my reporting in Juárez in the spring of 2019. My conversations with him, as well as his work elsewhere, made a tremendous impact on how I understood the violence in Juárez. He has had an immense influence on the work and thinking of numerous other reporters covering the drug war, and I and others owe him a great debt. I wish I had gotten to know him better, and I am grateful to have spent the small amount of time with him that I did, and even more grateful for the wisdom he imparted.

209 *from 1999 to 2002, he'd worked as the city's chief of forensics:* Cecilia Ballí, "Ciudad de la Muerte," *Texas Monthly,* June 2003, accessed July 21, 2020.

209 *Later, he'd worked in an advisory role:* Interview with Oscar Maynez in Ciudad Juárez, June 4, 2019.

209 *"The violence in Juárez is going to be there always":* Ibid.

210 *On October 22, 2008, federal police had clapped handcuffs on El Rey Zambada:* Ken Ellingwood, "Major trafficking suspect arrested," *Los Angeles Times,* October 23, 2008, https://www.latimes.com/archives/la-xpm-2008-oct-23-fg-mexarrest23-story.html.

210 *El Rey had specialized in bribing high-ranking officials:* Testimony of Jesús Zambada, November 20, 2018.

210 *Vicentillo was in Mexico City on an unusual mission:* "Government's Response to Defendant's Motion to Dismiss Based on the Extradition Proceedings," 1:09-cr-00383 Document #:105, filed on September 9, 2011, in United States District Court, Northern District of Illinois, Eastern Division, accessed via PACER.

211 *In 2010, El Chapo's longtime partner Ignacio "Nacho" Coronel:* Jo Tuckman, "Death of Drug Lord Ignacio 'Nacho' Coronel Deals Blow to Mexican Cartel," *Guardian,* July 30, 2010, https://www.theguardian.com/world/2010/jul/30/mexico-drugs-lord-shot-dead, accessed January 17, 2021.

212 *a huge number of those missing people:* See *Undeniable Atrocities.*

212 *Calderón's defenders sometimes argued:* Embassy Mexico, "The Battle Joined: Narco Violence Trends in 2008," Wikileaks Cable: 09MEXICO193_a, January 23, 2009.

213 *But EPN had skeletons in his closet:* This passage on the campaign and election of Enrique Peña Nieto is based on contemporaneous news articles, as well as Chapter 2 of Francisco Goldman's fantastic book *The Interior Circuit: A Mexico City Chronicle.*

213 *had presided over a brutal police crackdown against a protest in the town of Atenco:* José Meléndez, "Mexican government, guilty of rape and torture against

women in Atenco," *El Universal*, December 24, 2018, https://www.eluniversal.com.mx/english/mexican-government-guilty-rape-and-torture-against-women-atenco.

CHAPTER 12: THE INVISIBLES

215 *belonged to a country club in Bogotá that cost half a million dollars to join:* Author interview with law-enforcement sources on September 16, 2019.

215 *His older brother Francisco . . . had attended a military academy:* Testimony of Alex Cifuentes on January 15, 2019, p. 5205.

215 *A younger brother, Alex, was overseeing the family's business interests in Mexico:* Testimony of Jorge Cifuentes on December 13, 2018, pp. 3079–84.

215 *carried on a longtime affair and had two children with Jaime Uribe:* "Hermano de Uribe tuvo otro hijo con Dolly Cifuentes diez años después de la primera hija," *La Nueva Prensa*, October 10, 2019, https://www.lanuevaprensa.com.co/componente/k2/hermano-de-uribe-tuvo-otro-hijo-con-dolly-cifuentes-diez-anos-despues-de-la-primera-hija.

215 *Another sister was dating a powerful general in the Colombian Army:* Testimony of Alex Cifuentes on January 15, 2019, p. 5312.

216 *There, a young Alex hung around with bodyguards:* Testimony of Alex Cifuentes on January 15, 2019, pp. 5209–10.

216 *When Alex was just fifteen:* Ibid., pp. 5210–17.

216 *Jorge headed to Mexico in the late 1980s as an envoy:* Testimony of Jorge Cifuentes on December 11, 2018, pp. 2847–48 and December 13, p. 3116.

216 *Although he'd worked with El Mayo for years, it was not until 2003:* Testimony of Jorge Cifuentes on December 12, 2018, p. 2837.

216 *By this time, the Cifuentes-Villa business portfolio was a sprawling and diversified octopus:* Details on the Cifuentes-Villa network's front businesses is via the Department of the Treasury Office of Foreign Assets Control (OFAC), https://home.treasury.gov/system/files/126/cifuentes_villa_entities_022011.pdf.

216 *The Cifuentes family were part of a new class of Colombian cocaine traffickers dubbed "the Invisibles":* Jeremy McDermott, "The 'Invisibles': Colombia's New Generation of Drug Traffickers," *InSight Crime*, March 15, 2018, https://insightcrime.org/investigations/invisibles-colombias-new-generation-drug-traffickers/.

217 *"Oh, he got very excited":* Testimony of Jorge Cifuentes on December 12, 2018, pp. 2,877–2,881, *USA v. Guzmán Loera*, 1:2009cr00466.

217 *some half-trained goon of a pilot crash-landed the thing:* Testimony of Jorge Cifuentes on December 12 and December 13, 2018, pp. 2881 and 3113.

217 *In a sit-down with El Chapo, his son Iván Archivaldo, and Dámaso López:* Testimony of Jorge Cifuentes on December 12, 2018, pp. 2892–93.

218 *The big break for the Cifuentes Crew came in 2007:* Testimony of Juan Carlos Ramírez Abadía on December 3, 2018, p. 1975.

218 *The Cifuentes clan was in crisis mode as well:* Testimony of Jorge Cifuentes

on December 12, 2018, pp. 2897–98; *"Crimen de informante de la DEA en Medellín provocó estampida de narcos a Nueva York,"* *El Tiempo*, July 11, 2019, https://www.eltiempo.com/archivo/documento/CMS-5615488.

218 *Alex, a longtime alcoholic, had seen better years:* Testimony of Jorge Cifuentes on December 12, 2018, p. 2901.

218 *After surviving his surgery:* Testimony of Alex Cifuentes on January 10, 2019, pp. 4995–96.

218 *The best thing to do, El Chapo said, would be to press on:* Ibid., pp. 4997–98.

219 *Francisco had five widows:* Ibid., p. 4999.

219 *They weren't totally cut off:* Testimony of Alex Cifuentes, January 14, 2019, pp. 5024–27.

219 *life had settled into a routine:* Details of El Chapo's life in the mountains come from the testimony of Alex Cifuentes on January 14, 2019; and Isaias Valdez Ríos, aka Memín, on January 24, 2019.

220 *One guard in particular, a guy named Toronjo:* Testimony of Alex Cifuentes on January 14, 2019, p. 5084.

220 *At that party, El Chapo's sons gifted him a camouflage Hummer:* Ibid., p. 4029.

220 *According to Alex, El Chapo liked his women young:* Document 569-1, filed on October 9, 2018, and unsealed on February 1, 2019. Available via Pacer in *USA v. Guzmán Loera et al.*

220 *El Chapo would strongly deny this:* Kristine Phillips, "El Chapo raped girls as young as 13 and called them his 'vitamins,' witness says," *Washington Post*, February 3, 2019, https://www.washingtonpost.com/nation/2019/02/03/el-chapo-raped-girls-young-called-them-his-vitamins-witness-says/.

220 *his personal email address was "Illuminatixxx13@gmail.com":* That address now appears to be inactive: when I came across this fun fact in court documents, I sent an email to the address, but it bounced back. Oh, well. Judge Brian M. Cogan, "Order as to Joaquin Archivaldo Guzman Loera denying 410 Defendant's first motion for reconsideration," Case 1:09-cr-00466-BMC-RLM Document 440, filed November 12, 2018, unsealed September 21, 2020, accessed via PACER.

221 *Alex once saw El Chapo buying snake oils:* Document 569-1, p. 7, filed on October 9, 2018 and unsealed on February 1, 2019. Available via Pacer in *USA v. Guzmán Loera et al.*

221 *"There was a lot of security":* Testimony of Jorge Cifuentes on December 12, 2018, p. 2902. *USA v. Guzmán Loera*, 1:2009cr00466.

221 *"He looked like a mini-general":* Testimony of Jorge Cifuentes on December 12, 2018, p. 2908.

221 *There's a picture of them together in those days:* This photo was entered into evidence as GX1H.

222 *In one meeting during Jorge's visit to Mexico in late 2007:* Testimony of Jorge Cifuentes on December 12, 2018, pp. 2917–24.

222 *On the first journey, they successfully managed to ship six tons of cocaine from Ecuador to Mexico:* Ibid., p. 2963.

CHAPTER 13: THE IT *GÜEY*

223 *Christian Rodriguez peered out the porthole window:* Testimony of Christian Rodríguez on January 9, 2019, pp. 4802–4.

223 *Despite being a college dropout:* Testimony of Christian Rodríguez on January 9, 2019, p. 4793; author interviews with federal law-enforcement agents familiar with the case.

224 *which they referred to as "the Spark":* Interview with federal law-enforcement agents on September 16, 2019.

224 *If Christian had felt any pangs of guilt:* Ibid.

224 *Christian's anxiety only increased:* Testimony of Christian Rodríguez on January 9, 2019, pp. 4802–4.

225 *Christian found himself face-to-face with El Chapo:* Ibid., p. 4805.

225 *"Joaquín was very active and very receptive":* Testimony of Alex Cifuentes on January 14, 2019, p. 5058.

226 *pulling up a digital slideshow:* Testimony of Christian Rodríguez on January 9, 2019 and Alex Cifuentes on January 14, 2019.

227 *including one particularly rogue company that later did business with drug traffickers in Mexico:* I refer here to "Phantom Secure," the encrypted-phone company run by Vincent Ramos: Joseph Cox, "The Network: How a Secretive Phone Company Helped the Crime World Go Dark," *Motherboard*, October 22, 2020, https://www.vice.com/en/article/v7m4pj/the-network-vincent-ramos-phantom-secure.

227 *About a month and a half after Christian's first trip to the mountains:* This anecdote is built from the testimony of Christian Rodriguez on January 9, 2019; Alex Cifuentes on January 14 and January 15, 2019; the testimony of FBI Special Agent Stephen Marston on January 8 and January 9, 2019; and author interviews with federal law-enforcement agents familiar with the case.

230 *Back in the late 1980s:* Testimony of Miguel Ángel Martínez Martínez on November 27, 2018, p. 1483.

230 *"Mr. Guzmán always liked communications":* Ibid., p. 1484.

231 *In 2003, he and El Mayo coughed up more than half a million dollars:* This anecdote about the surveillance equipment and the resulting murder of a drug trafficker named Julio Beltrán is drawn from my own notes on the testimony of Vicente Zambada Niebla on January 4, 2019, rather than from a transcript of the testimony.

231 *Not one to disappoint his boss, Christian did some research and soon settled on a program called FlexiSPY:* This passage is based on the testimony of Christian Rodríguez on January 9 and January 10; the testimony of FBI Special Agent Stephen Marston on January 8 and January 9, 2019; documents entered

into evidence by the prosecution in *USA v. Guzmán*, and interviews with fed-eral law-enforcement sources with knowledge of the case in September of 2019.

233 *"El Señor needs this fixed"*: Testimony of Christian Rodríguez on January 9, 2019, p. 4831.

233 *On February 3, 2010, Christian Rodriguez found himself in a hotel suite over-looking Times Square:* This passage is based in part on the testimony of Spe-cial Agent Stephen Marston and on author interviews with law-enforcement sources familiar with the case who spoke with me on background in order to speak freely.

CHAPTER 14: OPERATION SERVER JACK

This chapter is based largely on author interviews with federal law-enforcement sources familiar with the investigation of Christián Rodríguez.

235 *"There's all this technical computer stuff"*: This quote is based on the recollec-tion of sources familiar with the investigation.

CHAPTER 15: WE NEED TO TALK

241 *Christian's final trip to the mountains:* This passage is based on the testimony of Christian Rodriguez on January 10, 2019, an the testimony of Alex Cifuen-tes on January 14, 2019.

241 *Would Christian be able to install spyware on every single public computer in Culiacán:* Testimony of Christian Rodríguez on January 10, 2019, pp. 4847–49.

243 *Throughout the whole ordeal, El Chapo remained utterly composed:* This epi-sode was reconstructed from the testimony of Christian Rodriguez on Janu-ary 10, 2019 (pp. 4848–50) and the testimony of Alex Cifuentes on January 14, 2019 (pp. 5061–64).

243 *Special Agent Bob Potash stood in the arrivals terminal:* This passage is based on author interviews with law-enforcement sources familiar with the investi-gation conducted in September 2019.

243 *the agents had been building what's referred to as a "pattern of life":* Ibid.

244 *"Hey, we're with the FBI":* Ibid.

245 *"I was frightened," Christian recalled later:* Testimony of Christian Rodríguez on January 10, 2019, p. 4853.

246 *Potash stood up and grabbed a laptop:* Author interview with law-enforcement sources on September 16, 2019.

246 *Like a balloon deflating, Christian exhaled a long breath:* Ibid.

247 *Christian ordered a forty-dollar steak:* Ibid.

248 *"We did not want to leave a footprint from the FBI":* Testimony of Stephen Marston on January 8, 2019, p. 4513.

249 *it was a relatively easy sell to convince El Chapo:* Testimony of Stephen Marston on January 8, 2019, pp. 4505–4512.

250 *In early April 2011, Potash and Marston sat in the office:* Author interview with law-enforcement sources on September 16, 2019.

251 *"Well, you taught us to be a wolf":* The transcript of this phone call was entered into evidence on January 8, 2019, as "Government Exhibit 601I-2BT."

251 *El Chapo appeared to be having trouble paying his men:* ibid.

252 *had suffered huge losses in Ecuador:* Testimony of Jorge Cifuentes on December 12 and December 13, 2018.

253 *shelling out between $150,000 and $200,000 a month:* Testimony of Alex Cifuentes on January 14, 2019, pp. 5044–45.

253 *that was a pittance compared with the bill for bribery, which exceeded $1 million per month:* Testimony of Dámaso López on January 22, 2019, pp. 5850–51.

253 *El Chapo's extension went dark:* Testimony of Stephen Marston on January 8, 2019, p. 4511.

253 *The FBI intercepted a phone call between El Chapo and his brother:* Testimony of Alex Cifuentes, January 14, 2019, pp. 5050–54.

254 *Every FlexiSPY report that El Chapo or one of his minions read:* "Memorandum of Law in Opposition to the Defendant's Motion to Suppress," aka Document 276, filed by the prosecution on July 30, 2018, in *USA v. Guzmán Loera.* Accessed via Pacer.

254 *In December 2011:* Ibid.

254 *On December 22, 2011, Christian logged into his FlexiSPY account:* "Defendant's Motion to Suppress Evidence (lexiSPY Data)," aka Document 263, filed by the defendant on July 9, 2018. Accessed via Pacer.

255 *El Chapo appeared to be increasingly relying on a handful of girlfriends:* I base this on the testimony of Stephen Marston on January 8 and January 9; Christian Rodríguez on January 9 and January 10; government exhibits showing intercepted communications; and interviews with law-enforcement sources on September 16, September 23, and September 27, 2019.

255 *Lucero and El Chapo had been seeing each other occasionally:* Testimony of Lucero Sánchez López on January 17 and January 22, 2019.

255 *Lucero's instructions were simple:* Ibid., January 17, 2019, pp. 5709–14.

255 *During her trips to the Sierra, El Chapo . . . became a model communicator:* Ibid., 5710; Government Exhibit 516, entered into evidence on January 17, 2019.

255 *"I thought it was unfair":* Testimony of Lucero Sánchez López on January 17, 2019, p. 5711.

255 *"I didn't want to leave it there":* Ibid., p. 5124.

256 *"Look, the mafia kills people who don't pay":* This exchange comes from a transcript of a BBM conversation on January 31, 2012, between El Chapo and Lucero, entered into evidence on January 17, 2019, as Government Exhibit 602F-5BT.

256 *Agustina Cabanillas Acosta, appeared to have earned an especially high degree of*

trust: This is based on the testimony of Stephen Marston on January 9, 2019, as well as BBM exchanged between the two, including those labelled Government Exhibit 511-8; Government Exhibit 511-13; and GX 511-15, entered into evidence on January 9, 2019.

256 *In one exchange, the agents read along:* These conversations are transcribed and translated in GX511-15 and were discussed during the testimony of Stephen Marston on January 9, 2019, pp. 4690–4718.

258 *Agustina revealed her deep suspicion of El Chapo:* Ibid., p. 4690.

258 *Born in California and raised in Durango, Emma was the daughter of Ines Coronel Barreras:* "Affidavit of Special Agent Eric S. McGuire in Support of Application for a Criminal Complaint and Arrest Warrant," filed on February 17, 2021, in *USA v. Coronel Aispuro.*

258 *In a 2019 interview with the* New York Times, *Emma described her relationship:* This phenomenal scoop by Emily Palmer was published to virtually everyone's envy, surprise, and admiration as she and I and the rest of the El Chapo press corps held vigil at the Brooklyn federal courthouse as we awaited the verdict. Emily Palmer, "El Chapo's Wife Emma Coronel Aispuro: 'I Admire Him,'" *New York Times,* January 30, 2019.

259 *The "simple ceremony with family and close friends" was, according to Mexican media reports, a massive party:* "La boda del Capo Mayor," *Proceso,* November 8, 2008, https://www.proceso.com.mx/nacional/2008/11/8/la-boda-del -capo-mayor-29307.html; William Finnegan, "The Kingpins," *New Yorker,* June 25, 2012, https://www.newyorker.com/magazine/2012/07/02/the-kingpins

259 *According to Alex Cifuentes, she rarely visited:* Testimony of Alex Cifuentes on January 14, 2019, pp. 5045–46.

259 *She gave birth at a Los Angeles County hospital to twin girls:* "Emma Coronel, esposa de 'El Chapo' Guzmán, dio a luz mellizas en California," Univision, September 27, 2011, https://www.univision.com/noticias/narcotrafico/emma-cor onel-esposa-de-el-chapo-guzman-dio-a-luz-mellizas-en-california; Tracy Wilkinson and Ken Ellingwood, "Wife of fugitive Mexican drug lord gives birth in L.A. County," *Los Angeles Times,* September 27, 2011, https://www.latimes.com /world/la-fg-mexico-twins-20110927-story.html.

259 *"Or maybe it's best if mommy makes them for you":* The line about enchiladas raised eyebrows among some of the reporters covering the trial, who had a hard time imagining Emma ever cooking. Later, in an interview with *Proceso* reporter Jesús Esquivel published in full at the end of his 2019 book, *El Juicio: Crónica de la Caída del Chapo,* Emma admitted that this portion of her conversations with her husband was pure role play. "I don't know how to make enchiladas. . . . I don't know how to cook."

260 *"Our Kiki is fearless":* All text messages quoted here are from Government Exhibit 602F-2B, entered into evidence on January 9, 2019, *USA v. Guzmán et al.,* 1:09-cr-00466.

CHAPTER 16: CLOSE CALL IN CABO

261 *On February 22, 2012, FBI special agent José Moreno stood:* This passage is based largely on the testimony of Moreno on January 7, 2019.

261 *the state of Baja California Sur, of which Los Cabos is part, had remained relatively calm:* In 2011, Baja California Sur registered just forty-two homicides, the lowest number in Mexico. During the worst of the Calderón years, he homicide rate never exceeded seven homicides per 100,000 residents, among the lowest rates in the country: "En 2011 se registraron 27 mil 199 homicidios," Instituto Nacional de Estadística y Geografía, press release number 310/12, NEGI, August 20, 2012. Accessed via: https://www.direccioneszac.net /en-2011-se-registraron-27-mil-199-homicidios/.

261 *the past few days had been hectic:* Info on Obama and Clinton via the archives of the Obama White House: https://obamawhitehouse.archives.gov /photos-and-video/photogallery/g20-summit-los-cabos-mexico; Alex Cifuentes testified as to the headaches—"There was a lot of security, from Mexico, from the U.S. The city was being heavily guarded"—on January 15, 2019, pp. 5154–56.

261 *El Chapo had been spending time in Los Cabos:* Ibid., pp. 5152–53.

261 *In Cabo, he tended to travel around in a gold Suburban:* Ibid., p. 5155.

262 *Alex Cifuentes had recently moved to Cabo as well:* Ibid., p. 5152.

262 *he had felt sidelined in the state capital, where Dámaso López was increasingly acting as El Chapo's right-hand man:* Ibid.

262 *an iPhone that Christian had told him was encrypted:* "I thought that iPhone was encrypted and, according to Cristian [sic], he had fixed it so that it wouldn't give away my location." Via testimony of Alex Cifuentes on January 15, 2019, p. 5157. This was corroborated in the testimony of Stephen Marston and in author interviews with law-enforcement sources familiar with the case in September 2019.

262 *in mid-February, El Chapo reached out to tell Alex that he was in town:* Testimony of Alex Cifuentes on January 15, 2019, pp. 5154–56.

262 *Thanks to intel cobbled together by the FlexiSPY reports:* Interview with law-enforcement sources familiar with the investigation on September 27, 2019.

262 *Moreno and his team suspected that El Chapo was holed up in a tony section of Cabo called Hacienda Encantada:* Testimony of José Moreno on January 7, 2019, pp. 4303–4.

262 *"They were supposed to be there in twenty minutes":* Ibid., p. 4307. The time frame of the operation is based on Moreno's testimony, as well as that of special agent Marston on January 9, corroborated by FlexiSPY data showing a gap in communication between El Chapo and Emma Coronel between 2:54 p.m. and 6:22 p.m. Testimony of Stephen Marston, p. 4664.

263 *El Chapo was texting with his wife:* Transcript and translation of this exchange is from GX602F-2BT, compiled in GX511-15, p. 38.

263 *the federal agents began arriving at the rendezvous spot where Moreno was wait-ing:* Testimony of José Moreno on January 7, 2019, pp. 4309–10.

263 *"I have no idea why they did that":* Ibid., pp. 4310–11.

263 *Out on the street, Moreno and the other U.S. agents waited anxiously for about five minutes:* Ibid., 4311–13.

263 *Moreno began to take stock of the place:* Ibid., and from video entered into evidence as "GX218-29A."

264 *In the papers recovered at the safe house:* Testimony of José Moreno on January 7, 2019, pp. 4314–20, and photos of the crime scene entered into evidence as GX218-12.

264 *But El Chapo had vanished:* Ibid.

264 *"Joaquín just left":* Testimony of Alex Cifuentes on January 15, 2019, p. 5160.

265 *Emma checked in on her husband:* Transcript and translation of this ex-change via GX511-15 and testimony of Stephen Marston on January 9, 2019, pp. 4665–69.

265 *Alex Cifuentes watched with mounting dread:* Testimony of Alex Cifuentes on January 15, 2019, pp. 5158–60.

266 *"The mosquitos have already arrived where I am":* This conversation between Alex and Carlina, held at 5:19 p.m. on February 23, 2012, is based on the prosecution's transcript and translation. I've condensed it slightly to re-move interruptions by Alex trying to get off the phone. Government Exhibit 603D–5T, entered into evidence on January 15, 2019, *USA v. Guzmán et al.,* 1:09-cr-00466.

266 *Thanks to Christian:* According to testimony by Alex Cifuentes and author interviews, as well as law-enforcement sources familiar with the case, the con-versation between Alex and his mom was held on iPhones that Christian had set up, having convinced the Cifuentes family that they were secure.

266 *In the wake of the raid in Los Cabos:* Author interview with law-enforcement sources on September 27, 2019.

267 *they began to use the GPS location:* Ibid.

267 *They had a local team on the ground in Culiacán:* Ibid.

267 *The various members of the Cifuentes family, on the other hand, were merrily chatting away:* Testimony of Alex Cifuentes on January 15, 2019, p. 5157; author interview with law-enforcement sources on September 16, 2019.

267 *taking cover in a slum on the outskirts of Caracas:* Details of Jorge Cifuentes's time on the lam in Caracas are via author interview with law-enforcement sources on September 16, 2019.

268 *Venezuelan authorities tracked him down, arrested him, and paraded him in front of the cameras:* "Así fue la captura de Jorge Cifuentes Villa, el enlace del 'El Chapo'," *El Tiempo,* November 9, 2012, https://www.eltiempo.com/archivo/documento/CMS-12368753.

268 *Christian had been slowly but surely extricating himself from El Chapo's orbit:* Testimony of Christian Rodríguez on January 10, 2019, p. 4851.

268 *on the FBI's servers in the Netherlands:* Author interview with law-enforcement sources on September 23, 2019; the operation and search of the servers is discussed at length in "Defendant's Motion to Suppress Evidence (Dutch Servers)"—docket number 264—and "Defendant's Motion to Suppress Evidence (FlexiSPY Data)"—docket number 264—and in the testimony of Stephen Marston on January 8 and January 9, 2019.

268 *He and the fugitive drug lord had not spoken . . . they didn't think he could stay cool under that kind of pressure:* Testimony of Christian Rodríguez on January 10, 2019; author interview with law-enforcement sources on September 23 and September 27, 2019.

268 *He continued to field questions:* Testimony of Christian Rodriguez on January 10, 2019, p. 4682.

268 *The double—or triple—life was beginning to wear on Christian:* Ibid., p. 4866. Info on money is via author interviews with law-enforcement sources on September 27, 2019.

268 *In addition to his girlfriend and their young children, he had a secret family:* Testimony of Christian Rodríguez on January 10, 2019, pp. 4934–36.

269 *"And tell him that Christian was the one who blew the whistle.":* Transcript and translation of phone call via GX604H-7T, read aloud during testimony of Alex Cifuentes on January 14, 2019, pp. 5076–77.

269 *Alex was texting his secretary, a woman named Andrea Fernández Velez:* Transcript and translation of this exchange via GX6604H-98T, entered into evidence and read aloud on January 14, 2019, pp. 5077–80.

269 *When Christian saw those two exchanges, he was terrified:* Testimony of Christian Rodríguez on January 10, 2019, pp. 4098–99.

269 *He and his family had already relocated to the United States:* Author interview with law-enforcement sources on September 23, 2019.

269 *Christian suffered what he described as a "nervous breakdown":* Testimony of Christian Rodriguez on January 10, 2019, p. 4867 and pp. 4934–36.

269 *FBI paid Christian more than half a million dollars in expenses and compensation:* Ibid., 4953–54.

269 *he was still in therapy:* Ibid., p. 4867.

CHAPTER 17: THE DRAGNET

270 *They needed someone who, like Christian, was a bit of an outsider:* Author interview with law-enforcement sources familiar with the case.

270 *They settled on Andrea Fernández Velez:* Ibid.

270 *including a pair of five-hundred-dollar sheets:* Testimony of Alex Cifuentes on January 16, 2019, pp. 5403–4.

270 *Eventually her duties included:* Testimony of Alex Cifuentes on January 15 and January 16, 2019; author interviews with law-enforcement sources in September of 2019.

270 *As Alex's assistant, Andrea was a conduit through whom many of the boss's decisions flowed:* Ibid., and testimony of Stephen Marston on January 9, 2019, pp. 4762–67.

271 *Special Agents Potash and Marston had plenty of dirt on Andrea:* Ibid.

271 *They wanted to confront her in Colombia:* Ibid.

271 *On the first day of their stakeout:* Unless otherwise noted, all details of the cooperation of Andrew Fernández Velez are via author interviews with law-enforcement sources familiar with the case conducted in person and over the phone in New York on September 16, September 23, and September 27 2019.

271 *Finally, on the seventh day, Andrea strolled into the terminal:* This passage and the following details regarding Andrea's cooperation are once again via interviews with law-enforcement sources unless otherwise and specifically noted.

272 *Alex had sent her to Ecuador to meet with a corrupt army captain:* Testimony of Alex Cifuentes on January 15, 2019, pp. 5170–75. The captain in question was a man named Telmo Castro, who was connected with the Cifuentes-Villa operation in Ecuador.

273 *agents with Homeland Security Investigations . . . set up a series of wiretaps:* Testimony of HIS Special Agent John Zappone on January 17, 2019, starting p. 5656.

273 *BlackBerry Messenger, or BBM, can be quite secure:* Author interviews with law-enforcement agents familiar with the case; Jordan Pearson and Justin Ling, "Exclusive: How Canadian Police Intercept and Read Encrypted Black-Berry Messages," *Motherboard*, April 14, 2016, https://www.vice.com/en/article/mg77vv/rcmp-blackberry-project-clemenza-global-encryption-key-canada.

273 *El Chapo and his pals were basically using store-bought BlackBerrys on the company's main servers:* Author interviews with law-enforcement sources on September 23, 2019.

273 *Investigators had begun to get a glimpse:* Details of the Tepic raid are via interviews with law-enforcement sources familiar with the case.

273 *El Chapo, ever paranoid about his communications, devised this new system:* Testimony of Alex Cifuentes on January 15, 2019, pp. 5161–62.

273 *El Chapo's mirror system was based on a series of levels, or tiers:* Ibid., and testimony of John Zappone on January 17, 2019, pp. 5669–72; *see also* GX515-1, entered into evidence by the prosecution on January 17, 2019.

274 *It was far less high-tech than Christian's system, but a hell of a lot harder to infiltrate:* Author interviews with law-enforcement sources on September 23, 2019.

274 *"It was a very unique method of communication that we basically hadn't seen before":* Testimony of John Zappone on January 17, 2019, p. 5668.

274 *slowly began to illuminate portions of El Chapo's network:* The details of this paragraph come from GX515-2, GX515-3, and GX515-4, entered into evidence on January 17, 2019.

275 *In November 2013, a team of Mexican agents raided a small ranch on the outskirts of Culiacán:* Testimony of Alex Cifuentes on January 15, pp. 5188–90 and January 16, pp. 5392–96.

275 *Even after the arrest of Alex, Andrea continued to pass information to the FBI:* Author interviews with law-enforcement sources on September 23 and September 27, 2019.

275 *Special Agent Drew Hogan coordinated with the HSI agents as more and more texts came in:* Most of the details regarding Drew Hogan come from author interviews with Hogan in May 2019. Hogan wrote about the investigation into El Chapo in his book *Hunting El Chapo: The Inside Story of the American Lawman Who Captured the World's Most-Wanted Drug Lord* (HarperCollins, 2018), co-written with Douglas Century. I used details from the book sparingly. In the interest of disclosure, I should mention that Hogan and I have the same literary agent.

275 *Hogan had arrived in Mexico in 2012, after assignments chasing money launderers from Tijuana to Bolivia:* Ibid.

276 *Every thirty days or so, or every time El Chapo's people got spooked, many of the devices would drop off the map:* Ibid.

276 *they were careful to get warrants:* Testimony of John Zappone on January 17, 2019, pp. 5657–62.

276 *That had happened before:* Details on the abduction of Humberto Álvarez Machain and the eventual dismissal of charges come from *United States v. Alvarez-Machain*, 504 U.S. 655 (1992), https://casetext.com/case/united-states-v-14.

276 *the doctor now runs a taco restaurant in Guadalajara:* Fox News reporter Lara Logan tracked down Álvarez Machain in Guadalajara, where she confronted him about his alleged role in the death of Camarena. Speaking through an interpreter, he denied having anything to do with the crime: "Tell her that since I left the United States prison, I've been here at this little business and keep enjoying it. . . . I feel very proud that I was able to get out of a federal court trial in the United States": Matt London, "Exclusive: Lara Logan Confronts Alleged Mexican Cartel Doctor Accused of Torturing DEA Agent," Fox News, January 6, 2019, accessed January 18, 2021, https://www.foxnews.com/media/mexico-cartel-doctor-torture-dea-lara-logan.

276 *The U.S. government knew it couldn't make the same mistake:* The case of the doctor, Humberto Álvarez Machain, eventually made its way to the U.S. Supreme Court, which ruled that his abduction and extralegal "extradition" should not have been grounds for dismissal. Still, prosecutors and federal agents were aware that evidence against El Chapo would have to meet U.S. legal standards.

276 *the arrest of Ines Coronel in Agua Prieta:* Coronel and his son—Emma's brother—were arrested along with three other men. Authorities told reporters the men were caught with 255 kilos of marijuana, four long arms, and a pistol: Fabiola Martínez and Gustavo Castillo, *"Capturan en flagrancia a Inés Coronel Barreras, suegro de El Chapo Guzmán," La Jornada,* May 2, 2013, https://www .jornada.com.mx/2013/05/02/politica/023n1pol, accessed January 18, 2018.

277 *And, at an increasing rate, the powerful synthetic opioid fentanyl:* Based on author interviews with drug traffickers in Sinaloa involved in the production and trafficking of fentanyl along with overdose data showing an increase of ODs involving fentanyl over time, it appears the Sinaloans began moving fentanyl in large quantities in 2014.

277 *For anyone who violated the traffickers' mandates:* Over the past decade, reported rates of kidnapping and extortion have been lower in Sinaloa than in states like Michoacán and Tamaulipas, a fact that allows some people involved in the drug trade or sympathetic to it to claim that kidnappings don't happen in Culiacán because El Chapo or El Mayo oppose them. This is absurd. Forced disappearances are a fact of life in Sinaloa as in many other areas of the country, and the rate—six a day, according to one recent estimate—is likely considerably higher than what is reported to authorities. Furthermore, I would argue that, given the "social cleansing" nature of some disappearances, such as the car thieves, it is within the realm of possibility that police are involved in or at least give sanction to such killings: Iliana del Rocio Padilla, "The Two Black Thursdays in Culiacán and the Challenge to the Codes of Urban Space," Center for U.S.-Mexican Studies, the Noria Mexico-Central America program, and Revista Espejo, accessed October 15, 2020; Andrés Villarreal, *"Autos de juguete y muerte," Riodoce,* August 13, 2019.

277 *For civilians in Culiacán:* This paragraph is based on interviews I conducted in Culiacán in April, June, August, and October 2019 and by Iliana del Rocío Padilla, *"Nelson Arteaga Botello: Códigos de la violencia en espacios económicos en Culiacán, Sinaloa, México,"* Papers: *Revista de Sociología* 104, no. 1, pp. 25–45.

CHAPTER 18: THE LION'S DEN

278 *On the afternoon of February 13, 2014, four Black Hawk helicopters:* The details of this passage are based on the testimony of DEA Special Agent Victor Vazquez on January 16, 2019, as well as a video of the flight and the raid entered into evidence that day and narrated in part by Vazquez during his testimony.

278 *Sitting with his back to the cockpit:* Video of the flight was entered into evidence as GX219-22 on January 16, 2019. Details on noise via testimony of Victor Vazquez on January 16, 2019, pp. 5526–28.

278 *Born in the state of Durango, he had served in the U.S. Marine Corps:* Ibid., pp. 5509–11.

278 *He had mostly been focusing on La Familia Michoacana:* Ibid., p. 5511. For more on La Familia Michoacana, see William Finnegan, "Silver or Lead," *New Yorker,* May 24, 2010, https://www.newyorker.com/magazine/2010/05/31 /silver-or-lead.

278 *Vazquez, along with fellow DEA agent Drew Hogan:* Drew Hogan was not mentioned by name at trial. However, I spoke with him regarding the events separately described in the testimony of Victor Vazquez. Most of the details here are via Vazquez, unless otherwise noted.

278 *spent the intervening weeks running training exercises, a cover for their true mission:* Testimony of Victor Vazquez on January 16, 2019, p. 5522.

279 *They were there for three men:* Ibid., p. 5512.

279 *A state judge had ordered that Caro Quintero be released:* "Rafael Caro Quintero, Infamous Mexican Drug Lord, Released after 28 Years in Prison," Associated Press, August 9, 2013, accessed October 21, 2020.

279 *When they got intel that El Mayo had been spotted at a ranch on the outskirts of Culiacán, they got ready to move:* Testimony of Victor Vazquez on January 16, 2019, pp. 5524–25.

279 *"I'm there with a hundred Marines":* Testimony of Victor Vazquez on January 17, 2019, p. 5608.

280 *"It's any corner, a specific location, and their job is to look out all day":* Testimony of Victor Vazquez on January 16, 2019, p. 5529.

280 *If a gringo gets off the plane in Culiacán, chances are someone at the airport is making a phone call:* This truism about *halcones* has become a staple of corny documentaries about the drug trade in Sinaloa, but it's not untrue. I've seen it in action. During an interview I conducted with drug traffickers at a heroin-production lab in Sinaloa in August 2019, they received warning over the radio about troop movements.

280 *The whole state is going to be on alert:* I've seen this in action. During an interview with a heroin cook at a makeshift outdoor lab outside of Culiacán, we had to make a hasty exit when their walkie-talkies lit up with reports from associates closer to the city about a column of military vehicles headed in our direction.

280 *The choppers flew low as they made landfall, sweeping above the scrubby Sinaloa countryside:* Visual details of the flight via GX219-22.

280 *Vazquez, dressed in full camo and toting an assault rifle:* In GX219-21, a video shot by Vazquez from a camera affixed to his helmet, Vazquez can be seen briefly reflected in a mirror. He also discussed his attire during his testimony on January 17, 2019, p. 5607.

280 *They swept into the house, checking it once, twice, three times for any signs of recent life:* Testimony of Victor Vazquez on January 16, 2019, pp. 5529–30.

280 *Night had fallen save for a sliver of light:* Visual details via helmet camera footage aka GX219-21.

281 *As Vazquez and his comrades searched the house, a pair of Marines stood on the front patio guarding the caretaker:* Ibid.

281 *They spent the next two days searching the nearby hills, but they came no closer to finding El Mayo:* Testimony of Victor Vazquez on January 16, 2019, p. 5530.

281 *Back in La Paz, Special Agent Drew Hogan was pissed:* Author interview with Drew Hogan on May 7, 2019.

282 *Compared to El Chapo, Hogan considered Caro Quintero a nobody:* Ibid.

282 *For Hogan, the ideal plan had been to wait for El Chapo to take a trip to the ranch and nab him there:* Ibid., and separate author interviews with law-enforcement sources familiar with the case.

282 *The unit in La Paz was mainly focused on organized crime groups in other regions of Mexico:* Hogan (2018), p. 186.

282 *On February 16:* See testimony of Victor Vazquez, January 16, 2018, p. 5540.

283 *The first location was a dud:* Testimony of Victor Vazquez on January 17, 2019, pp. 5540–41.

283 *"Drew, the fuckin' cops won't leave us alone":* This quote is drawn from "Hunting El Chapo," and circumstances corroborated by testimony from Vazquez. It's unclear, however, if they were being tailed by actual cops or by gunmen driving cloned cop cars. Later, after the Marines seized a cop car parked outside a safe house, the chief of the municipal police department insisted that the patrol car had been cloned, which is at once a common practice by Mexican traffickers and also a handy excuse for local authorities when cop cars end up in places they should not. "Se revisarán las patrullas que circulen por la ciudad," *El Debate de Sinaloa*, February 21, 2014, accessed August 19, 2019, at Archivo Histórico del Estado de Sinaloa.

283 *Hogan couldn't shake the sense of dread he felt as his fellow agent and the Marines rolled through the city:* Author interview with Drew Hogan on May 7, 2019.

285 *Lucero had begun working with El Chapo and his associates to set up front companies:* Testimony of Lucero Sánchez López on January 17, 2019, pp. 5736–38, and on January 22, 2019, pp. 5811–14.

285 *"I would just be there in the house":* Ibid., pp. 5738–39.

285 *"Tío, [Juancho] died":* This quote, attributed to Condor by Lucero on January 17, 2019, p. 5744, refers to Juancho as "Uncle Virgo," another nickname for Juancho.

285 *El Chapo suspected that his nephew had been lying to him:* Details of Juancho's death via testimony of Dámaso López Nuñez on January 22, 2019, pp. 5893–95.

286 *"He said from that point on, whoever betrayed him was going to die":* Testimony of Lucero Sánchez López on January 17, 2019, pp. 5744–45.

286 *"The relationship had ended, but it seemed like it actually would never end.":* Ibid.

286 *Finally... Lucero got the call:* Ibid.

287 *Condor came into the room to tell them that El Chapo had to move locations:* Ibid., pp. 5746.

287 *Lucero lay awake, unable to doze off:* Ibid., p. 5748.

287 *Victor Vazquez, meanwhile, was on the hunt for Nariz:* Testimony of Victor Vazquez on January 17, 2019, p. 5541.

288 *"Something told me to focus on the nose.":* Ibid., 5543.

289 *"Tu eres Nariz":* The details of the capture of Nariz are via testimony of Victor Vazquez on January 17, 2019, pp. 5541–50.

290 *It would be more unusual if Nariz had not suffered torture:* Patrick Radden Keefe, "Was Torture the Key to Bringing Down a Kingpin?" *New Yorker,* May 1, 2014.

290 *"Listen, when [Nariz] tells you to make a left":* Original quote edited for clarity: "I told the Marine driving, I said, 'Listen, when he tells you to make a left, make a left." Testimony of Victor Vazquez on January 17, 2019, p. 5551.

290 *Vazquez wanted them close to the safe house:* Unless otherwise noted, this passage is via testimony of Victor Vazquez on January 17, 2019, pp. 5551–58.

290 *SEMAR trucks had been rolling through town:* Details of the effects of the operation on the city come from articles published in *El Debate de Sinaloa* on February 18, 2014, August 19, 2019, at Archivo Histórico del Estado de Sinaloa.

290 *HSI fed the intel to Vazquez:* Testimony of Victor Vazquez on January 17, 2019, p. 5553. Transcripts of BBMs intercepted by HSI on February 17, 2014, were entered into evidence as GX610N-6.

291 *"Nariz told me that once I make this right the house is on this street":* Unless otherwise noted, this passage is via testimony of Victor Vazquez on January 17, 2019, pp. 5551–58

291 *"Don't waste your time with the upstairs":* Ibid., 5553.

291 *As Lucero finally started to drift off:* Testimony of Lucero Sánchez López on January 17, 2019, p. 5748.

292 *Groping her way along the side of the tunnel:* This passage is based entirely on the testimony of Lucero Sánchez López on January 17, 2019, pp. 5748–52.

292 *Finally, after what felt like an eternity but was likely just a few second, his radio crackled to life:* The exact quote is "I waited maybe what seemed to be forever but it was more like 10, 15 seconds . . ." Testimony of Victor Vazquez on January 17, 2019, p. 5555.

293 *Inside the house, the Marines were so close to their prey that they could hear footsteps:* Ibid., p. 5556.

293 *Once she caught a second to take in her surroundings:* Lucero's POV in this

passage is via her testimony on January 17, 2019, pp. 5751–52, and from January 22, 2019, pp. 5761–65.

293 *Finally, the little group emerged from the drainage tunnel:* Narration is via testimony of Lucero. Physical description of the tunnel outlet is my own, based on observations made at the scene on April 14, 2019.

294 *After about an hour of scouring the safe house and the tunnel:* Testimony of Victor Vazquez on January 17, 2019, pp. 5558–65, and via video of the scene, entered into evidence as GX219-31.

294 *With a crackling sound the grout sealing the tub to the black wall tiles broke free:* Ibid., and video taken of Nariz operating the tub, entered into evidence GX219-32.

294 *This time, however, they didn't linger:* Ibid., p. 5564.

294 *the Marines blocked off streets with white pickup trucks marked with the SEMAR logo:* Physical description of the scene via photos published in *El Debate de Sinaloa* on February 18, 2014, August 19, 2019, at Archivo Histórico del Estado de Sinaloa.

294 *2,800 packages of methamphetamine:* Info on seizures is from testimony of Victor Vazquez on January 17, 2019, pp. 5574–79.

295 *That evening, the Marines arrested Picudo:* Ibid., p. 5582.

295 *As they headed to Mazatlán:* Ibid., pp. 5584–87.

295 *Standing outside the Hotel Miramar:* Testimony of Victor Vazquez on January 17, 2019, pp. 5587–92.

296 *"Eres tu":* Ibid., p. 5591.

CHAPTER 19: DÉJÀ VU

297 *To prove it, the government released a photo:* "Details emerge in drug lord's capture," CNN, February 24, 2014, https://edition.cnn.com/videos/world/2014/02/24/tsr-dnt-todd-el-chapo-drug-lord-capture.cnn.

297 *Much later, another picture emerged:* Dominic Midgely, "Hunting El Chapo: How ex-DEA agent took down world's most wanted drug lord," *Express*, April 28, 2018, https://www.express.co.uk/life-style/life/952408/Hunting-El-Chapo-worlds-most-wanted-drug-lord-DEA-agent-Andrew-Hogan.

297 *a team of Marines in black face masks paraded him in front of news cameras in Mexico City:* "El arresto y traslado de Joaquín 'El Chapo' Guzmán," Univision Noticias, January 11, 2016.

298 *El Chapo's new home was a forbidding place:* Patrick Radden Keefe, "El Chapo Escapes Again," *New Yorker*, July 12, 2015, https://www.newyorker.com/news/news-desk/el-chapo-escapes-again.

298 *Observers cautioned that El Chapo's organization . . . was likely to keep chugging along:* Mary Speck, "The Arrest of El Chapo: What's Next for Mexico?" International Crisis Group, February 27, 2014, https://www.crisisgroup.org/latin-america-caribbean/mexico/arrest-el-chapo-what-s-next-mexico.

298 *To let him escape once more, the president said, would be "unforgivable":* William Neuman, Randal C. Archibold, and Azam Ahmed, "Mexico Prison Break by 'El Chapo' Is a Blow to President Peña Nieto," *New York Times*, July 13, 2015, https://www.nytimes.com/2015/07/14/world/americas/mexico-joaquin-guzman-loera-el-chapo-prison-escape.html.

298 *But El Chapo was already planning his next moves:* Testimony of Dámaso López Nuñez on January 22, January 23, and January 24, 2019.

299 *El Chapo ordered the murder of his chief of security:* Testimony of Dámaso López on January 23, 2019, pp. 5913–15.

299 *Negro had had a hand in numerous kidnappings:* According to Dámaso López, El Negro was involved in the kidnappings of Juan Guzmán Rocha, alias Juancho, and his secretary José Miguel "Güero" Bastidas in December of 2011; and Leopoldo "Polo" Ochoa in December of 2012. Isaias Valdez Ríos, alias Memín, testified that El Negro was personally involved in several other killings. Testimony of Dámaso López on January 22, 2019, pp. 5894–98, and testimony of Isaias Valdez Ríos on January 24, 2019.

299 *El Negro's body, showing signs of torture: "El mito del teniente 'Bravo'"* Riodoce, April 13, 2014, https://riodoce.mx/2014/04/13/el-mito-del-teniente-bravo/.

299 *Observers at the time speculated*: Joan García and Jesús Bustamente, *"Matan a 'El Bravo', jefe de seguridad de 'El Chapo,'"* Excelcior, April 11, 2014, https://www.excelsior.com.mx/nacional/2014/04/11/953453.

299 *In letters that El Chapo wrote from his cell at Altiplano and smuggled out via his attorney:* Testimony of Dámaso López on January 23, 2019, pp. 5914–36. Letters entered into evidence as GX806-1T, GX806-2T, and GX806-3T.

299 *Writing to them in April, he shared a bit of fatherly advice:* Ibid.

300 *"Hire accountants throughout the state":* Ibid.

300 *"I wanted to tell you that although nothing here is easy":* Ibid.

300 *"My compadre was sending the message":* Ibid., p. 5937.

300 *teaming up with his former rival, the drug trafficker known as La Barbie, to organize a hunger strike:* Anabel Hernandez, *"'El Chapo' y 'La Barbie' ponen de cabeza el penal del Altiplano,"* Proceso, July 19, 2014, https://web.archive.org/web/20140812211800/http://www.proceso.com.mx/?p=377621.

300 *Lucero Sánchez . . . now an elected state deputy of the PRI:* Testimony of Lucero Sánchez López on January 22, 2019, pp. 5773–76.

301 *Mexican authorities insisted he was being held "in isolation":* Marguerite Cawley, "'El Chapo' Works with Rival 'La Barbie' in Mexico Prison Hunger Strike," *InSight Crime*, July 22, 2019, https://insightcrime.org/news/brief/el-chapo-teams-up-with-rival-la-barbie-for-mexico-prison-hunger-strike/.

301 *At 5:52 p.m., on July 11, 2015:* Catherine Schoichet, Ed Payne, and Don Melvin, "Mexican drug lord Joaquín 'El Chapo' Guzmán escapes," CNN, July 13, 2015, https://edition.cnn.com/2015/07/12/world/mexico-el-chapo-escape/index.html.

301 *With El Chapo safely on the back of the bike:* Testimony of Dámaso López on January 23, 2019, pp. 5942–45.

302 *The escape was more than a year in the making:* Ibid., pp. 5936–42.

302 *It was on of the most well-worn tricks in El Chapo's book:* Larry Buchanan, Josh Keller, and Derek Watkins, "How Mexico's Most Wanted Drug Lord Escaped from Prison (Again)," *New York Times*, January 8, 2016, https://www.nytimes .com/interactive/2015/07/13/world/americas/mexico-drug-kingpin-prison-escape .html.

302 *By the spring of 2015, El Chapo's rescuers grew so close:* Testimony of Dámaso López on January 23, 2019, p. 5942.

302 *it took eighteen long minutes:* Denise Hassenzade Ajiri, " 'El Chapo' escape: Why did it take 18 long minutes to notice Guzmán was missing?" *Christian Science Monitor*, July 15, 2015, https://www.csmonitor.com/World/Global-News /2015/0717/El-Chapo-escape-Why-did-it-take-18-minutes-to-notice-Guzman-was -missing.

303 *President Enrique Peña Nieto was on a state visit to France:* "Mexico arrests seven officials over El Chapo jail break," *Irish Times*, July 18, 2015, https:// www.irishtimes.com/news/world/mexico-arrests-seven-officials-over-el-chapo-jail -break-1.2289925.

303 *"He would come back when you least expected it, and there he was":* Author interview with El Chapo relative in May 2019, in La Tuna.

303 *About a week after the jailbreak, El Chapo summoned his partners and lieutenants:* Testimony of Dámaso López on January 23, 2019, pp. 5941–42.

303 *Less than six months later, in predawn gloom, a team of heavily armed soldiers:* My reconstruction of this scene is based on video published in the wake of El Chapo's capture, available online at https://www.youtube.com /watch?v=ljt7KbFv35g&t=34s.

304 *Reportedly using the baby as a human shield:* José Córdoba and Juan Montes, "El Chapo's Obsession with Actress Led to His Capture, Officials Say," *Wall Street Journal*, January 13, 2016, https://www.wsj.com/articles /el-chapos-obsession-with-actress-led-to-his-capture-officials-say-1452669900.

304 *In October, the authorities laid siege to Culiacán:* Author interview with Oscar Loza Ochoa on August 18, 2019; Daniel Hernandez, "The People Displaced by the Hunt for El Chapo tell of Helicopter Attacks," *Vice News*, December 23, 2015, https://www.vice.com/en/article/ev954a/the-people-displaced -by-the-hunt-for-el-chapo-tell-of-helicopter-attacks.

305 *the hunters zeroed in on a home in Los Mochis:* Azam Ahmed, "How El Chapo Was Finally Captured, Again," *New York Times*, January 16, 2016, https:// www.nytimes.com/2016/01/17/world/americas/mexico-el-chapo-sinaloa-sean-penn .html.

305 *a team surveilling the house spotted a white van picking up a large carry-out order of tacos:* Ibid.

305 *Under intense fire from the Marines, the surviving cartel gunmen pulled back:* Video of the raid: https://www.youtube.com/watch?v=ljt7KbFv35g&t=34s.

306 *Sitting side by side in the backseat:* This photo was entered into evidence as GX1-E.

306 *Less than forty-eight hours later:* Sean Penn, "El Chapo Speaks: A secret visit with the most wanted man in the world," *Rolling Stone*, January 10, 2016, https://www.rollingstone.com/politics/politics-news/el-chapo-speaks-40784/.

307 *Peña Nieto's attorney general swore:* María Verza, "Mexico: Captured drug lord to stay put, María Verza, Associated Press, January 28, 2015, https://apnews .com/article/0fbcdfcab6f94b268c74cd651a35b932.

307 *Mexican officials were already moving to clear the way for El Chapo's transfer:* "'El Chapo': Mexico signals extradition to US," BBC, January 10, 2016, https://www.bbc.com/news/world-latin-america-35274547.

307 *"[Emma] told me that my compadre sent his regards:* The full quote, edited for clarity is "My *comadre* told me that my *compadre* sent his regards and that he would send word to say that he was going to make a huge effort to escape again, and he would also send word to ask me to, to ask me if I could help him." Testimony of Dámaso López on January 23, 2019, p. 5945.

307 *With $100,000 of El Chapo's money:* Ibid., p. 5946.

307 *sending a whopping $2 million bribe to a top prison official:* Ibid., p. 5947.

307 *As the plane landed, a horrified El Chapo, his eyes welling with tears:* The DEA released images to the media on February 12, 2019, showing the arrival in 2017 of El Chapo, including a photo that appeared to have been intentionally edited to highlight his tearful eyes.

EPILOGUE

310 *"She recommended to Señor Joaquin":* Testimony of Alex Cifuentes on January 14, 2019, p. 5056.

310 *In the world of Mexican narcos, this wasn't that unusual:* For more on *narcopelículas,* see Grillo (2011), Chapter 10.

310 *these are not the best movies:* At one film premiere I attended in Culiacán— for a picture about the tragic story of a doomed trafficker who got into the drug game to satisfy the materialist wishes of his girlfriend—the lighting and sound mixing were way off, the plot made little sense, and one character, a hit man dressed in distinctive camouflage fatigues, showed up fighting at various points in the movie for two opposing factions.

310 *La Barbie, the captured narco told police he had forked over $200,000 to a movie producer:* I. Longhi-Bracaglia, "'La Barbie,' la película," *El Mundo*, January 9, 2010, https://www.elmundo.es/america/2010/09/01/mexico/1283353149.html.

310 *with the help of a ghostwriter, El Chapo would draft his life story:* Testimony of Alex Cifuentes on January 14, 2019, pp. 5056–57, and on January 16, 2019, pp. 5424–26. This is also based on details submitted by the prosecution in its

"Memorandum of Support for the Government's Second Motion in Limine," filed on September 21, 2018, and unsealed as docket number 611-6 on May 5, 2019.

310 *Alex eventually settled on a Colombian producer named Javier Rey:* Ibid.

311 *Rey journeyed to Sinaloa:* Document 611-6, pp. 18-19.

311 *Over a series of interview sessions, El Chapo held forth on his life:* Ibid., and testimony of Alex Cifuentes on January 16, 2019, pp. 5425–26.

311 *another is sitting on an FBI server:* Author interview with law-enforcement sources in September 2019.

312 *Rey survived:* This information is gleaned from documents filed by the prosecution. I was unable to reach Rey to get his side of the story. Case 1:09-cr-00466-BMC-RLM Document 611-6, filed May 5, 2019.

312 *his lawyers even reached out to a* New Yorker *writer:* The writer, Patrick Radden Keefe, declined: Patrick Radden Keefe, "The Tragic Farce of El Chapo," *New Yorker,* January 10, 2016, https://www.newyorker.com/news/news-desk/the-tragic-farce-of-el-chapo.

312 *officials in Arizona had made the largest-ever seizure of fentanyl:* David Schwartz, "Largest-ever U.S. border seizure of fentanyl made in Arizona: officials," *Reuters,* February 1, 2019, https://www.reuters.com/article/us-arizona-opioids-seizure-idUSKCN1PP35J.

313 *the DEA announced the seizure of 50 pounds of fentanyl:* see DEA press release, https://www.dea.gov/press-releases/2019/06/05/more-50-pounds-fentanyl-recovered-investigation-trafficking-group.

314 *Just after 3 p.m. on October 17, 2019:* I've reconstructed this scene from video released by SEDENA of the raid, with some details via news coverage from outlets in the United States and Mexico: *"'Ya paren todo, ya me entregué': Sedena da detalles del operativo fallido contra Ovidio Guzmán," Animal Político,* October 30, 2019, https://www.animalpolitico.com/2019/10/sedena-detalles-operativo-fallido-ovidio-guzman-hijo-chapo/.

316 *"Usually a shooting lasts half an hour, an hour, and it's over":* Author interview with "Sergio" on November 28, 2019, in Culiacán.

317 *"Take off your uniform!":* This anecdote was told by Ernesto Martínez in "The Plan to Rescue El Chapo's Son: Chaos, Guns, and Fear," *New York Times, The Weekly,* December 8, 2019, https://www.nytimes.com/2019/11/15/the-weekly/el-chapo-guzman-son.html.

317 *Later, there were reports that the gunmen were offering 20,000 pesos:* Ibid.

317 *At a prison on the western outskirts of Culiacán:* Author interview with law-enforcement sources on November 28, 2019, in Culiacán.

317 *at a housing complex for military families:* "The Plan to Rescue El Chapo's Son."

318 *Among the civilians caught by the gunfire:* Author interview with "Miguel" on November 28, 2019, in Culiacán.

318 *"They were very hard workers, very responsible":* Ibid.

319 *In a photo taken that day: "José Arturo, Nicolás y Noé, víctimas del fuego cruzado en Culiacán," Riodoce,* October 27, 2019, https://riodoce.mx/2019/10/29/jose-arturo-nicolas-y-noe-victimas-del-fuego-cruzado-en-culiacan/.

319 *According to officials in Sinaloa, a total of fourteen people died:* Author interviews with residents of Culiacán in November 2019, and *"José Arturo, Nicolás y Noé, víctimas del fuego cruzado en Culiacán," Riodoce,* October 27, 2019, https://riodoce.mx/2019/10/29/jose-arturo-nicolas-y-noe-victimas-del-fuego-cruzado-en-culiacan/.

319 *President Andres Manuel Lopez Obrador announced that he had personally given the order:* Pedro Villa y Caña and Alberto Morales, *"Yo ordené liberar al Ovidio Guzmán, hijo de 'El Chapo': AMLO," El Universal,* June 19, 2020, https://www.eluniversal.com.mx/nacion/politica/amlo-ordeno-liberar-ovidio-guzman-hijo-de-el-chapo.

320 *López Obrador has leaned on the military even more than his predecessors:* Kate Linthicum and Patrick J. McDonnell, "Mexico's military gains power as president turns from critic to partner," *Los Angeles Times,* November 21, 2020, https://www.latimes.com/world-nation/story/2020-11-20/the-military-is-consolidating-power-in-mexico-like-never-before.

320 *most notably an attack in 2015 by the Cártel de Jalisco Nuevo Generación:* Jose Luis Osorio, "Gunmen open fire on Mexico Army chopper as violence roils major state," Reuters, May 1, 2015, https://www.reuters.com/article/us-mexico-violence/gunmen-open-fire-on-mexico-army-chopper-as-violence-roils-major-state-idUKKBN0NM4CA20150501?edition-redirect=in.

321 *But within a few days, the rhythms of everyday life resumed:* I base this on interviews I conducted in Culiacán in November 2019, but my thinking on the matter is deeply influenced by the work of Ilana del Rocio Padilla Reyes, notably her essay "The Two Black Thursdays in Culiacán and the Challenge to the Codes of Urban Space," published October 15, 2020, by Noria Mexico and the Mexico Violence Resource Project (available online: https://www.mexicoviolence.org/battles-after-battle/the-two-black-thursdays-in-culiacan) and her 2019 paper with Nelson Arteaga Botello: *"Códigos de la violencia en espacios económicos en Culiacán, Sinaloa, México," Papers: revista de sociología 104*(1), pp. 25–45.

321 *A measure of local feelings:* All data via INEGI, https://www.inegi.org.mx/programas/ensu/?ps=microdatos.

322 *the contract killer Chino Ántrax:* Alberto Nájar, *"Matan en México al Chino Ántrax, el narcotraficante que presumía en Instagram de su vida de lujo,"* BBC News Mundo, May 19, 2020, https://www.bbc.com/mundo/noticias-america-latina-52717553.

322 *So too did El Mayo's son Ismael Zambada Imperial, aka Mayito Gordo:* Keegan Hamilton, "Sinaloa Cartel Kingpin's 'Chubby' Son Lived Large on Twitter

Before He Got Busted," *Vice News*, November 16, 2014, https://www.vice.com/en/article/a38pve/sinaloa-cartel-kingpins-chubby-son-lived-large-on-twitter-before-he-got-busted.

322 *El Mayo waxed poetic:* Julio Scherer García, *"Proceso en el guarida de 'El Mayo' Zambada,"* *Proceso*, April 3, 2010, https://www.proceso.com.mx/reportajes/2010/4/3/proceso-en-la-guarida-de-el-mayo-zambada-8150.html, accessed January 22, 2021.

323 *"Mayito Flaco, they say, that kid stays in the mountains":* Author interview with "Antonio" on May 15, 2019, in Culiacán.

323 *"Dámaso was a lawyer, wrapped up with the narcos, but not a man of arms":* Author interview with Ismael Bojórquez on August 22, 2019, in Culiacán.

324 *"He likes to show off gold and jewelry":* Javier Valdez, *"Preso Dámaso, el hombre que quiso suplir al 'El Chapo',"* *Riodoce*, May 8, 2017, https://riodoce.mx/2017/05/08/preso-damaso-el-hombre-que-quiso-suplir-al-chapo/.

324 *I met up with Bojórquez:* Interview with Ismael Bojórquez, August 22, 2019, in Culiacán.

324 *When Dámaso testified at the trial of El Chapo:* Testimony of Dámaso López on January 23, 2019, pp. 6050–51.

325 *"I would be the first one to admit here in open court":* Statement of Judge Ruben Castillo on May 30, 2019, p. 20.

325 *In 1969, under the guise of counternarcotics work, the Nixon administration launched Intercept:* Patrick Timmons, "Trump's Wall at Nixon's Border," NACLA, (March 2017).

326 *In a brief, finger-wagging editorial:* "Operation Intercepted," *New York Times*, October 12, 1969, https://timesmachine.nytimes.com/timesmachine/1969/10/12/89138294.html.

326 *"Operation Intercept has been called a failure—but only by those who never knew its objective":* G. Gordon Liddy, *Will: The Autobiography of G. Gordon Liddy* (New York: Macmillan, 1980), p. 135.

326 *So much illegal drug money flows through big banks:* Rajeev Syal, "Drug money saved banks in global crisis, claims UN advisor," *Guardian*, December 12, 2009, https://www.theguardian.com/global/2009/dec/13/drug-money-banks-saved-un-cfief-claims.

327 *The Federal Bureau of Narcotics saw repeated budget cuts:* Lisa N. Sacco, "Drug Enforcement in the United States: History, Policy, and Trends," Congressional Research Service, October 2, 2014, https://fas.org/sgp/crs/misc/R43749.pdf.

327 *When Nixon formed the DEA in 1972:* Budget figures via the DEA, https://www.dea.gov/staffing-and-budget.

327 *in which security forces:* Defense spending rose from $2 billion in 2006 to $9.3 billion in 2009. Peter Chalk, "The Latin American Drug Trade: Scope, Dimensions, Impact, and Response," RAND, Project Air Force, 2011, https://

www.rand.org/content/dam/rand/pubs/monographs/2011/RAND_MG1076
.pdf, accessed January 21, 2021.

328 *allies such as Juan Orlando Hernández:* See *USA v. Hernández* and *USA v. Fuentes Ramirez.* See also https://www.theguardian.com/world/2021/jan/09 /honduras-president-bribes-drug-traffickers-juan-orlando-Hernández.

328 *for the mayor and chief of police of Columbus, New Mexico: USA v. Ignacio Villalobos et al.,* accessed via Pacer. Info on the police force being dissolved: "New Mexico town dissolves police dept after gun smuggling scandal," Yahoo News, July 12, 2011, https://news.yahoo.com/blogs/lookout/mexico-town-dis solves-police-dept-gun-smuggling-scandal-184408968.html.

328 *Arms manufacturers in the United States and gun stores along the border:* For more on the flow of weapons to Mexico, see Ioan Grillo, *Blood Gun Money: How America Arms Gangs and Cartels* (New York: Bloomsbury, 2021).

328 *how can lawmakers deny much-needed funds:* For a glimpse inside the process by which military officials shake their alms cup before Congress, see the testimony of Vice Admiral Charles D. Michel, Deputy Commandant for Operations, U.S. Coast Guard, before the House Committee on Transportation and Infrastructure, June 16, 2015, accessed January 17, 2021.

329 *while deflecting attention away from large-scale mining or timber interests:* My thinking on this aspect of violence in Mexico is deeply influenced by the work of scholars like Dawn Paley, whose excellent 2015 book, *Drug War Capitalism,* deals with these issues extensively.

329 *Nowhere was this been more clear:* "Reforma: Guerreros Unidos Mató a 20 indigentes para que PGJ 'tuviera pruebas' del caso Iguala," SinEmbargo, January 21, 2021, https://www.sinembargo.mx/21-01-2021/3927563.

330 *Less than two weeks after I walked through downtown Agua Prieta:* Lupita Murillo, "Sinaloa Cartel Shootout in Agua Prieta Leaves Nearly a Dozen People Dead," News 4 Tucson, June 11, 2019, https://kvoa.com/news/local -news/2019/06/11/sinaloa-cartel-shootout-in-agua-prieta-leaves-nearly-a-dozen -people-dead/, accessed January 21, 2021.

330 *In November 2019, the city exploded:* Daniel Borunda, "10 Killed, Bodies and Buses Burned in Violent Night of 'Revenge' in Juárez, Mexico," *El Paso Times,* November 6, 2019, https://elpasotimes.com/story/news/local/Juárez /2019/11/06/bodies-and-buses-burned-deadly-night-revenge-Juárez-mexico /2508506001/, accessed January 21, 2021.

330 *The "iron law of prohibition" states:* Leo Beletsky and Corey S. Davis, "Today's fentanyl crisis: Prohibition's Iron Law, revisited," *International Journal of Drug Policy* 46 (August 2017): pp. 156–59, doi: 10.1016/j.drugpo.2017.05.050 (Epub July 18, 2017, PMID: 28735773).

331 *Entire families are being driven out of the Sierra:* Author interviews with Oscar Loza Ochoa and displaced Sinaloans.

331 *In August 2019, I drove out to the outskirts of Culiacán:* Author interview with displaced family, August 22, 2019.

332 *The new normal is four times worse:* All homicide data via INEGI, https://www.inegi.org.mx/sistemas/olap/proyectos/bd/continuas/mortalidad/defuncioneshom.asp?s=est.

333 *Iván Archivaldo Guzmán Sálazar gave an interview:* This quote is from an English-language write-up of the interview. Ernesto Rodriguez Amari, *"Exclusief interview met de zoon van drugsbaron 'El Chapo': Trump zal de strijd nooit van ons winnen," Knack,* March 27, 2018, https://www.knack.be/nieuws/wereld/exclusief-interview-met-de-zoon-van-drugsbaron-el-chapo-trump-zal-de-strijd-nooit-van-ons-winnen/article-longread-982307.html, accessed January 21, 2021.

INDEX